Palgrave Studies in European Political Sociology

Series Editors
Carlo Ruzza
Department of Sociology and Social Research
University of Trento
Trento, Italy

Hans-Jörg Trenz
Department of Media, Cognition and Communication
University of Copenhagen
Copenhagen, Denmark

Palgrave Studies in European Political Sociology addresses contemporary themes in the field of Political Sociology. Over recent years, attention has turned increasingly to processes of Europeanization and globalization and the social and political spaces that are opened by them. These processes comprise both institutional-constitutional change and new dynamics of social transnationalism. Europeanization and globalization are also about changing power relations as they affect people's lives, social networks and forms of mobility. The Palgrave Studies in European Political Sociology series addresses linkages between regulation, institution building and the full range of societal repercussions at local, regional, national, European and global level, and will sharpen understanding of changing patterns of attitudes and behaviours of individuals and groups, the political use of new rights and opportunities by citizens, new conflict lines and coalitions, societal interactions and networking, and shifting loyalties and solidarity within and across the European space. We welcome proposals from across the spectrum of Political Sociology and Political Science, on dimensions of citizenship; political attitudes and values; political communication and public spheres; states, communities, governance structure and political institutions; forms of political participation; populism and the radical right; and democracy and democratization.

More information about this series at
http://www.palgrave.com/gp/series/14630

Birte Siim • Anna Krasteva • Aino Saarinen
Editors

Citizens' Activism and Solidarity Movements

Contending with Populism

Editors
Birte Siim
Department of Culture and Global
Studies, Aalborg University
Aalborg, Denmark

Anna Krasteva
Department of Political Sciences
New Bulgarian University
Sofia, Bulgaria

Aino Saarinen
Aleksanteri Institute
Helsinki, Finland

Palgrave Studies in European Political Sociology
ISBN 978-3-319-76182-4   ISBN 978-3-319-76183-1   (eBook)
https://doi.org/10.1007/978-3-319-76183-1

Library of Congress Control Number: 2018937108

© The Editor(s) (if applicable) and The Author(s) 2019
This work is subject to copyright. All rights are solely and exclusively licensed by the Publisher, whether the whole or part of the material is concerned, specifically the rights of translation, reprinting, reuse of illustrations, recitation, broadcasting, reproduction on microfilms or in any other physical way, and transmission or information storage and retrieval, electronic adaptation, computer software, or by similar or dissimilar methodology now known or hereafter developed.
The use of general descriptive names, registered names, trademarks, service marks, etc. in this publication does not imply, even in the absence of a specific statement, that such names are exempt from the relevant protective laws and regulations and therefore free for general use.
The publisher, the authors, and the editors are safe to assume that the advice and information in this book are believed to be true and accurate at the date of publication. Neither the publisher nor the authors or the editors give a warranty, express or implied, with respect to the material contained herein or for any errors or omissions that may have been made. The publisher remains neutral with regard to jurisdictional claims in published maps and institutional affiliations.

Cover credit: Krassimir Terziev

Printed on acid-free paper

This Palgrave Macmillan imprint is published by the registered company Springer Nature Switzerland AG
The registered company address is: Gewerbestrasse 11, 6330 Cham, Switzerland

ACKNOWLEDGMENTS

The results of the comparative RAGE project have been published in national reports from eight countries, namely Austria, Bulgaria, Denmark, Finland, France, Greece, Italy, Slovenia and the UK. We would like to thank all the members of the national teams who have worked on Work Stream 3 of the RAGE project, "Militants from the Other Side: Antibodies to hate speech and behaviour". The following researchers have in different ways contributed either to the country reports or have been involved in research concerning the country cases: Birgit Sauer and Edma Ajanovic worked on the Austrian Report; Anna Krasteva, Evelina Staykova, Ildiko Otova, Denitza Kramenova, and Vanya Ivanova on the Bulgarian Report; Birte Siim, Susi Meret, and Jeppe Fuglsang Larsen on the Danish Report; Aino Saarinen, Heini Puurunen, Airi Markkanen, and Anca Enache on the Finnish Report; Etienne Pingaud and Annie Benveniste on the French Report; Gabriella Lazaridis, Don Flynn, and Steve King worked on the Report from the United Kingdom; Gabriella Lazaridis and Mariangela Veikou on the Greek Report; Giovanna Campani and Giovanni Stanghellini on the Italian Report; and Mojca Pajnik, Živa Humer, and Iztok Šori worked on the Slovenian Report. Last but not least we thank the movement activists who in different ways took part in the observed events, campaigns, and forums, in particular the individual interviewees and focus group discussants.

Contents

1 Citizens' Activism and Solidarity Movements
   in Contemporary Europe: Contending with Populism   1
   Birte Siim, Aino Saarinen, and Anna Krasteva

2 Dilemmas of Citizenship and Evolving Civic Activism
   in Denmark   25
   Birte Siim and Susi Meret

3 Against Romanophobia, for Diversity and Equality:
   Exploring the Activism Modes of a "Movement Within
   a Movement" in Finland   51
   Aino Saarinen, Heini Puurunen, Airi Markkanen,
   and Anca Enache

4 Forging "the People" in the UK: The Appeal of Populism
   and the Resistant Antibodies   79
   Don Flynn and Gabriella Lazaridis

5 The (Im)Possibility of Creating Counter-Hegemony
   Against the Radical Right: The Case of Austria   111
   Birgit Sauer

6 We Are Still Here and Staying! Refugee-Led Mobilizations
  and Their Struggles for Rights in Germany 137
  Susi Meret and Waldemar Diener

7 The Anti-discrimination Activism in a Backlash Context:
  A Panorama of the French Situation 167
  Etienne Pingaud

8 Racism, Post-democracy, and Economy That Kills: The
  Challenges of Civil Society Movements in Italy 185
  Giovanna Campani

9 Being a Citizen in Times of Mainstreaming of Populism:
  Building Post-communist Contestatory and Solidary
  Citizenship 213
  Anna Krasteva with Evelina Staykova and Ildiko Otova

10 Feminist Movements' Acts of Citizenship: Experiences
   from Post-Socialist Slovenia 243
   Mojca Pajnik

11 Citizens' Activism for Reimagining and Reinventing
   Citizenship Countering Far-Right Populism 265
   Anna Krasteva, Aino Saarinen, and Birte Siim

12 Activist Citizens: An Afterword 293
   Donatella della Porta

Index 305

NOTES ON CONTRIBUTORS

Giovanna Campani is Full Professor of Intercultural Education, Gender Anthropology and Intercultural Communication at the University of Florence. She holds a PhD in Ethnology from the University of Nice (1988) on "Family, Village and Regional Networks of Italian Immigrants in France" and a Master of Philosophy from the University of Pisa on "History, Science and Sociology in Max Weber's Thought". Her research has focused on topics such as social movements, social inclusion, comparative education, the sociology of migration and gender issues. Gender (in the intersectionality with class and ethnicity) has become her main field of study over the last ten years. She has been principal coordinator of the Italian team of numerous EU projects and has coordinated EU projects in the field of migration and gender. Her most recent books include: *Understanding the Populist Shift: Othering in a Europe in Crisis* (2017, ed. with G. Lazaridis); *The Rise of the Far Right in Europe: Populist Shifts and 'Othering'* (2016, ed. with G. Lazaridis and A. Benveniste); *I populism nell a crisi europea* (2014, with Giovanni Stanghellini); *Precarious Migrant Work in Europe* (2011, with M. Painik); *Genere e Globalizzazione* (2010) and *Migrant nel mondo globale* (2007).

Donatella della Porta is Professor of Political Science, Dean of the Institute for Humanities and the Social Sciences and Director of the PD program in Political Science and Sociology at the Scuola Normale Superiore in Florence, where she also leads the Center on Social Movement Studies (Cosmos). She has directed a major ERC project Mobilizing for Democracy, on civil society participation in democratization processes in

Europe, the Middle East, Asia and Latin America. Among her very recent publications are *Late Neoliberalism and Its Discontents in the Economic Crisis. Comparing Social Movements in the European Periphery* (Palgrave, 2017); *Movement Parties in Times of Austerity* (Polity, 2017); *Where Did the Revolution Go?* (Cambridge University Press, 2016); *Social Movements in Times of Austerity* (Polity, 2015); *Methodological Practices in Social Movement Research* (Oxford University Press, 2014); *Spreading Protest* (ECPR Press, 2014, with Alice Mattoni); *Participatory Democracy in Southern Europe* (Rowman and Littlefield, 2014, with Joan Font and Yves Sintomer); *Mobilizing for Democracy* (Oxford University Press, 2014); *Can Democracy Be Saved?*, Polity Press, 2013; *Clandestine Political Violence*, Cambridge University Press, 2013 (with D. Snow, B. Klandermans and D. McAdam (eds.). *Blackwell Encyclopedia on Social and Political Movements*, Blackwell. 2013; *Mobilizing on the Extreme Right* (with M. Caiani and C. Wagemann), Oxford University Press, 2012; *Meeting Democracy* (ed. with D. Rucht), Cambridge University Press, 2012 and *The Hidden Order of Corruption* (with A. Vannucci). Ashgate 2012.

Waldemar Diener holds an MA degree in Culture, Communication and Globalization from Aalborg University, Denmark, with a specialization in International Migration and Ethnic Relations. During his studies, he spent one year at the University of KwaZulu-Natal (Centre for Civil Society) in Durban, South Africa, researching attitudes toward migrant traditional healers and later xenophobia against Nigerian migrants in South Africa. Living currently in Hamburg, he strives to keep balance between militant activism and academic research.

Anca Enache is a PhD student in Social and Cultural Anthropology at the University of Helsinki. In her doctoral thesis Enache examines the transnational practices of Roma migrants, particularly the marginal locations attributed to Roma families, versus individual and family migration strategies. Enache has conducted research in multinational projects on mobility, gender, hate speech, race and minority issues concerning populism, racism and othering in Europe (Rage) at the Aleksanteri Institute, Finnish Centre for Russian and Eastern European Studies of the University of Helsinki; language, identity and authenticity among Roma in Eastern Europe (2013–2017) at the University of Helsinki; and Inequalities of mobility: relatedness and belonging of transnational families in the Nordic migration space (2015–2019) at the University of Eastern Finland. She works as an Eastern Europe specialist of the Helsinki Deaconess Institute. As a leader of the Hirundo drop-in center, she has significant experience from the grassroots and policy levels and has contributed to different working groups on Roma migrant issues.

Don Flynn has been involved in work around migration and the rights of migrants since the 1970s. He has worked as an immigration caseworker in community law centers in London and as a policy officer for a national migrant welfare organization. From 2006 until 2016 he was the director of the Migrants Rights Network, a UK-wide network of community-based organizations working to support the rights of migrants. He had had a long involvement in European migrant anti-racist and solidarity networks, for many years chairing the UK section of the European Network Against Racism and working as the president of the Platform for International Cooperation on Undocumented Migrants. Previously published work includes *Unease About Strangers: Leveraging Anxiety as the Basis for Policy* in *Community, Citizenship and the 'War on Terror': Security and Insecurity* (Patricia Noxolo and Jef Huysmans (eds) 2009); *The politics of immigration in hard times* in *Labour Migration in Hard times: Reforming Labour Market Regulation?* (Bernard Ryan (ed) 2013); *The politics of immigration in hard times* in *Labour Migration in Hard Times: Reforming Labour Market Regulation?* (Bernard Ryan (ed) 2013); and *The securitisation of disadvantaged communities: The case of British-Somalis* (with Awale Olad) in *The Securitisation of Migration in the EU* (Gabriella Lazaridis, Khursheed Wadia, (eds) 2015).

Anna Krasteva is Professor of Political Sciences, Doctor Honoris Causa of University Lille 3, France, and founder and director of CERMES (Centre for European Refugees, Migration and Ethnic Studies) at the New Bulgarian University, Department of Political Sciences. She has authored and edited 29 books and published numerous articles in about 20 countries. Her main fields of research and teaching are migration policies and politics, far-right populism and civic mobilizations on- and offline. Last year she led the project "Securitization and its impact on human rights and human security"; this year she leads the project on labor migrations in the Western Balkans. She takes part currently in two Horizon 2020 projects: "Representations of the crisis and crisis of representation" and "Evaluation of the common European asylum system under pressure and recommendations for further development". She took part at the World Forum for Democracy (2017). She has been guest professor at the Institute of Political Studies in Paris and Lille; Institute of European Studies at Paris 8 University; Ecole Normale Supérieure de Lyon; Laval

University, Quebec; Metz University; and Institute for Advanced Studies in Nantes and lectured at numerous European universities. She is editor-in-chief of *Southeastern Europe* (Brill) and member of the editorial boards of *Nationalism and Ethnic Politics* (Routledge) and *Europeana* (Shanghai and Paris). She is member of the Board of the Diplomatic Institute and of numerous international scientific boards.

Gabriella Lazaridis is a sociologist who has recently retired from being Senior Lecturer at the University of Leicester in the UK. She has published extensively in the fields of EU policies, inclusion exclusion and social divisions, migration, ethnicity, racisms and gender. Her latest work has been on the rise of the far right in Europe and "othering". She was the PI and director of the multidisciplinary multi-method comparative RAGE project and has co-edited two books from the RAGE project: *Understanding the Populist Shift: Othering in a Europe in Crisis* (2016; with G. Campani) and *The Rise of the Far Right in Europe: Populist Shifts and 'Othering'* (2016; with G. Campani and A. Benveniste). Her latest books include *International Migration in Europe: From Subjects to Abjects* (monograph) and *Securitization of Migration in the EU: Debates After 9/11* (co-edited with Khursheed Wadia), both published by Palgrave.

Airi Markkanen has focused on Finnish Roma since the early 1990s. Her dissertation in Cultural Studies was published in 2003 as *Luonnollisesti: Etnografinen tutkimus romaninaisten elämänkulusta* [Naturally. An ethnographic study of Roma women's life course]. From 2009 she has done fieldwork with Romanian Roma in Finland and Romania. In 2012, she co-edited the anthology titled *Huomio! Romaneja tiellä* [Attention! Roma on the road] (with Heini Puurunen and Aino Saarinen) (Like 2012). Markkanen has published several (other) articles about Romanian Roma. In 2013–2015, she was involved with the Rage team at the Aleksanteri Institute. At present, she is working in the multinational project *Inequalities of mobility: relatedness and belonging of transnational families in the Nordic migration space* at the University of Eastern Finland. She is co-editing the anthology *The Culture of the Finnish Roma* for the Finnish Literature Society.

Susi Meret is Associate Professor in Comparative Migration Politics and Ethnic Relations in the Social Sciences, Department of Culture and Global Studies, Aalborg University (AAU), Denmark. She is affiliated with the research group CoMID, the Center for the Studies of Migration and Diversity. Her main expertise is within populist radical right parties in

Europe, populism and political extremism. She coordinated the research network on Nordic Populism and participated in several Nordic and European projects. Recent publications include *Populist political communication in mediatized society*, Routledge 2017 (with Pajnik, Mojca); *Right-wing Populism in Denmark: People, Nation and Welfare in the Construction of the 'Other'*, Palgrave Macmillan 2016 (with Siim, Birte), *Men's parties with women leaders: A comparative study of the right-wing populist leaders Pia Kjærsgaard, Marine Le Pen and Siv Jensen*, Routledge 2016 (with Siim, Birte & Pingaud, Etienne), and *Spaces of resistance and re-actuality of Gramsci in refugees' struggles for rights: The Lampedusa in Hamburg between exit and voice*, Pluto Press, 2016 (with Della Corte Elisabetta). She has been researching and actively participating in migrant solidarity movements in Germany, Denmark and Italy, and she is co-editor of the forthcoming book *The Refugee Movement is the Movement of the 21st Century: Refugee-Led Movements and the Politics of Solidarity in the European Migrant Metropolis*.

Ildiko Otova is a research assistant in CERMES (Centre for European Refugees, Migration and Ethnic Studies). She holds a PhD in Political Science from New Bulgarian University and is a laureate of the Mozer Scholarship for excellence in the study of Political Science and civil courage. Her main teaching and scientific interests are in the fields of migration, integration, populist and nationalist parties, citizenship and Internet politics. She works on different national and international research projects in this area.

Mojca Pajnik is Associate Professor at the Faculty of Social Sciences, University of Ljubljana, and senior research advisor at the Peace Institute in Ljubljana. Her research focuses on political and communication theory, citizenship, populism, racism, migration and gender. Among her recent books are *Populism and the Web: Communicative Practices of Parties and Movements in Europe* (co-edited with B. Sauer, Routledge, 2017); *Communicating Citizens' Protests, Requiring Public Accountability: Case Studies from Albania, Bosnia and Herzegovina and Macedonia* (co-edited with S. Hodžić, Mediacentar, 2016); and *Contesting Integration, Engendering Migration: Theory and Practice* (co-edited with F. Anthias, Palgrave, 2014). Currently (2018) she coordinates the project GEN-MED, *Gender Differentiation in Media Industry* (Slovenian Research Agency), and is a partner in MEET, *Media Education for Equity and Tolerance* (Erasmus+). She is member of editorial board of *Journal of Alternative and Community Media* and of *Migracijske i etničke teme* (*Migration and Ethnic Themes*). She was awarded for scientific excellency from the Faculty of Social Sciences, University of Ljubljana in 2014.

Etienne Pingaud is presently a "legal rapporteur" in the French National Justice Court. He has been a postdoctoral researcher at the Université de Paris 8 and holds a PhD in Sociology from the School for Advanced Studies in Social Sciences (EHESS/Paris). His main research fields include the development of Islam and the related rise of Islamophobia, the "identitarian" transformations of the far right and, in a more general way, the political construction of cultural identities. He has recently published articles and chapters on these topics in several books and reviews (including "Men's parties with women leaders: A comparative study of the right-wing populist leaders Pia Kjærsgaard, Siv Jensen and Marine Le Pen", in G. Campani and G. Lazaridis eds. *Understanding the Populist Shift* (2016; with S. Meret & B. Siim); "Far-Right Movements in France: The Principal Role of Front National and the Rise of Islamophobia", in Lazaridis, G, Benveniste, A., & Campani, G. (eds.); *The rise of the far right in a Europe under crisis* (2016; with Benveniste, A.); "Les temporalités de la lutte. Evénement, urgence et changements de rythme dans un mobilization locale pour Palestine" in *Politix* (2014); and "La costruzione del national-populismo" in Campani (2014)).

Heini Puurunen holds an MA in West and South Slavonic Languages and Cultures and prepares a doctoral dissertation in Area and Cultural Studies at the University of Helsinki. Her main research interests concern agency and mobility of Roma women and marginalized minorities in the Balkans and in Finland. Puurunen has been involved in multinational research projects on migration, welfare, gender, racism and populist othering, including the RAGE project at the Aleksanteri Institute. Currently she works at a NGO "No Fixed Abode" as an immigration specialist. During the past ten years, Puurunen has been participating in several civic initiatives and projects with an aim to improve the fulfillment of the fundamental human rights of Balkan Roma migrants in Helsinki, primarily in the fields of housing and employment. She has co-edited *Huomio! Romaneja tiellä* (with Markkanen and Saarinen).

Aino Saarinen (DSocSc) is a Senior Research Fellow (Emerita) at the Aleksanteri Institute and a Docent in Women's Studies (Tampere) and Sociology (Oulu). In the late 1990s to the early 2000s, she worked as the Head of Research at the Nordic Institute for Gender Research (Oslo) and as the Nordic Visiting Professor at the Nevsky Institute (St. Petersburg). Presently, she is in charge of the Co-operative Trialogue. Saarinen has been leading Nordic-Russian projects on gender violence and crisis centers in the Barents Region; on Russian women as immigrants in Nordic countries; and on gender, welfare and agency in Russia. She has also been responsible for Finnish EU teams in the field of migration; gender violence and minority women; and populism, racism and othering in Europe (Rage). Saarinen has published in Finnish and Nordic journals, and internationally, for example, in *Signs* and *Post-communist Studies*, and in books by Edward Elgar, Palgrave and Routledge. Among the volumes she has co-edited are *Builders of a New Europe: Women Immigrants from the Eastern Trans-regions* (with Marina Calloni, Kikimora, 2012); *Huomio! Romaneja tiellä* (with Markkanen and Puurunen); and *Women and Transformation in Russia* (with Kirsti Ekonen and Valentina Uspenskaya) (2014). *Mobilizing for mobile Roma*, edited by Saarinen, will come out from Trialogue Books in 2018.

Birgit Sauer is Professor at the Department of Political Science at the University of Vienna, Austria. She has published on gender, governance and democracy, on gender and right-wing populism and on affective labor and state transformation. She is member of the Executive Committee of European Consortium for Political Research. She held visiting professorships in Seoul (South Korea), Florida Atlantic University (USA) and Södertörn University (Sweden). Recent publications include: Gender and Citizenship: Governing Muslim Body Covering in Europe, in: Gemzöe, Lena et al. (eds.); *Contemporary Encounters in Gender and Religion. European Perspectives*, Cham: Palgrave Macmillan, 2016, S. 105–129; Intersections and inconsistencies. Framing Gender in Right-Wing Populist Discourses in Austria, in: *NORA. Nordic Journal of Feminist and Gender Research*, 2014, together with Edma Ajanovic and Stefanie Mayer; Affective governmentality: A feminist perspective, in: Hudson, Christine/Rönnblom, Malin/Teghtsoonian, Katherine (eds.): *Gender, Governance and Feminist Analysis. Missing in Action?*, London/New York: Routledge 2017, S. 39–58, together with Otto Penz.

Birte Siim is Professor in Gender Research in the Social Sciences, Dept. of Culture and Global Studies, Aalborg University (AAU), Denmark. She has been responsible for the Danish EU teams on citizenship, democracy, gender, migration and populism. Her publications include: *Gender and Citizenship. Politics and Agency in France, Britain and Denmark* (2000); *Negotiations of Gender and Diversity in an Emergent European Public Sphere* (co-ed. with M. Mokre) (2013); "Citizenship", in K. Celis et al. (eds.) *The Oxford Handbook on Gender and Politics* (2013); "Gender

Diversities – Practicing Intersectionality in the European Union", *Ethnicities* (2014) (with L. Rolandsen Agustin); "Political Intersectionality and Democratic Politics in the European Public Sphere", *Politics & Gender* (2014); "Gendering European welfare states and citizenship – revisioning inequalities", in P. Kennett and N. Lendvai-Benton (eds.) *Handbook of European Social Policy* (2017) (with A. Borchorst); "Men's parties with women leaders. A comparative study of the right-wing populist leaders Pia Kjærsgaard, Siv Jensen and Marine Le Pen", in G. Campani and G. Lazaridis eds. *Understanding the Populist Shift* (2016) (with S. Meret & E. Pingaud); "Rightwing Populism in Denmark: People, Nation and Welfare in the Construction of 'the other'", in *The Rise of the Far Right in Europe. Populist Shifts and 'Othering'*, ed. by G. Lazaridis et al. (2016) (with S. Meret).

Evelina Staykova is program director at the department of Political Sciences and coordinator of Centre for European Refugees, Migration and Ethnic Studies (CERMES). She is doctor of Political Sciences and assistant professor in the Department of Political Science of the New Bulgarian University (NBU). Her teaching and research interests are in the fields of migration, citizenship and urban studies. Evelina Staykova is experienced in coordinating and participation in national and international scientific projects. She is an author of numerous articles published in Bulgarian and foreign editions.

LIST OF FIGURES

Fig. 9.1	A comparison of three types of citizenship	235
Fig. 9.2	Mapping post-communist mobilizations and citizenships	236
Fig. 11.1	Mapping citizens' activism	283

LIST OF TABLES

Table 4.1　Participants in focus groups　96
Table 6.1　The Lampedusa in Hamburg (LiHH) main actions and messages (2013–2014)　162

CHAPTER 1

Citizens' Activism and Solidarity Movements in Contemporary Europe: Contending with Populism

Birte Siim, Aino Saarinen, and Anna Krasteva

INTRODUCTION: THE TRANSFORMATION OF THE POLITICAL LANDSCAPES

Populism and right-wing nationalism (the radical right) are contested, multi-dimensional, and contextual phenomena (Mudde 2005). One of the crucial elements of the populist discourse is the rejection of diversity, immigration, Islam, and LGBT rights (Müller 2016). Not only grass roots supporters have been activated; in the last two decades, numerous political leaders, in Eastern and Western, Northern and Southern Europe, have

---

B. Siim (✉)
Department of Culture and Global Studies, Aalborg University, Aalborg, Denmark

A. Saarinen
Aleksanteri Institute, Helsinki, Finland

A. Krasteva
Department of Political Sciences, New Bulgarian University, Sofia, Bulgaria

© The Author(s) 2019
B. Siim et al. (eds.), *Citizens' Activism and Solidarity Movements*,
Palgrave Studies in European Political Sociology,
https://doi.org/10.1007/978-3-319-76183-1_1

expressed openly exclusionist, xenophobic, racist positions. In the 2000s–2010s, a few party leaders and/or members of parliament have even been convicted for "othering". More recently, however, one part of the right-wing populist discourse and self-portraying has increasingly emphasized itself as a combatant of Western values and norms like freedom of opinion (the cartoon crisis in Denmark and Charlie Hebdo in France), gender equality, secularism, and sexual freedom. The political landscapes and legacies in the European Union are very different. Many populist, right-wing actors want a regime change; other actors protect Western democracies and welfare states, even minorities' human and fundamental rights.

These contradictory trends exist even in well-established democracies. Even the Nordic countries, which have long been praised for respect for human rights, equality and inclusiveness, have opened access to numerous "anti-phenomena". "Critical" discourses on the cornerstones of the regime have taken the floor and placed the mainstream parties on defense. Anders Widfeldt (2015), who has analyzed the rise of right-wing populist parties and their gradual integration in representative politics and governments in Scandinavia, points out that today the ideal called the Nordic model can even have a negative ring. Populist right-wingers are attacking the principle of all-inclusiveness, which not so long ago was re-examined in order to valorize new migration- and refugee-related forms of inequalities. These new forms of inequalities have inspired a constructive re-analysis of the regime (Kvist et al. 2012). The concept of "welfare nationalism" associated with social democracy (Brochmann and Hagelund 2012) has been replaced by concepts such as "welfare national chauvinism" (Siim and Meret 2016: 131) or even "welfare exclusionism" (Keskinen 2016), which indicates a turn toward limiting welfare to people with citizenship. Political hate expressions such as "welfare shoppers", "anchor children", and so on in social media and in formal parliamentary arenas as well target the most vulnerable groups who are refugees from war and are persecuted as old and new minorities and internal "deviants". At the same time, these parties polish their image by supporting Western liberal values such as gender equality and tolerance of sexual minorities, especially if this "liberalism" can be used to criticize Muslim newcomers (Siim and Meret 2016; Saarinen et al. 2018).

Similar analyses of the emergence of populist right-wing or far-right party family can also be found outside the Nordic countries. The literature on Eastern European post-socialist countries in transition from authoritarian one-party socialism toward multi-party liberal democracy has long neglected the negative aspects of the political transformation and focused mainly on EU membership. Over the last two decades, this picture has changed dramatically, and nationalist, populist, and Euro-skeptic forces have been characterized as expressions of nativism, that is, exclusionary versions of nationalism (Widfelt 2015: 33–61; Kriszan and Siim forthcoming). Paradoxically, simultaneously with accessing the EU and confronting suspicion and exclusion, Eastern European EU citizens have themselves, to cite Andrea Pirro (2015: 2–8), developed "organized intolerance" toward the "outsiders" in their own countries. Inclusion and exclusion have therefore been curiously intertwined. It has been argued that populist radical right parties in Central and Eastern Europe are more anti-democratic and militant than their Western European counterparts (Pirro 2015: 5; Mudde 2005; Minkenberg 2002). An additional special feature, which is not found to the same extent in Northern Europe, is hostility against internal, that is, the historic others, like Turks and Muslims in Bulgaria, and Roma who are more numerous in many East European countries than anywhere in the West (Mudde 2005).

In Continental and Southern European countries with a legacy of Nazism and fascism such as Austria, Germany, and Italy, the political developments and characteristics of right-wing populism are somewhat different (cf. Lazaridis et al. 2016; Lazaridis and Campani 2016). In Austria, the far right has moved from the margin to mainstream and entered the government (FPÖ) (Sauer and Ajanovic 2016). In Italy and Germany, the far right has long been marginalized. The Alternative für Deutschland is thus a very recent phenomenon. The Republican France is in many respects a special case, since right-wing populism has proved to be relatively strong in the presidential elections but has not directly managed to influence mainstream politics (Benveniste and Pingaud 2016).

It is worth noticing that in Western Europe, in particular, green and left party families (Pirro 2015: 33) have been on the move and engaged in forming solidarity movements, counter-publics, and counterforces to populist and right-wing actors. In addition, new forms of civic activism and solidarity have emerged "from below", initiated by diverse groups in civil society associations, often at the local level and sometimes bridging the local, national, and transnational arenas. This complex phenomenon, which is the focus of this book, has arguably not received the attention it deserves in normative, theoretical, and empirical studies of democracy and citizenship.

Making the Counterforces Visible

One of the main challenges is to make the diverse counterforces in contemporary Europe, which are often locally based and situated in civil society, visible. The dynamic transformations of the political landscape, the deconstruction of welfare states, and the strengthening of exclusive nationalisms across Europe create new challenges to democratic counterforces and solidarity movements and to their strategies and practices to combat othering and exclusion. An additional challenge is the paradox that part of the democratic opposition to right-wing populism defending cultural diversity, migration, and sexual inclusion sometimes shares the right-wing's criticisms of deficits in accountability of political and economic elites, the so-called the crisis of responsibility (Della Porta 2015: 6), and decreasing representativity and legitimacy of representative European politics. In brief, hate speech and hate acts flourish and increase around Europe, even in regimes that have previously been characterized as tolerant and inclusive (Widfeldt 2015: 37–42).

The authors in this volume theorize these political challenges and paradoxes by exploring the democratic counterforces, that is, pro-diversity and pro-equality movements, in Europe, historically and today, with focus on nine national contexts: Austria, Bulgaria, Denmark, Finland, France, Germany, Italy, Slovenia, and the UK. The political transformations are approached in macro-level analyses within diverse political regimes characterized by liberal democracy: (a) transitions brought about by migration in the Nordic welfare states and Britain, (b) combats against fascist and Nazi xenophobic legacies in Continental and Southern Europe, and (c) on-going transition from post-socialist/communist rule toward representative democratic rule. Growing divisions between North and South and East and West are investigated as well. Attention must be paid to the relationships between civic actors, both at the grassroot level and in relations with the local and national state and the EU. Another key theme, mobilization of "victim" actors who are facing discrimination but are struggling for their equal rights as citizens and residents, is a phenomenon topic in regard to democracy and citizenship (Isin 2008; Isin 2009; Mendez-Shannon and Bailey 2016; Bhimji 2016).

The Theoretical and Methodological Frames and Key Concepts

This book is motivated by a desire to understand the new forms of populism and nationalism in contemporary Europe linked to globalization, European integration, migration, and multiculturality/multiculturalism.

One of the theoretical ambitions is to move beyond the nation-state in order to overcome the "methodological nationalism" connected with key concept such as citizenship, democracy, the public sphere, and the welfare state (Wimmer and Glick-Schiller 2002; Fraser 2013). We focus on transnational civil society and "social movements in times of crisis" (della Porta and Mattoni 2014) such as the global justice movement from the 1990s, the World Social Forums, the Occupy Wall Street movements from the 2000s, and the social movements that are emerging in the current times of austerity, at regional, national, and even local levels. They are all networked with each other and have, in brief, turned into "movements of movements" (della Porta 2005; della Porta 2015).

The main aim is thus to critically reflect upon these expressions of transformative politics by re-exploring numerous key concepts in the social sciences, such as citizenship, democracy/public sphere, social movements, power/empowerment, and conflicts and cooperation around race/ethnicity, class, gender, and sexuality. Values, frameworks, claims, as well as action modes are changing. Flexibilities, hierarchies, and novel forms of multiple belongings are today intertwined with upward shifts toward transnational waves of contention, regional and global anti-austerity, and pro-democracy protests for vulnerable social groups amidst economic and financial crisis and new protest repertoires, also around the European Union (della Porta and Mattoni 2014; della Porta 2015).

Paradoxically, more focus is needed on the local level. "Urban citizenship" (Nielsen 2008) is a very recent phenomenon; it is cultivated in great metropolises, in multicultural cities where the most vulnerable groups, old and new, may act together to combat poverty and homelessness—people who are both "non-residents" and "illegals" but in different ways and who have no voice and formal representation. The sub-local level is also interesting for explorations of participation: squatters and people building camps as spaces for survival and action bring up what William Walters (2008), provocatively, calls "non-citizenship". They destabilize formal statist regimes of power and citizenship and show that the tension between residency and need is indeed one of the most topical issues in the 2010s. Concerns of ethics-based politics are therefore relevant for all levels, from global to neighborhoods.

On the analytical level, one of the main issues refers to citizens' activism and the struggles around citizenship rights and obligations in contemporary Europe. The fundamental questions, outlined by Hannah Arendt (1951, 1958), are concerned with all marginalized and vulnerable people's "right to have rights". The chapters in this volume address citizenship as a contested concept (contestatory citizenship; Krasteva 2016), which asks questions about inclusion/exclusion of actors in democracy. These contested issues are crucial in times when mobility and migration have become the road to work and welfare for an increasing number of people moving, circulating, or living in contemporary Europe. T. H. Marshall's normative model of equal rights (1950) was limited to the nation-state, and scholars like Nira Yuval-Davis (2011) and Nancy Fraser (2005, 2013) have reformulated the classic notions of citizenship and democracy from transnational perspectives.

EU citizenship is a supranational model of citizenship, but the meaning and perspectives of EU citizenship are highly debatable. On the one hand, EU citizenship has given new rights to citizens of member states to move freely across borders and to work and reside legally in other member states. On the other hand, EU citizenship is a secondary citizenship derived from national citizenship (Bauböck 2006), which has increased the gap between citizens from EU member states and third-country nationals. Moreover, the "free movement" directive does not apply everywhere and to everyone, for example, new mobile Roma and travelers within the EU, and it is arguably one of the major causes of the result of the Brexit referendum in 2016.

INTERSECTIONALITY

Intersectionality has become a key concept concerned with interrelations between different forms of inequalities in civil society and the public and private arena as well as on the regime level (Ferree et al. 2002; Yuval-Davis 2011: Siim and Mokre 2013). The book adds intersectional, comparative, and transnational analytical perspectives (Fraser 2013) to the citizenship and social movement theories focusing on the intersections of inequalities and differences across class, race/ethnicity, gender, sexuality, and religion. The objective is to both reframe and contextualize the dominant public sphere models of democracy and citizenship (Siim and Mokre 2013; Krasteva 2016) using an intersectional approach that is sensitive to time, space, and place. The analytical framework is inspired by diverse bodies of literature: Hannah Arendt's crucial question about "the right to have rights" for old and new groups of marginalized and vulnerable people; Engin Isin's "acts of citizenship"; Donatella della Porta's global social movement model; and Nancy Frasers' transnational model of social justice under conditions of crisis, austerity, and post-democracy in contemporary Europe (2005, 2013). The intersectionality approach provides sensitivity to multiple equalities and differences within and between marginalized social groups conceptualizing the interrelations of categories such as class, race/ethnicity, gender, sexuality, and religion and other social divisions. It thus encourages a focus on collaborations, negotiations, and conflicts between and within marginalized and vulnerable groups. The analytical framework explores who has the rights, to what kind of rights, where are these rights situated—the public or private arena—and how are these rights employed in practice in everyday life?

Through these theories, concepts, and approaches, the book discusses many of the most pressing contemporary problems and issues, such as hate speech and acts, in view of democracy and excluded and marginalized minorities. Specifically, it explores the developments of counterforces and pro-actors in defense of human and fundamental rights, not only horizontally, in civil society and in relation to parties, but also vertically, in transactional relations to the national, European and global institutions and human rights regimes (Jacobsson and Saxonberg 2013; Císař 2013). It introduces and critically evaluates pro-actors' values, aims, strategies, and action repertoires, as well as attitudes and practices of civil disobedience, a problematic that is of great importance in analyses of hate speech and hate acts. Confronting othering from the perspective of democracy and three-dimensional justice (economic-social, cultural, political) (Fraser 2013) will, also, encourage an exploration of possibilities for transversal dialogues (Yuval-Davis 2011) between right-wing populists and human rights pro-actors.

Marginalized Actors onto the Scene

Confrontations regarding flows of human movements inside the EU, across internal borders from East to West, across the regimes outlined above, are especially interesting in view of the rise of xenophobic right-wing populism and pro-actors who fight for inclusive human rights. To quote a team of Nordic scholars (Djuve et al. 2015): "when affluence meets poverty" is an issue that should not be viewed only from the social-economic and cultural perspective but also from the call for inclusive political rights, not only in civil society but in representative institutions as well, on all levels, including the EU. This problem is far from solved in any of the regimes, not even in the idealized Nordic regime and certainly not in the countries of origin in the Eastern states of the EU (Mudde 2005).

The issue formulated by Nancy Fraser (2005, 2013), among others, to include in decision-making "all affected" is a vision only, not only in view of "external" others from outside the national borders but of "internal others" as well. Roma, for instance, must move "from victimhood to citizenship" (Guy 2013), transforming the position from those acted on to agents, or, at least co-actors (Saarinen et al. 2018/forthcoming). They, like so many other marginalized minorities, have to take steps toward not a reactive but a proactive role that includes new identity formation, self-organizing, and formulation of action strategies on multiple levels, from bottom-up, local, and national levels to regional and even global levels. The increasingly complex political context calls for a "boomerang" strategy (see Keck and Sikkink 1998: 8–10): combining mobilization from below, civil society and pressure from above, particularly from the global level, the United Nations' human rights regime, to be implemented at lower levels, in the European Union, and in the nine nation-states investigated in this book. This multi-level strategy thus turns our attention to actors from below.

As decisions are now made in regional, supranational, and transnational contexts, we have to discuss the issue of post-national political and cultural belonging. Castles and Davison (2000: 84–102) have emphasized the need for "open and flexible belongings" and new forms of participation that transcend state boundaries. In brief, it is about "becoming a citizen" in the middle of contextual change. This is one of the fundamental challenges to democracy today because people in increasing numbers are without formal rights, outside the political institutions in the country they live in. This implies, self-evidently, a transition from being a passive citizen as a bearer of rights to becoming an "active citizen" who is willing and able to participate in the exercise of political power. Engin F. Isin and Greg M. Nielsen (2008) go further in emphasizing the processual approach and working out active and new forms of engagement. In brief, instead of focusing on formal status (only), scholars in citizenship studies have to turn toward actual politics, that is, practices, the "doers". Investigating "every day deeds" or "everyday citizenship" implies a call for "*activist* citizenship", aiming at disruption and identifying new possibilities, claiming new rights, formulating "creative moments", where the established status and order and related practices are questioned.

This demands urgent attention to "pro-actors" and "victims" as well as their interconnections, overlapping collaboration—not only as uprisings and protests but also, as social movement scholars recommend, as movements with intended outcomes and, more generally, a formation of a new kind of "movement society" (Jenkins et al. 2008; Meyer and Tarrow 1998). Another important issue is creating alternative visions of democracy in practice through "acts of resistance" in the local, national, or transnational arenas. The chapters address the spread of protest movements in civil society (della Porta and Mattoni 2014) through everyday activities and political activism in diverse anti-austerity, anti-racism, solidarity and resistance movements, and pro-diversity, pro-equality, feminist, and LGBT agency. The chapters address how the movements communicate through conflicts, cooperation and negotiation, and diverse forms of communication across civil society movements, for example, between anti-discrimination/racism/anti-racist movements and networks and feminism/anti-feminism movements and networks. Overall, transnational—regional and global—activism is an urgent research challenge and calls for new frameworks and concepts. In this, the book will continue debates and explorations.

Exclusion and Inclusion

This, however, brings along multiple ambiguities as it implies a dual focus on inclusion and exclusion. Irrespective of "post-national belonging" (Soysal 1994: 29), which is based on universal human rights, the nation-state is still, as Castles and Davidson (2000: 19) claim, the key reference point for citizenship and will likely remain so even if the borders become more and more porous. Moreover, analyses of formal and actual rights within national contexts have become increasingly critical and nuanced. Castles and Davidson 2000: 94–100), for instance, talk about "denizens", "quasi-citizens", and "margizens" when they discuss national citizenship; Isin and Nielsen (2008) partly call non-citizens "strangers", "aliens", and "outcasts".

Moving to the global level and its human rights regime, however, implies that no one is, or should be, totally without rights. An actually "no-one is illegal" is one of the most urgent challenges, both in theory and in practice (Nyers 2008). However, pro-actors often refer to border-crossers, displaced persons, asylum-seekers, and refugees as "victims". Also here, we have to shift our focus from helplessness to self-mobilization, self-empowerment, and self-organization. Even in the harshest settings, people seem to constitute themselves as subjects regardless of their status. In the 2010s, "refugee activists" (Bhimji 2016) organized, at least sporadically, against deportations and for regularization of their status. This uprise is, claims Peter Nyers (2008), deeply paradoxical: self-identifying as a non-status person leads to engagement in an act of citizenship, vocalization of justice/injustice. It shows that formal citizenship is not a precondition for having a political voice and asserting influence. People with uncertain or precarious status, resident non-citizens and those in the underground, are often called "paperless" or even "illegals", moving in and out, between statuses, also challenge the ideal of a welfare state "safeguarded" by populist right-wingers (Saarinen and Calloni 2012).

In this context, various pro-activists including "victims" have to find ways and means to respond to these welfare chauvinist or exclusionist rightwing populist parties and forces who tend to make use of "uncivil" repertoires, hate acts and hate speech, in order to draw the line between "deserving" and "undeserving" of welfare rights. When doing this, these populist groups build up what Petr Kopecký and Cas Mudde (2012) have conceptualized as "uncivil society". It is now, they argue, flourishing in particular in post-communist Europe where pro-actors are maybe more marginal or at least more on the defensive than in Western Europe (see also Jacobsson and Saxonberg 2013). However, these trends are visible in other parts of EU as well. Here, the "undocumented experience" (Mendez-Shannon and Bailey 2016) of excluded groups from their own, proactive welfare authorities' and various civil actors' perspective is worth exploring.

Acts of Citizenship and Acts of Friendship

This phenomenon also calls for a more thorough exploration, and even invention, of new political concepts and practices. In addition to "acts of citizenship", there is the Danish model of "acts of friendship" based on kindness, curiosity, and respect for diversity (Fenger-Grøndal 2017) as well as actions conceptualized by William Walters (2008) as "acts of demonstration", which aim at revealing injustices and bringing forth new claims. Acts of demonstration are often seen as the start of processes of including people without formal (or any) political and/or social rights. They create scenes and call witnesses for confirmation of actors and their claims, in one word, empower them.

This brings us to exploration of innovative action repertoires. Now in particular, the politics of aesthetics and performances, that is, visualization and symbolization of actions (Nyers 2008), has become a new focus in studies of political activism. Events such as art exhibits, graffiti, film, music, and theater festivals addressing different audiences, prospective supporters, the general public, even power holders confronted on the stairs of representative institutions. This offers new opportunity structures to new kinds of actors, today's outsiders, "beings with claims" to use Isin and Nielsen's (2008) provocative expression (see also Jacobsson and Saxonberg 2013). Pop-up performances benefit especially activists who have to stay underground, for example, asylum-seekers and those who have been denied residence permit, who appear and disappear in a minute or in the middle of the night.

Deliberative Mini-Publics: Transversal Dialogues

In order to look forward, to identify prospects for transformative politics, it is important to bring out new and innovative forms of making politics that open access to equal participation and, importantly, reciprocal deliberation. James S. Fishkin (2014) presents the principle of "non-tyranny" to emphasize the problematic of meetings of majorities and minorities, those with full, partial, or non-rights even in "well-intended" pro-actor contexts. In cases where the potential participants are from the outset unequal—cultural, gender or sexual minorities, fully or gradually excluded newcomers—this is indeed worthy of special attention. One innovative method for analyzing collaboration between "victims" and solidarity actors explores articulation of needs and claims as well as structures of opportunities for this—in brief, internal cultures in joint enterprises.

Increase of multicultural actors with extremely different experiences of participation and democracy (or non-democracy) has challenged the theorizing of participative and deliberative democracy (Guttman and Thompson 1996; Grönlund et al. 2014). Among democratic innovations within the so-called deliberative turn is, for instance, the Danish model of consensus conferences. More recently, multiple kinds of transnationally inspired civic forums for justice and multiculturality have emerged (della Porta 2013). One is "deliberative mini-public", a forum where participants representing different viewpoints are gathered to deliberate on a particular issue in small groups (Landwehr 2014; Grönlund et al. 2014). These kinds of laboratories, which are often used in focus groups interviews, are of interest because they involve outsiders, "victims", as well as citizens.

These types of arenas can be approached as political innovations, constructions for "learning democracy" (Grönlund et al. 2014). However, besides choosing the participants, the internal practices must also be ordered and analyzed in detail. In brief, to be effective, this talk-centric method for reasoned and balanced deliberation must be based on genuine inclusion and equal participation to arrive at what in deliberative democracy is called "enlightened understanding" (Saward 2000).

More generally, experiments with preconditions for critical and constructive dialogue, explorations of interests, needs and claims across divisions and differences have turned us toward hermeneutic theorizing of democracy, that is, Habermas' idea on the "ideal speech situation": a rational, argument-oriented discourse. Today, as more and more people live in countries that are not their own, in refuge, travels or more permanently, in diaspora, outside their homelands, this demands innovative, courageous, and sensitive methods. This is confirmed by focus groups interviews, such as in the RAGE project (cf. Lazaridis et al. 2016; Lazaridis and Campani 2016; Pajnik and Sauer 2017).

This challenge is similar to what Nira Yuval-Davis (1997: 130) has discussed and developed as a practice of "transversal dialogue", the process of "rooting" and "shifting", and "civility". To set up coalitions and formulate solidarity politics, one has to keep one's own perspective while emphasizing and respecting others and bearing in mind that interests are not always compatible. Yuval-Davis warns about the risk of "uncritical solidarity" and of identity politics, of not homogenizing the other participants. In brief, the other groups should not be approached *en bloc*. In both ingroups and out-groups, gender, sexualities, educations, and so on do make a difference. Here, we have to address the problem of scaling up deliberation, mini-publics, and transversal practices (Niemeyer 2014), which brings us to the macro-level challenges in regard to the nation-states and multi-level political formations as well as the three regimes discussed in this volume.

THE COMPARATIVE RAGE PROJECT: EXPLORING COUNTERFORCES TO NATIONAL POPULISMS

The book employs a comparative theoretical and methodological approach to analyze the nine national case studies outlined by national teams. The teams are in different ways related to the comparative RAGE project[1]: *Hate-Speech and Populist Othering through the Racism, Age and Gender Looking Glass* (cf. Lazaridis et al. 2016; Lazaridis and Campani 2016;

---

[1] Greece was part of the national case-studies of the first three books of the RAGE project but is unfortunately not included in this book. We decided to include a chapter focusing on Germany instead in order to study examples of migrant self-organization.

Pajnik and Sauer 2017). This closing section presents the case studies and their critical analyses of the state of democracy and rule of law with the aim of exploring counterforces to national populisms in the nine national- and three regime-level contexts. Othering and exclusion in various parts of the Europe Union are approached with similar theoretical and methodological frames analyzing framings and understandings of ethnic, religious, sexual, and gender-related divisions and diversities: various expressions of anti-migration, Romanophobia, Islamophobia, and homophobia, which are on the rise in the twenty-first century. The methodology is based on in-depth studies and narrative analyses of a diversity of civil society actors at the local, national, and transnational level, including focus group interviews, participant observation, and the internet.

Situating National Cases of Resistance in Geopolitical Regimes

The national case studies illustrate the great diversity in issues and actors and in the opposition they encounter from right-wing and mainstream state and civil society actors influenced by historical legacies, political institutions, and cultures of the different regimes in Europe. These analyses of diverse counterforces and resistance aim to uncover prospects for respect and tolerance in the increasingly multicultural Europe. The nine countries are situated in three geopolitical regions: Denmark and Finland are grouped together in Northern Europe with the UK; Austria, Germany, and France are grouped together in Continental and Southern Europe with Italy—the so-called old Europe; and Bulgaria and Slovenia are grouped together in Central and Eastern Europe—the so-called new Europe. The question is what characterizes these regimes in terms of right-wing populism and civil society activism, to what extent these geopolitical divisions still make sense in contemporary Europe. Most importantly, what are the prospects for a diverse and equal Europe that respects human rights and democratic participation by "all affected"?

The Transformations of the Northern European Welfare Regimes and the UK

The analysis of civic activism in Denmark and Finland is situated within the Nordic welfare states in transition characterized by growing welfare chauvinism. The two chapters identify new types of actors, new forms of transversal activism and acts of citizenship, which aim at transcending the division between national citizens and vulnerable and marginalized groups of non-citizens. The chapters confirm that despite the mainstreaming of right-wing populism in both countries, the welfare state model is still important and is even defended by right-wing populist parties such as the Danish People's Party and the Finns Party. It is worth mentioning that civil society actors usually perceive the national and local (and supranational) state as a potential ally despite the involvement of right-wing populism either directly in the government or indirectly as its support party. This picture in many ways contrasts with the UK case where populism usually refers to a more general movement in politics emphasizing political rhetoric across the left-right divide, a sense of general decline by the loss of political support for democratic management of national economies. The UK case focuses on strategies to both contain and combat racism and other forms of discrimination by state actors, NGOs, and civil society.

Chapter 2 by Birte Siim and Susi Meret explores the dilemmas of citizenship and evolving civic activism in Denmark addressing the new forms of differentiated and activist citizenship. The focus is on key organizations mobilized in the struggle against discrimination and othering in civil society associations that work on behalf of migrants, refugees, and asylum-seekers. The chapter shows that migration presents new challenges for Danish citizenship. It is a significant fact that the majority of the activists in the analysis are Danish citizens who oppose anti-migration, anti-Muslim discourses, and policies and act in solidarity with migrants, refugees, and asylum-seekers. The chapter elaborates on the notion of "everyday activism" used by many of the Danish activists to characterize their motivation behind their own activism. This concept is interesting since it refers to the dual objective to "act with and for" marginalized and vulnerable groups. Other groups understand themselves as acting mainly to support refugees and asylum-seekers, while only a minority is engaged in activism based on self-organization of refugees and asylum-seekers against discrimination and fighting for their rights to have rights. Despite the mainstreaming of right-wing populism, some of the activists refer to the evolving civic activism, for example, "the acts of friendship" by the Friendly Neighbors, which represents activist citizenship transcending the division between citizens and non-citizens.

Chapter 3 by Aino Saarinen, Heini Puurunen, Airi Markkanen, and Anca Enache explores a "movement within a movement" focusing on pro-actors who work to improve conditions for Eastern European Roma. The "beggars" arrived in Finland in the late 2000s as EU citizens after the Eastern enlargement and under the free movement directive. The chapter brings up surprisingly numerous pro-actors both in the third sector and civil society and shows, by analyzing internet information, campaign observations and focus group discussions, how they have come together to promote the cause of Roma and human rights. The typology of activism modes—service production, advocacy work, radical protesting, civic self-organization, and periodic mass mobilization—reveals transformative acts of citizenship, even civil disobedience. Finnish Roma are on the move in the name of common identity and solidarity, but mobile Roma participate only rarely, mostly for their own economic interests. In the background are the populist and right-wing actors who in 2015, after a great electoral victory, joined the center-right government, where they have successfully pressured for deconstruction of the Nordic model in favor of welfare nationalism/chauvinism. Interestingly, the "migration-critical" faction that took over the Finns Party in the summer of 2017 is currently in opposition.

Chapter 4 by Don Flynn and Gabriella Lazaridis shows how UK populism emerged as the seemingly standard way of doing mass politics in an epoch marked by the steady demise of leftist and Christian forms of social democracy. The first part offers an account of populism in Britain looking at three political parties with focus on political rhetoric used to constitute and mobilize a specific version of "the people" and discusses whether a particular political party operates with this element of populism consideration. The second part discusses how the confrontation between radical right populist parties and opposing actors results in the evolution of anti-racist and anti-discrimination attitudes, politics, strategies, and activism at the individual and organized level. Here the focus is on strategies to both contain and combat racism and other forms of discrimination by state actors, NGOs, and civil society. The analysis shows how Thatcher's "authoritarian populism" and Blair's "progressive populism" built the momentum for the "insurgent populism" in the UKIP/Farage-led revolt. It called for "people vs elite" confrontation and fiercely criticized the EU and Eastern European immigration, and it all crystallized in the Brexit vote in 2016. In this context, the British antibodies, although internally split, seek to build a shared agenda in the anti-capitalist/anti-globalist framework of the twenty-first century, which might lay the foundation for transnational networks and collaboration, which, however, will be challenging in post-Brexit Europe.

Continental and Southern European Regimes: Old Europe

Austria, Germany, and Italy share a common past influenced by Nazism and fascism. They are losers of the World War II, while Republican France emerged as one of the winners despite the authoritarian influence of the Vichy regime. Today, three of the four countries have strong right-wing populist movements and parties. Only in Germany is the growth of rightwing populism in parliamentary politics a more recent phenomenon. One of the crucial questions is if and how civil society organizations are able to fight right-wing populism and racism by organizing a counter-hegemonic discourse. A major difference between the countries is the role of the state. The Austrian chapter shows how the anti-immigrant and anti-Muslim consensus draws on a strong tradition of "institutional racism" as wells as on xenophobic opinions of the Austrian population. In contrast, the French chapter emphasizes the recent paradigmatic shift in antidiscrimination policies. This has, on the one hand, created new opportunities for associations and victims of racism, othering, and hate speech and hate crimes and, on the other hand, mobilized strong counter-movements in civil society against anti-discrimination policies. The German chapter finds that the case of Germany is paradigmatic and characterized by the emergence of new forms of migrant rights activism and mobilization practices, compared to the past. The Italian chapter proposes that Italy is in an era of post-populism since no forces have the strength to obtain hegemony with Berlusconi losing support. It emphasizes that the broad forces opposing anti-immigrant policies, racist discourses, and hate speech, such as the anti-racist movements, trade unions, and some religious organizations, face dramatic challenges after years of economic crisis, high unemployment, and reduction of the welfare state.

Chapter 5 by Birgit Sauer addresses the (im)possibility of creating counter-hegemony against right-wing populism. Austria has since the mid-1980s been characterized by a strong right-wing populist party, the Austrian Freedom Party (*Freiheitliche Partei Österreich*, FPÖ). Austria's integration into the European Union in 1995, economic globalization, the neoliberal restructuring of the country, and cuts in social welfare opened a window of opportunity for nationalist right-wing populists. The FPÖ's strategy to maximize votes and constituency has since then been to form "the people" as a community of "us" against the "others" based on ethnicity and nationality by the construction of others such as Muslims, intellectuals, the political elite, the EU, feminists, and LGBT people. The chapter shows that this anti-immigrant and anti-Muslim consensus draws on a strong tradition of "institutional racism" as wells as on xenophobic opinions in the Austrian population. These attempts to forge an anti-immigrant consensus triggered counterforces in Austrian civil society, but the chapter also illustrates how difficult it has been to create counter-hegemony against right-wing populism within political organizations of the strong Austrian social partnership.

Chapter 6 by Susi Meret and Waldemar Diener focuses on refugee-led mobilizations and their struggles for rights and belonging in Germany. It deals with recent forms of collective mobilization and resistance among non-status refugees across Europe who are protesting against stricter asylum and migration laws, policies of securitization, and control and criminalization at national and European level. The authors build on efforts to conduct research based on participatory action in Hamburg and Berlin, and they insist on the need of academics and researchers to critically reflect upon their positioning and to expound the often avowed purpose within critical migration studies to give the subalterns a voice. They suggest that the case of Germany is paradigmatic with the emergence of new forms of migrant rights activism and mobilization practices, also compared to the past. The chapter looks at the different phases of the struggles, particularly within the urban contexts of Hamburg and Berlin, at how these groups have emerged and organized with others and how they have challenged notions of citizenship, human rights, and democracy. It reflects upon the importance of the urban space in terms of past and present social movements, networks and resources, and on the way mobilization strategies have eventually been "transformed" by and with the refugee struggles. The chapter illustrates that despite the increasing efforts by refugee groups to get organized, the activities rarely achieve continuity, political power, and permanent victory, partly because of a lack of strategic direction, coherence, and continuity in the various phases of the mobilization.

Chapter 7 by Etienne Pingaud looks at the anti-discrimination activism in a backlash context exploring current mobilizations against discrimination in France, through the examples of LGBT and anti-racist movements. It shows that these movements are at a turning point as they are facing a strong intellectual and political conservative trend rejecting their demands in the name of French identity. The French case is seen as paradoxical: on the one hand, there has been an evolution of anti-discrimination mobilization since France has changed its legal approach to discrimination to conform to EU directives. This has created new opportunities for associations and victims, for example, the new key role of the law in the actions of activists. On the other hand, the far right reaches higher scores in each election, and conservative ideas are increasingly present in public debates. LGBT rights have been targeted for the first time by huge demonstrations against same-sex marriage. This has sparked new internal debates and controversies increasing the difficulty for all these organizations to unite forces, be heard and promote French republicanism or multiculturalism with recognition of minorities.

Chapter 8 by Giovanna Campani studies the challenges of social movements in Italy in times of racism, post-democracy, and "an economy that kills". It proposes that Italy is experiencing a period of "post-populism" since Berlusconi has lost political appeal, and the Northern League, which belongs to Marine Le Pen's group in the European Parliament, has no hope to become hegemonic, even allied with a few neo-fascist organizations. Nevertheless, the chapter shows that the forces that have opposed anti-immigrant policies, racist discourses, and hate speech, that is, anti-racist movements, trade unions, and some religious organizations, face dramatic challenges after eight years of economic crisis, high unemployment, and reduction of the welfare state. The chapter illustrates that hostility toward immigrants—including the countless refugees who have arrived in the past few years—is often the consequence of a war among the poor for what is left of the welfare system. The results show how complex it is to separate anti-racist battles from a broader critique of the current neoliberal system.

CENTRAL AND EASTERN EUROPE: NEW EUROPE

The analyses of Bulgaria and Slovenia are situated within the Central and Eastern European region. In these post-communist countries, the extreme right and nationalist actors have taken on more authoritarian forms. Despite this, both chapters end on an optimistic note. The Bulgarian chapter emphasizes the potentials of counterforces of human rights militants and pro-diversity civic actors as laboratories for citizenship between "the no more and not yet", and the Slovenian chapter studies the potentials of the feminist social movements to create new ways of thinking and being in the world.

Chapter 9 by Anna Krasteva with Evelina Staykova and Ildiko Otova focuses on the challenges of contestatory and solidary citizenship in times of mainstreaming of populism in post-communist Bulgaria. It analyzes the (in)capacity of the civic countering to the unprecedented wave of nationalist and xenophobic discourses and to the diversification and multiplication of extremist actors, theorizing the emergence and development of the civic agency through a variety of approaches. The focus is on human rights militants and pro-diversity civic actors. The chapter shows the unfinished and difficult combat against extremism but at the same time perceives the pro-diversity militancy as a laboratory for citizenship. It ends by mapping post-communist mobilization and citizenship labeled "green", "contestatory", and "solidaric". The anti-state activism captures contestatory citizenship—occupy and green; the human rights lawyers occupy the area marked by solidary citizenship; and anti-racist activists capture the place where civic activism unifies anti-racism and contestatory citizenship.

Chapter 10 by *Mojca Pajnik* addresses feminist activism, internetization, and alternative politics as experiences in post-socialist Slovenia. It starts from the thesis that social movements are not just about individual actions of protest but rather an opportunity to create new ways of thinking and being in the world. This is the only chapter with primary focus on the feminist movements' "acts of citizenship" as alternatives to patriarchy, neoliberalism, and racism via analyses of articulations and operations of movements in the context of post-socialist Slovenia. It is based on focus group discussions with various protagonists of feminist movements and on participant observation at events. The chapter discusses what the pertinent issues for these movements are, what are their ideas, as well as concrete actions and strategies of resistance. By comparing contemporary and "older" civil society feminist actors, the chapter provides interesting insights into their perceptions of democracy, meanings of anti-racial struggle, and tactics of civil disobedience as well as their operational strategies, that is, how they are connected and what tactics they use in struggle.

The concluding discussion by Anna Krasteva, Aino Saarinen, and Birte Siim reflects on the challenges for civic activism in times of mainstreaming of national populism and the crisis of democracy. It sums up the book's theoretical contributions to critical citizenship studies emphasizing the conception of contestatory citizenship and solidarity citizenship. In an overview of civic activism, it maps the diversity of civic actors, discourses, values, and strategies in contemporary Europe. The empirical studies demonstrate how the current growth of nationalism and right-wing populism fosters counter-forces that represent attempts to redefine citizenship in line with radical theorizing of the concept making it more liquid and dynamic. The studies illustrate that both the awakening nationalism and the mobilization of counter-forces take on different forms across Europe. They are useful reminders of both the specificities of the context and the commonality of the challenge. The book highlights that it is a future challenge how to transform these diverse forms of civic activism, so far operating at the margin of society, into broader political alliances and programs. It proposes that this will require a combination of transnational networking and local activism.

The afterword by Donatella della Porta discusses the constraints and potentials of activist citizens from the perspective of social movement studies. It proposes that in this context, one of the major contributions of the book is to create a dialogue between social movement studies and citizenship studies and to point at some potential innovations in both bodies of literature. Della Porta notices that the analysis of social movements for or against forced migrants' rights has rarely been addressed because social movement studies have mainly focused on "new", post-materialist actors. As a result, pro- and anti-migration movements have instead been addressed in citizenship studies, often with a normative concern. The afterword highlights four of such innovative contributions pointing at the importance of contextual opportunities and constraints of the mobilization of activist citizens around migration, the multitudes of internal characteristics of the mobilizations and the diversity of forms of pro-migrant mobilizations.

References

Arendt, H. (1951). *The origin of totalitarianism*. New York: Harvard Law School.
Arendt, H. (1958). *The human condition*. Chicago: University of Chicago Press.
Bauböck, R. (2006). Citizenship and migration: Concepts and controversies. In R. Bauboeck (Ed.), *Migration and citizenship. Legal status, rights and political participation* (pp.15–32). IMISCOE Reports, Amsterdam University Press.
Benveniste, A., & Pingaud, E. (2016). Far-right movements in France: The principal role of Front National and the Rise of Islamophobia. In G. Lazaridis, A. Benveniste, & G. Campani (Eds.), *The rise of the far right in a Europe under crisis*. London: Palgrave Macmillan.
Bhimji, F. (2016). Visibilities and the politics of space: Refugee activism in Berlin. *Journal of Immigrant & Refugee Studies, 14*, 432–450.
Brochmann, G., & Hagelund, A. (2012). *Immigration policies and the Scandinavian welfare states 1945–2010*. London: Palgrave Macmillan.
Castles, S., & Davidson, A. (2000). *Citizenship and migration: Globalization and the politics of belonging*. Houndmills/New York: Palgrave.

Cisař, O. (2013). A typology of extra-parliamentary political activism in post-communist settings: The case of the Czech Republic. In K. Jakobsson & S. Saxonberg (Eds.), *Beyond NGO-ization. The development of social movements in Central and Eastern Europe* (pp. 139–167). Farnham and Burlington: Ashgate.
della Porta, D. (2005). Multiple belongings, tolerant identities, and the construction of another politics: Between the European Social Forums and local social fora. In D. della Porta & S. Tarrow (Eds.), *Transnational protest and global activism* (pp. 175–202). Lanham: Rowman & Littlefield.
della Porta, D. (2013). *Can democracy be saved?* Cambridge, UK: Polity Press.
della Porta, D. (2015). *Social movements in times of austerity.* Cambridge: Polity Press.
della Porta, D., & Mattoni, A. (2014). Patterns of diffusion and the transnational dimension of protest in the movements of crisis. An introduction. In D. Della Porta & A. Mattoni (Eds.), *Spreading protest. Social movements in times of crisis* (pp. 1–18). Colchester: ECPR Press.
Djuve, A. B., Friberg, J., Tyldum, G., & Zhang, H. (2015). *When poverty meets affluence: Migrants from Romania on the streets of the Scandinavian capitals.* Oslo: FAFO.
Fenger-Grøndal, M. (2017). *Venligboerne – historien om en bevægelse* [The friendly neighbors: The story about a movement]. Copenhagen: Bibelselskabets Selskab.
Ferree, M. M., Gamson, W. A., Gerhards, J., & Rucht, D. (2002). Four models of the public sphere in modern democracies. *Theory and Society, 31,* 289–324.
Fishkin, J. M. (2014). Deliberative democracy in context: Reflections on theory and practice. In K. Grönlund, A. Bächtiger, & M. Setälä (Eds.), *Deliberative mini-publics: Involving citizens in the democratic process* (pp. 27–40). Colchester: ECPR Press.
Fraser, N. (2005). Reframing justice in a globalising world. *New Left Review, 36,* 69–88.
Fraser, N. (2013). *Fortunes of feminism: From state-managed capitalism to neoliberal crisis.* London: Verso.
Grönlund, K., Bächtiger, A., & Setälä, M. (2014). Introduction. In K. Grönlund, A. Bächtiger, & M. Setälä (Eds.), *Deliberative mini-publics. Involving citizens in the democratic process* (pp. 1–8). Colchester: ECPR Press.
Guttman, A., & Thompson, D. (1996). *Democracy and disagreement.* Cambridge, MA/London: The Belknap Press of Harvard University Press.
Guy, W. (2013). *From victimhood to citizenship. The path of Roma integration.* Pakiv European Roma Fund. Budapest: Kossuth Publishing Corporation.
Isin, E. F. (2008). Theorizing acts of citizenship. In E. F. Isin & G. M. Nielsen (Eds.), *Acts of citizenship* (pp. 15–43). London/New York: Zed Books.
Isin, E. F. (2009). Citizenship in the flux. *Subjectivity, 19,* 367–381.

Isin, E. F., & Nielsen, G. M. (2008). Introduction. In E. F. Isin & G. M. Nielsen (Eds.), *Acts of citizenship* (pp. 1–12). London/New York: Zed Books.

Jakobsson, K., & Saxonberg, S. (2013). Introduction: The development of social movements in Central and Eastern Europe. In K. Jakobsson & S. Saxonberg (Eds.), *Beyond NGO-ization: The developments of social movements in Central and Eastern Europe* (pp. 1–26). Farnham/Burlington: Ashgate.

Jenkins, J. G., Wallace, M., & Fullerton, A. W. (2008). A social movement society: A cross-national analysis of protest potential. *International Journal of Sociology*, 38, 12–35.

Keck, M. E., & Sikkink, K. (1998). *Activists beyond borders: Advocacy networks in international politics.* Ithaca: Cornell University Press.

Keskinen, S. (2016). From welfare nationalism to welfare chauvinism: Economic rhetoric, the welfare state and changing asylum policies in Finland. *Critical Social Policy*, 36, 1–19.

Kopecký, P., & Mudde, C. (Eds.). (2012). *The uncivil society: Contentious politics in post-communist Europe.* London/New York: Routledge.

Krasteva, A. (2016). Occupy Bulgaria or the emergence of the post-communist contestatory citizenship. *Southeastern Europe*, 40, 158–187.

Kriszan, A., & Siim, B. (forthcoming). Gender equality and family in European populist radical-right agendas: European parliamentary debates 2014. In T. Knijn & M. Naldini (Eds.), *Gender and generational division in EU citizenship.* Cheltenham: Edward Elgar Publishing.

Kvist, J., Fritzell, J., Hvinden, B., & Kangas, O. (Eds.). (2012). *Changing social equality: The Nordic welfare model in the 21st century.* Bristol/Chicago: The Policy Press.

Landwehr, C. (2014). Facilitating deliberation: The role of impartial intermediaries in deliberative mini-publics. In K. Grönlund, A. Bächtiger, & M. Setälä (Eds.), *Deliberative mini-publics. Involving citizens in the democratic process* (pp. 77–92). Colchester: ECPR Press.

Lazaridis, G., & Campani, G. (2016). *Understanding the populist shift: Othering in a Europe in crisis.* Milton Keynes: Routledge.

Lazaridis, G., Benveniste, A., & Campani, G. (Eds.). (2016). *The rise of the far right in Europe. Populist shifts and 'othering'.* London: Palgrave Macmillan.

Marshall, T. H. (1950). *Citizenship and social class.* Cambridge: Cambridge University Press.

Mendez-Shannon, C. E., & Bailey, J. D. (2016). Sobresalir: The undocumented experience. *Journal of Ethnic & Cultural Diversity in Social Work*, 25, 98–113.

Meyer, D. S., & Tarrow, S. G. (1998). *The social movement society: Contentious politics for a new century.* Lanham: Rowman & Littlefield.

Minkenberg, M. (2002). The radical right in postsocialist Central and Eastern Europe: Comparative observations and interpretations. *East European Politics & Societies*, 16, 335–362.

Mudde, C. (2005). Central and Eastern Europe. In C. Mudde (Ed.), *Racist extremism in Central and Eastern Europe* (pp. 267–285). London/New York: Routledge.
Müller, J.-W. (2016). *Hvad er populisme? [What is populism?].* Viborg: Informations Forlag.
Nielsen, G. M. (2008). Answerability with cosmopolitan intent: An ethics-based politics for acts of urban citizenship. In E. F. Isin & G. M. Nielsen (Eds.), *Acts of citizenship* (pp. 266–286). London/New York: Zed Books.
Niemeyer, S. (2014). Scaling up deliberation to mass publics: Harnessing mini-publics in a deliberative system. In K. Grönlund, A. Bächtiger, & M. Setälä (Eds.), *Deliberative mini-publics: Involving citizens in the democratic process* (pp. 177–202). Colchester: ECPR Press.
Nyers, P. (2008). No one is illegal between city and nation. In E. F. Isin & G. M. Nielsen (Eds.), *Acts of citizenship* (pp. 160–181). London/New York: Zed Books.
Pajnik, M., & Sauer, B. (2017). *Populism and the web: Communicative practices of parties and movements in Europe.* London/New York: Routledge.
Pirro, A. (2015). *The populist radical right in Central and Eastern Europe. Ideology, impact, and electoral performance.* London/New York: Routledge.
Saarinen, A., & Calloni, M. (2012). Feminised migration across the East-West Borders: A challenge to a "New Europe". In A. Saarinen & M. Calloni (Eds.), *Builders of a New Europa. Women immigrants from the Eastern trans-regions* (pp. 2–17). Kikimora Publications: Helsinki.
Saarinen, A., Puurunen, H., & Enache, A. (2018). Eastern European Roma as a new challenge for research. In A. Saarinen (Ed.), *Mobilizing for mobile Roma: Pro-actors in Helsinki, Finland in the 2000s–2010s.* Trialogue Books; and A. Markkanen & Kaj Åberg (Eds.), *The culture of Finnish Roma.* Helsinki: Finnish Literature Society.
Sauer, B., & Ajanovic, E. (2016). Hegemonic discourses of difference and inequality: Right-wing organizations in Austria. In G. Lazaridis, G. Campani, & A. Benveniste (Eds.), *The rise of the far right in Europe: Populist shifts and othering.* London: Palgrave Macmillan.
Saward, M. (2000, April). *Direct and deliberative democracy.* Paper for ECPR session in Copenhagen. Open University.
Siim, B., & Meret, S. (2016). Right wing populism in Denmark: People, nation and welfare in the construction of the "Other". In G. Lazaridis, A. Benveniste, & G. Campani (Eds.), *The rise of the far right in a Europe under crisis.* Houndmills, Basingstoke/Hampshire: Palgrave Macmillan.
Siim, B., & Mokre, M. (Eds.). (2013). *Negotiating gender and diversity in an emergent European public sphere.* Houndmills, Basingstoke/Hampshire: Palgrave Macmillan.
Soysal, Y. N. (1994). *Limits of citizenship: Migrants and post-national membership in Europe.* Chicago/London: University of Chicago.

Walters, W. (2008). Mapping the territory of (non-)citizenship. In E. F. Isin & G. M. Nielsen (Eds.), *Acts of citizenship* (pp. 182–206). London/New York: Zed Books.
Widfeldt, A. (2015). *Extreme right parties in Scandinavia*. London/New York: Routledge.
Wimmer, A., & Glick-Schiller, N. (2002). Methodological nationalism and beyond: Nation building, migration and social sciences. *Global Networks, 2*, 301–334.
Yuval-Davis, N. (1997). *Gender & Nation*. London/Thousand Oaks/New Delhi: Sage.
Yuval-Davis, N. (2011). *The politics of belonging: Intersectional contestations*. London: Sage.

CHAPTER 2

Dilemmas of Citizenship and Evolving Civic Activism in Denmark

Birte Siim and Susi Meret

SETTING THE SCENE: CIVIC ACTIVISM IN POPULIST TIMES

Research shows that civic engagement, activism, and motivations to act are deeply embedded in time, place, and space (della Porta and Caiani 2010; della Porta and Mattoni 2014). In the case of Denmark, mobilizations and motivations to act in the past two decades are rooted in the transformation of the country from a liberal and open approach to immigration and asylum to the most restrictive in the Nordic context (Brochmann and Hagelund 2012). In addition, new political parties and new political cleavages have emerged since the beginning of the twenty-first century and have affected Danish voting behavior and party structure. The value dimension in Danish politics (*værdipolitik*) became apparent in the 1990s. Especially the refugee question (Borre 2016: 118) triggered a polarized debate about the Danish asylum and migration system, which some claimed was too generous. Since the 2000s, immigration, asylum, and other value-related issues have been considered to be among the most

---

B. Siim (✉) • S. Meret
Department of Culture and Global Studies, Aalborg University,
Aalborg, Denmark

© The Author(s) 2019
B. Siim et al. (eds.), *Citizens' Activism and Solidarity Movements*,
Palgrave Studies in European Political Sociology,
https://doi.org/10.1007/978-3-319-76183-1_2

salient issues. Compared to the economic left-right dimension, value politics do not necessarily correspond with the parties' placement on the "old" economic dimension (Borre 2016).

The Danish People's Party (DPP) is the most influential representative of the so-called new right in Denmark. After its establishment at the end of the 1990s (Meret 2010), it achieved a prominent role due to its nativist and anti-immigration positions, especially against Islam, coupled with populist appeals to the Danish people against the political and intellectual elites. The formation of a majority government in 2001 of the Liberals and the Conservatives was secured with the support of the Danish People's Party, which delivered the necessary seats and support to achieve the parliamentary majority. This legitimization of the populist "new" right contributed to a bi-polar system, sustained by the nativist ideological core of the DPP. Once the DPP had achieved this position, the center-right parties were committed to getting tough on immigration, asylum, crime and welfare "abuses", integration, and citizenship rules. The decade 2001–2011 was thus marked by increasingly polarized positions in politics and society toward immigrants and refugees, in particular Islam and Muslim minorities (Meret 2010).

Most of the scholarly attention has focused on the impact of the populist new right and the effects of the emergence of value politics on Danish politics, while relatively few studies have been concerned with the response from civil society. Our contribution focuses in particular on the dilemmas of differentiated citizenship (between status and non-status) and democratic challenges of civic activism against racism, othering, and Islamophobia (cf. Siim and Meret 2016). One question is how Danish society and politics tackled the challenges of new forms of diversity and inequality, and what makes people act in response. The chapter also discusses the responses to the so-called European refugee crisis by mainstream politics and civil society activists.

Situating Citizenship: Welfare, Nationalism, and Citizens' Activism

Historically, the Danish nation state is marked by the triad construction of the people, democracy, and the welfare state (Korsgaard 2004: 422). Since the 1930s, the Social Democratic Party (SD) contributed to linking the nation state and its people with the Scandinavian version of "welfare nationalism" (Brochmann and Hagelund 2012). In particular, the discursive struggle about the meaning of "the people" was redefined by the SD with the formation of the universal welfare state to include almost everybody living legally within the nation state. Arguably, the emergence of welfare chauvinist positions is rooted in a nativist understanding of the people reframing the meaning of "welfare nationalism" (Siim and Meret 2016). In addition, the Danish approach to democracy has a history of civil society mobilization "from below" through associations, cooperatives, and unions organized in the peasants' and workers' movements. During the 1970s and 1980s, the women's movement, the peace movement, and the anti-nuclear and environmental movements reframed ideas about participatory democracy (cf. Siim and Meret 2016). From the 1990s, these movements lost momentum and were replaced by an array of diverse and much less cohesive grassroots organizations that focused on more specific issues and often received economic support from the state (Mikkelsen 2002).

At the same time, the rightwing populist ideology of the Danish People's Party started to gain momentum, informed by a nativist understanding of "the people", which translated into a gradual normalization of rightwing populist issues and claims also among mainstream parties (Meret 2010; Widfeldt 2015). Danish rightwing populism has from the beginning been characterized by exclusionary forms of welfare nationalism/nativism (cf. Siim and Meret 2016; Betz 2017) premised on a distinction between those who belong to the community and those who are not entitled to welfare benefits and services. In addition, it has advanced the culturalist position that Danish values are essential components of Danish democracy, welfare, and way of life and thus difficult to acquire (cf. Siim and Meret 2016). Especially Muslim minorities are constructed as "others" and undeserving due to their faith, loyalty, and cultural heritage.

Right-wing populism has increased political tensions and conflicts around migration issues, but at the same time, it has triggered new forms of civic activism to counteract discrimination, populist othering, and racism. The 2015 refugee crisis directed media and political attention to the impact of immigration at the national and EU level. At the national level, the Liberal Party has since the 2015 election formed a minority government with the Conservatives and Liberal Alliance, which again still largely depends on support from the DPP. The Social Democrats, the Social Liberals, the Socialist Peoples' Party, the new green grassroots party, the Alternative, and the Red-Green Alliance are now in opposition. However, this past year, a new form of cooperation between DPP and SD on welfare, migration, and integration issues has emerged, for example, for strict border control and family unification rules and a reduction of welfare benefits to newly arrived refugees.

It is not yet clear what the Danish implications are of the recent social and political transformations and new forms of exclusionary nationalisms in Europe (Siim and Meret 2016). The present analysis of the resistance against rightwing populism and nativism focuses on the response of civic activism in civil society organizations (CSO), non-governmental organizations (NGOs), voluntary groups, and individuals. It compares diverse forms of civic activism and mobilization based on in-depth interviews and participatory fieldwork conducted between 2010 and 2017. The selected groups, organizations, and individuals oppose what they perceive as increasingly unjust and discriminatory policies against migrants and refugees.

Analytical Focus and Empirical Method: In-Depth Case Studies

Our study examines what kind of activism can be found in Danish society that is mobilizing by, for, and with immigrants and refugees, by looking at the main claims, motivations, and action frames. How do the groups understand themselves, and what forms of activism do they practice? Another concern is to what extent the activism of these groups and individuals is encouraged by ideas of "acting for and/or with" the groups that are subject to discrimination, racism, and/or unjust treatment in Danish society. What kind of strategies are used and with what consequences for the people involved? What are the similarities and differences in their framings and practical activities? How have these groups developed since 2010, especially after the refugee "crises" in 2015?

The selected groups and organizations represent a diversity of issues, goals and values, strategies, and collective actions. They focus on pro-refugees, asylum seekers, LGBT, anti-racism, and anti-discrimination. The empirical material was collected between 2013 and 2014 in relation to the RAGE project and expanded in 2016 and 2017 to capture the effects of the recent political transformations. In the first round, five groups were selected for in-depth case studies, including document analysis, individual narratives, and focus group interviews with activists: SOS Against Racism, the Danish branch of a European-wide organization founded in 1984 targeting forms of racism in society with around 200 paying members in Denmark[1]; Sabaah, an LGBT group founded by immigrant youth inspired by the

---

[1] https://www.facebook.com/sosmodracis//

Danish LGBT organizations[2]; the Trampoline House [Trampolinhuset], a local activity house for and by asylum seekers[3]; and LGBT Asylum[4] and Refugees Welcome,[5] which both provide legal support to refugees and asylum seekers. In the second round, three recently founded groups were added: the Friendly Neighbors [Venligboerne, VB],[6] an informal network directed toward local refugees; the Danish chapter of Black Lives Matter (BLM), focusing on the exclusion, discrimination, and institutional racism against black people[7]; and Castaway Souls of Denmark, a refugee-led movement that started in the so-called repatriation camp Sjælsmark.[8]

Conceptualizing Citizens' Activism

One body of literature aims to reframe classic citizenship approaches emphasizing new forms and practices of in/exclusion of groups of citizens, immigrants, and marginalized groups in contemporary society (Bauböck 2006; Isin and Turner 2007; Isin 2009). Another body of literature focuses on the active role of social movements in shaping deliberative, radical, and participatory democracy, emphasizing the quality of democracy, inclusion, and empowerment (della Porta 2013), the key role for ordinary people in democracy and the activism of critical citizens. These approaches can arguably supplement each other, since both focus on the agency and voices of (non-)citizens, marginalized social groups, immigrants, refugees, and asylum seekers. Both are in different ways concerned with the participation and deliberation of civil society actors and social movements in the democratic process, with the quality, learning, and transforming of democracy, as well as with marginalized groups' claims for equality and social justice (della Porta 2015).

The rediscovery of the concept of citizenship has many roots (Isin and Turner 2007; Mouritsen 2015). One inspiration is Hannah Arendt's influential approach in *The Origins of Totalitarianism* (1951), which describes the social and political challenges posed by the increasing number of stateless people in pre- and post-WWII society. Arendt's concept of

---

[2] http://sabaah.dk/om-sabaah//
[3] https://www.facebook.com/trampolinhuset/
[4] https://www.lgbtasylum.dk/
[5] http://refugeeswelcome.dk/
[6] http://www.venligboerne.org/
[7] https://www.facebook.com/BlackLivesMatterDenmark/
[8] https://www.facebook.com/Rejected-souls-of-DenmarkEurope-222564811413741/

statelessness refers to all people who—for any reason—could no longer benefit from the rights granted by citizenship and belonging to a community. The right-less are excluded from the triad "nation-people-territory", which leaves them in a condition of deprivation from legal personhood and of the formal right to act as subject, to have a voice, to decide where to stay. Paradoxically, as Arendt suggests, once humans are stripped of their social, political, and juridical attributes, it becomes even more difficult to re-claim and exercise the "natural rights of being born human". Arendt's work challenges the idea of citizenship and universal human rights acquired by birth and shows that in practice the guarantees and privileges of human beings rely strongly upon membership of a community, defined by the borders of the nation state.

Arendt also develops a vision of citizenship premised on the power of action, the value of civic engagement, and collective deliberation as essential characteristics of human existence (1958: 246–247). Arendt's vision of human plurality, equality, and claims for social justice of marginalized social groups such as immigrants, refugees, and stateless peoples has proved an inspiration for theorizing the position of migrants and refugees in contemporary Europe (cf. Isin 2012).

In contemporary Europe, migration and mobility have challenged established theories, and new approaches to social justice, transnational citizenship, and global democracy have emerged (Siim 2013; Fraser 2013; della Porta 2013). Scholars analyzing modern citizenship suggest that citizenship needs to be invigorated (Isin and Turner 2007) and study the empowerment and self-empowerment of marginalized social groups (see, e.g. Monforte and Dufour 2011). Engin Isin (2009: 383–384) proposes a new vocabulary of "activist citizenship" making claims to justice as the emerging figure of contemporary global politics. Here, citizenship is enacted through struggles for rights among various groups, and the focus is on "acts" rather than on status or habitus—on citizenship as political subjectivity. Isin (2012) analyzes how "citizens without frontiers" traverse social, cultural, and geographical frontiers for social justice, creating relations between "those who are no longer and not yet citizens". In a similar vein, Baubäck's work (2006) studies the divisions between and within racial, social, civil, political categories of people, such as national citizens, EU citizens, and so-called third-country nationals, as well as the tensions between rights of refugees and asylum seekers and national citizens. These divisions have created what we call "differentiated citizenship" between categories of people.

From a social movement perspective, one issue is how to reconcile the tensions between participation and deliberation (della Porta 2013), between equality and diversity (Fraser 2013; Galligan 2015) and how to regulate the democratic dialogue within movements and organizations, for example, between the leaders/coordinators and initiators of citizens' activism and the excluded and marginalized (target) groups, such as immigrants, refugees, and asylum seekers. One way to address these issues is to reframe Habermas' deliberative model of the public spheres by asking: "who is in/excluded, what issues/demands are in/excluded, how do the actors communicate and what is the outcome of the process" (cf. Fraser 2013; della Porta 2013). To this we add the intersectional approach with focus on the intersecting inequalities and diversities, especially in relation to gender, nationality, ethnicity/race, and religion (cf. Siim and Mokre 2013; Meret and Siim 2013).

In addition, the notion of "learning democracy" from the social movement literature premised on dialogue and mutual learning proves to be a useful concept from the bottom-up perspective of social movements and civil society organizations (della Porta 2015). This perspective enables a focus on the ability to build trust and create dialogue within and across social groups and social movements, to diffuse ideas within and between social movements/associations cross-time and cross-nationally. Engaging in transversal and transnational dialogues (Yuval-Davis 2011) is an example of a learning process concerned with the challenge of working together across social groups according to gender, class, nationality, religion, and citizenship. The intersectional approach to citizens' activism is a similar perspective that focuses on the dilemma of integrating equality with diversity. Intersectionality can be interpreted as a methodological approach that emphasizes the need to be sensitive to diversity between and within categories (Yuval-Davis 2011; Siim and Mokre 2013).

The above theories of citizenship, democracy, and social movements provide a useful starting point for analyzing dilemmas of activist and differentiated citizenship with focus on civic activism that emphasizes equality, inclusion, participation, recognition, and empowerment of marginalized social groups. The empirical analysis combines the citizen approach with emphasis on peoples' claims to justice with models reframing democracy and the public sphere in times of rightwing populism and new forms of exclusionary nationalism. It addresses four dimensions: (1) *in/exclusion* of various groups of citizens and non-citizens in agency and voice addressing particular issues; (2) *recognition*, the sensitivity to diversity within and between social and cultural groups; (3) the *dialogical learning process* involving citizens and non-citizens, that is, the quality of deliberation and communication within and between activists and groups (also transversally); and (4) the *outcome* of the activities in terms of influencing people and transforming politics and society.

MOBILIZATION AGAINST HATE SPEECH, OTHERING, AND RACISM

One objective of the RAGE project[9] was to compare the national political cultures, democratic traditions, and civil society organizations in contemporary Europe and to analyze the resistance to rightwing populism, anti-migration, and anti-discrimination policies (cf. Lazaridis et al. 2016). Our analysis identified diverse forms of civic activism: (a) advocacy citizens "fighting for" vulnerable groups, for example, by providing legal support; (b) everyday activism—citizens fighting "for and with" vulnerable groups sharing everyday activities; (c) citizens collectively fighting together for empowerment/self-empowerment; and (d) civic activism and mobilizations by marginalized people such as refugees, asylum seekers, and stateless people. The analysis thus distinguishes between advocacy, everyday activism, and more radical forms of active protests that claim access to basic rights and aim to influence and change policies. The next section presents several examples of these various forms of activism and discusses the characteristics of civic activism and the dilemmas of activist citizenship primarily within a Danish context.

The interviews, fieldwork, and participatory observations thus aim at studying forms of democratic resistance to hate speech, othering, and racism in Denmark, initially including a representative number of so-called victim organizations and democratic anti-bodies targeting mainly immigrant, refugee, and LGBT issues. As already mentioned, five voluntary associations[10] were identified as most prominent in addressing asylum

[9]The RAGE project: *Right wing Populism and Hate Speech through the Racism, Gender and Age Looking Glass* (2010–13) was funded by the Fumandamental Rights and Citizenship Programme of the European Union thorugh EUs Justice and Home Affairs. It included national case studies from eight European countries. See the national Danish reports (Siim and Meret 2013; Siim et al. 2013, 2014, 2015). The Danish team consisted of Birte Siim and Susi Meret with research assistants Jeppe Fuglsang Larsen, Helene Møller Larsen, and Anna Stegger Gemzøe.

[10]The empirical material includes document analysis and interviews with ten civil society organizations (CSO) active in the public debate about discrimination against migrant and Muslim minorities. The first round of interviews in 2014 included the Documentation and

seekers and refugees, racism, immigrants, and LGBT minorities. In the second round, interviews with three newly formed groups were added as examples of diverse forms of local activism.

Refugees Welcome[11]

Refugees Welcome (RW) got its name in 2012 and grew from the former Committee for Underground Refugees. Since 2008, it has been led by Danish activist Michala Clante Bendixen (MCB). Primarily based in the Copenhagen area, RW also visits the asylum camps regularly. RW's main activity is giving legal advice and advocacy to refugees and asylum seekers as well as doing advocacy work for their rights. Another goal is to inform the Danish population and asylum seekers about facts and truths concerning the Danish asylum and refugee situation and conditions, mainly by means of a home page in English and Danish.[12] RW has office hours one day a week at the Trampoline House, which opened in 2010 as an independent community center in Copenhagen offering refugees and asylum seekers a place of support, community, activities, and events. The RW Facebook home page states:

> We give free, confidential advice. Please try to write in English or Danish. But if necessary, we can translate Farsi, Dari, Arabic, Tigrinyia, Somali. One of our advisers will get back to you as soon as possible. You can also call or email us or talk to us in person Tuesdays 16-19 at Trampoline House, Copenhagen.[13]

Refugees Welcome is an example of civic activism that gives priority to the advocacy role premised on the equal rights and equal respect of all human beings, increasingly also "working for and with" former refugees who are

---

Counselling Centre on Racism and the European Network Against Racism (ENAR) and organizations of migrants and Muslim minorities such as Ethnic Minority Women's Council and New/Now Danish Youth Council, SOS Against Racism, Sabaah, and the Trampoline House. Focus group interview with three selected groups, the Trampoline House, LGBT Asylum, and Refugees Welcome, was conducted in September 2014. The second round of interviews was conducted with the Friendly Neighbors in 2016 and with Refugees Welcome, Black Lives Matter, and refugees of the Castaway Souls of Denmark in 2017.

[11] Interview with Michala Clante Bendixen (MCB), present leader of Refugees Welcome, Copenhagen, August 15, 2017. https://www.facebook.com/refugeeswelcomedenmark/
[12] https://www.facebook.com/refugeeswelcomedenmark/
[13] https://www.facebook.com/pg/refugeeswelcomedenmark/posts/?ref=page_internal

now working as activists in RW. An experienced board of activists and legal experts on refugee matters works closely with official refugee organization channels such as the Red Cross and the Danish Refugee Help. Its growing legal expertise has gradually increased RW's visibility and influence in society and the media. MCB mentions a number of activist initiatives such as starting a doctor's clinic for undocumented, which was later taken over in a professional way by Red Cross. In 2015/16, RW members traveled to Lesbos to welcome boat refugees. The home page reports individual cases where RW made a difference for asylum seekers, that is, improving the practice regarding family unification, changing the law with regard to children's needs/interests in asylum cases, pressuring to get asylum children out of the camps. MCB finds that one positive effect of the repressive Danish asylum system is that refugees are spread across the country when being granted asylum. This forces local citizens, businesses, and politicians to deal with the situation, and people often realize that refugees are also an advantage for the local community. Asked about racism, MCB finds that the Danish situation is an example of fear of opposition to and discrimination of strangers, especially Muslims. She finds that Muslim women wearing the veil are the most discriminated group in Danish society and adds that one third of the refugees are women, and their situation should prompt more and better organized activities directed at improving their situation and staying in the country.[14]

RW has a growing number of Facebook supporters; MCB explains that RW plans to fund its activities through membership fees and not be dependent on public and private funding. MCB is highly critical of the present immigration policies that explicitly test the human rights system, for example, by writing "process risk" when there is a risk that the government will lose the case at the European Court of Justice. One example is RW's struggle for respect for the human rights convention, which is under pressure from the government due to the introduction of new and stricter regulations of family reunification, making it virtually impossible to apply before three years of stay in the country. The new rules about work internship are also described as ambiguous: Although it is good that refugees work, the 12-month internship makes it possible for employers to exploit refugees as cheap labor. Asked how the present political situation influences RW's work for refugees and asylum seekers, MCB underlines what

[14] This is the aim of a new Facebook group founded in 2016: https://www.facebook.com/WRRoute/

she interprets as a paradox: On the one hand, the anti-immigration politics and the media discourse have made it virtually impossible to talk about human rights without the debate becoming contentious and polarized also on the political left wing. On the other hand, she notices that the practical support from civil society for pro-refugee groups has increased in recent years. However, the greatest political challenge is whether and how activists' pro-refugee, pro-migrant work and engagement translates into a wider societal and political support for changes in Danish immigration policies toward less restrictive and more solidarity-based solutions.

The Trampoline House

The Trampoline House (TH) was initiated by Danish artists Morten Goll (MG) and Tone Olaf Nielsen in 2010 with the dual goal: close the refugee camps and start integration of refugees and asylum seekers from day one. TH's vision is "a user-driven culture center where asylum seekers and Danish citizens can meet to share experiences and learn from one another" (cf. Messel 2016: 9). The House has a formal organization with a flat structure but has in the past years been professionalized with a board that includes a lawyer and a fundraiser. The House is situated in an old factory in Northwest Copenhagen, and the organization is dependent on public and private support. MG explains that the present goal of the House is driven by what he calls "everyday activism", aimed at changing the daily life of the users of the House by creating a space for daily activities and mutual encounters, which make users feel "at home". MG further explains that the main aim is to change the Danish asylum system by practicing "the good example", by creating a "we"—not only for the left but also to win over the political "center" and be able to change the approach to immigration and asylum. The TH was supported by public funding from 2011 to 2014 and is presently supported by private donations. This enables the House to keep running and even expand its activities, for example, to hire a person 37 hours a week who is in charge of communication and media strategy and organizing the weekly democracy workshop for asylum seekers, refugees, and student interns with MG.

The dual aim acting for and with the users of the house is attractive, but it also bears many challenges. The House is a welcoming space based on all members' equal claims to membership of the House. Activities include art exhibitions, sports, language and religion classes, community eating and meetings. There is a "learning process" based on mutual trust that is going on in the House. This aspect of TH has been interpreted as a "project of recognition" in three ways: (a) foster self-confidence, (b) create equal relations in interaction within the house, and (c) create solidarity in the community about a common goal (Messel 2016).[15] Despite this vision, tensions do exist in practice between "them and us"—organizers and users—between participation and deliberation, between "empowerment" and "self-empowerment" of (immigrant and refugee) activists. For example, to involve the "users of the house" actively in the planning and decision making of the weekly house meetings on-equal terms with the leaders who run the House; There is arguably a tension between creating a dialogue from below and getting users involved in the actual decision-making of running the House. One key question is how and to what extent these activities in practice contribute to the self-empowerment and agency of the asylum seekers and refugees participating in the House activities. Strategic challenges also exist between "everyday activism" aimed at improving the daily life of refugees "here and now" and the long-term strategies "to change the whole system", that is, by closing the asylum camps.

TH is an innovative community center for various forms of civic activism "for", "with", and partly also "by" refugees, but the future depends both on mobilization, funding and politics. According to MG, one of the main challenges is the Danish government's plans to close most asylum camps in the Copenhagen area and to send refuges and asylum seekers to the Jutland peninsula. This would make the future work and activities of the TH difficult and open the question whether the TH model can be transferred to other places.

The Friendly Neighbors: A Volunteer Network in and from the Periphery

The Friendly Neighbors (VB) is a recent example of local citizens practicing everyday activism by mobilizing individually in voluntary groups interacting with refugees and asylum seekers from local asylum centers. VB is in many respects a rather unusual group. It started in 2014 in the remote

---

[15] Kajsa Minna Böttcher Messel's Master's thesis argues that the Trampoline House can be interpreted as a project of recognition in the sense of Honneth's recognition theory (2016: 82). She argues that the Trampoline House also facilitates the refugees' possibilities for autonomous navigation without antagonism premised on all members' equal claim to the house.

town of Hjørring, Northern Jutland, and originally aimed at welcoming newcomers to Hjørring. In 2015, VB activities were impacted by the arrival of 500 refugees during the fall, since then the aim of the network has become primarily to welcome refugees and asylum seekers. The group has no formal organization or formal leadership, and most members use Facebook to coordinate and communicate (Fenger-Grøndal 2017). All local groups are formed around three guiding principles: (1) be friendly in the meeting with others; (2) be curious when you meet people who are different from you; (3) meet diversity with respect.

The original group grew from 500 to 150,000 members in less than a year, and during 2016 it spread across several Danish cities. Today VB is well established also in the Copenhagen area. New local groups are started by Danish citizens or refugees with residence status to help people with everyday problems meeting over a cup of coffee or tea. In Hjørring, they are physically situated in the Café Venligbo and in Copenhagen in VenligboHus. The strength is the flexibility, since it is easy to form new local groups by local citizens or refugees who receive residence and move from Hjørring to another locality. The weakness is the lack of formal organization, and conflicts emerged from the start between groups in Hjørring and Copenhagen. The matter of dispute was two diverse strategies. Hjørring VB prefers to focus on the local and everyday character of the activities and avoid getting involved in national politics. Copenhagen VB prefers a critical political approach that includes criticizing the government's asylum, migration, and integration policies (see also Fenger-Grøndal 2017: 103).

The strength and uniqueness of the VB is their vision of friendship based on curiosity and mutual respect and the practice aimed at changing the everyday lives of refugees and asylum seekers by creating personal friendships by means of local activism. VB is a flexible, informal group that has currently spread to more than 100 cities, and the local groups are started either by Danish citizens or former refugees. VB now has a joint home page inspired by the three founding principles with links to all local chapters and cafes: http://www.venligboerne.org/ Lack of coordination and cooperation between local groups has been a growing problem over the past two years. VB is an innovative group practicing everyday activism "from below" directed toward asylum seekers. Its activism is dependent on local support and can be interpreted as a practical response to the Danish asylum policies.

Black Lives Matter Denmark[16]

The Danish chapter of the American organization, Black Lives Matter (BLM), was founded in 2016 by black activist Bwalya Sørensen (BS), strongly inspired by the US movement with the same name. It understands itself as a "chapter" of this organization with connections to the US leaders of BLM, who paid a visit and gave a speech in July 2017. BS came to Europe from Zambia when she was 12 and arrived in Denmark at 18 spending two years in an asylum center. She has a long history as full-time individual activist and explains that BLM in Denmark, as well as the USA, is about community [*fællesskab*] "to do things together to be stronger" and the social aspect is important for her. She is working as an IT consultant (interview notes).

BLM-DK was established to protest deportation, prisons at Vridsløselille and Ellebæk, police racial profiling, and arrests of black migrants. The incarceration of black and brown people for long periods without conviction or on weak evidence is a major concern for BLM-DK that collaborates with the Danish Radio (DR) about a documentary on this. BLM-DK is a partner with No Deportation Without Resistance protests and was in Kastrup the day an Afghan heart patient was deported last February (2017). BS is inspired by Martin Luther King, Mandela, and Gandhi, is against violence, and is active in No Pegida[17] once a month. She explains that she is pro-Muslim, pro freedom, pro respect, and pro equality for all religions. Her daughter is raised with those principles, and she is petrified the far right (No Pegida/For Frihed) will persecute Muslims like the Nazis did with the Jews. She tells that she is very motivated in the struggle against the far right, also because her daughter is married to a Muslim and her grandchildren are Muslims.

BLM is a protest group based on "call to action" activities relying on empowerment and self-empowerment practices using FB and other social media to communicate to the outside. It can be described as a political activist platform that aims to mobilize people to political activities against racism and discrimination through forms of self-empowerment. BS finds that there are many similarities in the issues connected to racism in the Danish and US organizations. One of the differences in their practice con-

---

[16] https://www.facebook.com/BlackLivesMatterDenmark/ Interview with the founder Bwalia Sørensen (BS) August 15, 2017.
[17] https://www.facebook.com/nopegidadk/

cerns the membership. BLM Denmark is a broad activist group that meets several times a month in the Peoples' House or in the Women's Building. The 21 activists of the Danish chapter are a mixed group of black and white people, whereas the members in the USA are predominantly black. BLM has an emphasis on freedom and justice for black people, but according to the home page, it works with a number of relatively diverse issues depending of the members' interests,[18] for example, freedom, equality, and justice for all, notwithstanding race, religion, and sexual orientation. BLM also supports feminism and environmental issues with a focus on black people.

BS emphasizes that despite the similar focus on local activism, it is not always easy for activist groups to work together. The radical left often contrasts "the real activists" such as the autonomous and anarchist groups with the activists of TH and VB who focus mainly on "positive work", calling VB "hat-wearing ladies". BS does not agree with this. She finds that VB's friendly form of activism is extremely powerful and calls it "humanitarian activism in its best form". She started the VB Albertslund group and VB Vridsløse Ellebæk herself but felt that she had to create BLM-DK, since VB does not organize protests. She emphasizes that despite their differences they are all real activists and that BLM-DK works comfortably with all activist groups fighting racism and discrimination. One of the future challenges for BLM is to what extent its model fits for Denmark and whether it is able to create a space for mutual learning across racial, religious, and gender differences within the BLM and possibly between similar groups.

Refugee-Led Mobilizations and Activism: The Castaway Souls of Sjælsmark/Denmark

Civic activism by non-status refugees also takes place in Denmark. One interesting example is the members of the Castaway Souls of Sjælsmark, a group of refugees who were refused asylum and who mobilized, protested, and disobeyed in the Sjælsmark repatriation/deportation camp.

On December 22, 2016, the non-status refugees in the Danish deportation camp of Sjælsmark organized and mobilized for the first time under the motto: *Empty the Camp*! The initiative came from a few activists inside the camp who "were suffering and [decided] we have to do something

---

[18] https://www.facebook.com/pg/BlackLivesMatterDenmark/events/?ref=page_internal

and talked about making a group" (interview with M, 15-06-2016). This was the first of many demonstrations and initiatives organized by the refugee-led group. Sjælsmark is one of two established deportation centers in Denmark; the other is Kærshovedgaard near Ikast on the Jutland peninsula. Sjælsmark is a former military facility that holds up to 200 men and women (now primarily families) in old military barracks. Its capacity is planned to be expanded to more than 400 if necessary. Both Sjælsmark and Kærshovedgaard are internally run by the Danish Prison and Probation Service (*Kriminalforsorgen*), whose mission, as described on the webpage "[...] is to contribute to reducing criminality" (Kriminalforsorgen 2011). The buildings at Sjælsmark are in a very poor state and have not been renovated since they were converted from military barracks to deportation center. The place is situated in a remote area about 35 km north of Copenhagen that is enclosed by barbed wire. Visits at the center are regulated and controlled by police: ID identification and a formal invitation from the internee are required. Visitors are given a badge to carry visibly during their stay. It is not allowed to take pictures; it is not allowed for visitors and refugees to eat together in the camp, to enter the gym or visit other buildings in the area besides the room of the confined. The visit generally takes place in the host's small room, which is tiny (about 20 m^2) and shared by two people. Toilets and showers are located in the corridors outside, and they are often filthy. In these conditions live the "deportables", who according to Danish Minister for Immigration, Integration and Housing Inger Støjberg "must be sent out of the country as soon as possible", and their life here made as "intolerable as possible".[19]

The Castaway Souls group is an example of radical refugee-led activism that is also found in other EU countries, whose aim is to become visible and to fight against deportation and for freedom of movement, stay, and a life in dignity. At the end of January 2016, the Castaways group organized a demonstration against the further tightening of the asylum laws with the support of several pro-refugee and pro-migrant and activist platforms in Copenhagen (Trampoline House, Common Ground, The Bridge Radio, the No-Borders). About 200 people marched from Sjælsmark deportation center to nearby Sandholm asylum center. On that occasion the refugees authored a public Refugee Manifesto with six main issues: (1) the right of

[19] https://www.dr.dk/nyheder/politik/video-stoejberg-til-asylansoeger-det-nytter-ikke-noget-du-skal-ud; https://politiken.dk/indland/art5624285/St%C3%B8jberg-vil-%C2%BBut%C3%A5leligg%C3%B8re%C2%AB-t%C3%A5lt-ophold

all migrants to be free and decide over their future; (2) the right to have rights (to work, to move freely, to stay, to education, to healthcare, to voice, etc.); (3) the right to move, be free, or stay and not to be forcefully confined to Sjælsmark, nor deported by force; (4) the right to resist deportation; (5) the demand to close camps like Sjælsmark where people are criminalized and forced to live without dignity, in a state of intolerable uncertainty, poverty, and isolation; and (6) the right to resist the criminalization of refugees and their being represented as the source of all evils and problems in society. The event had some media resonance, but it remained virtually ignored by the politicians in Parliament. At the end of January/February 2016, the Castaway Souls organized a presidium/protest camp in Copenhagen on the so-called Red Square/Tadhamoun Square with the aim of mobilizing civil society to fight against the conditions for refugees in Sjælsmark. The group's printed flier read: "We are not criminals. It is not a crime to be a refugee and seek asylum. We are not criminals. Do not treat us like criminals … Camps are dehumanizing. We demand the closing of camps. We did not flee for our life only to die in your dehumanizing camps". Slogans on banners read "Sjælsmark is a factory making people crazy" and "Stop killing us slowly". A spokesperson of the group stated: "We are here to protest. We have been through a lot without anybody saying anything … we are punished, forced, treated like criminals … our life has been taken away from us, we are being killed slowly".

The protest camp raised awareness about the situation at Sjælsmark but remained too local. There were not enough participants to be able to challenge the hegemonic public discourses and political debate demanding marginalization, isolation, and ultimately expulsion of the rejected asylum seekers. Even so, the Castaway Souls of Sjælsmark managed to organize a new public event in April 2016, asking Danish authorities for a dialogue and performing in front of the Danish Immigration Service (*Udlændingestyrelsen*) in Copenhagen, wearing Guantanamo orange jumpsuit. As they stated:

> … we have walked from Sjælsmark deportation camp to Sandholm camp. We had a demonstration in Allerød, and another in the streets of Copenhagen. We have resisted social, civil and political death. We have challenged the idea that we cannot be visible, that we do not have the right to have rights, and that we cannot contribute to society. Through these mobilizations we have built a community with refugees from other camps, immigrants, Danes and non-Danes who understand that our struggle is legitimate and just. We have

brought to public attention the inhumane conditions in Sjælsmark, the deportations, and the unjust laws and policies that violate our freedom and dignity. We now take the struggle a step further, and continue forging our freedom. We do not wait for anyone to give us rights. We take the right to participate in the construction of a world where freedom of movement is not a privilege for the few, where the camps are abolished, and where it is unthinkable to create death and destruction. We welcome more people to join this struggle, people who understand that our struggle is necessary and just: Join us on the 27th of April in front of the Danish Immigration Service at 3pm.

At the time of our interviews, the movement had come to a standstill. However, the Castaways Souls of Sjælsmark demonstrate how practices of radical forms of civic activism protesting against unjust asylum laws can take place also in isolated and surveilled conditions as in a deportation center. Their fight for rights and for justice and dignity resembles the practices and citizenship acts described by Arendt and Isin. For non-status refugees, the future challenge[20] remains how to mobilize refugees and pro-refugee groups among Danish citizens and at the same time gain public recognition and attention to their cause.

One illustrative example of an activist fighting for her right to stay in Denmark is the narrative of the rejected asylum seeker E. E. has been denied asylum in Denmark and any other EU country and cannot be sent home either since she lacks official papers. She was born in Ethiopia and arrived to Europe in 2009 through the Balkan route and has lived in the Danish asylum camp, Sandholm, since 2012. She lives with her young son, who attends a Danish kindergarten, speaks Danish, and will soon start school. It is a difficult life as a single mother living on the generosity of people she knows. She maintains that her belief as an orthodox Christian helps her to endure her life, particularly in these past years. E. explains that she lives an "almost" normal life; she is doing an internship in one of the major international organizations, gives lectures at schools, and actively participates and contributes to the activities organized by the Trampoline

---

[20] One of the founders commented: "We were strong, but the government broke us. All the people, where are they now? They have removed them. They have displaced them. They have worn them out ... We want our rights. We are refugees not criminals. If you don't have the rights in your country, you flee ... and in Denmark you hear they believe and practice human rights ... but it is not true ... They are moving people to Ikast (Kærshovedgaard). If they cannot send you back to [the country you fled from] you are going to rot in Ikast!"

House. Her biggest dream is to take an education as journalist, but as a stateless person she does not have any rights to take an education or a job. She is grateful to be part of a community in TH where she can meet with other women activists like her. She argues that more places like TH should be opened and accessed by refugees, since the worst part of a refugee life is the long days spent awaiting a reply. Although E. is not allowed to learn Danish or study, she believes the most important thing for her is to become part of Danish life and society.

E.'s narrative as a woman activist is influenced by her family situation as a mother. Her practices of civic activism as a stateless person show her courage and strong conviction that visibility, voice, and self-empowerment are the refugees' main means to fight for their rights and for social justice, also by informing others about the conditions of refugees. E.'s example can illustrate the situation of the stateless refugees living in the asylum camps caught in a legal and moral dilemma between the home country refusing to accept them back and the Danish authorities refusing to grant them asylum.

Dilemmas of Activist Citizenship and Challenges of Civic Activism

The above analyses illustrate that different forms of civic activism against racism, discrimination, and hate speech exist in Denmark. Our empirical material raises a number of questions about how to conceptualize and contextualize the findings, and how to interpret different forms of activism and the relations among the activists. Indeed, it is difficult to distinguish between different types of activism because they often interact and change over time.

In the Danish context, "everyday activism" seems to be a key concept, for instance, used by several interviewees at the TH. Here, the term refers to civic activism initiated by Danish artists working "for and with" marginalized social groups by means of interactive/everyday learning opportunities, dialogues, and practices. VB's "everyday activism" is premised upon "acts of friendship" in the everyday lives of refugees. Refugees Welcome and LGBT Asylum work mainly as advocacy groups "acting for" asylum seekers and refugees in order to reform the legal rules and procedures and make the Danish system live up to the international human rights conventions. In this chapter, we also identified radical forms of civic activism as practiced by BLM and the Castaway Souls of Sjælsmark. BLM practices a strategy interpreted as empowerment/self-empowerment to combat racism and discrimination against black and brown citizens and more generally refugees. The Castaway Souls of Sjælsmark and E. practice forms of activism with right-less refugees in the front seat, by choosing visibility and political acts in the fight for their rights to stay and to move.

We developed the concept "everyday activism" further by linking it to theories about democracy and social movements on the one hand and to the concept of participatory democracy on the other hand. Our understanding of everyday activism is different from the literature on deliberative democracy, where everyday activism and everyday democracy often refer to the everyday talk and practice of ordinary people.[21] We thus suggest that the notion and practice of everyday activism and learning democracy are influenced by the Danish tradition for bottom-up democracy based on mutual dialogue. Nevertheless, it remains a challenge to combine the roles as advocates "for" with acting "with" vulnerable groups by creating frameworks where self-empowering practices can emerge that remain a stated long-term goal.

The "everyday activism" as practiced by the TH and the VB fits the Danish context as innovative examples of civic activism by Danish nationals fighting for justice for vulnerable groups, which in this sense is different from Isin's idea of "activist citizenship". They can be interpreted as diverse "acts of friendship" and/or "politics of friendship" creating both continuity and resistance strategies through everyday activities as a way to overcome "the politics of fear" (Wodak 2015) of rightwing populism. One remaining challenge is how to empower the agency of migrants and refugees by developing their own action-oriented capacity through forms of self-empowerment. Another is to overcome the gap between "working for" vulnerable groups who need the support of activists and "working with" them toward empowering the agency and political subjectivity of these people. The forms of self-empowerment are best represented in our interviews by the civic activism practiced by Black Lives Matter and the Castaway Souls. In this case the main challenge is to sustain the radical forms of protests by citizens and non-citizens alike.

[21] Interview with Jane Mansbridge—Everyday activism and change: "Jenny contends we need to understand that change comes from 'the everyday talk" and daily practice through which 'ordinary' women – from different political standpoints or none – "make their everyday lives more equal, and stay alive, and not go under". Jenny has long argued for the importance of everyday activism as a precursor to micro politics": http://dangerouswomenproject.org/2017/03/08/4863/.

Concluding Reflections: Reframing Citizenship

This chapter explored some of the dilemmas of citizenship confined to the boundaries of the nation state by focusing on the challenges of civic activism and resistance against the spreading and mainstreaming of rightwing populism, against hate speech, racism, and othering in a contemporary Danish context (Lazaridis et al. 2016). The comparative studies of the RAGE project aptly illustrate that European rightwing populism is embedded in particular historical and political contexts and that democratic resistance is articulated in various ways, influenced by the national/local particularities and heritage (Lazaridis and Campone 2017). The present study had the dual aim to understand the conception of citizenship and civic activism from a Danish perspective, also involving history and conceptions of welfare and democracy that have contributed to reframing citizenship understandings in contemporary Europe, particularly in order to counteract rightwing discourse and politics contributing to a "politics of fear" (Wodak 2015).

Our analysis raises theoretical, normative, and political issues about what concepts and strategies are possible and desirable for understanding and reframing citizenship within, beyond, and across national borders. Research shows that the Danish political elite and public policies, including the position and policies of Social Democracy, have contributed to mainstreaming the discourse and values of neo-nationalism and rightwing populism (Betz and Meret 2012; Borre 2016). The present political climate has made it more difficult to practice citizenship in the form of advocacy, everyday activism, and learning democracy and to engage in more radical forms of activism. It is, however, worth noticing that some activists find that it has become easier to mobilize ordinary citizens against exclusionary welfare nationalism, anti-immigration discourses, and policies for pro-refugee, pro-immigrant activities at the local level.

Our first research question asks who the actors are. In our empirical material, all activists can be seen as fiery souls [*ildsjæle*], founders, and coordinators of voluntary associations and groups mobilized against rightwing populism, othering, and racism. These activists mainly work either for or with immigrants, LGBT groups, refugees, and asylum seekers. The investigated groups were mainly, but not all, founded by Danish activists, and the analyses clearly illustrate the dilemmas of citizenship and civic activism. It raises questions about how to overcome the differentiated citizenship by transversal interactions between Danish citizens, immigrant/

asylum seekers, and marginalized groups. The activism of the Castaway Souls initiated and run by non-status refugees forms a clear exception to the dominant picture.

Our second research question asked what kind of civic activism they practice. The Danish cases include a variety of civic activism: a focus on advocacy, on everyday activism, as well as on more radical forms of activism including forms of self-empowerment initiated by marginalized and vulnerable groups. The majority of examples of civic activism by voluntary civil society groups are examples of everyday activism acting "for, with, and by" vulnerable groups. "Everyday activism" can be understood as examples of civic activism fighting for refugees' and asylum seekers' "right to have rights". It is clearly different from the civic activism of marginalized groups such as BLM and Castaways Souls premised on self-empowerment, which comes closer to Isin's concept of activist citizenship. The short-lived mobilization and radical protest of Castaway Souls show the difficulties and obstacles involved in this form of activism and illustrates the authorities' efforts to disturb and eventually stop practices of activist citizenship by non-status refugees, based on the premise that they are "no longer, not yet, and have never been citizens" and therefore not entitled to be part of the society. Arguably, the variety of forms of civic activism supporting refugees and opposing rightwing populism can be interpreted both as strength and as weakness.

Activists also frame the issues in different ways. Discrimination according to racism, religion, sexuality, and nationality was clearly seen as the main categories. It is somewhat surprising that gender and women refugees' issues were seldom part of the agenda, since the empirical material contains a large number of female activists, initiators, leaders, coordinators, and members of old and new organizations. Activists are generally aware that female migrants and asylum seekers have specific problems as women and mothers that need to be addressed; that is, women usually do not have an individual right to asylum and mainly arrive via family unification, and after getting a residence permit they have difficulties getting a job. Another problem for female refugees and asylum seekers is the lack of camps designed specifically for women and children.

The third research question concerns cooperation among and between activist groups. Denmark is a small country, and it is not surprising that many activities, except VB, are still centered in the capital, Copenhagen, or in Aarhus. The interviewees experience that activists from different organizations/groups usually coordinate their activities against rightwing populism, "othering", and racism. Groups working on similar issues, such as LGBT organizations and anti-racist or advocates of asylum seekers and refugees, usually collaborate and support rather than compete with each other. There is a learning process going on in organizations such as the TH, which serves as organizer of activities within and outside the House for refugees and asylum seekers, for example, at Roskilde Festival or at the Peoples' Meeting on the isle of Bornholm [Folkemødet]. The groups share mutual knowledge about their area of expertise, such as referring refugees and asylum seekers to RW for legal help and to VB for help with clothes and furniture. Nevertheless, there is a need to overcome diversities and strengthen transversal cooperation among activists working to support vulnerable groups.

Our last and perhaps most difficult research question concerns the impact of activism, especially over time. In our case, organizations such as RW and the TH are relatively successful in terms of mobilizing people and get economic and moral support for their politics. It is probably too early to evaluate the impact of the other more recently founded group such as the VB and Black Lives Matter. It is worth noticing that despite an increasingly hostile political and media atmosphere against immigrants, refugees, and asylum seekers since 2015, RW and the TH experience growing support in terms of members, activities, visibility, and funding. In addition, the more recently founded VB is expanding fast locally as the Facebook groups testify. The mainstreaming of the neo-nationalist and anti-migration discourses has thus created opportunities for new forms of local mobilization of citizens for solidarity and human rights and against restrictive anti-immigration policies.

Global mobility and the European crisis have inspired political and theoretical rethinking about transformative politics and the need to create more inclusive forms of democracy, citizenship, and solidarity (Fraser 2013; della Porta 2013). The aim of this chapter has been to explore questions such as: Who counts as citizens, what counts as acts of citizenship and "activist citizenship", how to understand participatory democracy and democratic learning? These questions remain contested and need to be further explored by comparative and transnational research. Hannah Arendt's vision of citizenship, Engin Isin's claims for social justice, and Donatella della Porta's research on solidarity and inclusion against austerity politics and rightwing populism invite researchers to investigate examples of activist citizenship and conceptualize citizens without frontiers. This speaks for developing the notion of differentiated citizenship by transcending normative categories applied to people and their rights to open up for alternative and more inclusive understandings of belonging and of European and transnational citizenship.

References

Arendt, H. (1951). *The origin of totalitarianism*. New York: Schocken Books.
Arendt, H. (1958). *The human condition*. Chicago: University of Chicago Press.
Bauböck, R. (2006). Citizenship and migration: Concepts and controversies. In R. Bauboeck (Ed.), *Migration and citizenship: Legal status, rights and political participation, IMISCOE reports* (pp. 15–32). Amsterdam: Amsterdam University Press.
Betz, H.-G. (2017). Nativism across time and space. *Swiss Political Science Review*. https://doi.org/10.1111/spsr.12260.
Betz, H.-G., & Meret, S. (2012). Right-wing populist parties and the working class vote: What have you done for us lately? In J. Rydgren (Ed.), *Class politics and the radical right*. Abingdon: Routledge.
Borre, O. (2016). Tyve år med værdipolitik. In *Fra krisevalg til jordskredsvalg. Vælgere på vandring 2011–2015*. Frederiksberg: Frydenlund Academic.
Brochmann, G., & Hagelund, A. (2012). *Immigration policies and the Scandinavian welfare states 1945–2010*. London: Palgrave Macmillan.
della Porta, D. (2013). *Can democracy be saved?* Cambridge: Polity Press.
della Porta, D. (2015). *Social movements in times of austerity*. Cambridge: Polity Press.
della Porta, D., & Caiani, M. (2010). *Social movements and Europeanization*. Oxford: Oxford University Press.
della Porta, D., & Mattoni, A. (Eds.). (2014). *Spreading protest: Social movements in times of crisis*. Colchester: ECPR Press.
Fenger-Grøndal, M. (2017). *Venligboerne – historien om en bevægelse* [The friendly neighbors – The story about a movement]. København: Bibelselskabets Selskab.
Fraser, N. (2013). *Fortunes of feminism: From state-managed capitalism to neoliberal crisis*. London: Verso.
Galligan, Y. (2015). *States of democracy: Gender and politics in the European Union*. Abingdon: Routledge.
Isin, E. (2009). Citizenship in the flux. *Subjectivity, 19*, 367–381.
Isin, E. (2012). *Citizens without frontiers*. London: Bloomsbury Academic.
Isin, E., & Turner, B. (2007). Investigating citizenship: An agenda for citizenship studies. *Citizenship Studies, 11*, 5–17.
Korsgaard, O. (2004). *Kampen om folket. Et dannelsesperspektiv på folkets historie i 500 år*. Copenhagen: Gyldendal.
Kriminalforsorgen. (2011). http://www.kriminalforsorgen.dk/Om-os-5720.aspx
Lazaridis, G., & Campani, G. (Eds.). (2017). *Understanding the populist shift*. Abingdon: Routledge.
Lazaridis, G., Campani, G., & Benveniste, A. (Eds.). (2016). *The rise of the far right in Europe: Populist shifts and "othering"*. Basingstoke: Palgrave Macmillan.

Meret, S. (2010). The Danish people's party, the Italian northern league and the Austrian freedom party in a comparative perspective: Party ideology and electoral support. In *SPIRIT PhD series*. Aalborg: Aalborg University.
Meret, S., & Siim, B. (2013). Gender, populism and politics of belonging: Discourses of rightwing populist parties in Denmark, Norway and Austria. In B. Siim & M. Mokre (Eds.), *Negotiating gender and diversity in an emerging European public sphere*. Basingstoke: Palgrave Macmillan.
Messel, K. M. B. (2016). *My house, your house. On recognition, autonomy, and membership in communities of Danes and refugees*. Master thesis, Global Refugee Studies, Aalborg University.
Mikkelsen, F. (Ed.). (2002). *Bevægelser og demokrati. Kollektive bevægelser og foreninger i Danmark*. Aarhus: Aarhus University Press.
Monforte, P., & Dufour, P. (2011). Mobilizing in borderline citizenship regimes: A comparative analysis of undocumented migrants' collective actions. *Politics & Society, 39*, 203–232.
Mouritsen, P. (2015). *En plads i verden. Det moderne medborgerskab*. København: Gyldendal.
Siim, B. (2013). Citizenship. In G. Waylen, K. Celis, J. Kantola, & S. L. Weldon (Eds.), *The Oxford handbook of gender and politics*. Oxford: Oxford University Press.
Siim B., & Meret, S. (2013). *State of the art. Literature review: Danish populism*. National Report from the RAGE-project (WS 1). Aalborg: Aalborg University.
Siim, B., & Meret, S. (2016). Right-wing populism in Denmark: People, nation and welfare in the construction of the 'other'. In G. Lazarides, A. Benveniste, & G. Campani (Eds.), *The rise of the far right: Populist shifts and othering*. London: Palgrave Macmillan.
Siim, B., & Mokre, M. (Eds.). (2013). *Negotiating gender and diversity in an emergent European public sphere*. Basingstoke: Palgrave Macmillan.
Siim B., Fulgsang Larsen, J. & Meret, S. (2013). *Danish populism: Hate speech and populist othering. Analysis of Interviews*. Report from the Rage project (WS1). Aalborg: Aalborg University.
Siim, B., Fuglsang Larsen, J., & Meret, S. (2014, May). *State of the art. Militants from the other side. Anti-bodies to hate-speech and behavior in Denmark*. National Report from the RAGE project (WS3). Aalborg: Aalborg University.
Siim B., Fuglsang Larsen, J., & Meret, S. (2015). *Militants from the other side: Anti-bodies to hate-speech and behavior in Denmark: Analysis of focus group interviews* (WS3). Aalborg: Aalborg University.
Widfeldt, A. (2015). *Extreme right parties in Scandinavia*. Abingdon: Routledge.
Wodak, R. (2015). *Politics of fear: What right wing populist discourses mean*. London: Sage.
Yuval-Davis, N. (2011). *The politics of belonging: Intersectional contestations*. London: Sage.

Links

http://dangerouswomenproject.org/2017/03/08/4863/
http://refugeeswelcome.dk/
http://sabaah.dk/om-sabaah//
http://www.venligboerne.org/
https://www.facebook.com/BlackLivesMatterDenmark/
https://www.facebook.com/pg/BlackLivesMatterDenmark/events/?ref=page_internal
https://www.facebook.com/refugeeswelcomedenmark/
https://www.facebook.com/Rejected-souls-of-DenmarkEurope-222564811413741/
https://www.facebook.com/sosmodracis//
https://www.facebook.com/trampolinhuset/
https://www.lgbtasylum.dk/

CHAPTER 3

Against Romanophobia, for Diversity and Equality: Exploring the Activism Modes of a "Movement Within a Movement" in Finland

Aino Saarinen, Heini Puurunen, Airi Markkanen, and Anca Enache

THE POLITICAL LANDSCAPE: "OTHERERS" VERSUS "EQUALIZERS", ECONOMY AND SECURITY VERSUS HUMAN AND FUNDAMENTAL RIGHTS

In Finland, the turn of the 2010s was marked by a significant political transformation. It was exemplified by the reception of Eastern European Roma from the EU-10 states. The contrast between the interior ministry's

---

A. Saarinen (✉)
Aleksanteri Institute, Helsinki, Finland

H. Puurunen • A. Enache
University of Helsinki, Helsinki, Finland

A. Markkanen
University of Eastern Finland, Joensuu, Finland

© The Author(s) 2019
B. Siim et al. (eds.), *Citizens' Activism and Solidarity Movements*, Palgrave Studies in European Political Sociology,
https://doi.org/10.1007/978-3-319-76183-1_3

work groups in 2008 and 2010 was dramatic. The first approached Roma in the framework of human and fundamental rights, whereas the second recommended strict supervision of camping and begging by Roma. Legislative proposals initiated by populist and right-wing MPs even aimed at turning Roma out of the country. On this basis the government, then led by the center party, presented a "compromise" that featured prohibition of "camping without permission" and "aggressive begging" (Puumalainen 2009; Hirvonen 2012).

The interior and police minister, in reply to a fellow coalition party member (and policeman), felt that "officials should direct [Romani] beggars towards quarters that help them" (Saarinen 2012). By helpers the minister of course did not refer to populist actors. These "immigration-critics" or "otherers", as they sometimes provocatively call themselves, have repeatedly stated that full social, cultural, and health-related rights only belong to citizens and other permanent residents. In the group of the "undeserving", they include asylum seekers, refugees, undocumented people, and mobile EU citizens like Roma. In addition, an electoral program titled *Nuiva manifesti* [Bitter (or Sour) Manifesto] (2011) was released on the internet by the Finns' immigration-critical faction; in 2015 it was further developed into a party platform. This does much to explain their electoral success in what was called the *jytky* in 2011 and its continuation in the *jatkojytky*[1] in 2015.

The following phase began when the populist Finns and the more politically correct center and right-wing parties enhanced their cooperation. The manifesto is indirectly visible, through the Finns' party platform, in the government program for 2015–2019 dealing with immigration policies (Perussuomalaisten 2015; Pääministeri Juha Sipilän 2015[2]). The pro-multicultural and immigrant-friendly left alliance, the greens, and the Swedish People's (minority) Party are all in the opposition (2017) (Saarinen 2017).

The restrictive trend was due to anticipation of an increase in the number of asylum seekers, but as mentioned, there were also other new targets for racist othering, namely, mobile Roma. The Finnish Roma who arrived

---

[1] *Jytky* and *jatkojytky* are Finns' linguistic innovations referring to particularly great electoral victories.

[2] Note: the Finns split right after the party convention in June 2017 into the "immigration-critical" Finns (in opposition) and the Alternative (in government), a party in the making that is to be called the *Blue Future*.

in Finland over 500 years ago still experience discrimination. They are, however, acknowledged as Finnish, while the "new Roma" are, in spite of their EU citizenship, outsiders, strangers, or even aliens (Isin and Nielsen 2008). As poor people without permanent income, they do not have the right to settle in Finland that is given either by the EU's free movement directive or by the National Aliens Act (Puumalainen 2009). On the contrary, they are targeted by antiziganism or Romanophobia (Georghe 2013), that is, hate speech and hate acts, as shown by analyses of regular and social media and by field observation of face-to-face encounters in the street (Oksanen 2012; Markkanen 2012). No wonder that Ari Hirvonen (2012) emphasizes in our anthology *Huomio! Romaneja tiellä* [Attention! Roma on the road] (Markkanen et al. 2012) that new Roma are being defined as a burden, a threat to economy and security, and not people with human and fundamental rights. Even though Finland has been proclaimed a "model country" by the Advisory Board on Romani Affairs (www.romani.fi)—founded in 1956 as the "Gypsy" board—in its strategic declaration for the 2010s (Friman-Korpela 2014: 135), a look at these homeless new Roma on the "rocky streets" of Helsinki (Markkanen 2012) gives us a critical perspective on Finland in the 2010s.

The same mood is found elsewhere in Scandinavia, as recently reported by Anne Britt Djuve et al. (2015) and Ada I. Engebrigtsen et al. (2014). The era in which the Nordic countries could be perceived as the world's "paradise" is therefore over, and it is time to explore present trends, conceptualized as "welfare nationalism" and "welfare chauvinism", that are in conflict with national, regional, and global norms (see Keskinen 2016).

However, the full picture is not so simplistic. In the 2000s–2010s, many ministries have established new multimember committees, boards, and networks that seek to promote human and fundamental rights (Saarinen 2017). They support the work of the previously mentioned board on Romani affairs, and the Advisory Board for Ethnic Relations (1982) and special one-member authorities like the Non-discrimination Ombudsman. It is therefore topical to consider not only horizontal, that is, transsectoral links in civil society, but also vertical connections that are, in the words of Kerstin Jacobsson and Steve Saxonberg (2013), "transactional" and cross the public-civil divide. Civil actors are in a two-way relationship with these state and multinational bodies. Together they influence the development, implementation, and monitoring of formal norms and policies that promote human and fundamental rights.

In addition to the immigration-friendly parties and these public bodies, other "helpers" are also visible. They defend a permissive immigration policy and at their most radical even present visions of a borderless Europe and world. They could be called counterforces or, more positively, equalizers, that is, pro-equality and pro-diversity actors. Regarding new Roma they are organizational families, or in the words of Donatella della Porta and Alica Mattoni (2014) a "movement within a movement".

Research Questions

This chapter focuses on actors composed of civil groups, organizations, individuals, and networks and examines their values, targets, and, most, interestingly, action repertoires, a variety of different types of collective action (della Porta and Diani 1999: 3–12). In which framework do these pro-actors approach mobile Eastern European Roma and how does this affect their activity for change? What kinds of concrete claims and projects unite actors? What are the targets of action—the otherers, the general public, the state? How do demands for the implementation of human and fundamental rights and transcultural solidarity bring actors together in spite of their different histories and action repertoires?

The chapter presents some of those who, with regard to new Roma, appear to be the most important actors. The groups examined include a foundation-based institution from the third sector, two non-governmental organizations, and a militant network, all of which are located in political civil society. Because the aim is also to consider the mutual dynamics of the actors and their actions, shared events and projects will be included; these can be seen as knots (Konttinen 2010), points of connection, and collaboration. Moreover, the chapter considers the role of churches and naturally of Finnish Roma, who also address the situation of Eastern European Roma in their search for a shared identity and solidarity across internal Romani divisions, as recently analyzed by Raluca Roman (2018).

The major actors are all pro-Roma in emphasizing the indivisibility of human value. The delineation of the group under discussion has employed basic discursive concepts that are referred to by Scandinavian researchers Anne Britt Djuve et al. (2015: 15, 55–63) and Ada I. Engebrigtsen et al. (2014: 16–18), as well as numerous Romani scholars, including Martin Kovats (2013) and Nicolae Georghe (2013). In brief, populist otherers define mobile Roma negatively as "beggars" or "welfare tourists"; equalizers see them as "undocumented migrants" or "people who work on the street who also beg", or who seek employment and income and who should be treated with solidarity and respect. The prospect of factual inclusion will be further evaluated based on Nancy Fraser's (2005) idea of three-dimensional justice: in addition to economic-social and cultural rights, marginalized people must have a voice and opportunity to participate in decision making at all levels and in all ways.

The research questions will be explored by drawing on the materials collected in Helsinki, mostly in 2014, in the third period of the RAGE project, which studied the rise of equalizers and the challenges they presented to otherers and formal decision makers. The materials are comprised of the observation of actors on the internet, field notes on campaigning (FN) (18), and focus group discussions (FG) (3). For the Rage research team in Helsinki, the reason for focusing in this chapter on mobile Roma is the possibility to continue the ongoing three-step project: mapping out the situation upon arrival, analyzing pro-actors, and giving a voice to the newcomers themselves.[3]

THE EQUALIZER: PRO-EQUALITY, PRO-DIVERSITY— MOVEMENT IN FINLAND

A broad definition of social movements says that they consist of collective challenges by groups and people with a common purpose and solidarity, in sustained interaction with elites, authorities, and civic opponents (Jacobsson and Saxonberg 2013; Tarrow 1998: 4) In Finland, the number of collective actors on the move to defend new Roma has risen to dozens in the 2010s, according to the internet material that has been collected (Saarinen et al. 2015). This organizational family includes actors that promote the Roma's rights in general as well as actors that focus on a specific vulnerable group as "insider others" (Kovats 2013), for example, mothers and children.

The analysis is inspired by the five-part typology of "activism modes" developed by Ondřej Císař (2013). Service activism, advocacy activism, radical activism, civic self-organization, and periodic mass mobilization concern the abovementioned four elements in the collective mobilization: frameworks and values, goals and claims; targets; and action repertoires. We will also discuss civil disobedience, non-violence vs. violence, and the issue of empowering mobile Roma as political actors.

---

[3] The first book, *Huomio! Romaneja tiellä* [Attention! Roma on the road], was published in 2012; the next two anthologies will come out in 2018–2019.

Activism brings together old actors from the nineteenth century and the post-WWII period and new ones from the late twentieth and early twenty-first century. Their organizational models are different: they include actors that, according to Esa Konttinen (2010), are content with the Finnish habit of conventional, legal actions and cooperation with the state and underground actors that are characterized by a readiness to employ radical repertoires and harsh confrontations. The chapter also looks at the individuals on the move that inspired Engin F. Isin and Greg M. Nielsen (2008) to create the concept of "activist citizenship". Finally, it turns to the numerous annual anniversaries and other mass events. Also under discussion is the previously mentioned human rights regime and how the transactional relationships between civil actors and human rights bodies seem to play a growing role. This leads to a consideration of the prospect of moving toward "transversal dialogue" (Yuval-Davis 1997: 125–133) and "deliberative mini-publics" (Grönlund et al. 2014); both proved useful in organizing the Rage focus group sessions. A thesis discussed near the conclusion says that the pro-Roma movement is more and more capable of acting together across different activism modes.

Service Activism: Institution-Building in the Third Sector

Service production activism in the third sector is not included as such in Císař's (2013) politics-centered typology. However, as these actors are involved in numerous actions that are more or less directly political, there is cause to discuss them as part of equalizers, in terms of "service activism". By modifying Císař, it includes organizations that are able and willing to cooperate with other collective actors and, moreover, have good access to the political system and administration.

The oldest of the actors, the Helsinki Deaconess Institute (HDI) [Helsingin Diakonissalaitos] was founded in the mid-nineteenth century (1867) in the Russian era of Finnish autonomy that ended in independence in 1917. This institute—now a "social foundation" and one of the key actors in the social and healthcare branch—represents an early philanthropic-religious mobilization that had its roots in Germany (Paaskoski 2017: 19–28). In collaboration with other religious-minded organizations and actors, including the Lutheran and Pentecostal churches, it supports socially, culturally, and politically marginalized people. This commitment has led to cooperation with groups that have anti-state goals and radical action repertoires.

The Deaconess Institute has always prioritized work among the "poorest of the poor" and emphasized the indivisibility of human value (www.hdl.fi). It is therefore natural that Finnish Roma have been one of its major target groups. The HDI has supported them, for example, by opening the drop-in center "Kaalo". No wonder, then, that many of the HDI projects have included Romano Missio (originally Gypsy Missio (1906), another old organization that has also kept its religious framework and is closely connected to the Pentecostal church (www.romanomissio.fi; Roman 2018). Today the Deaconess Institute takes a step toward Fraser's (2005) three-dimensional justice in seeking to increase participation by its clients.

As Anca Enache (2012) and Airi Markkanen (2012) have already shown, Roma arriving from Romania and Bulgaria took up their "street work" in Finland immediately after the countries joined the EU in 2007. Soon the Institute received a suggestion from Helsinki's social center to map the situation. It reacted swiftly by starting a two-year project called "Rom po drom" [Roma on the road] for 2008–2010 (Leinonen and Vesalainen 2009). The Federation of Parishes joined the project as the third partner. The steering group expanded the circle of both transsectoral and transactional participants as it also had representatives from the Finn Church Aid, the local police department, and the umbrella organization of Finnish Roma (Fintiko Romano Forum), which was founded in 2006 (www.SuomenRomanifoorumi.fi; www.hdl.fi).

The three major participants were united in their view that Roma were in a difficult economic situation, but each had a different goal (www.hdl.fi). The HDI felt that the project was about "victims" who must be helped; it was also aware of the risks resulting from the "cultural stigma" related to this group. The federation framed the task by speaking about "the beggar project", "loving your neighbor", but also "keeping the human rights perspective out in the open". The social center was the most reserved. It emphasized that "beggars" should be helped not by giving them services in line with the residence-based welfare model but by keeping them from becoming an "economic burden", preferably by pushing them back to their country of origin; naturally, the EU should also be reminded of its duties.

The Roma, who had dispersed to the streets and to events that offered opportunities to make money, were located through traditional outreach work (Enache 2012, 2018). The collaboration quickly led to institutionalization. In 2011, the low-threshold drop-in center with the poetic Latin name "Hirundo" [Swallow] was created to be a place for daily care, relaxation, and meetings. At present, the number of clients is close to a hundred out of the approximately 300 Roma staying in Helsinki in the summer. The center relies on paid staff, among them Finnish and non-Finnish persons and one or two new Roma, as well as volunteers, some of whom are local Pentecostal Roma. Moreover, as the HDI is also a vocational university whose program includes training in multiculturality, students of the field are also working at Hirundo (Puurunen et al. 2016, 2018; FG-1).

The funding draws on the Institute itself, the city and the federation, and, importantly, Finland's Slot Machine Association[4] (SMA), a semi-public organization with a monopoly on gambling (www.rahaautomaattiyhdistys.fi). In regard to the human rights regime, the work done by Hirundo is greatly appreciated: Hirundo has representation in the board on Romani affairs, and in 2014 its efforts were acknowledged by the European Economic and Social Committee as one of civil society's "top projects" (www.hdl.fi).

Cooperation has also developed across the borders. In 2014, the HDI began a three-year village project in Romania that focuses on the well-being of women and children and fights the lack of birth and identity certificates, which prevents access to health-related rights in countries of departure and arrival (www.hdl.fi; Puurunen et al. 2016, 2018; Enache 2018). Like Hirundo, the project includes many other religiously affiliated actors. The extended steering group is both transactional and transsectoral as there are representatives from the city, the church, and Fintiko Romano Forum. All these actors were represented in the interior ministry's work group on the new Roma in 2008; however, in the second work group in 2010, they were marginalized as "opinion givers"; in the previously mentioned government proposal, they were present as "commentators".

In 2011, right after founding Hirundo, the Deaconess Institute progressed to a new phase by cofounding a transnationally inspired institution. The Global Clinic is a low-threshold unit for undocumented people, who were systematically called "paperless" in these contexts in 2014. They are, like mobile Roma, stigmatized, but even more so as they are often

---

[4]The Funding Center for Social Welfare and Health (STEA) is currently cooperating with the social ministry and health (www.stea.fi/web/en/).

referred to as "illegal" immigrants (www.hdl.fi). The Clinic provides free health and dental care at a secret address. The HDI thus practices a kind of civil disobedience. Funding comes from individual activists, associations, and in general nonpartisan actors. The Clinic's resources are wholly inadequate, and the range of medicine and research equipment is limited. Notably, the Clinic is not directly involved with the state human rights regime.

The service is operated by volunteer professionals, that is, doctors, nurses, lawyers, social workers, and, as the only group getting paid, interpreters. They are all committed to absolute confidentiality and strict care ethics, which is important as the attitude of Roma to services offered is everywhere characterized by fear, particularly of the activities of police and security firms (Mudde 2005; see also Djuve et al. 2015: 106–108; Engebrigtsen et al. 2014: 9–10).

According to the HDI's estimates, over two thirds or even three fourths of clients were Roma from Romania and Bulgaria in 2013. As mentioned, the project seeks to remind people of how Roma, due to their poverty and lack of relevant certificates, are often excluded from health insurance in their home countries (Rat 2012; Puurunen 2012) and therefore have no opportunity to receive non-urgent services in other EU countries. More than ten institutional partners are mentioned and involve much the same actors as Hirundo as well as the radical Free Movement Network (to be discussed later).

The Clinic is not only a service but a political project that makes use of pressure and campaigning both nationally and locally. It targets the state directly and thus becomes part of advocacy or even radical activism. Already when it was in its early stages, an appeal was made to the state: the ministry of social issues and health to begin preparing a bill that would oblige municipalities to offer undocumented foreigners more than just emergency healthcare services. The Deaconess Institute again spoke particularly in favor of "mobile EU citizens", that is, Roma. The actors behind the appeal included medical and healthcare sources, international organizations that promote the rights of undocumented people, the Free Movement Network, and of course the (then) ongoing Refugee Advice Centre's "Paperless" project. This action is also linked transnationally with Picum, a platform and network working to ensure the rights of undocumented migrants (http://picum.org/en/).

Advocacy Activism: Petitions, Pressures, and Campaigns

The Global Clinic leads us to another pro-actor that can be discussed according to Císař's (2013) typology. It is based on small advocacy actors that organize many events with few participants and tend to make use of petitions, that is, work in a manner that, in line with Margaret Keck and Kathryn Sikkink (1998: 8–10), can be described as "advocacy activism". The Refugee Advice Centre (1988), run by professional and paid staff, defines itself as a "legal office and a NGO" that serves refugees and other foreigners and distributes information in order to influence both the state and the general public to challenge information released by populist otherers (www.pakolaisneuvonta.fi/eng). It is involved in many bodies of the human rights regime—for instance, the parliament's Human Rights Center and the foreign ministry's Advisory Board for human rights—and is often at hearings in parliamentary committees. The foreign ministry is among its sources of funding (Saarinen 2017).

The organization is also responsible for a permanent knot, a horizontal umbrella network including, among others, the Refugee Council, Amnesty, the Red Cross, and the International Evangelical Church. The Centre is also an INGO, a member of the UN Commission of Human Rights and the European Council on Refugees and Exiles (www.pakolaisneuvonta.fi/eng). The Advice Centre itself is familiar with the practice of civil disobedience but does not encourage breaking laws.[5] Even as it speaks in the name of the most vulnerable groups, it chooses to campaign and pressure decision makers conventionally, in many kinds of cooperation with its network's civil actors with similar aims.

Eastern European EU Roma were briefly on the Centre's agenda in the early 2000s when Roma from Slovakia and the Czech Republic applied for "economic asylum" in Finland and lived in reception centers. Asylum was not granted because it was stated that there are no human rights violations in the EU, even though violations of the rights of Roma had repeatedly been investigated and discovered by the EU itself (Markkanen 2003: 105).

In the second Eastern enlargement phase, the position of Roma as a group without full substantial rights, "quasi citizens" (Castles and Davidson

---

[5] This was emphasized by the organization's representative in a focus group of the Speak Out! EU project that studied violence against minority women (Saarinen 2013).

2000: 94–95), became a problem that the organization has addressed. The three-year "Paperless" project in 2012–2014, funded by the Slot Machine Association, was the first of its kind in Finland. A guide named "Paperless people's right to health" (www.pakolaisneuvonta.fi/eng) presented solutions to making a wider range of services available to those in need and not only children and women who were pregnant or had just given birth. The guide also discussed the Global Clinic and other units maintained by volunteers. With reference to the Deaconess Institute, the guide paid special attention to "people in a situation that resembles being paperless" or, directly, "Eastern European Roma".

The Centre made a political statement in emphasizing that securing human and fundamental rights is the duty of the state and mentioned the UN Economic and Social Council (Saarinen 2017). It was especially persistent when targeting the state. At the turn of 2014–2015, the Centre followed every phase of a law proposal to extend healthcare rights for undocumented people. It participated in a ministerial hearing and received strong support from the public expert institutions and the human rights administration. For instance, both the Non-discrimination Ombudsman and the National Institute for Health and Welfare, which did the groundwork for the proposal, drew special attention to the exclusion of EU Roma (www.thl.fi/en).

In the following phases, the Advice Centre mobilized actors from its umbrella network, as well as a few from outside. It harshly criticized the government's December 2014 proposal and made an appeal to the parliament's Bureau of the Chairs to present the proposal during the legislative period that was about to conclude. Next, it organized an appeal that was signed by ten organizations, including old and new actors, focused on the well-being of children and mothers (www.pakolaisneuvonta.fi/eng).

The pressure succeeded as the bill was presented for voting in the final days of the period. However, it lapsed due to tactical cooperation by the "bitter" Finns and a key social democrat, a former interior and police minister. The Advice Centre did not give up but appealed to MP candidates, but as the election ended in the Finns' *jatkojytky*, the Centre had to turn to the former to the coming government by "demanding" that health services for the undocumented be secured. The number of signatories had increased to nearly 20, this time including a prestigious umbrella organization titled Monika—Multicultural Women's Association (1998). Today, the somewhat extended right for more than acute public services is still restricted to the most vulnerable groups (www.paperittomat.fi/). Some municipalities, for instance Helsinki, are more generous, but volunteers and organizations like the Clinic still play a key role.[6]

Amnesty International Finland [Amnesty Suomi] has been under the umbrella of the Advice Centre since the mid-1960s (1967). In Keck and Sikkink's words (1998: 12–13), it is an "activist beyond borders", an INGO. Unlike the previously discussed service and campaigning institutions, Amnesty focuses on political civil society. It is especially aware of "donor dependency" (Jacobsson and Saxonberg 2013), and to underline and secure its political independence, it receives no public funding but relies on private donors to whom it appeals on the web (www.amnesty.fi/frontpage).

On the other hand, Amnesty is among the organizations that have become especially well integrated with the human rights regime. It is present at most hearings, and its membership includes boards and network run by the social ministry, foreign ministry, as well as the government and the parliament (Saarinen 2017). In brief, it is part of the entire political process, that is, initiating, making, monitoring, and assessment of norms and programs. As an advocacy actor, Amnesty practices both persuasive lobbying and harsh pressure on its public targets, nationally and internationally, and it makes active use of awareness-raising methods when turning to the general public.

A cross-border campaign started by the Finnish Division in 2010, polemically titled "Roma are treated like trash", targets European governments by demanding legal and political reforms. The campaign spreads information about why Roma leave their homelands to make "existential mobility" (Enache 2012) or "circular migration" (Gheorghe 2013) understandable and acceptable. On International Romani Day, 8 April in 2014, the Division urged grassroots activists to send postcards to authorities in Romanian villages under threat of forced eviction. Amnesty has also had a separate Roma work group (FG-3), which has included Finnish Roma—but thus far no mobile Roma—since 2016; this development is in harmony with Amnesty's and Fraser's (2005) call for third justice that Roma themselves must be heard and made part of decision making.

---

[6] In 2017, the Helsinki Board of Social and Health Services voted in favor of expanding the rights to "necessary health services" to all undocumented migrants. To come into effect, this has to be accepted by the city board and council (https://www.hel.fi/sote/en).

As part of the organizational family, the Division is involved in the actions of other local advocacy actors, for example, the Advice Centre's project to promote healthcare for undocumented people and cooperation with an NGO named All Our Children (http://www.pakolaisneuvonta.fi/eng). Among their most visible joint cultural contributions was a short movie filmed in Romania and an education package, which are distributed widely throughout Europe. In Finland, they were presented at an event on EU's Europe Day, in which Romano Missio and the Fintiko Romano Forum also participated (FN, 9 May, 2014).

RADICAL ACTIVISM: DIRECT CONFRONTATIONS, THE EU, THE STATE, AND OTHERERS AS TARGETS

According to Císař (2013), a radical network is mainly based on loose platforms and individual activists, and it often works with a small number of participants and militant strategies. The Free Movement Network [Vapaa Liikkuvuus Verkosto], on the move since the 1990s, is a prime example of this kind of pro-actor. It has roots in the squatter movement (Jokela 2017) and is the most radical of the actors presented here. In Pierre Rosanvallon's (2008: 8) words, it is "counter-cultural": it employs flamboyant visual symbols and emotive language and targets primarily public institutions and decision makers. The Network fights to empower marginal groups politically and give them a voice with a militant action repertoire that includes open confrontations, protests, and demonstrations. For example, in 2006, before the advent of new Eastern European Roma, the Network made an effort to transform asylum seekers into "refugee activists" (Bhimji 2016) by arranging a hunger strike by those denied asylum. The setting for the event outside parliament was one of the most central democratic spaces (www.vapaaliikkuvuus.fi/).

The Network's criticism is aimed at both Finland and the EU, in particular its border management Frontex and the Dublin agreement. It presents ideas about a borderless Europe and world and does not hesitate to speak of "state racism" and "European apartheid". The Network collaborates with similar actors all over Europe (Jokela 2017). Unsurprisingly, it is not represented in the state human rights regime (Saarinen 2017).

Since the 2000s, the Network has focused on people it persistently refers to as "undocumented" and "migrants", and it has recently begun to support "roaming migrants", that is, "mobile Roma" specifically. So far, the most significant project has been "Social Centre Harbour" [Sosiaalikeskus Satama], which follows transnational examples (Jokela 2017). It was founded in 2009 in the Helsinki area of Fish Harbour, which was set for demolition. Social Centre Harbour went beyond the work of the drop-in center Hirundo by helping Roma build living infrastructures for their camp. However, the maintenance required external resources and the permission of the city. This forced the Network to assume a transactional strategy and build an alliance system (della Porta 2005). An organization called "Free Roof" [Vapaa Katto] was set up in 2010 to cooperate with the Helsinki city youth center (Jokela 2017; Peth 2011).

This of course reveals that the youth center had a different view of Roma than the social center and the public order authorities; it is programmatically multiculturalist and has a history of working with Finnish Roma (www.hdl.fi/). However, while cooperation was still ongoing, the city emptied the Harbour in order to "keep order", "guarantee physical security", and "avoid health risks". Police arrived wearing riot gear and took down the heating and electrical wires that had been built. Similar clashes took place elsewhere in Scandinavia and Europe (Engebrigtsen et al. 2014: 69–70). The emptying of the camp was preceded by numerous protests and demonstrations that also mobilized Finnish Roma (Roth 2012).

As a whole, even if new Roma did not offer any physical resistance, the event was dramatic by Finnish standards (Konttinen 2010). It received wide publicity in both regular and social media. In the activists' own words, Roma, whom they referred to as "squatters" as a sign of their solidarity and an imagined common history, were evicted from their "homes". In "immigration-critical" social media, the pro-actors were called "anarchists" who "refused to renounce violence" (Saarinen et al. 2015; www.vapaaliikkuvuus.fi/). The demolition was followed by a demonstration that lasted several days and again took place on an iconic site, the Senate Square. On the stage were politicians from the left alliance, the greens, and anarchists shouting "End to racism, roof for Roma". The demonstration continued with the "Flowers and beggars", a carnival-like performance where Roma handed out roses to passersby. Most of these events had, at least indirectly, elements of civil disobedience; yet despite the presence of anarchists, they did not lead to violence (Jokela 2017).

Despite their defeat in the Harbour, the Network continued the struggle, now with more conventional means. In a discussion convened by the Network at the parliament's Visitors' Center in 2013, panelists—who included representatives from all council parties—were asked about their views on improving the living conditions of Roma: the most moderate alternative was general camping areas, the most daring a dormitory. None of the party panelists made a direct statement in support of even opening free camping areas due to "the lack of public funds" or fear that this "would increase the number of arrivals" (FN, 23 May, 2013). It is worth noting that this struggle is not a minor matter because it involves the law-based "everyman's right", which is an essential part of the Finnish legal system (Hirvonen 2012).

Irrespective of its radicalism, the Free Movement Network is not isolated, which is demonstrated by these events and the transactional cooperation with the city's youth center, not to mention their role in long-term underground institutionalization. Legal counseling for undocumented people was initiated by the Network (Interview with a Free Movement activist, 15 April, 2014); at the moment it shares premises with the Global Clinic. Through this action, the Network received recognition from the widely respected Deaconess Institute and numerous professional volunteers and organizations in the background. Importantly, the Advice Centre's previously mentioned project for healthcare services to undocumented people was also on the agenda. The latest project, "9 Gatherings", is significant as it is funded by the ministry of education and culture; through this the state recognized a rebel as an official pro-actor. It aimed at practical benefits, that is, the self-production of items for sale by Roma. In this initiative, the Network also collaborated with the Danish Trampoline House (FN, 13 June, 2016; see also Siim and Meret 2018).

In all, the Network wants to offer a "political space" (Bhimji 2016) to promote the Roma's politicization and their own projects. More generally, the Free Movement aims at the borderless world, deconstructing thinking about "us/them" and creating spaces for friendly encounters between "citizens and foreigners, strangers and city-dwellers" (www.vapaaliikkuvuus.fi/). It thus fights for all three of Fraser's (2005) justices, economic-social, cultural, and, importantly, political.

Civic Self-Organization: Sporadic and Courageous Deeds

Special attention should be paid to efforts by individuals or loose, spontaneous groups not sponsored by any formal organization: actions that can be defined, in line with Císař (2013), as *civic self-organization*. They also offer knots to other, more disciplined actors, and expand the repertoire in an essential way. Radical individual or group activism is practiced widely by various church-related actors as well as a few Romani actors. A readiness to face antiziganism and Romanophobia came up repeatedly in focus group discussions, in particular the one that focused on the "Romani issue" (FG-1). This kind of sporadic activity assumes many forms, even militant ones, and transforms people into what Engin F. Isin and Greg M. Nielsen (2008) call "activist citizens" targeting formal political institutions and the general public as audiences and, hopefully, participants. Creative "everyday deeds" (Isin 2008) result from feelings of frustration that are due to experiences of powerlessness but also from commitment to human rights. They are done both *for* Roma and *against* otherers and raise the issue of the nature of civil disobedience: how do pro-actors respond to violence from the side of populist otherers or even state institutions like the police?

As mentioned in the section on the political landscape, the preparation in parliament and ministries of the law to prohibit or restrict camping and begging took place in the "bitter years" from 2010 to 2011 onward. Other motivations for mobilization came from the social center's immigration-hostile plans and actions (FN, 8 May, 2014). As a sign of their personal devotion, church-related activists even discussed the possibility of acting as "beggars" themselves, the targets of hate speech and hate acts, so that they might see whether passers-by or police would treat local people like they treat Roma "beggars" (FG-1; see also Markkanen 2012).

Regarding sporadic acts, artists were often on the front line. Many of them wanted to remind people of the human rights of Roma through softer means. A couple of Finnish Roma musicians offered much-needed help by bringing food and clothes to people in the Harbour area (Roth 2012). The "Poor Box Granny" [Vaivaismummo] sculpture by a local artist stood outside chapels with the support of the church but without formal permission by local authorities. The sculpture was visually arresting, encouraged solidarity and also recalled a centuries-old tradition of sharing in Finnish churches. The artist asked passers-by to leave their comments in the closed box and was present in order to enter into a dialogue (FG-1; FN, 15 May, 2014). An accordionist, well-known in concert halls and on the streets, trained mobile Roma to transform them from "beggars" into "working people", even street artists (www.vapaaliikkuvuus.fi/). Another artist collaborated on a long-term basis with many of the aforementioned organizations to empower Roma economically.

Activist citizens also included journalists and educators who, through publicity and educational work, sought to inspire the majority to look at Roma from the framework of human rights and solidarity. A few "ordinary" individuals offered Roma, without much publicity, a place to sleep in their own homes, again as had been done elsewhere in Scandinavia (Engebrigtsen et al. 2014: 73–78). A one-week "skiing holiday", indirectly supported by the church, also provided Roma with short-term private homes. These innovative campaigns, which did not demand any additional funding, received attention in both social and regular media. The sporadic "night services" can be seen as an extension of the day services offered by Hirundo as well as an expression of support for permanent dormitories. Unsurprisingly, as was discussed in the focus group, some of these actors, those who came out in the public, received hate mail and threats (FG-1).

The most central donor, the Slot Machine Association, once again joined the action by offering a platform for what can be conceptualized as "transversal dialogue" (Yuval-Davis 1997: 130–131). In its social media, one of the meetings in the "Human News" [Inhimillisiä Uutisia] (www. inhimillisiauutisia.fi) featured a known pro-actor and an MP of the Finns party, at present a social minister. Supported by the SMA, a famous style and design artist made a short film in which Roma working on the streets were interviewed as ordinary people about their individual life stories, hopes, and dreams. All these can be viewed as elements of political empowerment in the spirit of Nancy Fraser's (2005) triple rights.

Periodic Mass Mobilization: Knots of Pro-actors and Actions

Excluding the actions of the Free Movement, no episodic mass event (Císař 2013) took place for mobile Roma. However, it is also necessary to bring up actions that include elements for advancing the Roma cause and could be called *periodic mass mobilization*. This kind of minor modification of the five-divided typology seems necessary as it makes major mass events visible as dynamic knots (Konttinen 2010). It is important that different actors regularly come together and strengthen the pro-Roma organizational family. Annual campaign days, like the International Romani Day and Europe Day, and other events call together organizations, groups, and individuals both vertically and horizontally. This also gives evidence of the transnational, even global, diffusion of ideas and practices (della Porta and Mattoni 2014).

The happenings mobilize all of the pro-actors discussed in this chapter. Some of the events are impressive by local and national standards. The Finnish version of Social Forum has over a hundred organizers and an audience of almost a thousand (www.sosiaalifoorumi.fi). In 2014, the Forum had a workshop called "Romani stories" about the situation of mobile Roma. Among the five organizers were Hirundo and the Finnish Rage team; the previously mentioned church-related video was shown here for the first time. The new Roma were also represented by a panel discussant.

New Roma were also addressed in an annual event in 2014 that makes us all members of a "neighborhood" and deconstructs the "us/them" division symbolically through its title. The "World Village Festival" [Maailma Kylässä] (1995) gathers the largest number of organizers and has the biggest audience, over a hundred thousand people (www.maailmakylassa.fi/festivaali). The latest books from pro-actors are also presented; mobile Roma were discussed in 2012's book exhibitions of our "Huomio" [Attention!] collection, first launched on Europe Day.

The Festival is co-funded by the ministry of education and culture. Again, collaboration between civic actors and the pro-diversity and pro-immigration parties (primarily the left and the greens) is characteristic. The participation of the human rights regime shows the sustainability and continued development of the alliance system. Members or supporters of well-established civic organizations did not view participation as a problem either, as shown by the discussion in the focus groups (FG-2). Moreover, Roma who benefit economically by collecting returnable goods and selling their artifacts are no longer "beggars" but "working people" who in this role are visible even at the annual Pride week gatherings (FN, 29 June, 2014).

These transnational inspirations must be seen as connected to the global human justice movements analyzed by Donatella della Porta and Alice Mattoni (2014). The action repertoires are relatively moderate as they consist mainly of seminars, workshops, or happenings such as pop-up restaurants, which thus makes them more like celebrations and performances than direct political challenges, much less militant ones. This nonetheless indicates that the events do offer some channels for direct participation and therefore have elements of third justice in the spirit of Fraser (2005).

Conclusion and Discussion

"Otherers" who work within a framework of welfare chauvinism and welfare nationalism emphasize economic benefit and security; they represent antiziganism and Romanophobia, fear and hatred of Roma; for them new Roma are "beggars" or "welfare tourists". Otherers include, at least occasionally, the center-right government that has partial roots in the immigration-critics' "manifesto" and the related policy program of the Finns. A human rights framework is represented by the opposition, which is composed of the left-green forces; for them new Roma are "migrants" in need of help and welfare rights and services.

Simultaneously with the growth of high-level right-wing populism, however, collaboration between public bodies and pro-actors has intensified: civic actors are represented in the human rights bodies; on the other hand, state actors take part in civil society events and support them financially. These civil actors, civil servants, and politicians form a kind of alliance system which can be found at the local level as well. Helsinki's youth center, which operates a multiculturalist program, is a viable partner to civil pro-actors. But there are also clashes as the social center—without forgetting the police—often seems to have taken a stand against the rights and welfare of the Roma. In all, the public decision makers and administration are not only collaborators but also the target of actions aiming at a kind of pro-regime—multinationally, nationally, and locally.

In this chapter, civic actors, analyses of the internet, event observations, and focus group discussions have revealed the existence of an organizational family, a lively "movement within a movement": there are intensive and sustainable networks and knots where participants overlap, are active in many organizations, and move from between groups. The movement brings together old, established service producers as well as advocacy actors, not to forget actors from radical underground initiatives, networks, and institutions. A remarkable phenomenon is mobilization from below, sporadically and through annual events.

The five-part typology—service activism, advocacy activism, radical activism, civic self-organization, and periodic mass mobilization—helps reveal the complex and flexible collective pro-Roma movement. Notably, even sub-state actions criticizing the state receive support from respected third sector and political advocacy institutions. The analysis brings up interesting divergences in action repertoires. Dependence on funding and membership in the human rights regime demand careful consideration of methods and alliances from both NGOs and INGOs. Many focus group discussants assured us that they can participate in demonstrations and projects that are not part of the action repertoire of their own organizations, if not as salaried staff then at least as individuals. Radical activists are free to engage in daring actions that target both the state and populist forces as well as the general public in the streets. Artists often participate through acts of demonstration (Walters 2008) or performances that seek to appeal to media and passers-by. Many "ordinary" activists prefer relatively soft means, such as providing shelter for the night.

They are all activist citizens who may respond, directly or indirectly, to populist hate speech and acts. They do, however, not mirror "uncivil" actions (Kopecký and Mudde 2012). Regarding civil disobedience, no actor, individual or collective, tolerated verbal or physical attacks on persons or groups or spoke for it; they were "decidedly non-violent" (Císař 2013). The anarchists (not discussed in this chapter) who intervened at some happenings were treated with caution.

The most massive events are part of the activism mode classified as periodic mass mobilization. They bring together great numbers of participants from a wide spectrum and make visible the alliance system, the "movement within a movement". In addition to their periodic mass mobilization, umbrella organizations and their projects are also interesting because they are linked with international anniversaries that function as knots both horizontally and vertically, between the state human rights regime and civic actors.

Many acts, especially by people classified as civic self-organization, can be called "political deeds" or "political demonstrations" (Isin 2008). They target both the wider audience, media, and established institutions, including decision makers and the human rights regime, and call for sympathy and solidarity by making use of symbols, visual artifacts, and multi-sensual performances. At times they approach democracy as a processual institution by arranging "mini-publics" (Grönlund et al. 2014). There are some signs of transversal dialogue between equalizers and right-wing populists, which was discussed in one focus group in particular. Populists and pro-actors were both wary of and spoke for transversal dialogue, at least in principle (FG-3).

Observation of forms and flows of funding reveals that those who are active on behalf of mobile Roma constantly come together in many forums. The financial support for Roma and pro-actors draws on several sources. Aid comes from the public sector, occasionally from semi-public sources which can be seen as part of the pro-actor movement. Resources also come from membership fees and donations as well as from tickets bought for performances.

Worth a special mention are the churches, religious organizations, and individual actors on the move across the whole spectrum of activism modes. The Lutheran Church is active transnationally, through its European and global connections, and sub-locally at the parish level; in small neighborhoods "acts of friendship" (Isin 2008) take place. A few church-related actors have become publicly known for their radical activism, courageous political deeds, and—as confirmed in the focus group discussion—readiness for "acts of resistance" (Isin 2008) in case the ban of begging would be adapted; they if any can be characterized as activist citizens. Furthermore, the churches participate in service and institution-building together with the city administration and the major service institution, the Deaconess Institute and with advocacy and radical actors pressuring the state. Also, they are present in periodic mass events with transnational links.

Epilogue

The agendas remind us of the plight of Finnish Roma before the construction of the residence-based welfare state in the 1970s. There is great concern for children and mothers. Because the settling of children is monitored at least in regard to street work, projects also become transnational and involve the countries of departure. This activity in particular draws on a wide array of national, already established organizations.

The mobilization and organization of Roma are therefore of great interest. Finnish Roma can be found in many places: in their own traditional and newly politicized organizations, in building service institutions, the advocacy fight for undocumented Roma's rights, and in civic self-organizing that provides first-aid for camps. Elements for building a common identity with new Roma through memories of the history of Finnish Roma must be recognized as well—even if many local Roma are wary of attracting some of the hate aimed at newcomers (Roman 2018).

However, mobile Roma themselves have not organized. They participate in events rarely and singly. It is clear that the networks and politics that were built in the 2000s–2010s, which now extend to the European and global levels, mainly reach the well-integrated elite. On street level, inclusion only takes place through small projects. They often have a clear connection to the Roma's own economic interests, such as different art and artifact projects for production of items to be sold on the streets and at events. In any case, the idea of Finland as a "model country" for Roma strategies seems questionable from the perspective of new Roma, who are far from the right to have rights, in particular Nancy Fraser's triple citizenship including economic-social, cultural, and substantial political rights.

The burning issue is, without doubt, the question of "importing" democratic, long-term activism into circularly mobile groups such as the Roma. This will be approached by the Helsinki team's second anthology, now in progress, through interviews of individual pro-actors including the "target" group. The third part will focus exclusively on mobile Roma as speakers, participants, and even political actors. This will, as shown in our methodological analysis (Saarinen et al. 2018), call for experiments for "learning democracy", developing practical innovations in the spirit of deliberative democracy (Grönlund et al. 2014). To involve mobile Roma in the democratic process, we as "processual facilitators" must also turn to critical self-reflections. This challenge that started in the 2000s (Markkanen et al. 2012; Saarinen et al. 2018) will come to a synthesis in the late 2010s.

Rage Sources

Field Notes (FN), Helsinki

Panel Discussion on New Roma's Housing, 23 May, 2013; Social Forum Finland: European Spring, 27 April, 2014; Humanist Association: On Romani Beggars, 8 May, 2014; Europe Day (Tampere), 9 May, 2014; International Romani Music (HDI/Kaalo), 14 May, 2014; Alm Granny, 15 May, 2014; World Village Festival, 24 May, 2014; 9 Gatherings, 23 May, 2014; Pride Festival, 29 June, 2014; Trampoline House (Copenhagen), 13 June, 2016.

Focus Groups (FG), Helsinki

FG–1: Mobile Roma issue group, 20 May, 2014; FG–2: Multi-issue group, 27 May, 2014; FG–3: Transversal dialogue group, 3 June, 2014
Interview for Rage with a Free Movement activist, 15 April, 2013.

References

Bhimji, F. (2016). Visibilities and the politics of space: Refugee activism in Berlin. *Journal of Immigrant & Refugee Studies, 14*, 432–450.
Castles, S., & Davidson, A. (2000). *Citizenship and migration. Globalization and the politics of belonging.* Houndmills/New York: Palgrave.
Císař, O. (2013). A typology of extra-parliamentary political activism in post-communist settings: The case of the Czech Republic. In K. Jacobsson & S. Saxonberg (Eds.), *Beyond NGO-ization. The development of social movements in Central and Eastern Europe* (pp. 139–167). Farnham/Burlington: Ashgate.
della Porta, D. (2005). Multiple belongings, tolerant identities, and the construction of another politics: Between European social forums and local social fora. In D. della Porta & S. Tarrow (Eds.), *Transnational protest and global activism* (pp. 175–202). Lanham: Rowman and Littlefield.
della Porta, D., & Diani, M. (1999). *Social movements. An introduction.* Malden: Blackwell Publishing.
della Porta, D., & Mattoni, A. (2014). Patterns of diffusion and the transnational dimension of protest in the movements of the crisis. An introduction. In D. della Porta & A. Mattoni (Eds.), *Spreading protest. Social movements in times of crisis* (pp. 1–18). Colchester: ECPR Press.
Djuve, A. B., Friberg, J. H., Tyldum, G., & Zhang, H. (2015). *When poverty meets affluence. Migrants from Romania on the streets of the Scandinavian capitals.* Oslo: FAFO.
Enache, A. L. (2012). Köyhyyden kiertokulku – Romanian romanien viimeaikainen muutto Helsinkiin eloonjäämisstrategiana. In A. Markkanen, H. Puurunen, & A. Saarinen (Eds.), *Huomio! Romaneja tiellä* [Attention! Roma on the road] (pp. 42–71). Helsinki: Like.
Enache, A. (2018). Reflections on doing critical ethnography: Fieldwork with mobile Roma. In *Mobilizing for mobile Roma in Finland in the 2000s–2010s* (working title). Helsinki: Trialogue Books. Manuscript.
Engebrigtsen, A. I., Fraenkel, J., & Pop, D. (2014). *Gateliv. Kartlegging av situationer til utenlandske personer som tigger*, NOVA Rapport 7/2014. Oslo: NOVA.
Fraser, N. (2005, November–December). Reframing justice in a globalizing world. *New Left Review*, 69–88.
Friman-Korpela, S. (2014). *Romanipolitiikasta romanien politiikkaan. Poliittisen asialistan ja toimijakonseption muutos 1900-luvun jälkipuoliskon Suomessa.* Jyväskylä: University of Jyväskylä.
Georghe, N. (2013). Choices to be made and prices to be paid: Potential roles and consequences in Roma activism and policy-making. In W. Guy & Pakiv European Roma Fund (Eds.), *From victimhood to citizenship. The path of Roma integration* (pp. 41–99). Budapest: Kossuth Publishing Corporation.

Grönlund, K., Bächtiger, A., & Setälä, M. (2014). Introduction. In K. Grönlund, A. Bächtiger, & M. Setälä (Eds.), *Deliberative mini-publics. Involving citizens in the democratic process* (pp. 1-8). Colchester: ECPR Press.

Hirvonen, A. (2012). Karkotetut kansalaiset vapaan liikkuvuuden alueella. In A. Markkanen, H. Puurunen, & A. Saarinen (Eds.), *Huomio! Romaneja tiellä* [Attention! Roma on the road] (pp. 183-213). Helsinki: Like.

Isin, E. F. (2008). Theorizing acts of citizenship. In E. F. Isin & G. M. Nielsen (Eds.), *Acts of citizenship* (pp. 15-43). London/New York: Zed Books.

Isin, E. F., & Nielsen, M. G. (2008). Introduction. In E. F. Isin & G. M. Nielsen (Eds.), *Acts of citizenship* (pp. 1-12). London/New York: Zed Books.

Jacobsson, K., & Saxonberg, S. (2013). Introduction: The development of social movements in Central and Eastern Europe. In K. Jacobsson & S. Saxonberg (Eds.), *Beyond NGO-ization. The development of social movements in Central and Eastern Europe* (pp. 1-26). Farnham/Burlington: Ashgate.

Jokela, M. (2017). Kaupungin rajat. Sosiaalikeskus Satama, nuorisopolitiikka ja romanit. *Sosiologia, 64*, 63-78.

Keck, M. E., & Sikkink, K. (1998). *Activists beyond borders: Advocacy networks in international politics*. Ithaca: Cornell University Press.

Keskinen, S. (2016). From welfare nationalism to welfare chauvinism: Economic rhetoric, the welfare state and changing asylum policies in Finland. *Critical Social Policy, 36*, 1-19.

Konttinen, E. (2010). Suomalaisen ympäristöliikkeen valtiosuhteet. In E. Konttinen & J. Peltokoski (Eds.), *Verkostojen liikettä* (pp. 58-78). Jyväskylän yliopisto. Kansalaisyhteiskunnan tutkimusportaali. Available at http://kans.jyu.fi. Accessed 29 Apr 2016.

Kopeckŷ, P., & Mudde, C. (Eds.). (2012). *Uncivil society. Contentious politics in post-communist Europe*. London/New York: Routledge.

Kovats, M. (2013). Integration and politisation of Roma identity. In W. Guy (Ed.), *From victimhood to citizenship. The path of Roma integration* (pp. 101-127). Pakiv European Roma Fund. Budapest: Kossuth Publishing Corporation.

Leinonen, T., & Vesalainen, M. (2009). *Päivästä päivään, maasta maahan, tavoitteena toimeentulo. Rom po drom – romanit tiellä – projektin väliraportti ajalta 3.6.-31.10.2008. Raportteja 1/2009*. Helsingin Diakonissalaitos: Helsinki.

Markkanen, A. (2003). *Luonnollisesti – etnografinen tutkimus romaninaisten elämänkulusta*. [Naturally: An ethnographic study of Romani women's life course] Joensuu: Joensuun yliopisto.

Markkanen, A. (2012). Romanien elämisen ehdot Suomessa ja Romaniassa – onko romaneilla tilaa EU-Euroopassa. In A. Markkanen, H. Puurunen, & A. Saarinen (Eds.), *Huomio! Romaneja tiellä* [attention! Roma on the road] (pp. 72-104). Helsinki: Like.

Markkanen, A. (2018). Romanian Romani women and families on the move. Ethnography of othering. In A. Markkanen & K. Åberg (Eds.), *The Culture of the Finnish Roma*. Manuscript.

Markkanen, A., Puurunen, H., & Saarinen, A. (Eds.) (2012). *Huomio! Romaneja tiellä*. [Attention! Roma on the road]. Helsinki: Like.

Mudde, C. (2005). Central and Eastern Europe. In C. Mudde (Ed.), *Racist extremism in Central and Eastern Europe* (pp. 267–285). London/New York: Routledge.

Oksanen, K. (2012). Kuinka media löysi kerjäläiset. Havaintoja romanikerjäläisten ja tiedotusvälineiden suhteesta vuosina 2006–2011. In A. Markkanen, H. Puurunen, & A. Saarinen (Eds.), *Huomio! Romaneja tiellä*. [Attention! Roma on the road] (pp. 248–273). Helsinki: Like.

Paaskoski, J. (2017). *Ihmisen arvo. Helsingin Diakonissalaitos 150 vuotta*. Helsinki: Helsingin Diakonissalaitos/Edita.

Peth, A. (2011). *Vapaa Katto ry ja nuorisoasiainkeskus yhteistyössä Sosiaalikeskus Satamassa – selvitys Sosiaalikeskus Sataman vaiheisiin vuosina 2008–2011*. Helsinki: Helsingin kaupungin nuorisoasiainkeskus.

Puumalainen, M. (2009). Poissa silmistä, poissa mielestä: Romanikerjäläiset ja liikkumisvapaus. In V. Mäkinen & A.-B. Pessi (Eds.), *Kerjääminen eilen ja tänään* (pp. 121–170). Tampere: Vastapaino.

Puurunen, H. (2012). Matkalla Balkanilla. Bulgarian ja Serbian romanit perinteiden ja muutosten ristipaineissa. In A. Markkanen, H. Puurunen, & A. Saarinen (Eds.), *Huomio! Romaneja tiellä*. [Attention! Roma on the road] (pp. 105–136). Helsinki: Like.

Puurunen, H., Markkanen, A., & Enache, A. (2016). Päiväkeskus Hirundo – matalan kynnyksen palveluja ja kansalaisaktivismia muuttajaromanien puolesta. Kansainvälinen sosiaalityö. Käsitteitä, käytäntöjä ja kehityskulkuja. In M. Jäppinen, A. Metteri, S. Ranta-Tyrkkö, & P.-L. Rauhala (Eds.), *Sosiaalityön vuosikirja* (pp. 227–249). Tallinna: United Press. [See Puurunen, Markkanen, & Enache, 2018].

Puurunen, H., Markkanen, A., & Enache, A. (2018). Hirundo drop-in centre: Helping and supporting Eastern European Roma in Helsinki. In *Mobilizing for mobile Roma in Finland in the 2000s–2010s* (working title). Helsinki: Trialogue Books. Manuscript.

Raț, C. (2012). Romaninaiset ja lapset – Romanian uuden perhepolitiikan häviäjät. In A. Markkanen, H. Puurunen, & A. Saarinen (Eds.), *Huomio! Romaneja tiellä*. [Attention! Roma on the road] (pp. 164–182). Helsinki: Like.

Roman, R. (2018). Between (mis)recognition and belonging. Finnish Roma, migrant Roma and social outreach. In *Mobilizing for mobile Roma in Finland in the 2000s–2010s* (working title). Helsinki: Trialogue Books. Manuscript.

Rosanvallon, P. (2008). *Counter-democracy: Politics in an age of distrust*. Cambridge: Cambridge University Press.

Roth, K. (2012). Romanikerjäläiset Helsingin Manhattanilla. In A. Markkanen, H. Puurunen, & A. Saarinen (Eds.), *Huomio! Romaneja tiellä.* [Attention! Roma on the road] (pp. 26–40). Helsinki: Like.

Saarinen, A. (2012). Vapaa liikkuvuus: haaste suomalaiselle maahanmuuttopolitiikalle ja naisystävälliselle hyvinvointivaltiolle. In A. Markkanen, H. Puurunen, & A. Saarinen (Eds.), *Huomio! Romaneja tiellä.* [Attention! Roma on the road] (pp. 214–247). Helsinki: Like.

Saarinen, A. (2013). Helsinki: Looking for shared vocabularies. In F. Bimbi (Ed.), *Agency of migrant women against gender violence. Final comparative report of the project* SPEAK OUT! (pp. 97–129). Merano: Edizioni alpha beta Verlag.

Saarinen, A. (2017). An unpublished, Rage-related manuscript that focuses on the human rights regime in Finland.

Saarinen, A., Enache, A., Markkanen, A., & Puurunen, H. (2015). *The antibodies. Rage WS-3 Report: Finland.* Unpublished.

Saarinen, A., Puurunen, H., & Enache, A. (2018). Eastern European Roma as a new challenge for research. In A. Markkanen & K. Åberg (Eds.), *The culture of finnish Roma.* Manuscript.

Siim, B., & Meret, S. (2018). Dilemmas of citizenship: Democratic challenges, civic activism and resistance in Danish society. Chapter 2 in this volume.

Tarrow, S. (1998). *Power in movement. Social movements and contentious politics. Cambridge studies in comparative politics.* Cambridge: Cambridge University Press.

Walters, W. (2008). Acts of demonstration: Mapping the territory of (non-)citizenship. In E. F. Isin & G. M. Nielsen (Eds.), *Acts of citizenship* (pp. 182–206). London/New York: Zed Books.

Yuval-Davis, N. (1997). *Gender & Nation. Politics and Culture: A Theory, Culture & Society series.* London/Thousand Oaks/New Delhi: Sage.

Internet

9 Gatherings Project. Available at: www.vapaaliikkuvuus.net/2014/11/uusi-taidehanke-luo-itä-euroopan-siirtolaisnuorille-toimeentulomahdollisuuksia. Accessed 12 Nov 2014.

Amnesty Finland. Amnesty International. 2010. *Eurooppalainen ihmisoikeusongelma: Romaneja kohdellaan kuin roskaa.* Available at www.amnestyfinland.fi. Accessed 4 Aug 2014.

Funding Centre for Social Welfare and Health (STEA) operating in connection with the Social Ministry and Health. Available at: www.stea.fi/web/en/. Accessed 30 Aug 2017.

Helsingin Diakonissalaitos. Helsinki Deaconess Institute. Available at: www.hdl.fi. Accessed 4 Aug 2014.

Helsingin kaupunki, Nuorisoasiainkeskus, Monikulttuurisuus. Available at: www.hel.fi/hki/fi/Vapaa-aika/Monikulttuurisuus. Accessed 10 Oct 2014.
Helsinki Board of Social and Health Services. Available at: https://www.hel.fi/sote/en. Accessed 3 Sept 2017.
Maailma Kylässä. World Village Festival. 2014. Available at: www.maailmakylassa.fi/festivaali/. Accessed 10 Oct 2014.
National Institute for Health and Welfare. [Terveyden ja Hyvinvoinnin Laitos]. Available at: www.thl.fi/fi/web/thlfi-en/. Accessed 5 Aug 2014.
Nuiva vaalimanifesti. MMXI. 2011 [Bitter (or Sour) Manifesto]. Available at: www.vaalimanifesti.fi. Accessed 5 Aug 2015.
Oikeus terveyteen. Paperittomuudesta. Available at: www.paperittomat.fi/. Accessed 5 Aug 2014.
Pääministeri Juha Sipilän hallitusohjelma. 29.05.2015. Available at: www.valtioneuvosto.fi. Accessed 5 Aug 2015.
Perussuomalaisten maahanmuuttopoliittinen vaaliohjelma. 2015. Available at: www.perussuomalaiset.fi. Accessed 5 Aug 2015.
PICUM – Platform for International Cooperation of Undocumented Migrants. Available at: http://picum.org/en/. Accessed 30 Aug 2014.
Romano Missio. Available at: www.romanomissio.fi. Accessed 6 Apr 2014.
Suomen Pakolaisneuvonta. Refugee Advice Centre. Available at: www.pakolaisneuvonta.fi. Accessed 6 Aug 2014.
Suomen Romanifoorumi. Fintiko Romano Forum. Available at: www.romanofoorum.fi. Accessed 6 Apr 2014.
Suomen Sosiaalifoorumi [Finnish Social Forum]. 2014. Available at: www.sosiaalifoorumi.fi/. Accessed 4 Aug 2014.
Vapaa Liikkuvuus Verkosto [Free Movement Network]. Available at: www.vapaaliikkuvuus.net. Accessed 5 Aug 2014.

CHAPTER 4

Forging "the People" in the UK: The Appeal of Populism and the Resistant Antibodies

Don Flynn and Gabriella Lazaridis

INTRODUCTION

In recent decades, populism has emerged as the seemingly standard way of doing mass politics in an epoch marked by the steady demise of leftist and Christian forms of social democracy. In its post-Second World War heyday, these approaches shared the view that the business of governing a country meant attending to the welfare of its people, as well as providing the conditions for its economy to prosper. Social and Christian democrats did not believe in "trickle-down" theories of social improvement: if citizens were better housed, better educated, and enjoyed better health, it was because government-run programs were bringing about these desired ends.

The heyday of this approach began to unravel during the course of the 1970s with the onset of conditions that undermined the global Keynesian settlement, which had given the world stable currencies and national gov-

---

D. Flynn (✉)
Migrants' Rights Network, London, UK

G. Lazaridis
University of Leicester, Leicester, UK

© The Author(s) 2019
B. Siim et al. (eds.), *Citizens' Activism and Solidarity Movements*, Palgrave Studies in European Political Sociology,
https://doi.org/10.1007/978-3-319-76183-1_4

ernments the means to manage the economic affairs of their countries (Offe 1984). The crisis years loomed. Societies whose social stability had been underpinned by the state's role in providing a social housing market, public schools, and health services, a legal regime based on the sanctity of contractual undertakings, were pitched into cycles of constant fiscal crisis which produced a marked physical decline in the infrastructure of public life. The old certainties of life in stable parliamentary democracies, that things would constantly get better for the mass of the population and the good governance of the nation was the mechanism to achieve this, fell away at a rapid rate. Social identities forged by the assurance that the state would deliver for its citizens began to disintegrate, leaving ever larger numbers of people with the feeling that they had been forgotten by their political masters.

Populism is the movement in politics that addresses this sense of decline that takes root in nations buffeted by the loss of the public policy levers that support democratic management of national economies. Its mode of operation is to pull together bodies of public opinion that have become fragmented and diffuse as a consequence of the demise of forms of government that had the appearance of accountability and worked for them. It aims to speak directly to the self-identity of ordinary citizens, assuring them that they are indeed good people who have been made the victims of a great injustice at the hands of sinister forces that have robbed them of their autonomy and capacity for action (Albertazzi and McDonnell 2008: 1–11). The populist politician offers a program that summons a newly invigorated people back into existence, filled with energy and equipped to take on the task of renewing their national community.

This paper, which is based on the findings of the comparative multidisciplinary, multi-method project RAGE, a project looking at the rise of the far right in Europe, its "othering," and the resistant antibodies to this phenomenon,[1] is divided into two parts: in part one, we offer a standard account of populism in Britain looking at three political parties. To determine whether a particular political party operates with this element of populism, consideration is given to the rhetoric it uses to constitute and mobilize its version of "the people" and how it frames the question of the injustices they have endured and the correctives to which they are in need. The second part discusses the ways in which the confrontation between radical right populist parties and opposing actors results in the

[1] We thank the UK team for their help.

evolution of anti-racist and anti-discrimination attitudes, politics, strategies, and activism at the individual and organized level. We have focused on strategies to both contain and combat racism and other forms of discrimination by state actors, NGOs, and civil society. The UK is an interesting case due to the two migration flows: from the Commonwealth countries and the EU member states.

Part One: Populism in the Old and the New Political Parties

Discussion about populist political movements invariably centers on their innovation of "the other" in their political rhetoric. "The other" is the external force that acts to deprive the people of the entitlements they have earned by their loyalty, their service to the well-being of the community, and their fortitude in abiding by the rules and waiting their turn when the benefits that accrue to good citizens are being handed out. "The other" could take the form of "greedy bankers" who wrecked the economy through their selfishness; the dominant fraction of the ruling elite, which works to protect its own interests before considering others; or "the foreigners" who don't share "our" values and who are claiming things to which they have no moral entitlement. Really powerful populist narratives will find ways to combine all of these elements into its rhetoric, and often even more.

Margaret Thatcher and "Authoritarian Populism"

As the certainties of the post-war political settlement began to unravel, stripping the established parties of their power to govern within the framework of economic management and ordered social policies, they began to produce currents within their ranks that were prepared to experiment with populist modes of operation. The first significant advance for this new approach came with the rise of Margaret Thatcher through the ranks of the Conservative Party in the 1970s. Emerging as a radical, free-market politician, her ambition was to change the elite consensus that had governed the country. Offering a vision of an establishment made up of technocrats and upper-class civil servants running the show in ways that were indifferent to the moods of the popular masses, she claimed that Britain was stifled by "interests" ranging from the trade unions, the heads of nationalized industries and public services and utilities, and the elite professions (Hall 1979). In this setup, the policy direction of government emerged through a process of corporate tripartism, which meant that decisions were taken only after all the privileged "insiders" had shaped the agenda and made sure that, first and foremost, their own interests had been protected (Morris 2017: 19).

Thatcher's "people" did not extend to the whole population of Great Britain. It did not cover, for example, the 12.5 million trade unionists who had shown a propensity to support the interventionist, state welfare policies she abhorred (Leys 1986: chapter 5). Her rhetoric centered on the interests of groups of people who stood apart from the ideologies of collectivism, which had shaped post-war Britain. Small business people, wage earners who were not union members, housewives managing tight domestic budgets, and people aspiring to get an education for their children outside the confines of the state comprehensive system were the sort of citizens she offered up as a more authentic British people. Stoical, long-suffering, patients, but fed up with the red tape and pettifogging bureaucracy that encumbered plans for their businesses, were a force waiting to be unleashed to push the country forward to a new period of greatness.

Margaret Thatcher's political career was dedicated to breaking up the structures that were demoralizing her version of the people. What they needed to flourish was the energy that comes from minimally regulated free markets. Thatcher set out to craft an offer to the electorate that promised that their interests, as opposed to the elites', would be made the driving force of government action. Her style was famously described as "authoritarian populism" by cultural theorist Stuart Hall (1979). According to this analysis, authoritarian populism was a product of the conjunctural crisis of that period, arising from the failure of the post-war interventionist, Keynesian state to respond to the economic and political crises that had marked the decade of the 1970s. Blame for this inability to find a way out of the social and economic impasse had fallen most heavily on Labour as the party that had advanced the view that the expansion of the state was synonymous with the interests of the mass of working-class citizens. However, the interests of ordinary people were being squeezed in at least four areas of these state policies, namely, income policy, which aimed at restraining wage growth during a period of high inflation; progressive forms of school education, seen as holding back working-class children; and race equality and immigration policies.

This authoritarian version of populism had succeeded in defining its "people"; but who played the role of "the other"? Trade union leaders, the heads of nationalized industries, state planners, and professional classes all figured, but the rhetoric needed a figure that reached deep into the subconscious of Thatcher's main constituency of the chronically insecure, anxiety-laden strata of the lower middle classes. That was provided by a character invoking real dread over whiskey and soda in the bars of golf clubs across the country—the "colored" immigrant. So recently the colonial subjects who knew their place and showed the right amount of deference to the true citizens of the mother country, these dusky people had been showing up in increasing numbers in recent years and were to be found in all sorts of jobs and occupations, which generated the appearance of equality across the ethnic groups. Nothing presented itself as a more potent symbol of the decline of the British nation than the fact that the former residents of the Caribbean, the East African colonies, and the Indian subcontinent were making claims for equal treatment with the people who had so recently been their masters.

The large residue of support that existed for the agitation against immigration led by former Conservative government minister Enoch Powell sent out barely coded messages intended to convey sympathy for this viewpoint. It seems probable that Thatcher addressed herself to this strand of public opinion when she responded to an interviewer's questions during a television program in 1978, uttering her most quoted statement on immigration policy:

> If we went on as we are then, by the end of the century, there would be four million people of the new Commonwealth or Pakistan here. Now, that is an awful lot and I think it means that people are really rather afraid that this country might be rather swamped by people with a different culture.[2]

Yet despite the role that this negative view played in the politics of her version of populism, Thatcher was able to leave anti-immigrant sentiment at the level of rhetoric rather than concrete action in the form of policy and law. The recessions of the mid-decade and the restructuring and downsizing of manufacturing had on their own curtailed demand for fresh migration. While newcomers continued to arrive through the family reunion route, the category of primary migration—made up of people coming for

---

[2] For full interview, see https://www.margaretthatcher.org/document/103485.

the purpose of employment or establishing a business—had come to an end at the time of the energy crisis initiated by the OPEC oil price hikes after 1973. During the years when Thatcher occupied the office of prime minister, migration rates ran at net-zero levels, and anxious public moods had been placated on this score. The authoritarian populist crusade had other targets to aim for in the form of the power of the trade unions, the nationalized industries, the progressive teaching profession, and the local government role in running social housing and setting taxation. The efforts of "do-gooders" to promote the integration of immigrant communities through multiculturalism were constantly derided as the work of "lunatic lefties." The bulk of the work on this question was left to allies running the tabloid newspapers and required only the occasional affirmation of the Thatcherite party of its shared contempt for this approach.

By the end of her period of office, Thatcher had reshaped not just the form of government in Britain—with its deep aversion to economic intervention to support ailing industries and its downgrading of the ethos of non-commercial public service in areas like healthcare and education. The transfer of a range of public assets, from council housing to gas and electric utilities and the telecommunications industry into private hands through the "right to buy" and privatization, had bolstered the fortunes—though in most cases on a rather temporary basis—of many people in the lower middle-class ranks of society. This seemed to be a permanent change in the self-identity of many British citizens. Their lives would no longer be steadily improved because of the greater efficacy of social programs promoted by the state. The path to greater security and well-being would come from individuals acting on their own behalf to achieve more for themselves and their families. A decade of war on the old collectivisms of the social democratic past had reduced membership of the trade movement to a rump. Very few industries remained in public hands, and even local government had been divested of much of its power to improve the quality of life in the neighborhoods they covered. The British people presented themselves scarcely as a coherent society ("There is no such thing as society," Thatcher had famously declared[3]) and appeared instead as atomized individuals and families, each acting exclusively on their own singular behalves. Successor governments would have to work with this people, accepting that they constituted the community to which they were accountable, for a long time after Thatcher herself had disappeared from the scene.

---

[3] The statement was made during an interview with *Women's Own* magazine published on 23 September 1987. https://www.margaretthatcher.org/document/106689.

Tony Blair and "Progressive Populism"

The second major character in the British populist story is Tony Blair. Blair shared Thatcher's positive view of the role of markets, her skepticism toward the public sector as an efficient way to provide services, and the firm belief that political messages had to be conveyed directly by the leader to voters by making full use of the populist platforms provided by the mass media (Jordan 2010).

New Labour's approach to immigration, however, was different in that it saw past experiences of migration as having a role in creating the modern, vibrant, diverse Britain. If Thatcher's ideal member of "the people" was the small businessperson trading in a medium-size provincial town, filled with anxieties arising from the reducing state of the one collective that he or she identified with—the British nation—Blair addressed himself to a different audience. In his purview, there was a British identity to be consolidated out of a generation of citizens who had grown up with ethnic diversity and were excited by the prospect of living in a highly interconnected and globalized world. He offered up this vision in a speech to the Labour Party conference in 1995:

> This is a new age, to be led by a new generation. Let me talk to you about my generation. We grew up after the Second World War. We read about fascism and saw the Soviet Union and we learned to fear extremes of right and left. We were born into the welfare state and the National Health Service, into the market economy of bank accounts, supermarkets, jeans and cars. We had money in our pockets our parents never dreamt of, we travelled abroad, we have been through the sexual revolution of the 60s. Half the workforce now are women and the world of work revolutionised by science. We built a new popular culture, transformed by colour TV, Coronation Street and the Beatles.[4]

However, positivity is not enough for populism to create a deep bond with its audience: It needs a sense of visceral threat to the security and wellbeing of the putative member of "the people" that is being summoned into existence for this to happen. Blair was able to add this to his message:

---

[4] For this and the following quotes, see British Political Speech archive http://www.britishpoliticalspeech.org/speech-archive.htm?speech=201.

My generation enjoys a thousand material advantages over any previous generation and yet we suffer a depth of insecurity and spiritual doubt they never knew. The family weakened, society divided, we see elderly people in fear of crime, children abused. We live today with the knowledge that the world through nuclear weapons, chemical weapons and contempt for the environment can end a billion years of evolution.

It caught a mood and there was a clear sense of a "Blair generation" that played its role in bringing his New Labour party to power in the landslide election victory of 1997. Not wanting to rest on nostalgia for past greatness, Britain was to be a "young country" once again, united by a sense of:

common purpose, ideals we cherish and live up to, not resting on past glories, fighting old battles and sitting back, hand on mouth, concealing a yawn of cynicism, but ready for the day's challenge, ambitious, idealistic, united, where people succeed on the basis of what they did to their country, rather than what they take from their country, not saying, 'This was a great country,' but 'Britain can and will be a great country again.'

There were many ironies in the New Labour period of government, which saw this idealism thwarted by a reversion to what many saw as an old style of "greatness," which required the UK to sit at the world's top tables, dictating terms to other nations, much as it had in the days of its empire. New anxieties were admitted into the heart of its political project that had less to do with the declining state of welfare and well-being for families, and were directly connected to the fears invoked by the foreign and the alien. Blair's wholehearted commitment to joining the "war on terror" after the 9/11 terrorist attack in the USA was probably the pivotal issue that fundamentally changed the nature of the appeal of New Labour populism to its audience, but its record on immigration also figured as a significant moment.

In the early years of this experiment in progressive populism, the attitude of the British people to immigration had figured as a hopeful, positive element in the New Labour discourse. The narrative here spoke of communities that possessed sufficient good sense to turn away from the overt racism and antagonism to immigrants that had been a feature of the 1950s and 1960s and instead embrace the principles of racial equality and steady, organic progress toward the integration of ethnic minorities. One year after the election victory, the country was able to mark the 50th anniversary of the arrival of the *Empire Windrush* at Tilbury dock and the disembarkation of 492 citizens of Britain's Caribbean colonies, an event that was seen as the start of post-war migration from the countries of the "new" Commonwealth. The narrative that was implicitly read into this presentation of the historical event was that a Britain that could manage the task of building a united, multicultural people out of this diversity could certainly handle whatever would arise from the arrival of new immigrants at this later point in time.[5]

Blair's government followed up on this optimism with reforms to existing immigration policy that aimed to address labor shortages that existed at key points in industrial and service sectors at that time. It believed that as long as the arrival of new cohorts of migrants could be justified by evidence that they were adding to the productivity of the economy, then the people who had swept them into power would give them their acceptance. At the height of this confidence in the sophistication of the electorate, the then Home Secretary could declare in a widely reported speech that there "was no obvious limit" to the numbers of migrants being admitted each year.[6]

Yet, within just one year of this high watermark, it was clear that Blairite populism had lost control of the narrative, and the public mood was swinging strongly against migration. The trigger for this reaction was the government's failure to assess the impact of opening the labor market to citizens of the eight countries in central Europe and the Baltic that acceded to membership of the European Union in May 2004. The message that came out of the Home Office was that this was likely to involve relatively low numbers, on a range of around 13,000 to 20,000 people a year. In fact, in the region, 600,000 newcomers arrived by mid-2006.[7]

---

[5] See the opening paragraph of the white paper on immigration policy published in 1998, which lauded subsequent migrants for having "made an enormous contribution to today's British society. Every area of British life has been enriched by their presence. In politics and public life; the economy and public service; medicine, law, and teaching; and the cultural and sporting elements of our national life, individuals and communities have made a positive impact, helping Britain to develop. Part of that development is in our national identity, which now reflects our multi-cultural and multi-racial society" (Home Office 1998: para.1.1).

[6] See "Blunkett: no UK immigration limit" by Tom Happold, *The Guardian*, 13 November 2003. https://www.theguardian.com/politics/2003/nov/13/immigrationpolicy.immigration.

[7] See "'Nearly 600,000' new EU migrants," *BBC News*, 22 August 2006, http://news.bbc.co.uk/1/hi/uk_politics/5273356.stm.

This was a cardinal sin against the government's attempts at populist identification with the moods of the people. The charge that it was out of touch with what was really going on in the country at large echoed across the tabloid media. Labour's blunder was joined to a counter-narrative, coming from populist critics on the right of the political spectrum, who now claimed that their policies were part of a plot by metropolitan elites to change the fundamental character of the country by packing the population with foreign immigrants. Evidence for this claim was found in the text of a newspaper column written by Andrew Neather, a former speech-writer who had worked in the Home Office. Neather described conversations with government policy advisors working on immigration who had told him of an internal policy paper that was supposed to set out a plan to use "mass immigration" to "make the UK truly multicultural."[8] In years to come, the populist critics of New Labour ranging from the newspaper columnist Peter Hitchens, the anti-immigration lobby group Migration Watch UK, and the leaders of the UK Independence Party[9] cited this as evidence of a conspiracy on the part of the establishment to shape and mold British society without seeking the consent of the people.

The populist component of Blair's New Labour project ought to be acknowledged as a counterbalance to critics who see it as representing the entirely opposite phenomenon of technocratic elitism. It failed because the conventional "progressive" part of its message took it away from the moods of the people who had formed its original political base, going off in the direction of globalist adventures alongside powerful international allies. The citizens who marched in their hundreds of thousands against military interventions in Afghanistan and Iraq were also the people who, in the main, would have backed a Labour government pursuing liberal reforms to immigration policy. Their alienation from the Blairite cause

---

[8] See "Don't listen to the whingers – London needs immigrants" by Andrew Neather, *Evening Standard*, 23 October 2009, https://www.standard.co.uk/news/dont-listen-to-the-whingers-london-needs-immigrants-6786170.html.

[9] See "The slow-motion New Labour putsch that swept our nation away" by Peter Hitchens, *MailOnline*, 1 November 2009. http://www.dailymail.co.uk/debate/article-1224335/PETER-HITCHENS-The-slow-motion-New-Labour-putsch-swept-nation-away.html; "Was Mass Immigration a Conspiracy?", by Sir Andrew Green, Migration Watch UK, https://www.migrationwatchuk.org/press-article/83; and "Farage accuses Mandelson and Labour of 'rubbing our noses in diversity'," by Rowena Mason, 17 May 2016, *The Guardian*, https://www.theguardian.com/politics/2016/may/17/farage-accuses-mandelson-and-labour-of-rubbing-our-noses-in-diversity.

deepened when the government moved to compensate for its misjudgments on EU migration by a reversion to much tougher control policies that ramped up goals for detention and deportation and also repudiated its former commitment to human rights as the basis for refugee policy. After the "five-year plan" for immigration policy set out by a new Home Secretary, Charles Clarke, in 2005, the progressive moment in New Labour's vision of a country at ease with the people of the rest of the world had drawn to a definite close (Home Office 2005).

Nigel Farage, UKIP, and "Insurgent Populism"

For many commentators of the British political scene, the rise of the UK Independence Party (UKIP) under the leadership of Nigel Farage provides us with the only experience of populism worth talking about. The leading study of the phenomenon, by Robert Ford and Matthew Goodwin (2014), sees the rise of Farage and UKIP as *the* story of populism in Britain, implying that everything that went before was, at the most, a partial rehearsal for the real drama. In fact, the radical right-wing party operated in a political environment in which populism was already in the ascendency, giving it the task of going further than its rival versions in representing its radical logic.

The significance of UKIP is that it represents the moment when populism cut loose from its role, in Arditi's phrase, as "a recurrent feature of modern politics" which can be located within the rhetoric of established parties, and becomes "a threatening underside" of the democratic discourse (2005: 77). This happens when conflicts within the political order can no longer be represented in symbolic terms and the sense of fragmentation becomes more pervasive across society. The modes of populist representation, until now utilized by factions of the mainstream parties to seal a relationship with the voting public, become the site of more widespread social mobilization. "The people" is no longer required solely to sit in judgment on the performance of the charismatic leaders who have been striving on its behalf but to fill in the empty spaces that define the collective will and to act directly in support of the vision that has been conjured into existence. This was the role that UKIP came to play in British politics in the period after the turn of the millennium.

UKIP languished for the early part of its existence as a project with the single aim of bringing about British withdrawal from the EU. Its earliest protagonists had been a group of libertarian-minded intellectuals who were working with a critique of the EU as a democratically unaccountable, multinational bureaucracy. It was the volume of regulation that was coming out of the European Commission in Brussels that most provoked their ire, rather than any complaint about the intermixing of the European people as a consequence of mass migration. The explicitly anti-immigration theme was only developed as a major part of UKIP's program until triggered by the intervention of another figure from the political past—the former Labour Party Member of Parliament Robert Kilroy-Silk.

Kilroy-Silk ended his career as a politician in 1986 in order to present a daytime topical affair talk show on television. Using this to promote himself as a plain-talking man of the people, his style veered strongly in the direction of British nationalism if not outright xenophobia. The broadcaster canceled the program in 2004 in response to controversy over an article that Kilroy-Silk published in the *Sunday Express*, which was judged too racist in tone.[10] After a brief period sheltering from public criticism in Spain, he re-entered politics as a new recruit to UKIP, vowing to ramp up the explicitly anti-immigrant tone of its program.

Though his career in the party was brief,[11] the boost given to UKIP's profile arising from its contact with a person considered a celebrity impressed itself on other UKIP members, most notably Nigel Farage, who was then one of several people associated with the party's core leadership group. In 2005, the controversies around New Labour's approach to immigration were becoming more prominent on the political agenda. Farage became keen to find a way to bring discontent about the issue into the UKIP camp. His object was to latch onto the visceral anxieties that were showing themselves to be present in the mind of many voters and to hitch these onto the matter that had motivated UKIP from the start—membership of the EU.

In an interview with Ford and Goodwin (2014: 90–91), Farage sets out the evidence for "the rebirth of identity politics in this country." This ranges from the upsurge of Scottish nationalism to attendance at Remembrance Day parades, and the increased interest people had in "their history and what their grandparents did and where they come from" (Ford

---

[10] See "Anger at Kilroy 'anti-Arab rant'", *BBC News*, 8 January 2004, http://news.bbc.co.uk/1/hi/uk/3376633.stm.

[11] After a few months of internal fighting with other UKIP members, he left to set up a rival party, named Veritas, in January 2005.

and Goodwin 2014). For Farage this meant patriotism, and the way forward was for UKIP to present itself as the patriotic party.

The point at which UKIP's fortunes turned decisively upward was the Great Recession, which commenced with the bank crashes in 2007. As the economy plunged into months of zero growth, and unemployment rose by one million to reach 8% of the workforce, the sense that everything that had been done by the New Labour government then in office was producing chaos began to rise, creating the conditions for an outsider party to make significant breakthroughs in winning support.

For a large swathe of public opinion, it was immigration that provided the most readily comprehendible evidence of a social order that was breaking down. Concern about the issue had undoubtedly been increasing since the turn of the millennium (Blinder and Allen 2016). Ipsos MORI polls showed that anxiety over this rose to reach levels consistently in the range of 20–40% of voters throughout the years of New Labour government. This ratchetted toward the higher levels at all the points where the misjudgments of the Blair, and later the Brown government on levels of EU migration, were exposed by critics of the policy.

Further evidence for the role the EU was projected in playing in causing unwanted migration came during the summer of 2015 with the advent of the refugee crisis across the Mediterranean region (Tinti and Reitano 2016). Finding routes of clandestine entry into European territory, refugees gathered in what was presented in many news reports as overwhelmingly large numbers and set about a long trek in search of countries that would be prepared to offer a safe haven. As the crisis reached its height, German Chancellor, Angela Merkel, took the decision to suspend the provisions of the Dublin Convention as it applied to asylum seekers who had managed to enter Germany and offered recognition as refugees to all Syrians.[12] This all occurred at a time when the UK news was full of reports of a more local version of the refugee crisis, arising from the gathering of thousands of asylum seekers in the area around the port of Calais in the hope that they might find a way to board a ferry or the Eurostar train across the English Channel to apply for refugee status in Britain.

---

[12] See "Germany opens its gates: Berlin says all Syrian asylum-seekers are welcome to remain, as Britain is urged to make a 'similar statement'", by Allan Hall and John Lichfield, *The Independent*, 24 August 2015, http://www.independent.co.uk/news/world/europe/germany-opens-its-gates-berlin-says-all-syrian-asylum-seekers-are-welcome-to-remain-as-britain-is-10470062.html.

Labour's perceived mishandling of the management of migration was one of the main reasons for its eviction from office at the general election of May 2010.[13] Its replacement by a Conservative-led coalition, with the small Liberal Democrat party as its junior partner, helped move the UKIP insurgency against the establishment parties onto a new plane. Ill-considered promises by the new prime minister, David Cameron, to drive down net migration gave critics further to the right a metric by which his administration could be judged. It went very badly, as the difference between those entering the country and those leaving rose from 235,000 in 2010 to 336,000 five years later (ONS 2015).

Farage moved on with his attacks on the record of the Labour government to now cover the Conservatives, arguing that their net migration pledge was "utterly meaningless" because it was not possible to have "any control over who comes to Britain" while it remains a member of the European Union.[14] Striving for the persona of "the ordinary man in the pub" rather than political ideologue, the UKIP leader expressed his political ideas in the terms of "plain common sense," which would be acknowledged as such by any person who was prepared to accept that immigration had grown beyond reasonable numbers. He explained in any televised interview on one of BBC's prime political affairs programs that he toured the whole of England during the run-up to the 2013 English county elections. During this time:

> I met people everywhere who said: "Nigel, we've never had a problem with immigration – it jollifies the place and the food's better and all that – but how many people can we actually take? What chance have our kids got of getting jobs?"[15]

---

[13] The polling organization YouGov reported findings from its surveys on the 2010 general election result that 52% of the public believed that its stance on immigration was one of the main reasons why Labour suffered a heavy defeat. See "UKPOLLINGREPORT Views on why Labour lost" by Anthony Wells, 2 August 2010, http://ukpollingreport.co.uk/blog/archives/2769

[14] See "Nigel Farage: 'Immigrants have jollified Britain and made our food better'," by Georgia Graham, *Daily Telegraph*, 2 March 2014.

[15] Ford and Goodwin (2014) also make the point that in the period after 2010 UKIP was struggling to distinguish its message from that of the genuinely far-right British National Party. The BNP had also enjoyed an upsurge of electoral support for its anti-immigration message after 2010, but had used a language that was more overtly prejudicial and racist in tone than that which Farage was working hard to cultivate.

Ford and Goodwin (2014) make the idea of a "left-behind" cohort of British citizens central to their idea of the continued rise of populism during this period. This came to be defined as that part of the working class that had lost out during the decline of employment in the mass manufacturing industries that had been so important up until the downsizing of the 1970s and 1980s but who had not been able to find a secure place for themselves in the now dominant service sector. While supposedly so marginal to the political thinking of the professional political class, its viewpoint was well represented in the editorial lines of the largest selling daily newspapers. The populist journalism of *The Sun*, the *Daily Mail*, and the *Daily Express* affirmed the grievances of people defined as belonging to this segment with stories that hung around the vision of beleaguered white working-class people whose lives were being made harder by competition from migrants for ever-poorer quality job opportunities and a welfare state no longer able to deliver welfare.

The same basic approach to politics that had been used by Thatcher and Blair in earlier years was now taken up by UKIP and used to build momentum for its even more far-reaching insurgency against the political establishment. The bold use of a narrative that proclaimed the injustice inflicted on ordinary people by the inequities of the established powers, the commitment to conflict over consensus, the allure of a new identity for a people that had become fragmented and disillusioned, and the role of a charismatic leader in getting these messages across had become the way of doing politics that was now common to both the traditional parties and their outside challengers. The configuration of mass democratic politics in a period when the state's influence in directing the economy has been much reduced has necessarily inflated the role the sentiments of grievance and anxiety have played in mobilizing political activity.

However, the example of UKIP shows that as a pure outsider project, populism is unlikely to give rise to the stability and coherence of vision that would facilitate the transition from protest to government. As the conditions that favored UKIP's rise—anxiety about immigration, frustration with the bureaucracy, and elitism of the EU—cease to be center stage, the party's fortunes have rapidly declined. In the UK, the next contender for the mantle of radical populism seems to have been passed to a new people who are forging a strong identity with the leftism of Jeremy Corbyn's freshly invigorated Labour Party.

Part Two: Populism and Its "Antibodies"

The account provided above centers on the role political actors play in the formation of populist politics. Its discussion of the ways in which "the people" is summoned into existence to best further the aims of the populist party suggests a purely passive role for the population of atomized citizens. In reality this is not the case. In complex modern societies, populations have internal structures that reveal themselves as economic classes and social status groups. Filling the vast space between the political structures of the state and the purely individual world of the citizen, this is the world in which the interactions of civil society—made up of market exchanges, charitable groups, clubs and voluntary associations, independent churches, and publishing houses (Keane 2009)—facilitate other forms of social knowledge and experience that run parallel to those of politics.

This civil society can be enlisted into aspects of the projects being advanced by political parties and are often used by the latter to give moral force—such as patriotism (needed to gain assent to confrontations with foreign interests), charity (to reduce the fiscal cost of running public services), or family values (reinforcing the social roles that young people are expected to play when entering adult society). But civil society can be, and often is, thrown into contention with initiatives that have their origins in politics and become factors in resisting the programs they are attempting to impose. It is important to look at this capacity of civil society to resist in more detail, because this is how we learn more about the factors at play which lead populist projects to the point where they lose momentum and die away.

Over the three decades with Thatcher and Blair, a significant portion of civil society activism in Britain moved onto the political terrain, functioning as the opposition to the neoliberal turn which the traditional party system was failing to provide. Trade unions fought an ultimately doomed fight against the downsizing of manufacturing industries (Towers 1989); social movements drawn from youth culture campaigned against the racism that was constantly stirred by right-wing politics (Moliterno 2012); gay-rights activists pushed back against homophobic legislation (Kollman and Waites 2011); supporters of social housing resisted the growth of market-orientated policy (Woodward 2007). The perspective of the "two-thirds, one-third" society that was emerging in Britain during these years, in which market-driven social policies divided the population into prosperous, just-about managing, and clear loser segments, encouraged resistance across the fault lines that marked out disadvantage, with organizations, networks, and campaigns proliferating in scores of cities and communities. A tradition of "alternative" politics was born at this time which filled the space left by a hollowed-out party system, with electorates coming to the view that there was no real difference between any of the established formations across the center-right and center-left.

This tradition has remained a vital part of the political scene right up until the present time. Constantly shifting to form new points of resistance to the emerging features of neoliberal capitalism, it made its presence felt just when populist nationalism started to take the shape of the right-wing anti-EU parties. The following sections are based on research into civil society organizations during the time when the insurgent populism of UKIP was in the ascendency. We look at them to see what is embedded in the logic of their work that precipitates resistance to particular forms of populism, and causes them to act as the system's "antibodies."

This part of the chapter is a discussion and analysis of the ways in which the confrontation between right populist groups/parties and opposing actors (here termed "antibodies") results in the evolution of anti-racist and anti-discrimination attitudes, politics, strategies, and activism at the individual and organized level. We have focused on policies to both contain and combat racism and other forms of discrimination by state actors, NGOs, and civil society. Our strategy has been to assemble a broad cross-section of local, regional, and national antibodies and from across a spectrum running from prominent to small organizational forms.

The fieldwork was executed in 2014. We organized two focus groups (see Table 4.1). A core of participants was contacted directly, and the composition of this group was based upon previous contact with organizations and individuals. Thereafter, invitations were snowballed through the networks of our core group and direct approaches to organizational typologies not otherwise covered in our existing membership. More than 20 people approached us directly to request participation having "heard" of our plans.

We sought to identify the practices and experiences of a range of antibodies across a spectrum from long-established national organizations, small local groups driven by single issues or formed in response to transient local pressures, and individual campaigners who have moved between different causes over a prolonged "career" as a pseudo antibody. Participants from national organizations (see tables below setting out the

Table 4.1   Participants in focus groups

Focus group 1: Migrants and refugees
1. BT (Male: Former organizing officer for the Commission for Racial Equality)
2. HA (Female: Former investigation officer, British Council for Refugees)
3. CB (Female: The Brilliant Club)
4. AF (Female: Former policy analyst, MIND)
5. TG (Female: East Midlands Anti-Racism Network)
6. SJ (Male: Organizing agent, Refugee Council)
7. GM (Male: Campaigner for corporate responsibility)

Focus group 2: Political parties and youth organizations
NV (Female: Journalist)
LG (Male: Lean Left, anti-discrimination group drawn from the ranks of Labour Party youth wing)
LO (Male: Equalities spokesperson)
DFT (Female: Conservative activist)
PL (Female: UK Independence Party activist)
JK (Female: Former organizer, Scottish National Party)
GM (House of Commons researcher)

membership of the groups) had the resources of organizing committees, administrative infrastructure, and the funds to underpin (and often a de facto or legal remit for) extensive local, regional, and national campaigns. Our engagement in this respect included both state actors (Commission for Racial Equality, the Discrimination Commission) and charities and other bodies with an extensive national reach. These bodies have a role in either enforcing legislation as an arm of the state or are sufficiently well resourced to influence the formulation of national policies and legislation. A further distinguishing feature of these actors is that they have the legal means and capacity to undertake enforcement actions where laws have been or might be breached.

At the opposite end of the spectrum of participants were local and regional groups, including the East Midlands Anti-Racism Network, the Leicester Discrimination Commission, The Brilliant Club, and ProLac, a group campaigning in the English midland counties on behalf of immigrants with disabilities. Across our focus groups we achieved a broad balance of contributions from the perspective of gender, country of origin, ethnicity, and regional distributions.

We also observed a march against racism, in London, August 2014. This event attracted large audiences and several significant counter-demonstrations by a coalition of far-right and extremist groups. Materials available for analysis include observation reports based upon notes taken at the time and reflections thereafter, ad hoc interviews with participants and bystanders, usually of short duration.

In each group we considered the understanding of what we thought would be a common linguistic platform—fascism, racism, othering, and so on—and it rapidly became clear that no such common platform exists. In particular there was a very poor grasp of the meaning of "populism."

Three key observations are seen by our actors to have shaped the immediate landscape for antibody groups, and these map strongly onto academic research into such groups:

First, national umbrella groups (Muslim Council of Britain, the Refugee Council, etc.) have gained significant political and legislative influence, coming to be seen as core links between political elites and parties and the constituencies that they claim to represent. However, such bodies have sometimes themselves been fractious at the center and have had a variable reach over the activities and messaging of regional affiliates. As one of our actors noted, echoing Rhodes (2010), some antibody groups have had exactly the same messaging problems as far-right groups themselves.

Second, tensions between national and regional actors and local campaigning groups have been sustained and considerable (e.g. a periodic sense of betrayal between grassroots organizations and bodies such as the Muslim Council of Great Britain).

Third, there is a clear sense from our actors that the most effective voices in generating national legislative changes and influencing political opinion from the early 2000s have been those of "accidental antibodies." The term, coined by one of our respondents in focus group 1, refers to powerful charities, NGOs, General Medical Council, the Trades Union Congress, individual unions, and other groups who come to issues of racism, othering, and intolerance as part of an extension of their core mission. Nowhere is this clearer than in the work of the mental health charity MIND, which has gained remarkable influence on political groups as it extends its concerns to the particular mental health needs of immigrant groups. The Labour Party put this issue into their putative manifesto for the 2015 election.

The later 1990s and 2000s have seen a rich landscape for national, regional, and local antibody groups. Our actors confirm academic research findings that the most vibrant and radical agendas have been driven by bottom-up grassroots groups which have forced local and national political agendas. However, it is the fusion of national campaigning groups with the "accidental antibodies" from the early 2000s that has done most to create an enabling socio-political and cultural landscape for antibody groups. As many academic commentators acknowledge, however, the rise of UKIP-style identity politics, the reversing of social mobility, and the rise of radical Islam pose a toxic systemic threat to the gains already made.

Focus Group 1: Migrants and Refugees

Our participants were all driven to work in the area by personal experiences. BT, HA, and TG were first- or second-generation migrants from South Asia. SJ is involved in a "mixed marriage." Their identities were closely entwined with the organizations for which they worked. As CB noted of her work with The Brilliant Club: "This is just a way of life; it's indivisible from what you do and how you live." GM, who had successfully fought a deportation order, noted that "it's a strange feeling you know, to be like another subject to the full weight of the state's law and defined as unwanted." Yet it was striking how this broadly common identity did not translate into mutual respect for the work of each organization. GM accused AF's organization of "being late to the party" and an "accidental antibody." AF responded with a convincing overview of the achievements of the organization in terms of changing the law and influencing political climates.

CB and BT clashed over the visibility of the CRE in the localities, suggesting that it took on the easy-to-win cases and left organizations such as her own to be the visible face of tackling youth education and building a platform for "making the rhetoric of the right meaningless." The discussion moved on to questions of channels and definitions. There was no traction for the broad academic concept of populism. Moreover, the group had little time for concepts such as marginality. As one suggested, "I'm marginal because I've got ginger hair; it's nonsense." Broad concepts of racism, Islamophobia, and othering were well understood but not thought of as useful organizing or driving categories for the work of the organizations represented. CB suggested that "racism" was an accusative categorization on a par with Islamophobia or "poor white" and that her personal aims and that of her organization were better serviced by focusing on movable "isms" such as extremism.

This occasioned an important discussion on the relationship between categorization, labeling, and British culture. In this sense all of the actors agreed that the single most important channel for combatting extremism is education of the young. As HA noted, "our aim just has to be to engineer extremism out of the system from the bottom up." A broad agreement in this sense fed directly into the issue of strategies to combat extremism. The group was split on the question of the utility of political campaigning and attempts to enforce or extend legal rights. While SJ focused heavily on legal rights and restrictions, others were concerned that the extension of the law had two unintended consequences—to limit the freedom of action of antibodies themselves and to lead others to question the role, financing, and messaging of antibodies given growing assumptions that "this is covered by the law." CB noted that the key battleground was not the forum of parliament or the court but the classroom and the computer.

She recounted a series of stories about the engagement of her organization with extremist media, and the stories were widely appreciated. All of the participants agreed that there was insufficient collaboration between themselves and other third parties. BT called local organization of national bodies and local co-ordination of local and regional bodies a "dog's breakfast." Those representing national bodies felt constrained in their potential collaborations with more radical direct action groups, for fear that their standing and message would be diluted. The refugee-oriented participants felt the weight of state disapproval of any extension of their activities in the more direct areas given the attitudes of the government. The group was split on the question of direct action, violence, and civil disobedience. At one end of the spectrum, GM had participated frequently in such actions and believed that "it was the only way to get people to really take notice." At the other end of the spectrum, AF felt that direct action could never be countenanced. For the rest of the group, it was clear that the principles for which they fought might, in cases, involve confrontation but that there was a real and ingrained worry about sustaining their message. In particular, CB suggested that confronting "the idiot minority" with direct action in a place like Leicester would simply be counter-productive.

There ensued an interesting discussion of the place of Leicester as a multicultural city in which the divisions between different origin groups were as wide as traditional conceptualized divisions between, say, black and white. For this reason, local activists in the group were clear on the need to adopt a nuanced rather than a definitive rhetoric. As TG noted, "it's pointless talking to Mr Singh about anti-Muslim rhetoric and demonstrations; we have to speak the common language of extremism wherever we find it." All of the actors were planning to remain heavily engaged in this area, seeing it not as a job but as a way of life. All worried, however, that the decline of the middle class and the reversal of social mobility threatened the gains made, and all called for a significant extension of the work with schools of all sorts in order to engineer out extremism.

The discussion ended with a concerted discussion about gay marriage and Muslim refugees. In common with the other groups, gay marriage was not seen as an issue for most groups, though there was sustained discussion of the attitude of Muslim communities to the matter. Most of the actors were well aware of the sense that for young people this was a non-issue. Unsurprisingly, the discussion of Muslim refugees was long and involved. The actors were universally torn between personal experience, the purpose of their job roles and humanitarian and libertarian sentiment, and a sense that uncontrolled immigration would provide succor to newer right-wing groups such as UKIP. As HA said in summation, "The real problem is that uncontrolled immigration and physical concentration make UKIP [and others] seem reasonable."

Eight core conclusions were agreed at the end of the focus group:

1. While there is a consistent and insistent narrative against Muslim refugees (which intensifies or dwindles according to global political issues), in most places actively targeted groups are highly specific. As CB noted, "it's always small scale, like a drip drip, and we have to confront it drip by drip, but if we can start in the schools, we win."
2. While we can trace increasing concern about migrants and refugees, this is not a simple dichotomy between Muslim and Christian or immigrant and native. It is quite clear that concern about European migrants (white and otherwise) is rising fast and that there are real tensions between immigrant groups themselves. One of the biggest worries for the group was the splintering (on an intergenerational basis) of immigrant identities.
3. Following from this conclusion, we can trace a concerted upsurge in direct action against immigrants and immigrant symbols (such as religious buildings) and an increasing counter-reaction by local campaigning groups. The latter are different in their basic ideology to the nationally orientated groups also represented in the focus group.

For GM, the issue was simple: "all things start with the lowest level and you have to confront every little bit."

4. Antibody actors and organizations have seen an increasing squeeze on their funding and status, which affects their current campaigning capacity and their future thoughts about structure and focus. For the group as a whole, TG's observation—"In the end, if it's 'the law' then it's down to someone else to speak, act, run and fight, but the law is just words and words that deflect attention away from personal responsibility at the lowest level of our society"—had considerable resonance.
5. Most antibody actors have a dwindling faith in the ability of "the law" to make a difference to the lives of immigrants.
6. Legal restrictions on hate speech have paradoxically limited the ability and range of forums in which antibodies are able to challenge racist and discriminatory views, driving attitudes underground. GM sums this up for the group in one of our recap sessions: "At the local levels it's like a dance, right, because the righters [right-wing demonstrators] can sort of goad you, and when they do, you find yourself doing more than you should and saying stuff when you should be silent so that the police are on to you using the laws that are supposed to protect the very people I am interested in."
7. Antibody actors and organizations are strongly split on the desirability of direct action, though there is an acceptance that the threat of power for UKIP will necessitate more direct action.
8. There is a deeply ingrained tension between perceptions of "immigrants" as a negative stereotype and the often harmonious relations found in a city such as Leicester.

Focus Group 2: Political Parties and Youth Organizations

While divided by basic political ideology, all of our actors shared one common view: It remains difficult for youth to gain traction for their ideas in the current political system. As LG commented, "you might as well hit your head against a brick wall. They [party leadership] say all the right things but you have to believe it and facilitate it [opposition to racism] not pansy about when questions of Europe or Islam come up."

Our participants were not driven into their roles by any unified set of personal experiences and expectations. At one end of the spectrum, LO admitted to having "just drifted into it." At the other end of the spectrum,

JK had been an activist at school, university, and then in the youth wing of her party, coming to focus on discrimination and equality issues relatively late in her nascent political career. For her "it was like coming home." With the exception of JK and DFT, personal identity was not tied up with role/job. Indeed, PL went out of her way to disown a really strong connection, staring a theme that ran through the session: UKIP as essentially "normal" compared to the career politics and unhealthy focus of others involved in politics.

At the outset of this group, the team had expected the focus of the subsequent discussion to be a polarized exchange between UKIP and the other political parties. In fact, we detected three core divisions: between UKIP, which denied being "a discriminatory right-wing organization with racism at its core," and the other major political parties; between the English parties including UKIP and the Scottish National Party, which was accused four times of being jingoistic, nationalistic, and overtly racist; and between those with their roots in national politics versus those with their roots in local campaigning. An emblematic case study is the exchange between DFT and JK, in which the former accused the latter of "presiding over the most racist campaign in recent memory," while JK retorted, "Both you and the Labour party have overseen the continuance of institutional racism in its most unpleasant and ingrained form." The moderator subsequently moved the group to consider questions of channels and definitions. There was a strong definitional understanding of racism, extremism, homophobia, and Islamophobia. There was much less agreement on how far individual parties had gone in confronting these issues; all participants agreed with the statement from NV that "it's just a fact, we have not done enough, and whether we are writers or politicians or whatever, we have just not reacted quickly enough to the changing economic and social circumstances that shape the experience of racism and homophobia."

There was an interesting exchange in this context between LG and PL, in which PL reported a phenomenon recently highlighted in the British press, which is rising UKIP membership by second-generation immigrants concerned at the erosion of their material and cultural status by uncontrolled immigration. All actors agreed that there were strict limits to political power in this area, and we were struck by the remarkably shallow understanding of the channels through which racism might be confronted compared to the other group with which we have engaged. As GM noted in an ensuing discussion of Islamophobia: "The question is not one of UKIP versus Labour or the Tories. These are old questions and questions for a political elite. What you have to ask yourselves is how you fight these things at the coal face not through the Chamber." Perhaps unsurprisingly given the constituencies represented in the group, our actors were very positive about the value of political action.

There was an unprompted discussion in this context of "gay marriage" in which all of the political representatives claimed to have had a part and on which they all agreed political lobbying had been crucial. NV noted that "of course only UKIP actually wrote down their support for this measure in something that looked like a manifesto commitment." Our actors saw the gains in changing core attitudes to race and sexuality as essentially fragile. They agreed that there were strict limits to the purchase of the law and regulation on these issues. For LO the decline of the British middle class poses a systemic risk: "If they go then the whole Liberal impetus, the center ground, goes with them." For LG the issue has less to do with class and more to do with social mobility: "It has stopped, just stopped. And once you can't improve your chances, what then? Then we get Burnley [town in the north of England with strong BNP representation] or Dover [town on the English south coast with strong UKIP presence]."

Without exception, all of the actors responded to our question about the need for connectivity between the bodies that they represented in a positive fashion. Unfortunately, we found no evidence in the ensuing or preceding discussions that there was any appetite for such networked approaches. JK suggested that she hoped to be part of a different country before the 2020 election! This fracturing was repeated when the group moved on to discuss direct action. For representatives of UKIP, the SNP, and Lean Left, there was a common acceptance that direct action to combat racism and homophobia, as well as to achieve their wider political ends, was both desirable and necessary.

JK rejected the accusation that the campaigning in the Scottish independence referendum going on at the time had actually been characterized by direct action in support of racist rhetoric and policies. Both JK and PL drew attention to a disjoint between stated party policies and the attitudes and experiences of local activists. The group moved from this point to a discussion of the rhetoric of racism and othering. The group agreed with an observation from GM that the core problem for politicians is that extremist groups of all political and religious hues have moderated an underlying rhetoric of confrontation and instead adopted intellectual arguments about local and national identity as a vehicle for their views, policies, and attitudes. For GM, "It comes down to this: that extremist group are just more agile – more agile in their platforms, channels, finances, evolving rhetoric and headline policies – than mainstream political parties."

For this group five core conclusions were agreed:

1. Far-right (and far-left) extremist groups have taken on the strategies, organizational frameworks, and funding models of traditional antibodies as they seek to mainstream their views.
2. The language of extremism has moved away from confrontational to reasonable rhetoric, and this has made the activities of the antibody groups more difficult. Youth representatives were notably frustrated by their inability to gain traction in this increasingly sophisticated marketplace of ideas by taking them to the mainstream of debate in the political establishment. For GM the matter was simple: "Political expediency has made it palatable to ignore the increasingly sophisticated reinvention of those who would rein back success in the areas we are considering."
3. Actors in this group were comfortable with the concept of an antibody and with wider conceptual discussion of racism, othering, and populism. It was notable for NV that "othering is such a slippery concept that UKIP can appear and construct itself as other and then win seats in the house."
4. All of the actors made a distinction between themselves and government or opposition ministers, seeing these groups as essentially apologists for racism.
5. The UKIP actor claimed not to represent a racist party, and while this was challenged, it is clear that the status of the UK (a collection of four nations) complicates the political identification and challenging of racism. In our conversation, for instance, the Scottish National Party, and not UKIP, was accused of being inherently racist.

In addition to the focus groups, we undertook a large-scale observational event as described above. Four summative observations can be made based on the material collected:

1. There is a palpable fear among campaigning groups/antibodies that their gains are fragile, even though many of them have been written into law and practice. While the evidence for this in terms of direct counter-demonstrations and anything but periodic violence is slim,

activists elaborated and events embodied a clear sense that an underlying but often unspoken culture needs to be challenged with direct action and a continuing campaign of mixed educations/confrontations. Commentary on this matter included:

Male, 36 years old: "But it's not enough see, you have to come out every time. Look at UKIP. It came from nowhere and now look. They want to spread disharmony and conflict and to roll back the basic freedoms, and they will get a foothold and it will mushroom and we just can't stand by and watch this happen, we just can't."

TG, 28 years old: "I know what you University types think, that the law is the law but you never get it because we see it on the front line of life every day. We are hanging on by the fingertips most times, and if we make a gain here and there it's like crawling through treacle. There just can't be a let-up."

Female, 42 years old: "Look, look over there, does it look like we are secure? Does it? Everything we have done in schools and through education can be rolled right back. It's so easy, as easy as breathing, as easy as voting, as easy as well you know, as easy as letting go. If I don't come here who will, and when these idiots [pointing to a BNP counter demonstration] get a chance then it ends."

2. Many of the event speeches and informal interviews reveal a sophisticated analysis of current attitudes toward racism and discrimination by individual antibody activists. In particular the decline of the political influence of far-right bodies at local and regional level was correlated in the minds of activists with a withdrawal of many supporters or sympathizers from mainstream politics, allowing discriminatory attitudes to be rolled up into a wider and less challenging discussion of political disengagement in the UK. Commentary included:

Matthew, 51 years old: "Do you think they have gone away? I know there are not many of them here but they have not gone away. They are reinventing themselves, like a re-launch and repackaging to make them more acceptable. So now they wrap themselves up in the flag and recruit a few people with brown skin and they become respectable. The bastards will be debating with the prime minister at the election, you just wait and see."

Helen, 18 years old: "My father, yes that's why I'm here. He voted UKIP and then BNP, but he's never racist or a queer hater or anything, so he says. His mates are no different. It's all about our town our neighborhood, and the Asians are the same, and what's good for them is good for us.' I bloody hate it."

3. For immigrants and poor white communities in particular, the antibody groups and activists noted that failings in the basic ecology of support for poor communities (immigrants often end up concentrated in poor communities rather than contributing to that poverty) create path dependency in the way that "others" are constructed and limit the ability of antibody groups to gain traction for their messages in such communities. Crudely, the problem becomes that *both* antibody groups *and* extremist groups come to be seen as outsiders by these communities. Commentary included:

Jim, 46 years old: "Y'know the funny thing is that when we walk past Dunhill [pointing to a largely Muslim district], we are still seen as outsiders. Even though we are on their side. But they just get dumped there and left to rot so they come up with their own systems, systems for everything and we just don't get it. For them even we are the enemy."

Hannah, 21 years old: "Yes, you're right [talking to her friend]. It all comes down to hope. If you haven't got any then why should you care? When you feel abandoned then you just move to someone that promises hope. It will get worse though because people just can't get on the ladder, and if you've got no stake in society then any old tosh will reel you in."

4. There was a distinct sense in these engagements that racist and discriminatory discourse should not be isolated but rather confronted and engineered out of the social system through education, emblematic prosecution, and the creation of a wider program of support for the (poor white, black, and Muslim) communities that are the direct focus of extremist attentions. Commentary included:

Roger, 63 years old: "Them [pointing to a group of schoolchildren] it's about them. They need to see this and know what we are here for, otherwise there's no point. My grandchildren, now they are in a good school and they have, what's it called, um, diversity lessons and that's good, but you can't dress this stuff up. They have to feel it's real, but they are the way forward."

Bets, 19 years old: "Yes, we've just finished sixth form and it's important to be here. I wish that there were more of us; there should be because it's not like we don't know. Yeah, I just wish there were more of us."

Sam, 29 years old: "They've got to have their voice too, there's just no point in trying to close it down, otherwise its goes underground, right, and what then? You end up confronting this shit on the web and in the chatrooms, and when it gets there it's too late, you know what I mean?"

The synergy between some of the sentiments expressed and those arising out of our focus groups is important and speaks to a wider shared agenda, which came out very powerfully in all of the discussions elaborated here.

Concluding Remarks

In the first part of the chapter, we argued that populism is best understood as an approach to politics in the modern conditions of liberal democratic states, which have to frame their polities within the constraints of a globalized economic order. The stability that had once come from post-war Keynesian economic management and the welfare state had supported a way of doing politics that could be described as elitist and corporatist—in many ways the mirror-image opposite of populism. In Britain this approach succumbed to a much earlier populist revolt, under the guise of Thatcherism, which set out to disrupt a system of governance based on the expertise of an elite strata of corporate interests working together to plan the national economy. To win this battle, Thatcher conjured into existence a "people" that embodied the values of the market-orientated middle classes, with their dislike of official regulation and the red tape it was said to generate. Sustaining this viewpoint meant working with other values that were represented in these social strata. They included a marked tendency toward chauvinistic, anti-foreigner prejudice, which reduced itself to anti-immigrant sentiments.

New Labour did not seek a break with this fundamental approach. It worked with the same basic tools to motivate the mass of people to take on new challenges, with the themes of modernization, diversity, and global leadership becoming the tropes of its brand of populism. Was it inevitable that a populist reaction against New Labour's enthusiasm for globalization could only take the form of a revival of nationalism? Another version of "the people" was beginning to assemble during the same years when Farage and UKIP were making use of identity politics to bring about a mobilization of the "left behind." The arrival of migrants had never drawn universal hostility from local communities, which right-wing nationalist believed followed on from the mixing of people of different ethnicities. If Farage's people centered on a demographic that was older, less educated, and concentrated in coastal towns and northern cities that had been overlooked by economic prosperity (Ford and Goodwin 2014: chapter 3), they also repelled those in younger age groups, with higher levels of education, and who believed that diversity brought cultural and material benefits to the country. Networks were established across parts of the country where assistance be usefully rendered to people who were experiencing hardship either as refugees or workers who were vulnerable to exploitation.

The "tough" turn against these migrants by the government after the policy debacle of 2004 increasingly involved immigration enforcement actions, involving raids on workplaces, arrests, and detention of people deemed to be without rights, and this in turn provoked a resistance among the people who opposed this approach. In the multicultural city centers, on university campuses, among public service professionals in healthcare and education, a reaction to the role that the government was expecting people to play as informants and denouncers of "illegals" set in and converted many to the opposite role of defenders of the rights of migrants. Support for migrants' rights became in many places the new anti-racism and took root among the same sorts of people who, in the period of the first wave of authoritarian populism, had aligned themselves with the Anti-Nazi League and Rock Against Racism.

The discussions referenced in the second part of the chapter can be seen as the heirs of the reactions against the direction of mainstream politics which took the form of the anti-racist movements of the 1980s, which were an important part of the antibodies to Thatcherism, and the "Stop the War" movement of the 2000s which played the same role vis-à-vis the Blairite commitment to the neoliberal world order. There are signs, in the form of the surge of support for the Corbyn leadership of the Labour Party, that it might yet prove to be the basis for yet another populist movement, but this time most decidedly from a leftist standpoint. What seems clear is that, with the demise of the older form of social and liberal democratic governance, whatever comes in the future, it will work within the parameters of the new populism.

REFERENCES

Albertazzi, D., & McDonnell, D. (2008). Introduction: The sceptre and the spectre. In D. Albertazzi & D. McDonnell (Eds.), *Twenty-first century populism: The spectre of Western European democracy*. London: Palgrave.
Arditi, B. (2005). Populism as an internal periphery of democratic politics. In F. Panizza (Ed.), *Populism and the mirror of democracy*. Verso: London/New York.
Blinder, S., & Allen, W. (2016). *BRIEFING: UK public opinion toward immigration: Overall attitudes and level of concern*. Oxford: Migration Observatory at the University of Oxford.
Ford, R., & Goodwin, M. (2014). *Revolt on the right: Explaining support for the radical right in Britain*. London/New York: Routledge.
Hall, S. (1979, January). The great moving right show. *Marxism Today*.
Home Office. (1998). *Fairer, faster and firmer – A modern approach to immigration and asylum, Cm 4018*. Norwich: HMSO.
Home Office (2005). *Controlling our borders: Making migration work for Britain – Five year strategy for asylum and immigration*. Cm 6472, HMSO, Norwich.
Jordan, B. (2010). *Why the third way failed: Economics, morality and the origins of the "Big Society"*. Bristol: Policy Press.
Keane, J. (2009). *Civil society, definitions and approaches*. http://www.johnkeane.net/wp-content/uploads/2009/01/jk_civil_sciety_definitions_encyclopedia.pdf
Kollman, K., & Waites, M. (2011). United Kingdom: Changing political opportunity structures, policy success and continuing challenges for lesbian, gay and bisexual movements. In M. Tremblay, D. Paternotte, & C. Johnson (Eds.), *The lesbian and gay movement and the state: Comparative insights into a transformed relationship* (pp. 181–196). Farnham: Ashgate. http://eprints.gla.ac.uk/44250/1/44250.pdf.
Leys, C. (1986). *Politics in Britain*. London/New York: Verso.
Moliterno, A. G. (2012). What riot? Punk rock politics, fascism, and rock against racism. *Inquiries Journal/Student Pulse, 4*(01). http://www.inquiriesjournal.com/a?id=612
Morris, R. (2017). *Urban governance: Britain and beyond since 1750*. Abingdon/New York: Routledge.
Offe, C. (1984). *Contradictions of the welfare state*. London: MIT Press.
ONS (2015). *Migration statistics quarterly report: November 2015*. https://www.ons.gov.uk/peoplepopulationandcommunity/populationandmigration/internationalmigration/bulletins/migrationstatisticsquarterlyreport/november2015
Rhodes, J. (2010). White backlash, "unfairness" and justifications of BNP support. *Ethnicities, 10*, 77–99.

Tinti, P., & Reitano, T. (2016). *Migrant, refugee, smuggler, savior*. London: Hurst and Company.

Towers, B. (1989). Running the gauntlet: British trade unions under Thatcher, 1979–1988. *ILR Review*. http://journals.sagepub.com/doi/abs/10.1177/001979398904200201

Woodward, R. (2007). Mobilising opposition: The campaign against housing action trusts in Tower Hamlets. *Housing Studies*, 6. http://www.tandfonline.com/doi/abs/10.1080/02673039108720696

CHAPTER 5

The (Im)Possibility of Creating Counter-Hegemony Against the Radical Right: The Case of Austria

Birgit Sauer

RIGHT-WING HEGEMONY AND COUNTER-HEGEMONIC MOVEMENTS: INTRODUCTION

Austria's post-war political system was characterized by social partnership (*Sozialpartnerschaft*), consociational democracy with two major parties, the Social Democrats, SPÖ (Sozialdemokratische Partei Österreichs), and the Christian-conservative ÖVP (Österreichische Volkspartei), including workers' unions, the chamber of labor (Arbeiterkammer) and the chamber of the employers (Wirtschaftskammer) (Dolezal and Hutter 2007: 337). This constellation resulted in a rather closed system of consensual decision-making (Tàlos 2006) and a sort of "division of power", institutionalized in "great government coalitions" between the two parties. Thus, there was hardly any room for other parties or for social movements (Sauer and Ajanovic 2014,

---

B. Sauer (✉)
Department of Political Science, University of Vienna, Vienna, Austria

© The Author(s) 2019
B. Siim et al. (eds.), *Citizens' Activism and Solidarity Movements*, Palgrave Studies in European Political Sociology,
https://doi.org/10.1007/978-3-319-76183-1_5

2016), and social movements have been late-comers in Austria compared to other European countries (Dolezal and Hutter 2007: 347). The Austrian social-democratic project of modernization and democratization "from above" since the 1970s slowly opened the political system for new social movements. This brought a variety of single-issue and/or identity-based social movements such as women's liberation movements, gay and lesbian movements, peace and environmental movements as well as Third World solidarity groups into being. Most of these early movements were rooted in leftist organizations or the SPÖ party youth branch (Foltin 2004).

By the end of the 1970s, the Austrian two-party system as well as the social partnership model gradually lost legitimation. This situation created a window of opportunity for new parties, such as the Greens, but also for the right-wing FPÖ (Freiheitliche Partei Österreichs) to enter the political stage (Heinisch 2012: 372). Since then, Austria has been characterized by a strong right-wing populist party. After the turn of the century, the FPÖ is the major player in Austria's political landscape and a competitor to the SPÖ and the ÖVP (Pelinka 2002). After elections in 1999, the ÖVP entered a government coalition with the FPÖ until 2006. The FPÖ won 20.5% of the votes in the national elections 2013, 19.7% at the European elections in 2014 (BMI 2013, 2014), and 25.97% in the national elections on 15 October 2017. In the direct vote for the Austrian president in December 2016, the FPÖ candidate won 46.2% in the third ballot.

Most important for FPÖ's success is its way of organizing consent and creating hegemony by establishing an exclusive nationalist-populist project, which aims, for instance, at restricting access to social benefits to "nationals" and proving that Muslims and Islam do not fit into Austrian culture. This consensus against migrants and Muslims also challenges the social-democratic consensus of societal liberalization and equality that has prevailed since the 1970s. The right-wing struggle for consensus and hegemony evokes images of a natural binary constellation between "them" and "us", which not only creates migrants and Muslims but also LGBT people, feminists, gender researchers and gender mainstreaming officers, and "the" elite in general as "others". The right-wing discourse of an "exclusionary intersectionality" (combining class, nationality, religion, gender, sexuality) forges these narratives into a commonsense perspective of difference and inequality, of belonging and non-belonging and thus exclusion. The radical right's strategy of "exclusive intersectionality" builds on a "chain of equivalence" (Laclau 2005), which results in "anti-immigration", "anti-Muslim", and "anti-gender" as "empty signifiers"

(Laclau 1996: 36) for the new hegemonic project of exclusion, inequality, and solidarity of nationals only, of the nativist and homogeneous "we". On the one hand, the new political forces on the radical right developed into a challenge for Austria's social justice movements. On the other hand, the visibility of the radical right has since the 1990s triggered the formation of anti-racist groups and new civil society organizations that oppose exclusive policies and the mobilization of hate and resentment against immigrants. As a reaction to the FPÖ's referendum of 1993 "Austria first" (*Österreich zuerst*), calling to curb immigration and tighten immigration laws, 250,000 people gathered across the country to protest against this referendum in a "sea of lights" (*Lichtermeer*). These civil society organizations were able to unite with the leftist parties and trade unions against the exclusionary referendum. The success of the counter-forces created a momentum, and anti-racist and anti-discrimination movements spread all over the country. Since then, civil society organizations have mobilized against the FPÖ and its exclusive and racist claims.

Despite the huge mobilization capacities at the turn of the century, when the FPÖ entered a government coalition with the Christian-conservatives, it seems that these anti-right organizations were unable to stop the wave of success of the FPÖ and right-wing radical groups and to counter their practices and policies of inequality and exclusion. The right-wing hegemony of exclusionary intersectionality makes it difficult for anti-discrimination groups to establish a counter-strategy (Sauer and Ajanovic 2016).

While the rise and success of right-wing extremism in Austria is rather well researched, research on "anti-bodies" and on social movements that aim at countering Austria's right-wing forces, their racist claims, and exclusionary intersectionality does not exist.[1] This chapter wants to contribute to this field with a special focus on intersectionality at the interface of immigration, race, gender, and sexuality. The entry point for this study is civil society groups that counter the anti-immigrant discourse and (anti-Muslim) racism of right-wing forces. I examine the opportunities of these groups to counter the "exclusionary intersectionality" (Siim and Mokre 2013; Sauer and Ajanovic 2016) of the new right-wing hegemonic project by organizing a common counter-hegemonic discourse (Laclau 1996). How do the different anti-racist, anti-discrimination, and pro-diversity groups in Austria answer the exclusionary intersectional challenge of the FPÖ? Hans Pühretmayer (2002), for instance, regarded the rather poor

---

[1] See also Karner (2007), who analyzes the "counter-hegemonic regional press" in Austria.

cross-linkages between anti-racist organizations as a problem. Similarly, studies on European anti-racist groups talk about a "crisis" of anti-racism as a "viable movement", "lacking unity, workable strategy and public support" (Lentin 2000: 92). Lentin argues that a "reformulation of anti-racism as a viable form of collective action" needs alliances "that seek to go beyond identity politics" (Lentin 2000: 93; for Belgium Detant 2005).

Therefore, this chapter examines whether Austrian social justice movements have been able to forge alliances and to shift their activities towards solidarity with other activists and towards common strategic framing over the last 15 years. Or put differently: Do we find transversal politics and frames (Yuval-Davis 1997)? Do we encounter new forms of political intersectionality towards equality and difference, towards solidarity and emancipation? Are the anti-racist movements able to construct an "empty signifier" of social equality and social justice to counter racist notions of the migrant and Muslim "other"? Is this "empty signifier" able to unite the different social justice and anti-racist movements? This anti-right discourse should include the idea of recognition of immigration and plurality of the population, of gender equality and sexual difference, that is, an intersectional "chain of equivalence".

The chapter proceeds as follows: I first specify the Austrian context, the development of the radical right, and the situation of NGOs fighting right-wing extremism and racism. I then elaborate on the theoretical concepts and explain the methods of our study.[2] Finally, I present the findings of the study by focusing on the activities, strategies, and frames of anti-racist and anti-discrimination groups. The conclusion reflects on the possibilities of creating counter-hegemony against the radical right in the light of "inclusive intersectionality".

SETTING THE POLITICAL CONTEXT: RIGHT-WING POPULISM AND SOCIAL JUSTICE MOVEMENTS IN AUSTRIA

This section gives a brief overview of the development of the radical right in Austria in a historical perspective and the emergence of social justice movements in response to the right-wing challenge. The social democrats, who have been in power since 1971, strengthened civil society by mobiliz-

---

[2] The empirical work for this paper has been conducted in the context of two EU-funded projects, eEAV and RAGE. I thank Edma Ajanovic, who did the empirical study in the RAGE project, and Stefanie Mayer, who conducted research in the eEAV project, for their work.

ing for "more democracy" and at the same time forging a new welfare consensus based on Keynesian policies and welfare state expansion. As a result, a variety of new social movements emerged. Some of these groups organized as "identity movements" as, for instance, the women's or gay and lesbian movement, focusing on (supposed) commonalities in order to mobilize for gender equality, against sexism and homophobia. In 1979, the Homosexual Initiative (Homosexuellen Initiative, HOSI) was founded as a movement to fight for the rights of gays and lesbians.[3]

As early as the 1980s, the women's movement put issues of migration, racism, and women in the Third World on its agenda (Mayer 2015: 104f.). The first immigrant self-help groups were established in the 1980s like in other European countries (Ruzza 2000). In this area, feminist groups were rather active. The organization LEFÖ (Lateinamerikanische Frauen in Österreich, Latin-American women in Austria) was founded in 1985 by women from Latin America who migrated to Austria (http://www.lefoe. at/). Today, LEFÖ engages in empowering migrant women, especially sex workers, and strengthening their rights. A similar organization with an intersectional approach, Maiz in Linz, was founded in 1994 with the aim to fight for the rights of migrant women, to engage in anti-racism work, and to challenge "white, western European, patriarchal, (post-)colonial or heterosexual ideas" (http://www.maiz.at/).

In the mid-1980s, however, the FPÖ developed into a major political force in the country. In 1986, when Jörg Haider took over party leadership, the party "modernized" its ideology in the direction of a populist party in order to maximize votes and to gain electoral success. It pushed its German-national orientation and open Nazi discourse into the background and reorganized in hierarchical structures (Pelinka 2002: 286ff.; Campani and Sauer 2017). Since then, anti-immigration has become the party's main issue. Since the turn of the century, the FPÖ has systematically established a discourse of difference and exclusion towards immigration and migrants with focus on "the" Muslims. The "populist" turn was accompanied by a discursive strategy to form "the people" as a community of "us" against the "others", the immigrants, and thus joining the discourse of the new (radical) right (Mayer et al. 2016).

In response, the Austrian civil society landscape expanded in the late 1980s when another issue—Austria's Nazi past—appeared on the public agenda. Since the end of the Second World War, Austria's identity has

---

[3] Until 1971, homosexuality was criminalized in Austria.

been built up around being the "first victim" of Nazi Germany. After ÖVP's Kurt Waldheim won the presidential elections in 1986, a wave of international and national outrage shook the country because Waldheim had denied his membership in a Nazi student organization (Foltin 2004: 150ff.). Leftist organizations mobilized against his presidency and eventually a new perspective on Austria's responsibility as well as new forms of Holocaust remembrance developed. This was pushed forward by anti-Nazi organizations, originally founded by and for victims of the Nazi regime, for instance, the "Mauthausen Committee Austria"[4] (Mauthausen Kommitte Österreich, MKÖ),[5] the "Documentation Archive of the Austrian Resistance" (Dokumentationsarchiv des Österreichischen Widerstands, DÖW),[6] and the "Documentation and Information Centre of the Austrian Roma and Sinti association" (Dokumentations- und Informationszentrum der österreichischen Roma und Sinti).[7] These organizations are well connected with party organizations and the state administration. During and after the so-called Waldheim affaire, new anti-racist and anti-rightist organizations were founded, for instance, Asyl in Not (Asylum in Distress) founded in 1985 and Zebra founded in 1986 to implement human rights, equality, and integration and to fight racism (www.zebra.or.at/cms/cms.php).

Since the 1990s, Austria has seen growing protest mobilization (Dolezal and Hutter 2007: 338). SOS Mitmensch (SOS Fellow Human Being) was founded in 1992 by Vienna intellectuals as a mobilizing group against FPÖ's "Austria first!" referendum in 1993 (Foltin 2004: 228). The FPÖ's mobilization resulted in several waves of tightened asylum laws and right to asylum, which has been granted to refugees not least due to the country's National Socialist past. In 1992, deportation of asylum seekers became possible; in 2016, the right to family reunification was restricted. A new foreigner law in 1993 and the so-called *Integrationspaket* (integration law package) in 1997 tightened the conditions for staying in Austria. In 2005 a comprehensive shift in migration legislation, the "alien law package" (*Fremdenrechtspaket*), was pushed through by ÖVP, SPÖ, and

---

[4] The largest concentration camp on Austrian territory was located in the city of Mauthausen.

[5] The MKÖ is the successor organization of the Austrian Concentration Camp Community Mauthausen, whose founders were camp survivors.

[6] The DÖW was established in 1963 by former resistance fighters, concentration camp prisoners, persons returning from exile, and academics.

[7] Founded in 1997.

FPÖ/BZÖ votes demanding either assimilation or exclusion (Flecker and Kirschenhofer 2007: 158; Schumacher 2008: 1; Zerbes 2012). As a reaction to this paradigmatic shift in asylum and integration laws, several NGOs were founded to provide legal, social, and psychosocial assistance for migrants and asylum seekers and to protest and mobilize against the restrictive laws. One of these groups is Helping Hands, founded in 1993. These organizations also launch campaigns against racism, anti-Semitism, and homophobia and promote equality, human rights, and empowerment. "Pink Anti-fascists Vienna" (Rosa Antifa Wien), founded in 1995, mobilizes against right-wing extremism and neo-fascism. The group, which is connected to the gay movement, provides information and conducts research, and it emphasizes the existence of different discrimination mechanisms and organizes demonstrations (www.raw.at; Foltin 2004: 224). Zivilcourage und Anti-Rassismus-Arbeit (ZARA, civil courage and anti-racism work) was established in 1999 with the aim of fighting all forms of racism. Overall, during the 1990s and at the turn of the century, the issue of anti-racism was widely present in Austrian protest mobilization (Dolezal and Hutter 2007: 344).

The growth of the FPÖ and its electoral success since the 1990s are effects of a "crisis of representation", that is, a decline in Austrian consensus democracy. Moreover, Austria's integration in the European Union in 1995; economic globalization; the neoliberal restructuring of the formerly strong Austrian welfare state, austerity policies, and cuts in social welfare; and the creation of low-wage sectors resulted in rising unemployment, precarization of working conditions, growing social disintegration, and rising poverty (Penz 2010). These dramatic economic and social changes and the crisis of neoliberalism since 2008 have marginalized working people; nurtured fears of social degradation, marginalization, and insecurity of the working class and the lower middle class; and thus fostered the rise of the FPÖ (Poglia Mileti et al. 2002: 5; Heinisch 2012; Wiegel 2013; Sauer and Ajanovic 2014). The FPÖ has been able to transform these fears into resentment and anger against migrants, and it has exploited the rising numbers of refugees arriving in Europe and Austria to mobilize intensively against immigrants.

When the FPÖ entered a government coalition with the ÖVP in 2000, "Austrian civil society"—a large network of civil society organizations—organized weekly "Thursday demonstrations" against the radical right in power (Foltin 2004: 258). This mobilization was supported by the Green party and by parts of the Social Democrats.

In 2011, Offensive gegen Rechts (Campaign against the Right), a group of young people and students that mobilizes against right-wing events through campaigns and demonstrations, was founded. It was established specifically as an alliance to demonstrate against the "WKR Ball" (Wiener Korporiertenball), the Viennese Ball of the (right-wing) fraternities at the Vienna castle (Hofburg).

In 2012, an important self-organized group, Refugee Camp Vienna, emerged. It is a group of asylum seekers and supporters who aim to raise awareness about the dire conditions asylum seekers face in Austria. The group "squatted" the Votivkirche in Vienna (a church in the city center) and attracted broad public attention.

Although the FPÖ occupies the right-wing political space, small right-wing groups and organizations with single-issue strategies focusing on migration, Islam, gender, and sexual difference have gained importance and public visibility in recent years. Examples are citizens' initiatives against the construction of mosques, the Identitarian movement which claims to be a nationally oriented youth movement, and "parents" who protest against sexual education in schools (Mayer and Sauer 2017).

While the FPÖ promotes a neoliberal project of inequality within the Austrian society, that is, flat tax and competitiveness, party officials are able to present their world-view as common sense by referring to conflicts and antagonistic structures within Austrian society, for instance, social inequality and fears of social decline, and re-defining them as issues concerning immigration, feminists, and LGBT people. The anti-immigrant and anti-Muslim consensus draws on a strong tradition of "institutional racism", for instance, an exclusive citizenship regime based on *ius sanguinis* as well as xenophobia in the Austrian population.

The Austrian landscape of NGOs fighting racism and right-wing extremism is characterized by a plurality of groups that deal with intersecting issues of discrimination. Some are state or quasi-state institutions focusing on fascism and anti-Semitism in the context of the country's NS past. Others claim to be independent from state money and thus autonomous with respect to their activities. All these anti-racist, pro-immigrant, and pro-asylum groups were active in the spring and summer of 2015 when a large number of refugees arrived in Austria. As a sign of solidarity and compassion, they organized a so-called welcome culture in the country by providing care, food, and clothes for refugees. However, their fields of activity and their thematic and strategic issues are rather diverse. What could be a force might also be an obstacle in forming alliances and a strong counter-hegemony to the right-wing racist discourses (Pühretmayer 2002: 304).

Theoretical Foundations, Material, and Methods

The theoretical concepts presented in this section explain the main foci of analyzing the activities of Austrian anti-racist and anti-rightist NGOs. With these concepts the opportunities to create cross-movement cooperation, cross-movement communication, and cross-movement solidarity will be assessed (della Porta and Mattoni 2014). Moreover, the section explains the broader theoretical notion of counter-hegemony, which forms the basis for assessing the success of NGOs countering right-wing exclusionary intersectionality. Right-wing discourse actively creates interactions and intersections between a variety of differences—race, ethnicity, nationality, religion, and gender—in order to demonstrate, for instance, the supposed sexism of Muslim men and to connect these different structures of exclusion in one exclusive narration, in a chain of equivalence. As a result, one marker of difference and exclusion might be able to articulate with other markers and create an overall discourse of inequality and exclusion. Thus, gender might be articulated with immigrants or Muslims to fix the idea of the religious "other". Racism, for instance, is based on hegemonic social discourses and practices (Omi and Winant 2002: 129; Hall 1988; 2000). Hence, new and alternative discourse articulations and new forms of "political intersectionality" (Crenshaw 1991) are necessary to transform these hegemonic constellations and to create new chains of equivalence and start a counter-hegemonic project (Laclau and Mouffe 1985; Stavrakakis 2014: 120). This new discursive strategy needs to target the change of material conditions.

Framing reality is an important dimension of creating "exclusionary intersectionality" (Siim and Mokre 2013; Sauer and Ajanovic 2016). Frames are sets of "commonsense concepts and notions" (Detant 2005: 189), which interpret everyday situations (Rein and Schön 1994). Frames are part of "discursive/political strategies" (Karner 2007: 85). Racism can be perceived as an interpretative frame of the social, economic, and cultural situation in a country (Detant 2005: 189). Frames, moreover, can mobilize action of civil society organizations, they are usually contested in political struggles, but frame coalitions can also support alliances and joint activities. To create counter-hegemony, movements need to develop "counter-hegemonic 'interpretative repertoires'", that is, alternative "frameworks of meaning" (Karner 2007: 85). Thus, frames are important means to create new articulations and chains of equivalences.

Two important dimensions of a counter-hegemonic discourse are transversal politics and transversal mobilization (Yuval-Davis 1997): While social justice movements are often "rooted" in a common identity of their members, it is important to shift this identity towards a position of exchange and cooperation with groups with other identities in pursuit of the common aim of equality and justice. Hence, the history of new social justice movements in the West that started in the 1970s shows that solidarity across movements is premised on the erosion of movement organization borders. This transversal politics of joining forces, resources, and frames proved to be an important means for democratization and social justice. Movement coalitions that emerge out of transversality may also be able to mobilize a "transversal audience" (Roos and Oikonomakis 2014: 120).

Hybrid organizations and hybrid activists are specific forms of transversality. "Hybrid organizations" are "composed of two or more types that would not normally be expected to go together", for instance, identity movements like feminists or homosexuals that include anti-racist and/or anti-fascist aims (Albert and Whetten, quoted in: Heaney and Rojas 2014: 1051). "Thus, hybrid organizations traverse the boundaries that typically divide organizations in one category from organizations in another category" (Heaney and Rojas 2014: 1051). Hybridization of different "movements, constituencies, and political institutions" is a way to organize a great array of movements for one specific issue and to encourage coalitions and "crossover activists" to bridge multiple movements (Heaney and Rojas 2014: 1048f.). Hybrid activists amplify the identity of movements and the scope of their issues and themes, their frames, or their strategies. They are able to build "intermovement networks", which allow for "recombining 'knowledge, technology, or experiences'" and to "blend activism" (Heaney and Rojas 2014: 1049–1054).

Methodologically the paper draws on focus group interviews with representatives of nine Vienna-based civil society organizations that fight racism and discrimination. Moreover, we conducted face-to-face interviews with ten representatives from NGOs in the field. Overall, we talked with representatives of 12 organizations, which were introduced above.[8] The activities of these organizations can be divided into four strands: (a) education, information, and awareness raising; (b) counselling; (c) monitoring and documentation; and (d) campaigning, communication, events, and lobbying.

---

[8] We selected the most publicly visible and the most diverse civil society organizations. We did not take into account organizations such as Amnesty International, Caritas, the Austrian Red Cross, and Volkshilfe, which also help migrants and asylum seekers by providing mentorships or "integration buddy programs" and by raising awareness about discriminative issues in this field.

(a) Six of the interviewed organizations are active in the field of empowerment trainings and remembrance work. This includes training and workshops against discrimination and racism, for empowerment, civil awareness of racism, and conflict resolution for pupils, students, and companies. MKÖ and DÖW mainly engage in awareness raising and remembrance work with regard to the crimes of National Socialism and its victims, especially anti-Semitism and anti-Ziganism. MKÖ offers guided tours at the Mauthausen Concentration Camp (MKÖ Online). The most important event, organized together with other civil society organizations, is the *Fest der Freude* (Celebration of Joy) at the Viennese Heldenplatz, where Austrian masses welcomed Hitler and the accession of Austria to Nazi Germany in 1938.[9]

Helping Hands raises awareness about institutional racism, which is manifest in day-to-day legal actions and decisions, especially in asylum-seeking procedures. The organization especially wants to break stereotypes of civil servants and the police. Maiz uses its cultural work to promote equality and stop racism, sexism, and homophobia. The first strand also includes the umbrella organization of Vienna Youth centers, which deals with everyday racism of and against young people. ZARA offers training and workshops for students, for organizations, and companies to increase the awareness about anti-racism, anti-discrimination, and diversity (zara-training.at).

(b) Counselling for migrants, asylum seekers, and people who experience racism is the main field of activities of ZARA and Zebra. Counselling includes legal advice and psychosocial assistance for migrants and for victims of racist attacks as well as general information about possible action against racism. Asyl in Not's major strategy is to empower clients by informing them about their rights during asylum procedures. Information about migrants' and refugees' rights seems to be the core of anti-discrimination work, as people who are not aware of their rights are more often the target

---

[9] After WWII, right-wing dueling fraternities (*Burschenschaften*) gathered on 8 May at the Heldenplatz to remember the fallen Austrian Wehrmacht comrades and to grieve the end of the Nazi regime. Until 2013, only small (left-wing) groups demonstrated against this event, but since 2013, the Celebration of Joy has recoded this public space in the city center on 8 May to commemorate the liberation from National Socialism.

of discrimination by authorities and institutional racism. Helping Hands, Asyl in Not, and Zebra counsel migrants and asylum seekers, for instance, in the form of legal advice in asylum procedures.

In addition to counselling people affected by racism and discrimination, Helping Hands is also a contact point for information about neo-Nazi groups and right-wing popular culture such as symbols, signs, and music. HOSI counsels gay people, including asylum seekers who are being persecuted for their homosexuality. Maiz counsels migrant women, especially sex workers (*Maiz Online*).

(c) Monitoring of right-wing extremism, racism, and hate speech is a major focus of DÖW and ZARA. ZARA focuses on anti-racism and DÖW on documenting and monitoring the right-wing extremist scene. For its *Rassismus Report* (ZARA 2014), ZARA collects all racist statements and incidents (offline and online), hate speech incidents, and neo-Nazi and right-wing extremist incidents and statements.

(d) Campaigning against racism and right-wing extremism and for anti-discrimination is another pillar of most of the organizations we interviewed. SOS Mitmensch is concerned with communication, sensitizing activities, and campaigning against right-wing extremist and racist discourses.[10] SOS Mitmensch's main activity is political campaigning for human rights, refugees and asylum politics, anti-racism, citizenship, integration, and social justice. Likewise, Asyl in Not and Helping Hands are actively lobbying to change the asylum regime in Austria. Offensive gegen Rechts (Campaign against the Right) mobilizes against right-wing events and organizes demonstrations. FairPlay, founded in 1997, lobbies for anti-racism and anti-discrimination (racism, sexism, homophobia) in soccer-related contexts. HOSI mobilizes for non-discrimination of same-sex marriages and societal recognition of homosexuals and organizes the yearly Pride parade in Vienna.

The first focus group was attended by representatives from HOSI, Asyl in Not, Offensive gegen Rechts, MKÖ, ZARA Training, and Helping Hands. The aim was to identify central issues of the NGOs. We were able to

---

[10] In March 2017, SOS Mitmensch launched the campaign "Populistenpause", which called for a break in public and media reporting on the radical right.

identify two central common "issues", namely, anti-racism and anti-rightwing activities. The second focus group included one representative from ZARA, SOS Mitmensch, and HOSI and discussed anti-racists and anti-discriminatory activities. The third focus group on "anti-New Right" activities included one representative from Offensive gegen Rechts and MKÖ. We conducted face-to-face interviews with the other organizations.

My analysis concentrates first on cooperation, joint activities, and networks, second on the assessment of frames and narratives of the civil society organizations and their way of creating a "chain of equivalence" by mobilizing against antagonism in the fields of migration, Islam, gender relations, and sexual orientation. In short, I will focus on the organizations' "capability to create alliances" (Detant 2005: 185), on their transversal framings as a common basis for mobilization and finally their relationship with state institutions and with parties and trade unions.

The Struggle for Counter-Hegemony: Political Intersectionality of Civil Organizations Fighting Racism and Discrimination

In this section, I will elaborate on strategies and outline the possibilities of civil society organizations fighting the radical right and racism by creating transversal politics and establishing counter-hegemony. Counter-hegemony, I contend, requires, first, joint activities and networking and, second and most important, deconstruction of exclusionary intersectionality and hence of racist commonsense arguments by stressing the right to difference and the necessity of equality and equal treatment. As stated earlier, the entry point for this study is civil society organizations in the field of anti-racism and anti-radical right. While early social movements—such as women's or gay movements—were "identity based", anti-racist and anti-right groups share the common aim to fight the radical right and racism, although their notions of racism are rather different. Gender, sexuality, and class are not at the center of these groups. Only some civil society groups were explicitly founded as "hybrid organizations", taking gender, sexuality, race, and class into account. Nevertheless, in the following I want to point out how anti-racist and anti-rightist groups in Austria were able to shift their focus, to expand towards transversal themes and create conditions for transversal politics, intersectional framing, and a new inclusive "chain of equivalence".

Transversal Politics and Cooperation

Transversal politics points to the ability of movements to create interorganizational relations and cooperation. Cooperation has two dimensions: first, joint activities against racism and the radical right and second transversal activities, that is, joint activities that transcend the organizations' aims and strategies. Our interviewees are aware of the necessity to build broad alliances against racism and the radical right, and they all see joint activities as positive. The most important argument is that cooperation can make anti-racist and anti-rightist organizations more visible and therefore might reach and address a wider audience (OgR, focus 1): "The wider the cooperation is, the stronger and more successful the mobilization against the right will be" (MKÖ, focus 1). Offensive gegen Rechts reports that in the last years more networks and alliances against the right have been established across the country and outside of Vienna (OgR, focus 1).

Most focus group participants knew each other from jointly organized events. They actively seek strategic cooperation and synergies when organizing campaigns or demonstrations. For instance, HOSI cooperates with MKÖ in organizing Holocaust commemoration ceremonies as homosexuals were detained at the Mauthausen camp. HOSI also takes part in commemoration ceremonies at a camp for Sinti and Roma (HOSI, focus 1).

The umbrella organization Asylkoordination, a network with several member organizations, regularly organizes exchanges on issues of asylum and anti-racism. Some of our interviewees are members of this network and organize joint activities. Quite a few alliances against the radical right also include party youth organizations, mainly from the Greens and SPÖ in some parts of the country (OgR, focus 1).

Hence, we encountered a lot of cooperation at specific events, for instance, counter-demonstrations against the Viennese fraternity ball (WKR) or prohibiting a gathering of the "Identitarian movement" in Vienna (OgR, focus 3). ZARA and SOS Mitmensch jointly organize the "Clean Politics Campaign", which requests that politicians do not use racist or discriminating slogans during election campaigns, and HOSI organizes the yearly Vienna Pride parade in cooperation with other organizations.

Although all interviewees stressed the importance of creating alliances and of networking, they were also aware that they lack the resources to systematically organize transversal politics. Asyl in Not told us: "The problem of intensive networking is capacities and resources" (AiN, focus 1).

Lack of money, time, and personnel is seen as the main obstacle to cooperation and joint mobilization, and the social justice movements are increasingly competing for the same decreasing state funds.

SOS Mitmensch claims that networks are important but also have weaknesses, "because we need to coordinate, this is time consuming and resource intensive; we are not able to act quick and focused" (SOS, focus 2). HOSI has similar experiences and adds the problem of "personal differences" in civil society groups (HOSI, focus 2).

The HOSI representative was very clear that the organization still is identity based and therefore cooperates more with "similar community associations" (such as Queer Business Women or AIDS Help) than with other groups (HOSI, focus 2).

Hybrid Organizations

Hybrid organizations include more than one type of activity or have more than one political aim; they traverse the boundaries of clear-cut movements, and "hybrid activists" aim at combining several political aims by crossing movement boundaries (Heaney and Rojas 2014: 1048ff.). Several of the movements we interviewed might be labelled "hybrid organizations" as they combine several political issues or are networks composed of different anti-racism, anti-fascism, anti-right-wing extremism, and anti-discrimination groups. The following organizations carry out hybrid activities against racism and the radical right: Asyl in Not defines itself as an organization that works with asylum and foreigner law and fights against the radical right (AiN, focus 1). They collaborate with the youth organization of the Green party and have created a "loose network" with Offensive gegen Rechts (OgR, focus 1). Offensive gegen Rechts was founded as a hybrid organization per se, a network and "action alliance" of 14 anti-right organizations, but also works with racism and sexism (OgR, focus 1). MKÖ is mainly active in organizing civic education on the Holocaust but is also active against the right and neo-Nazism (MKÖ, focus 1). ZARA combines anti-racism work with empowerment of asylum seekers through membership in the network Klagsverband (Litigation Association of NGOs Against Discrimination), which supports claimants, that is, asylum seekers, in legal cases. HOSI was founded as an identity-based organization but developed into a hybrid organization, which includes an "antifascist committee" and the group MiGaY, homosexuals with migrant background, founded in 2009. However, it seems that MiGaY's primary goal is to become a member of the LGBTIQ community in Austria and is less interested the anti-racist scene (Kubicek 2014: 93).

SOS Mitmensch also presents itself as a hybrid organization with focus on racism in politics and right-wing extremism, as well as "intersections of racism, homophobia, anti-Semitism and sexism" (SOS, Focus 2). Rosa Antifa Wien is a hybrid organization that expands the struggle against racism and fascism to gender sexual discrimination. They mobilize, for instance, for the right to abortion (www.raw.at/schwerpunkte/pro-choice/). Maiz was explicitly founded as a feminist organization that tackles institutional racism and racist perspectives. Helping Hands connects economic questions of who gets jobs, nationals or migrants, with questions of marriage, gender, and sexuality, as policies and discourses against immigration target these issues (HH, focus 1).

Some interviewees were aware of multiple and intersecting forms of discrimination and therefore fight different forms of discrimination. Overall, the organizations in our sample have the potential to hybridize different issues of discrimination and to struggle against exclusionary intersectionality by mobilizing transversal politics.

Framing the Problem: The Success of Right-Wing Hegemony

An "adequate analysis of the racist phenomenon by anti-racist movements seems to be a precondition to develop efficient counter-strategies" (Detant 2005: 184). Some of our interviewees are very well aware of the right-wing hegemony and the paralysis of Austrian mainstream parties. Asyl in Not claims that it is difficult to work against the anti-immigration discourse because "the established parties and large parts of the society are clearly against liberal asylum and foreigner laws" (AiN, focus 1). In a similar vein, Offensive gegen Rechts argues "that FPÖ was successful in pushing diverse social debates towards the right" and that the established parties did not challenge this strategy but were defensive or even accommodative (OgR, focus 1). "The established parties leave a vacuum (of liberal immigration law, B.S.); and small NGOs like us are unable to fill this" (OgR, focus 1). Overall, the interviewees see themselves as weaker than the parties and thus powerless: "This is the problem; our arguments are never as strong as the voice of parties because they have a lot more resources" (OgR, focus 1).

The organizations we talked to agree that it is difficult to counter the right-wing hegemony and that "it is getting more and more difficult and complex to argue against right-wing extremist arguments and frames" (OgR, focus 3) as they are no longer openly neo-Nazi. The "Identitarian movement", for instance, explicitly claims not to be racist. The anti-right and anti-racist civil society organizations are thus aware that one of their main problems is how to address and mobilize more people and "appeal to a broader population or all ages", especially "young people" who "vote for the right" (OgR, focus 1).

SOS Mitmensch addresses the hegemonic problem as a discursive problem:

> It is always more difficult to work against prejudices than with them. [...] I think it is a basic problem that I experience in anti-racism work. It is, for instance, easier for environmental organizations as they work with peoples' fears, with the mainstream, but we have to work against people's fears. (SOS, focus 2)

A representative of ZARA was rather disillusioned with respect to possible changes of "institutionalized racism" in Austria: "I think it is an efficient system [...] and I can't see a way of cracking it" (ZARA, focus 2). Also, Helping Hands said that Austria does not have a political culture of a strong civil society (HH, focus 1). As the representative puts it: "In the dim past, we had the beautiful goal to change the legal framework in such a way that we would become unnecessary. But this is something we can archive as we probably will never achieve this goal" (HH, focus 1). Helping Hands sees the police, other state bureaucracies, and the media as a cause of right-wing hegemony (HH, focus 1). Especially the Austrian media landscape is perceived as a problem due to lacking plurality and neutrality of the print media (HOSI, focus 2).

However, they also witness "acts of citizenship" (Isin and Nielsen 2008), for instance, in cases of deportation where communities stand up for families to protect them (AiN, focus 1). The HOSI representative therefore claims that there are "opposing voices": "But they do not have a public forum" (HOSI, focus 2).

Framing the Struggle: Transversal Framing and Emancipatory Anti-racism

The two important mobilizing frames of our interviewees were racism and anti-right-wing extremism. However, some of the organizations explicitly differentiated between anti-racist and anti-right struggles and claimed not to combine the two frames, while others contended that anti-racist work necessarily includes struggles against the radical right. Our interviews revealed that the organizations have different self-understandings of their strategies. The organizations were aware that their frames and aims might hamper cooperation. Like racism and anti-racism, the concepts radical right or anti-right are perceived as fuzzy. SOS Mitmensch prefers "racism" as a clearer concept for their campaigns. The leftist Offensive gegen Rechts remarks: "It is a challenge how to frame our aims to be most inclusive [for cooperation] [...] not to abolish the state. First of all, it is important to have consensus, as it is most important to be a large group and to create pressure in order to be noticed by the right-wing extremists" (OgR, focus 1). However, during the focus groups, it became clear that all civil society organizations differ with respect to their aims—being anti-racist or anti-right.

It also became clear that the concept of racism and hence anti-racism were defined and conceptualized rather differently by the organizations and that not all NGOs frame racism in an intersectional or transversal mode. Racism and anti-racism are contested and multi-faceted frames. Hans Pühretmayer (2002: 294–299) discusses three "models of anti-racism", namely, "reactive" or "moral anti-racism"; "techno-economic anti-racism", which considers racism as a consequence of economic organization or of discriminatory laws (2002: 296); and "emancipatory anti-racism", which fights intersecting practices and structures of discrimination and exclusion (2002: 298). Our material shows that these differences in conceptualizing racism and, hence, anti-racist strategies exist in our sample of civil society organizations. And these differences might be connected to general strategies against discrimination and racism.

In general, our interviewees told us that it is difficult to mobilize with the frame "racism" as, for instance, public and state institutions as well as parties refuse to use the word racism but talk instead about integration (ZARA, SOS, focus 2). Anti-Nazi and anti-Semitism frames are able to build broad alliances with parties and unions, but anti-racism is much more difficult.[11] The concept of racism is "cumbersome" and is therefore not used by all NGOs. If it is used, it "creates communicative problems" (SOS, also ZARA, focus 2). Moreover, the representative of Offensive

---

[11] It seems to be much easier for MiGaY to cooperate with political parties' homosexual caucuses.

gegen Rechts claims that it is difficult to find a common understanding of the causes of the rise of right-wing extremism; criticizing capitalism and the economic situation seems to impede joint action: "It is much more difficult to agree than to mobilize against right-wing fraternities or the FPÖ" (OgR, focus 3). Overall, our study shows that "substantial ideological divides within the anti-racist movement [...] prevent co-ordinated action" (Ruzza 2000: 168). Hence, it is difficult to fight for emancipatory anti-racism and even more difficult to forge alliances under this frame. The next section looks at instances of transversal framing and thus of emancipatory anti-racism that exist even though anti-racist and anti-right movements are not united on common frames.

Counter-Hegemony and an Alternative "Chain of Equivalence"

A counter-hegemonic strategy needs new commonsense narratives as well as awareness to change material conditions. Common frames across the organizations we talked to are citizenship rights, human rights, (social) equality, and plurality. Moreover, all groups agreed on notions of anti-Semitism and anti-Muslim racism, but their definitions of racism differ. Issues of liberal rights and plurality and anti-Nazi mobilization allow frame coalitions with liberal print media, public broadcasting, TV, and leftist parties.

However, only some groups are aware of intersecting structures of exclusion and discrimination and of their complex articulations. Thus, only a few interviewees actively take, for instance, sexuality and gender into account. Maiz is most outspoken in fighting exclusive intersections of ethnicity, race, and gender. SOS Mitmensch monitors the "political sphere" in terms of its discriminatory discourses, not limited to racism but also sensitive to other "-isms". We thus encountered transversal framing and a mode of "emancipatory anti-racism". As one interviewee puts it:

> We have different emphases. First, racism in the political sphere where we follow the discourse and which laws are being passed. And then we try to identify where boundaries in terms of racism, homophobia, anti-Semitism and sexism are being crossed. Another area is state institutions, authorities like the police [...] where we try to identify if there is discrimination [...]. And the third would be the everyday racism. Here it is more difficult to decide where to react and where not. [...] Also we are not reacting to every incident because we focus more on the institutional dimension. (SOS, focus 2)

Similarly, ZARA stresses that they aim at strengthening the recognition of difference and plurality and that their fight against racism is combined with fighting other forms of discrimination (ZARA, focus 1). The *HOSI* representative also reported that the organization deals with "multiple discrimination" and pointed to the struggles of *MiGaY* (HOSI, focus 2).

Some of the representatives are aware that right-wing hegemony rests on the difficult situation on the labor market. The MKÖ representative claims that the "Identitarian movement" is successful among young people due to austerity policies, deregulation of the labor market, and precarization of labor (MKÖ, focus 3). The representative of Offensive gegen Rechts stated that a successful transversal campaign against the political right—especially to reach young people—needs to offer "social security", "a job and a carrier" for young people. The representative also addressed feelings of (social) insecurity and "fear of job loss" as causes of the success of the right (OgR, focus 1) and that right-wingers use "anti-capitalist arguments to mobilize for their aims, for instance against capitalists, however sometimes with an anti-Semitist tone" (OgR, focus 3). He concludes: "We have to open the discussion against 'the right'. We have to take into account social causes, for instance economic causes" (OgR, focus 3). Similarly, Helping Hands stresses that anti-immigration resentments are linked to the question of jobs (HH, focus 1). Hence, the issue of class is part of the imagery of organizations fighting the radical right and racism.

The active engagement in countering the radical right's exclusionary intersectionality, which rests in the empty signifier of "the migrant and Muslim other", is still rather weak in the Austrian civil society. While some of the groups we interviewed do engage in creating an alternative chain of equivalence by combining the struggle against racism with the fight against sexism, homophobia, and unequal social and economic relations, most of the groups do not have the capacities for such a strategy—and they do not engage in transversal framing with other groups.

The State as a Problem: State Racism, Institutional Racism, and Cooperation with the State

The view of Austrian state authorities, that is, ministries, police, judiciary, and asylum administration, is rather controversial within anti-racist and anti-rightist organizations. Some are dependent on state money, some refuse state funding and cooperation, and some have to cooperate with state institutions, for instance, with asylum bureaucracies or the police. For organizations that are dependent on state money, the lack of resources is a drawback in their struggle for counter-hegemony. SOS Mitmensch and Helping Hands depend on donations in order to be independent of state resources, and SOS Mitmensch explicitly refuses to be dependent on state money (SOS, focus 1).

SOS Mitmensch, Offensive gegen Rechts, Asyl in Not, and Helping Hands make the Austrian state responsible for racism and racist practices towards immigrants and refugees. They criticize "institutional" and "state racism", which is especially visible through restrictive immigration laws and—as the representative of Asyl in Not frames it— through the "criminalization of asylum seekers" (AiN, focus 2). These NGOs identify "racism as exercise of power" applied especially by civil servants and judges in the field of immigration policies. Due to institutional racism, migrants and asylum seekers encounter "systematic malignancies" by state institutions in legal procedures (AiN, focus 2). SOS Mitmensch furthermore identifies an increasing discriminatory practice in the context of citizenship laws and working possibilities for migrants (SOS, focus 2). Hence, these organizations mobilize against tight and exclusive asylum and integration laws and against restrictive citizenship regulations. Overall, they accuse the Austrian state of implementing exclusionary policies and thus being part of a hegemonic compromise against immigrants and refugees and supporting right-wing exclusionary hegemony.

Nevertheless, most of the NGOs perceive the state as a necessary ally. HOSI and ZARA cooperate with some state institutions, for instance, with the national and Viennese Ombud for Equal Treatment and antidiscrimination (focus 2). The representative of DÖW stresses that they try to establish networks with the police in order to sensitize the police for institutionalized racist practices. However, some organizations report that cooperation with state administration is becoming more and more difficult. Especially, the police is seen as repressing anti-rightist mobilization.

Overall, our interviews indicate a paradoxical situation: On the one hand, the civil society organizations see the state—as well as semi-state organizations such as leftist parties and trade unions, which could be political allies for an anti-rightist project—as collaborators in the racist system and as supporters of exclusionary politics. On the other hand, the organizations are aware of the necessity to ally with the state and with parties and trade unions to create counter-hegemony. However, our observation is that these alliances failed in the past, not least because Austrian mainstream parties moved to the right and implemented anti-immigrant laws, which have been on FPÖ's agenda for a long time.[12]

Conclusions

The rise of the radical right in Austria and the strong anti-immigration wave across Europe (Ruzza 2000: 167f.) have led to the emergence and public visibility of anti-racism, anti-exclusion, and anti-right-wing organizations. The fact that racism is inherent to Austrian society and that it is embedded in society and state institutions renders it difficult to fight racist discourses of difference and inequality. The intensification of these right-wing discourses and the commonsense status of their racist, exclusionary arguments, that is, the mainstreaming of the radical right discourse on immigration and immigrants, impede the work of civil society organizations.

The 12 civil society organizations in our analysis follow different strategies to counter the racist right-wing discourse. They engage in educational work with a focus on youth; in legal and psychological counselling of migrants, asylum seekers, and people who have experienced racism; and in campaigning and lobbying as well as in monitoring racism. In general, the study shows that in the context of commonsense racism and of exclusionary intersectionality of the political right, it is difficult to mobilize on a broad scale and especially to permeate social and institutional practices of racism, inequality, and exclusion towards counter-hegemony of equality and solidarity. Some interviewees were representatives of hybrid organizations, but their capacities to actively cooperate and forge transversal alliances and to promote transversal frames are rather low.

Pühretmayer and Görg's (1999) diagnosis still holds: As in the Belgian case, struggles over the meaning of anti-racism—the lack of consensus on an emancipatory anti-racism and an intersectional, transversal, anti-racist approach—partly explain the weakness of anti-racist movements in the country (see Detant 2005: 195). While our interview partners are aware that fighting for the rights of migrants and refugees includes fighting institutionalized racism, the focus on racism prevents cooperation with trade unions and the SPÖ as they refuse to talk about it. We encountered trans-

---

[12] Another example of the mainstreaming of the radical right is that both ÖVP and SPÖ before the latest elections sounded out possible coalitions with the FPÖ.

versal politics and alliances that go beyond identity issues but very few transversal framings of racism of the radical right that actively include feminism, gender, sexuality, and class. While feminist organizations would be "natural" partners of anti-racism and anti-rightist movements, the cooperation is rather weak.

I argue that framing, in addition to lack of resources and other practical issues, explains why it is difficult to successfully introduce counter-strategies to racism and practices of social exclusion. The engagement of Austrian civil society organizations would need a clearer shift towards discourses of equality and inclusion to be able to address the exclusionary common sense.

While anti-rightist and anti-racist groups are visible in the Austrian public and have the power to mobilize ad hoc activities, for instance, solidarity with refugees in 2015, their inability to liaise with anti-neoliberal equality frames obstructs cooperation with trade unions. And vice versa, the trade unions do not actively fight racist common sense. In the Austrian system of social partnership, this results in a lack of institutional power of NGOs. However, we found some changes since the 1990s: Some of the civil society organizations we interviewed explicitly linked the issue of hegemonic racism and voting preferences for the radical right to neoliberal transformations of work and family and thus started to connect anti-racism to issues of (in)equality and marginalization of the Austrian workers at the intersection of gender and race.

References

BMI. (2013). Wahl 2013. http://wahl13.bmi.gv.at/
BMI. (2014). EU Wahl 2014. http://euwahl2014.bmi.gv.at/
Campani, G., & Sauer, B. (2017). Neo-fascist and neo-Nazi constellations: The cases of Italy and Austria. In G. Campani & G. Lazaridis (Eds.), *Understanding the populist shift: Othering in a Europe in crisis*. London/New York: Routledge.
Crenshaw, K. (1991). Mapping the margins: Intersectionality, identity politics, and violence against women of color. *Stanford Law Review, 43*, 1241–1299.
della Porta, D., & Mattoni, A. (Eds.). (2014). *Spreading protest: Social movements in times of crisis*. Colchester: ECPR.
Detant, A. (2005). The politics of anti-racism in Belgium: A qualitative analysis of the discourse of the anti-racist movement Hand in Hand in the 1990s. *Ethnicities, 5*, 183–215.

Dolezal, M., & Hutter, S. (2007). Konsensdemokratie unter Druck? Politischer Protest in Österreich, 1975–2005. *Österreichische Zeitschrift für Politikwissenschaft, 36*, 337–352.

Flecker, J., & Kirschenhofer, S. (2007). *Die populistische Lücke. Umbrüche in der Arbeitswelt und Aufstieg des Rechtspopulismus am Beispiel Österreichs*. Berlin: Edition Sigma.

Foltin, R. (2004). *Und wir bewegen uns doch. Soziale Bewegungen in Österreich*. Wien: Edition Grundrisse.

Hall, S. (1988). *The hard road to renewal: Thatcherism and the crisis of the left*. London/New York: Verso.

Hall, S. (2000). Rassismus als ideologischer Diskurs. In N. Räthzel (Ed.), *Theorien über Rassismus* (pp. 7–16). Hamburg: Argument.

Heaney, M. T., & Rojas, F. (2014). Hybrid activism: Social movement mobilization in a multimovement environment. *American Journal of Sociology, 119*, 1047–1103.

Heinisch, R. (2012). Demokratiekritik und (Rechts-)Populismus: Modellfall Österreich? In L. Helms & D. M. Wineroither (Eds.), *Die österreichische Demokratie im Vergleich* (pp. 361–382). Baden-Baden: Nomos.

Isin, E., & Nielsen, G. M. (Eds.). (2008). *Acts of citizenship*. London: Zed books.

Karner, C. (2007). Austrian counter-hegemony. Critiquing ethnic exclusion and globalization. *Ethnicities, 7*, 82–115.

Kubicek, K. (2014). *Praxen politischer Intersektionalität. Eine qualitative Analyse der Zeitschriften und Veranstaltungen des Vereins MiGaY*. Diploma thesis, University of Vienna.

Laclau, E. (1996). *Emancipation(s)*. London/New York: Verso.

Laclau, E. (2005). *On populist reason*. London: Verso.

Laclau, E., & Mouffe, C. (1985). *Hegemony and socialist strategy. Towards a radical democratic politics*. London: Verso.

Lentin, A. (2000). "Race", racism and anti-racism: Challenging contemporary classifications. In social identities. *Journal for the Study of Race, Nation and Culture, 6*, 91–106.

Mayer, S. (2015). *Politik der Differenzen. Ethnisierung, Rassismen und Antirassismus im weißen feministischen Aktivismus in Wien*. PhD thesis, University of Vienna.

Mayer, S., & Sauer, B. (2017). "Gender ideology" in Austria: Coalitions around an empty signifier. In R. Kuhar & D. Paternotte (Eds.), *Anti-gender campaigns in Europe: Mobilizing against equality* (pp. 23–40). London/New York: Roman and Littlefield.

Mayer, S., Sori, I., & Sauer, B. (2016). Gendering "the people": Heteronormativity and "ethno-masochism" in populist imaginary. In M. Raniera (Ed.), *Populism, media and education: Challenging discrimination in contemporary digital societies* (pp. 26–43). London/New York: Routledge.

Omi, M., & Winant, O. (2002). Racial formation. In P. Essed & D. T. Goldberg (Eds.), *Race critical theories: Text and context* (pp. 123–145). Malden: Blackwell.

Pelinka, A. (2002). Die FPÖ in der vergleichenden Parteienforschung. Zur typologischen Einordnung der Freiheitlichen Partei Österreichs. *ÖZP, 31,* 281–290.

Penz, O. (2010). Vom Sozial- zum Wettbewerbsstaat. Arbeitsbeziehungen und politische Regulation in Österreich. In A. Grisold, W. Maderthaner, & O. Penz (Eds.), *Neoliberalismus und die Krise des Sozialen. Das Beispiel Österreich* (pp. 139–178). Böhlau: Vienna/Cologne/Weimar.

Poglia Mileti, F., Tondolo, R., Plomb, F., Schultheis, F., Meyer, M.-H., Hentges, G., Flecker, J., & Mairhuber, I. (2002). *Modern sirens and their populist songs: A European literature review on changes in working life and the rise of right-wing populism* (Literature review (Deliverable 1, SIREN)). Vienna: FORBA.

Pühretmayer, H. (2002). Antirassismus als emanzipatorisches Projekt und die Probleme antirassistischer Praktiken in Wien. In M. Bojadzijev & A. Demirović (Eds.), *Konjunkturen Des Rassismus* (pp. 290–311). Münster: Westfälisches Dampfboot.

Pühretmayer, H., & Görg, A. (1999). Antirassismus in Österreich. Strategische Potenziale gegen Rassismus. Auszug aus unveröffentlichtem Forschungsbericht. http://no-racism.net/article

Rein, M., & Schön, D. (1994). *Frame reflection toward the resolution of intractable policy controversies.* New York: Basic Books.

Roos, F. E., & Oikonomakis, L. (2014). They don't represent us! The global resonance of the real democracy movement from the *indignados* to occupy. In D. della Porta & Y. A. Mattoni (Eds.), *Spreading protest: Social movements in times of crisis* (pp. 117–136). Colchester: ECPR.

Ruzza, C. (2000). Anti-racism and EU institutions. *Journal of European Integration, 22,* 145–171.

Sauer, B., & Ajanovic, E. (2014). The rise of racism across Europe. In M. Sedmak, Z. Medaric, & S. Walker (Eds.), *Children's voices* (pp. 17–32). London: Routledge.

Sauer, B., & Ajanovic, E. (2016). Hegemonic discourses of difference and inequality: Right-wing organisations in Austria. In G. Lazaridis, G. Campani, & A. Benveniste (Eds.), *The rise of the far right in Europe: Populist shifts and "othering"* (pp. 81–108). London: Palgrave Macmillan.

Schumacher, S. (2008). Die Neuorganisation der Zuwanderung durch das Fremdenrechtspaket 2005. http://www.oeaw.ac.at/kmi/Bilder/kmi_WP12.pdf

Siim, B., & Mokre, M. (2013). European public spheres and intersectionality. In B. Siim & M. Mokre (Eds.), *Negotiating gender and diversity in an emergent European public sphere* (pp. 43–60). London: Palgrave Macmillan.

Stavrakakis, Y. (2014). Discourse theory, post-hegemonic critique and Chantal Mouffe's politics of passion. *Parallax, 20*, 118–135.
Talos, E. (2006). Politik in Schwarz-Blau/Orange. Eine Bilanz. In E. Talos (Ed.), *Schwarz-Blau. Eine Bilanz des 'Neu-Regierens'* (pp. 326–343). Münster: Lit-Verlag.
Wiegel, G. (2013). Rechtsverschiebung in Europa. In P. Bathke & A. Hoffstadt (Eds.), *Die neuen Rechten in Europa. Zwischen Neoliberalismus und Rassismus* (pp. 112–125). PapyRossa: Cologne.
Yuval-Davis, N. (1997). *Gender and nation*. London: Sage.
ZARA. (2014). *Rassismusreport*. Vienna: ZARA.
Zerbes, J. (2012). Österreich zuerst! http://www.univie.ac.at/unique/uniquecms/?p=1149

CHAPTER 6

We Are Still Here and Staying! Refugee-Led Mobilizations and Their Struggles for Rights in Germany

Susi Meret and Waldemar Diener

INTRODUCTION

The years 2012–2015 were characterized by demonstrations, protest camps and mobilizations initiated by undocumented/non-status refugees in several major German cities. Refugees without status engaged in acts of citizenship (Isin and Nielsen 2008) and in radical political performative acts (Butler 2015) alongside local communities, pro-migrant, pro-refugee and anti-racist networks. Their endeavors to self-organize and reclaim a voice of their own took place in a situation of fundamental insecurity for their own rights and life and in conditions of vulnerability and lack of certainty about the present and the future. The activities of refugee activists and refugee collectives have encouraged and established new political approaches and practices in Germany and prompted reflections about

---

S. Meret (✉) • W. Diener
Aalborg University (AAU), Aalborg, Denmark

© The Author(s) 2019
B. Siim et al. (eds.), *Citizens' Activism and Solidarity Movements*, Palgrave Studies in European Political Sociology, https://doi.org/10.1007/978-3-319-76183-1_6

137

their role as initiators and active subjects within the movements. The choice to become visible and to speak out in public became their counter-reaction against yet stricter laws marginalizing, isolating and rejecting them.

Migration is in itself a political act, and the collective mobilization for rights triggered by the refugee movement created more knowledge and awareness in the public consciousness about how certain laws target specific peoples. In this sense, the German refugee and migrant solidarity movements developed in the twenty-first century resonate strongly with what French scholar Étienne Balibar (1997) observed about the mobilizations of undocumented migrants in France in the mid-1990s. In a manifesto entitled "What we owe to the sans-papiers", he argues that:

> We owe them ... for having recreated citizenship among us, since the latter is not an institution nor a status, but a collective practice. They did it for themselves ... but also by stimulating new forms of activism and renewing old ones. Now, activism, although it is not the whole of active citizenship, it is clearly one of its indispensable components. We cannot both deplore democratic apathy and deny the importance of the recent mobilizations for the rights of immigrants resident in France (and, more generally, in Europe). They have thus contributed to giving political activity the transnational dimension that we so desperately need to open prospects for social transformation and civility in the era of globalization.

Like the French sans-papiers (Bloch et al. 2012), the refugee movement in Germany arose from conditions of social and physical isolation, geographical immobilization and deprivation in asylum centers. Non-status refugees made themselves active agents of contentious politics and of democratic processes, re-claiming and exercising the same rights they have been denied access to. With their resistance, struggles and political imagination they energized mobilizations of civil society for equal rights and a more inclusive democratic process. They also provided new political insights about how to engage *with* them rather than speak *for* them—in the transformative processes for rights and for social justice. In this sense, refugees' practices of political activism prompt questions about what processes of individual and collective political subjectivation take place among them and how organizational strategies and mobilizations affect the development of the refugee movement over time.

The rise, mobilization and struggles of these groups in Germany were initiated at the local/urban level and mostly in the (political) spaces of the contemporary migrant metropolis (De Genova 2015). These urban spaces have influenced the rise and development of the refugee movements' modes of organization, networking and (inter-)connecting within the overall urban environment. The "on-site" opportunity structures, the (good and bad) alliance formation, the political strategies and the repertoires of action have of course partly been elaborated in relation to the specific urban context of existing movements. The past and present in terms of the landscape of militant activism, political opportunities and social movements' activity shape diverse geographies of connections and articulations of messages. Relationships established between new and old movements can reveal the ability (or difficulty) to (re-)mobilize, integrate and "accommodate" new actors and new issues. In the case of the refugee movement in Germany, we examine whether the refugees' mobilizations and activism have prompted transformations, new alliance configurations and organizational patterns within the social movements' reality.

The refugees' background, their connections to networks elsewhere, their migratory patterns and their language skills are features than can facilitate and encourage transnational developments, which can take the movements' demands and grievances beyond the local/national level. New relations can thus help to redraw and negotiate new "maps of grievances" (Davies and Featherstone 2013) and signal practices through which actors engage with and contest "spatially stretched relations of power". For example, many of the non-status refugees we met look at Europe and more generally at transnational cooperation and activity as a means to strengthen and unify the refugees' voices and spread the word of political mobilization at different levels. Strategically, this can be a way to differentiate and directly address migration and asylum issues at multiple levels, that is, (1) at local and national levels (claim the right to stay, move freely within the national territory, work, access medical care, decent housing and education) and (2) at transnational and European levels (the right to move freely in Europe and decide where to stay, criticism of European policies of control and externalization of the borders, securitization and policing).

Below, we analyze the emergence and development of two of the main refugee-led movements in Germany that developed in the years 2012–2015: the Lampedusa in Hamburg and the Berlin-based Oranienplatz refugee movement (the Berlin Refugee Strike Movement or Berlin Refugee Movement and the Lampedusa in Berlin). We map some of the organizational strategies, activities, alliances and developments that characterized these movements at the local/national and the European level. We rely on participatory observations, interviews, dialogues and reflections elaborated by and with some of the refugee activists in the past four years. We have actively participated in demonstrations, seminars, protests at borders, conferences and debates. Dialogue and long-term involvement inspired us to reflect critically on our role as scholars when it comes to participating, thinking critically and reflecting on our research methods and positioning in relation to the movement. In particular, it made us think about the often avowed and perhaps rarely practiced intent in critical studies and academia to give refugees a voice (Desai 2013).

Refugee Protests and Claims: Between Exit and Voice

Refugees without status are among those voices that today organize and mobilize to reclaim their rights (Monforte 2014; Nyers 2008). Regardless of their situation, they establish themselves as subjects entitled to rights and together with others constitute themselves as "citizens" belonging to and living in a place. Especially asylum seekers and refugees increasingly attempt to engage in political practices, protests and demonstrations that reclaim the basic "right to have rights" (Arendt 1951; Isin and Nielsen 2008). Their protests and claims address the need to radically rethink and politically react against political and social exclusion, physical confinement, detention in removal camps, and against politics that deny them basic civil and political rights. To make their voices heard, non-status migrants overcome fear and invisibility to position themselves as political subjects, asking for political and social changes in a context that increasingly keeps them excluded and marginalized. Paradoxically, non-status refugees make use of precisely those rights that laws and authorities deny them. Their mobilizations and activities reveal patterns of individual and collective political subjectivation that also connect to and engage with others in their struggle. The emergence of the refugee movements in Europe opens up opportunities for solidarity and for transversal social and political alliances, particularly among today's dispossessed and "undesirables" (Agier 2012).

What is at stake is, among other things, the ways in which refugees are able to mobilize themselves and others by overcoming their situation of general deprivation and insecurity about their present and future. How do refugees generate and seize new political spaces of contention? How do they reach new audiences that can help shape and re-scale the geographies of resistance and solidarity? Do their role and activity challenge hegemonic representations of refugees and migrants as subaltern? How do their claims and activism address not only racial but also class and gender issues?

From the 1990s, stricter immigration and asylum laws in Europe (and beyond) have triggered resistance, mobilizations and militant activism among migrants at the local/national and the European level (Monforte and Dufour 2013; Monforte 2014). Collective acts of dissent and disobedience, protests and mobilizations have been replicated in several geographical spaces and places. The vast and increasingly shared repertoire of actions includes peaceful sit-ins and demonstrations, protest camps, (hunger) strikes, lip-sewing, theater performances and art installations, video screenings, public debates, seminars and conferences, squatting of buildings, church sanctuary, national and transnational walking caravans and so on. Many of these actions have been used by the refugee movements in Hamburg and in Berlin.

THE HAMBURG SETTING: URBAN SOCIAL MOVEMENTS AND THE RIGHT FOR ALL TO STAY

Are refugees given the opportunity and the voice to articulate their demands and organize their protests? Do anti-racist and pro-migrant groups, organizations, networks and parties act with them, or are alliances moved by the belief that they are supporting people they perceive as vulnerable victims or are they fighting their own fight (e.g. anti-capitalistic or anti-racist) "on the back" of the refugees?

Historically and politically, Germany has been a fertile setting for the emergence and development of pro-migrant, anti-fascist, anti-racist and pro-housing/anti-gentrification groups. This historical legacy has contributed to and encouraged the emergence and consolidation of (among others) the refugee group "Lampedusa in Hamburg" and strengthened the migrant solidarity movement in Hamburg in recent years.

The history of Hamburg documents a fast-developing trade, flourishing business and financial industries, and a very dynamic and flexible industrial sector. Hamburg's development dates back to the period of the Hansestadt, when the city was part of the Hanseatic League, which granted

Hamburg almost undisturbed expansion to trading activities and autonomy from central government. As the Hamburg maxim goes: "Wherever there's trade, there tread Hamburgers". The city has historically been a major center of maritime power (see Harreld 2015). Today it is still renowned for its industriousness, wealth and prosperity. But like other global, neoliberal, financial hubs (Sassen 1991), Hamburg's contemporary history documents significant economic fluctuations; the effects of global economic and financial crises have throughout history caused major structural changes in the city's labor market, economic activity and urban geography. The economic crisis of the 1980s had a large and immediate impact on the Hamburgers, triggering the shutdown of factories and industries related to the harbor. This produced rocketing unemployment rates, massive work precarization and growing economic uncertainty for the lower social classes, and particularly the manual workers and the dockers. These processes were met with increasing workers' mobilization (e.g. in relation to the closure of the shipyards in Hamburg and in Bremen) and social unrest by the younger generations of Hamburgers, who saw themselves destined for precarization and unemployment.

Historic social movements in Hamburg have thus been characterized by a predisposition towards the convergence or at least the intersection of the protests of diverse social groups in society. Particularly in the 1980s, workers and young people staged and performed their discontent and dissent in the St. Pauli workers' district. The protests were often backed by the resident population (see Birke 2016). The activity of the so-called Autonomen, who in 1981 occupied houses in the St. Pauli street Hafenstrasse, was part of the successful mobilizations of those years. This happened at the same time as the squatters' movement peaked in Berlin. The occupiers at Hafenstrasse resisted several attempts by the city government and the police to evict them. The squatters' movement was able to engage and mobilize thousands of supporters and sympathizers, who worked together to protect what was considered a liberated and politicized urban space. The plans and activities put in place locally and internationally to safeguard the squatted buildings from urban renewal and gentrification still make Hafenstrasse a contentious place with a history of "militant resistance, internationalism, self-empowerment and self-management practices and a collective structure" (Katsiaficas 2006: 125). For many German activists, the experience of Hafenstrasse shows how an organized struggle and strategic actions can become a mobilization pattern that includes many different claims and actors. It also proved how long-term resolutions can be achieved by bargaining with local authorities. To prevent the conflict from spinning out of control, Hamburg SPD mayor Klaus von Dohnányi (1981–1988) was forced to accept the squatters and to create a corporation between the council members and the residents, which allowed them to lease the houses to the occupants (at the cost of 1 DM). However, a new measure would in the future clear out any new attempts to squat a building in the city within 24-hours. A similar measure had already been implemented in Berlin (the so-called Berliner Linie). The Autonomen milieu remains the symbol of militant resistance and of the radical political activism in Hamburg, where many activists have socialized and passed the history on to the new generations.

The Right to the City for All

In the 1990s, the municipality plans for further privatizations, outsourcing of public resources and urban gentrification intensified in Hamburg. This reinvigorated mobilizations and political contestations among the social movements, trade unions and the wider Hamburg citizenry. The group Recht auf Stadt/Right to the City[1] was founded in 2009 as a network of initiatives in Hamburg that fights for affordable housing, non-commercial spaces, socialization of property and a new democratic urban planning for the preservation of public resources and green areas. The group also aims at connecting the history of social movements in Hamburg to the wider mobilizations for rights to the city for all (with and without papers) and against urban gentrification.[2] The Right to the City network was, for example, also involved in local initiatives and struggles for community participation in the restructuring (planned for 2020) of the former Esso-Häuser area in St. Pauli[3] and against the eviction (December 2013) of the internationally renowned social center, the Rote Flora.[4]

---

[1] http://rechtaufstadt.net/about.html

[2] A recent initiative is the so-called Hamburg Urban Citizenship Card. It was launched during the anti-G20 summit event, on 2 July 2017. Residents, activists and supporters temporarily occupied the green spot Grüner Jäger in St. Pauli to debate asylum, migration, urban citizenship and rights for all. The park was registered as a congregation where the "authority" of the "Free and Solidarity City Hamburg" issued the Hamburg Urban Citizenship Card, designed with a logo, a seal and a photograph and details of the card owner. See http://urban-citizenship-hamburg.rechtaufstadt.net/

[3] http://www.initiative-esso-haeuser.de/index.html

[4] https://rote-flora.de/

When the Hamburg nexus of groups, activists and networks protesting urban gentrification and fighting for the right of all to stay joined forces with the pro-refugee and pro-migrant solidarity groups, it created—as we shall see—an important foundation and opportunity for the refugee-led mobilizations to rise and grow. In November 2014, the newly formed sister network of the Right to the City group, Recht auf Stadt—Never Mind the Papers, started a formal alliance with the organized refugees in the city, including independent union activists (e.g. ver.di), Hamburg students, leftist groups and an array of other local initiatives. They state on their homepage[5]:

> We call ourselves Right to City – Never Mind the Papers because we believe that basic rights must be guaranteed regardless of race, color or residence status. …We fight for a city where all the people who live here have the same rights – against structural and everyday racism. In order to reach this goal, we organize demonstrations, position ourselves in discussions within the city, support the self-organization of migrants and refugees, and fight together – for example with the group "Lampedusa in Hamburg", with Roma or refugees from Syria and from Afghanistan. At the same time we are committed to living solidarity in everyday life.

Since late 2014, the Never Mind the Papers alliance has organized several major demonstrations and actions with the refugee movement in Hamburg, protesting in particular against the still precarious living conditions of migrants, refugees and destitutes in the city and asking for politics of solidarity first of all to be guaranteed at the urban level.

The urban dimension of the struggle—as we suggest below—was prompted by the lack of response to the refugees' reiterated demands of dialogue with the Hamburg authorities. The attempt to re-scale and translate the struggle for rights to the urban level also called for the engagement of all citizens and mobilization of all local resources. We argue that the recent developments in Hamburg refer back to the roots and lessons learned from past urban social movements, as much as it draws upon the right to the city of the non-status refugees living in it, such as the refugees of "Lampedusa in Hamburg" (LiHH).

[5] https://nevermindthepapers.noblogs.org/about/

Pro-Refugee, Pro-Migrant Solidarity Movements in Germany and Hamburg

Migrant solidarity organizations, networks and advocacy groups are rather established and consolidated realities in Germany, albeit their intent and work can be moved by different understandings of support and mobilization (Monforte 2014: 47–56). Towards the end of the 1990s, new pro-migrant organizations and anti-racist networks emerged whose activities promoted a more critical and active role to be played at the national level together with migrants and refugees with and without status. Networks and groups such as Kein Mensch Ist Illegal and Kanak Attak became platforms to encourage critical positions and support wider connections at the national level.

The Caravan for the rights of Refugees and Migrants (Die Karawane für die Rechte der Flüchtlinge und MigrantInnen, AKA Karawane) and the VOICE Refugee Forum are among the groups that since the end of the 1990s have more explicitly and consistently struggled for the rise of self-organized and self-empowered refugee movements in Germany. These two groups foster activities that encourage and support refugees to take up their own fight for a political voice and visibility. The VOICE Refugee Forum (the VOICE) is a result of such efforts; it was launched in the 1990s in the Eastern German city of Jena. Its members are refugees who protested and organized themselves against the German asylum and migration politics in the 1990s (Jakob 2016). Karawane is a "network of individuals, groups and organizations of refugees, migrants and Germans based on anti-imperialism and antiracism, (…) engaged in the struggle for socio-political justice, equality and respect for the fundamental human rights of everyone" (Karawane 2011). The network was founded in the late 1990s in response to the tightening of the German asylum laws and the escalation in racist attacks against refugees and migrants in Germany. Karawane differs from other pro-refugee/pro-migrant advocacy groups and networks in Germany by explicitly rejecting the humanitarian and white-European colonial hegemony (Monforte 2014: 47–55).

In the 1990s, the VOICE gave rise to a wave of German-based, self-organized groups of non-status migrants. Unlike other German anti-racist groups and pro-migrant advocacy organizations, the VOICE and Karawane highlight the right and duty of asylum seekers to be active and militant participants in the struggle concerning their own rights and conditions. This sets them apart from institutions and pro-migrant advocacy groups that act and speak *for* migrants instead of *with* them (see Monforte 2014). The VOICE has campaigned against the culture of isolation and deportation in what is referred to as *Lager* (= asylum centers) and was among the groups protesting the German practice of mandatory residence (the so-called *Residenzpflicht*). In recent years, this group has fostered practices of self-empowerment and autonomy among asylum seekers, refugees and migrants in Germany, by, for example, calling for meetings, seminars and debates where non-status refugees are the main initiators and participants. The VOICE strives to locally create and sustain support to refugee groups, but also aims at building and interconnecting the struggles at the national level. The support of both the VOICE and Karawane has been crucial for the development of the refugee-led movements in Hamburg, Berlin and several other cities in Germany (e.g. Munich).

"We Are Here to Stay" and Organize

In May 2013, a group of refugees who called themselves "Lampedusa in Hamburg" marched from Hamburg Hauptbahnhof (main station) to the Rathaus (City Hall). They asked to meet with Hamburg's SPD mayor Olaf Scholz. They wanted to know what the Hamburg Senate had planned to do with the Libyan refugees that had arrived from Italy and were now living on the streets. Hundreds marched together with them. They entered the Rathaus. The situation was very chaotic. Asuquo Udo, a group spokesperson, was stopped and questioned by a policeman in the City Hall:

> *Udo*: "We are the Lampedusa in Hamburg and we are here to demand our rights!"
> *Policeman*: "Where are your papers? Don't you know that you just violated the German law saying you have to keep 500 meters away from here? We will deport you all to Africa!"
> *Udo*: "Oh indeed sir, and what criteria will you use to deport us? We want to see the mayor, now!" They were confused at the question. They did not know what to answer.
> *Udo*: "We are going to stay here! We are not afraid!"

This episode is narrated by Asuquo Udo (interviews February 2014 and April 2015), spokesperson and main initiator of the Lampedusa in Hamburg refugee group. He described in detail the first public protest by what became known as the refugee group Lampedusa in Hamburg (LiHH). The demonstration inside the Rathaus launched a long season of important pro-migrant and pro-refugee street-level demonstrations, activities, mobilization and initiatives that involved several different actors in the Hanseatic city (see Table 6.1, appendix). The march from Hamburg Hauptbahnhof to the City Hall was organized by the group of refugees who had fled war-torn Libya back in 2011, landing on the Lampedusa shores. After two years, several of them reached Germany in spring 2013. Most had documents issued by the Italian government under the so-called Emergency North-Africa (Meret and Della Corte 2014). The organization, rise and mobilizations of LiHH demarcate a new phase and direction in the migrant and refugee rights solidarity struggle in Germany and Europe.

In his narrations of LiHH's initial phases, Asuquo Udo often mentions Hamburg-based Karawane's role in sparking the initial mobilizations and organization of the refugees from Lampedusa in the city. Udo met Karawane at a demonstration at Hamburg Hauptbahnhof, soon after his arrival. Udo, who is from Nigeria and has a past as a human rights activist, became involved and soon learned what they were demonstrating for and against and where to find them in Hamburg.

> I met up at their café gathering and I asked them if they could support me. I tell them I want to meet the mayor [Olaf Scholz, SPD] ... they look at me and say I have to go home and think about it twice. But I thought I could do something different. I wanted to ask him [the mayor] if human rights are really in practice in Hamburg. And since the law does not allow people to sleep on the streets, how would he explain the situation of us refugees? They [Karawane] said, "good, this is what we have been fighting for", and next day they suggested a few options: If you want to do anything with the mayor you should not be alone, bring your people with you. And I went to all the places where we usually meet to eat and talk to them and there were a lot of people. I was myself ready to face all consequences of this and I asked Karawane to prepare banners and flyers, which they did.

The mobilizations triggered by LiHH from May 2013 to spring 2014 (see Table 6.1) added a few new important components to the fight of and for refugee rights in Germany. In particular, the transnational composition and migration patterns of the group members, their previous experiences in Libya, their knowledge about different European asylum systems (for example in Italy) gave the members of the group diverse experiences to draw upon in their decisions about how best to organize together and what strategy to implement. Their early contact with German networks that work to sustain self-organization and self-empowerment also strongly impacted their political practices and mutual learning, building and reifying their self-awareness, identity and autonomy within the social movements' context in Hamburg. The culture of engaged participation encouraged by the group and the Hamburg activists became one of the foundations of LiHH.

"We are here to stay" is perhaps the group's strongest and most recognizable slogan clearly summoning the aims, demands and claims for recognition. The way LiHH organized and defined its positions and demands was crucial for the consolidation of the group and for the development of a strong identity of belonging. Collective decision-making and structured organization at the local level were decisive for sustained and enduring engagement and active participation in the struggles. LiHH was started by a few people, like Asuquo Udo, whose efforts helped shape a structured organization relying on four main spokespersons who worked actively to bring together the refugees of the Libyan war in Hamburg. In the initial phases, the spokespersons handled both internal and external communication. They shared similar migration pattern, but originated from different African countries and spoke several languages, which helped establish and broaden the network of communities to which they could reach out. Translations into the different languages spoken by the activists were a common procedure at the LiHH meetings, seminars and gatherings.

Several LiHH front figures had experiences with political and human rights activism before Hamburg and before Europe. Most of them had been politically active in Africa or, while staying in Libya, in student associations, trade unions, human rights organizations and so on. The LiHH spokespersons enhanced group visibility and facilitated communication with the wider Hamburg support network and citizenry. LiHH's media strategy was designed to reach out to larger parts of society and beyond the active groups and networks mobilizing at street level. The media strategy relied on an official group blog, a homepage,[6] various social media platforms and self-engagement in the media framing of the group.[7]

To promote a participatory decision-making model, LiHH convened twice a week (they still do, although with different procedures) to discuss

---

[6] http://lampedusa-in-hamburg.org/
[7] The Refugee Radio Network project was to a large extent kindled by this experience and motivation to be refugees organizing their own media outlets. See http://www.refugeeradionetwork.net/projekt.html

and coordinate actions, internally and then with the larger assembly of Hamburg networks, activists and supporters. A number of local community delegates ensured that the group was debriefed about discussions carried out ahead of the main gathering by the smaller community groups spread around in the city. The LiHH spokespersons then communicated decisions to the larger assembly of supporters and activists. The organizational structure had several advantages, but in the long term, it also bestowed some of the front members with more decisional power and connections than the others. This gave rise to internal disagreements regarding, for example, the greater visibility of the spokespersons and the management of economic resources. In particular, the four spokespersons were later held accountable by several group members for what many saw as the political failure to achieve concrete solutions.

LiHH sought from the beginning to achieve public visibility by organizing street actions, demonstrations and talks and by acting as the main referents when demanding a dialogue with the authorities. While LiHH gained sizable support at the street level, it continued to be ignored by the federal authorities. As LiHH member Ali Ahmet recently iterated (conversation, November 2017):

> Each of us wants to work and contribute with something positive to the shaping of this society. Many people in Hamburg still support us and our demands, but the Senate continues to refuse to talk directly to anyone of us, after four years.

The Hamburg Senate has never acknowledged the group and has systematically turned down all their demands for a constructive dialogue.

LiHH's activities particularly involved a process of political subjectivation: They questioned naturalized and internalized identities, power roles, belonging and institutional positioning. By occupying and inhabiting the public space in Hamburg, they purposely and visibly contested their exclusion and forced invisibility produced by their lack of a legal status in Germany. Their collective and organized dissent gave rise to a political platform and a framework of "their own", which gave the group a very strong political sense of belonging. This important asset has been internalized by the younger generation of LiHH activists, who have initiated and joined several new projects. According to Udo, however, the political within social movements still needs work because "most people are not ready to endure a long-term political movement and to fight back. They get tired of waiting for decisions by political parties and some of the supporters were frankly weak and inexperienced in long-term solutions" (Interview with Udo, April 2015).

POLITICIZING THE URBAN SPACE IN HAMBURG: WE STAY HERE!

LiHH's actions were unexpected. Although they never talked with Hamburg's mayor, the group activities gave them visibility and a voice in the public. A tent functioning as a 24-hour info point and as a meeting place transformed the area at Steindamm 2 between the pharmacy and the U-Bahn exit into LiHH's most visible spatial conquest and a political location within the city's topography of movements (St Pauli's Hafenstrasse been the most renowned). This political achievement resulted from another public street-level demonstration and from intense negotiations with the police and the city authorities. After four years of mobilizations and despite the eviction threats from the Hamburg City council, the tent is still up. The tent is the politically visible occupied space that, similarly to Oranienplatz in Berlin, has meant and still means a lot to the refugee movement. It is LiHH's place and space, almost a home, and the physical symbol of their fights and struggles.[8]

The way LiHH initially organized was decisive for the developments of the movement. It ensured a degree of flat democratic decision-making process and of structured action, also by encouraging the involvement of local groups staying in different parts of the city, although not all members had the same opportunity. For instance, some LiHH members sought sanctuary at the St. Pauli church and were given much fewer prospects to participate directly as they were rather seen and treated as victims in need of help.

The first phase of LiHH's mobilization struggle largely focused on the national/local level of politics, thus reflecting the specific demands characteristic of the group: the right to stay, to work and a decent life in Hamburg. LiHH also asked for group recognition based on §23 of the Residence

[8] On 1 May 2014, LiHH and Hamburg activists and supporters briefly occupied an empty public building (a former primary school) placed in Laeiszstrasse 12, St. Pauli. The plan was to establish a Refugee Welcome House, functioning both as an info point and as a sleeping place for those still without a place to stay in Hamburg. The squatters were evacuated by police soon after. LiHH and other activists continued for some days to hold public meetings in the schoolyard, but abandoned the project once it became clear that the Hamburg Senate would never let them in.

Act. However, this claim in itself contested individual approaches to asylum as well as the failure of the Dublin regulations. As formulated in a public statement by LiHH:

> To be constructive ... would mean to accept that we are not guaranteed the appropriate refugee protection in Italy, as a result of the failure of the Dublin II-system and that in Hamburg the refugees ... should not be made to pay for this failure ... we call the §23 of the Resident Act, which ...offers a solution to our existential crisis.

The claim for dialogue, based on LiHH's concrete political propositions to the Hamburg Senate, went together with the broader messages formulated by the network of supporters (e.g. Karawane), which until 2014 also included action frames dealing with: (1) structural problems such as racism, discrimination and Western European colonial mentality (We are here because you are there; United against colonial injustice; In the name of democracy and human rights: Stop this hypocrisy!; Self-determination and freedom for the people of the world), (2) promotion of new fundamental rights (Open Borders, Right to Stay for Everybody, Freedom of Movement, Solidarity without Borders, Kein Mensch Ist Illegal, No Borders, No Nations, No Deportations, etc.), and (3) awareness about European countries' role in the Libyan war and more generally in African conflicts.

From late spring 2014, LiHH initiated a close activity and mobilization strategy with the network Recht auf Stadt—Never Mind the Papers (see above). This encouraged the development of an agenda that increasingly referred to the urban dimension of the struggle and translated the agenda to include all other groups of non-status refugees, the poor and the precarious workers. The right of all people to access the same basic civil rights in the city became the main aim connecting all groups, networks and individuals within a broader alliance. To some extent, this recoupled and integrated the new refugee movement in Hamburg to the agenda of the past urban social movements active in the city. The urban dimension was further developed under the so-called refugee crisis in 2015, which triggered (new) initiatives across Hamburg to focus on urban space and its inhabitants as main subjects. These included, for example, the Bündnis Stadt des Ankommens/City of Arrival Alliance and the Hamburger Aktionsbündnis gegen Wohnungsnot/Hamburg Action Alliance Against Housing Shortage.

WE ARE ALL ORANIENPLATZ! THE REFUGEE MOVEMENT IN BERLIN

I just arrived in Berlin, they told me: "Sudanese are doing a demo in front of the [Sudan] Embassy". [I ask] Why? [They say] Because of this situation. People tell me the unbelievable. We are located from nowhere, we do not see people; other people do not see us. There is no transport; we live in the middle of nowhere. We just eat and sleep. And this for how long? Someone even longer than 20 years. The situation is not good and this is why they protest. This I was told. They don't have a place they can call home... But you know, a person cannot run from a problem, can only hide from it. I decided to stay in Germany. I will not run all the time. Let me start an organization. I can see what I can do. People replied, "You are illegal. You cannot make a community ... If you do not behave as the government wants, you will not get the papers." [I replied] This is not about politics; it is about our life. (Interview with Napuli Paul Langa, Rome, May 2017)

This is what Sudanese activist Napuli Paul Langa recalls during her visit in Rome with the World Refugee Let Fear Go Tour.[9] This is an account of why, how and where she started to get herself and others actively engaged in the struggle of and for refugees in Germany in 2012. It happened soon after Napuli's arrival in Germany from Uganda where she had lived for a few years in exile because of her political activism in Sudan. Napuli was a human rights activist in the Sudanese Organization for Nonviolence and Development (SONAD) and a student at Ahfad University for Women in Khartoum (Langa 2015).

In 2013, she joined a trip to Sweden and Germany and decided to stay in the latter, where she applied for asylum. As several other non-status refugees recall, their ideals of and expectations to the European democratic system were soon disbanded by reality:

> If you think about Europe, you think about human rights. In Africa, everybody thinks human rights come from Europe and particularly Germany because of the war, you know. And then, the first article of the constitution says human dignity is untouchable. But it is not right. [Then] I thought this is my right time to fight.

Napuli eventually joined the group which in 2012 decided to march from different asylum centers across Germany towards Berlin. The movement

---

[9] https://www.facebook.com/wrlfg/

was triggered by the suicide of Mohammed Rahsapar in a refugee camp in Würzburg, in Northern Bavaria. Mohammed's friends had started a protest in front of the camp, which later developed into the idea of mobilizing people from other camps and march to Berlin to protest the conditions of isolation, invisibility and lack of basic rights in the German asylum system. In about a month, they had marched over 500 km from Würzburg to Berlin, visiting several camps on their way, and joined by increasing numbers of refugees and supporters (from Antifa, anti-racist groups, Kein Mensch Ist Illegal, Pro Asyl, Karawane and so forth). The refugee activists arrived in Berlin with clear demands to the government:

> Our demands are and will remain: The abolition of *Lagers* and *Residenzpflicht*, the stopping of all deportations, permanent right to stay, the right to work, to education and to a self-determined habitation as well as the right to freedom of movement. We demand to be treated and respected as human beings. We demand our human rights! (See International Refugee Center 2015: 149)

Napuli joined the movement in the beginning. As she explains, it was in this context that she

> ... became experienced about what was going on. In the beginning, I was not talking [in public] because I did not know enough about the situation. I made translations from Arabic to English. But people went like: Hey, Napuli your voice is strong and they pushed me to talk, which I did for the first time in Hamburg.

When the people finally made it to Berlin early October 2012, the refugee activists held a major demonstration that gathered about 6000–7000 people on the streets. It was one of the largest ever organized by refugees without papers. In Berlin, the activists stayed initially at Pariser Platz in Berlin-Mitte. On 6 October, they got a two-month permission from the mayor of the Kreuzberg-Friedrichshain district to move to Oranienplatz in Berlin-Kreuzberg (Landry 2015: 403).

The move from central Berlin to Kreuzberg was perhaps a political maneuver of displacement that again attempted to make refugees marginalized and less visible to the public. However, at that point, the protesters did not have the opportunities and resources to decline the offer and negotiate with the local authorities. Additionally, the politicized past and present of the Berlin-Kreuzberg area later showed that Oranienplatz was actually a suitable location to organize sustained and effective resistance with the support of the residents.

However, there was internal disagreement in the group. Some went on hunger strike at the Brandenburger Tor, whereas another group—among them Napuli—decided to start a protest camp at Oranienplatz. The Brandenburger Tor became the place of action, but Oranienplatz became the refugees' new home. As Napuli explains (conversations with Napuli, March 2017):

> We say no to the hunger strike. We have more opportunities. Let us think about political strategies and we have ideas, but we have nothing, no support, no economy. But let us wait for some time and see how we can maintain this place and stay here until our demands are met. We stay here. No one is going home and we build more tents. Then others joined from Sweden, Italy, France. Even police led people to Oranienplatz. Before, if you were new [in Berlin] they took you to the camp, now they send people to Oranienplatz. They did not realize this was an occupied space ... [and] the more we were there, the more people in the neighborhood were getting to know us and supported us. Oranienplatz became the center, the meeting place, our home.

BERLIN, KREUZBERG, ORANIENPLATZ

The refugees called themselves the Berlin Refugee Strike Movement. Oranienplatz became the main site of political resistance, movement organization and public visibility, a vital spot to meet, discuss, organize the weekly meetings and come together with German activists and supporters. About 200–250 refugees lived permanently at Oranienplatz, among them Napuli. This was not a mere "place of survival" but a space for politics where refugees developed strong ties, networks and formed political and social structures (see Landry 2015; Bhimji 2016). In addition to the sleeping area, the common kitchen and the assembling space, the Oranienplatz refugees set up an info point, where supporters and activists were on a daily basis engaged to answer questions and inform local residents and passers-by about the reasons for their protest. Oranienplatz became a representational space, which stood in direct opposition to the state-administered asylum camps the refugees came from and which they had left feeling isolated, marginalized and invisible to society. Oranienplatz was the movement's self-earned political space, something very similar to what the LiHH's info tent at Steindamm represents to the Hamburg group (see above).

Kreuzberg is historically the working class and the immigrant neighborhood of West Berlin. Situated close to the Wall, this district accommodated most "guest workers" (the so-called *Gastarbeiter*—mainly Turkish migrant workers) and other economically disadvantaged groups (e.g. artists and students from West Germany) in the 1960s. Berlin-Kreuzberg (especially postal area SO36) was seen and constructed as the unattractive "Ghetto Kreuzberg" (see Stehle 2006). The name carried an easy racist equation: Immigrants and particularly Turks were to blame for the lack of living space and unemployment in Berlin. During the 1970s, the district became one of main centers of the Berlin radical and alternative subculture and of the squatter movement. In the 1980s, hundreds of houses were squatted in Kreuzberg (Bader and Bialluch 2009), and the strong squatter movement, with the support of local residents, played a major role in slowing down the modernist urban renewal plan and implementing instead a "cautious urban renewal/*behutsame Stadterneuerung*".[10] Tellingly, Kreuzberg was not part of the post-Wende neoliberal urban development, and gentrification reached this district relatively late (Holm 2013). Early attempts at urban renewal and privatization gave rise to strong opposition from local residents and to the proliferation of squatted buildings. Particularly from the 2000s, Berlin-Kreuzberg started to attract new types of residents while commodification, rocketing house prices and rents forced many long-time residents to move out. In early summer 2012, the tenant's initiative Kotti & Co[11] turned a summer street fair into a permanent protest camp at the southern Kottbusser Tor in Kreuzberg. Supported by neighbors and activists, the people from Kotti & Co protested against higher rents, privatization of social housing units and displacement of residents who had been living in Kreuzberg. Berlin-Kreuzberg residents have historically struggled for decades with lack of social and political opportunities, marginalizing practices and destitution; they have themselves experimented with alternative ways of living.

Furthermore, the arrival of non-status refugees from outside Germany influenced and expanded the direction of the demands of the refugees at Oranienplatz. From claims focusing on the lack of basic rights in the

---

[10] http://berlin-besetzt.de/#!id=687
[11] https://kottiundco.net/english/

German asylum system, the demands broadened to issues like transformation of the Dublin regulations, the right to work, education, healthcare and a critique of Europe-wide politics of deportations. "Lampedusa in Berlin" (LiB) were among the groups to arrive at Oranienplatz about a year later than the others. Their background was in many respects similar to that of LiHH; their members had also come from Italy and had previously fled Libya in 2011. Unlike the situation in Hamburg, the protest in Berlin included from the beginning activists from different countries and different backgrounds, migration patterns and demands. This diversity made it necessary to amplify and include a multi-scaled approach in the fight (federal, national, European, transnational). At the same time however it posed challenges and opened internal conflicts about where to go and what political strategies to use to achieve the goals. This became obvious later during negotiations with the Berlin Senate and district authorities. Since many of the LiB refugees had papers issued by the Italian government, their situation differed from other non-status refugees in the German system. For the latter, Oranienplatz represented the worksite for differentiated citizenship, a space of possibility, struggle, negotiation, hope and rights to be reclaimed. In a context of increasing neoliberal privatization of urban spaces and the displacement and marginalization of the destitute and "undesirables", the creation and maintenance of this public space was in itself an achievement for the refugee movement. For the destitute however, Berlin was itself a site of opportunity and hope for the future; a place where to stay, work and live. Something that could not be realized in the economic crisis ridden Italy.

You Can't Evict a Movement

Oranienplatz was evicted by the police on 8 April 2014, and Kreuzberg district mayor (Monika Herrmann) and the Senator of Integration of the State of Berlin (Dilek Kolat 2011–2016) maintained that the Oranienplatz refugees had agreed to evacuate voluntarily. However, this was not the case.[12] Authorities took advantage of the internal disagreements among refugees to achieve their objectives. The LiB members were told that had they signed the agreement to remove the tents from Oranienplatz, they would be granted most of their demands: a (temporary) residence

[12] See https://www.vice.com/en_us/article/jmbg8g/the-eviction-of-berlin-refugee-camps

and work permit and accommodation in Berlin. Yet, most of those who signed the agreement had already moved out from Oranienplatz to other temporary accommodations in town, although others were still living there. As Napuli recalls about those moments (conversations with Napuli, March 2017):

> I did not support the agreement. The police came to evict and refugees were fighting. We said that they could take away the sleeping places, but they should not touch the political space, the [Oranienplatz] info point.
> I could deny the clearance by occupying a tree for five days. The police and security services prevented me from all attempts to contact or to be supplied with food. They prevented hunger strikers from sleeping during the night. I demanded a conversation with the Integration Senator, Dilek Kolat, from the SPD to point to the promises. The promises were, for example, toleration of the Lampedusa group, transitional housing to Berlin, and a stop to deportations, which were the reasons for refugees to accept the Senate's offer. We also demanded to bring back our meeting place and the info point to Oranienplatz, which they told me was impossible. After all, I succeeded to bring the meeting place back.
> The woman from the Senate signed the paper and then they all signed. Also [the] refugees. Then I asked to read the paper. Everybody was crying because the doctor kept saying that I would die if I did not climb down the tree. [They] read the paper to me ... Then I came down and asked the policemen ... not to beat me. I was expecting to go to jail. But they said: You are not going to jail, you go to the hospital and then home ... when I came down the real pain came. I was not sleeping for a week. So that's how we got the Oranienplatz info point back ...

Oranienplatz was a vital place of visibility, solidarity and resistance achieved with the support of residents and German activists. For two years, they had peacefully occupied this space. From here they had promoted an alternative and differentiated approach to citizenship and belonging based on inclusive accounts that can ensure life, equal rights and recognition, and not just survival; a citizenship premised on politics of quality and equality, rather than on the politics of quantity and exclusion (Holton and Appadurai 1998).

In June 2014, the people from Oranienplatz, who in winter 2012 had occupied the empty Gerhart-Hauptmann-Schule in Ohlauer Strasse to accommodate families with children and women, were asked to leave the school. Similar to Oranienplatz, the school was understood by the refugees as a place of resistance and freedom, and after the eviction of the square, the occupants did not trust the promises made by authorities.[13] Yet, when it became clear that the space could not be maintained, most of the 200 people agreed to move to other accommodation provided by the district authorities. However, 40 refugees (with around a dozen still staying in 2017) and some supporters remained inside, and from the school's rooftop a banner was unfolded: "You Can't Evict a Movement". They also proclaimed: "We don't want to go back to the *Lager*". More than a thousand police were mobilized for nine days to clear out the school, fencing off large sectors of the surrounding area. This huge police presence triggered a reaction from the local population, and thousands of Kreuzberg residents rallied against the police action together with refugees who protested the state of emergency and that had been created and the generalized criminalization of the refugees.

BUILDING LOCALLY, LINKING GLOBALLY

Transferring the struggles from the local/urban to the national and the European level requires the development of political opportunities that can support the building of a broader network of contacts, actions and activities. Learning from each other's successes and mistakes can help consolidate a movement's position and future advances both within and beyond the national borders. These efforts are often constrained and prevented by authorities and institutional powers at local and national level, as we saw happen in Hamburg and Berlin. LiHH experienced this at a relatively early stage. By the end of October 2013, the Federal Senate of Hamburg asked LiHH members to accept the German status of *Duldung* (toleration status and temporary suspension of deportation), which implies living for years without a residence permit with restricted basic rights. Additionally, the Senate proposed a new asylum procedure in Germany, remitting the papers that many had been issued years back in Italy.

This occurred as the Senate and the church struck an agreement behind the LiHH's back, creating internal divisions and conflicts that ultimately divided the group. The unfolding events in 2013 and 2014 set off a phase

[13] https://www.youtube.com/watch?v=yilF-UWoICY

of uncertainties and decline, both politically and with regard to the street-level mobilization in Hamburg. However, if motivation was fading, the situation sparked reflections about the movement's need to create a broader network of activities and exchange ideas with other groups in Hamburg, Germany and Europe.

Similarly, the Berlin Refugee Strike Movement at Oranienplatz was weakened and destabilized by negotiations conducted before the police eviction and which purposely only included some of the refugees. This strategy played on the movement's internal contradictions and disagreements to achieve the goal of clearing the public space and moving the people away. As Napuli observes:

> We had difficulties ... in our movement due to clashes of interests, either strategically or tactically, as well as different demands, from several sides: Between refugees and refugees, between refugees and supporters, and between supporters and supporters. These clashes gave the government the chance to try to divide us ... The politicians used this for their divide-and-rule strategy at Oranienplatz, just like politicians did it in the colonies in Africa. [But] from my experience there is always a possibility, nothing is impossible. Gandhi said: "Be the change you want to see in the world". So, for you right now and right here do not be part of the problem. Rather, oppose! ...Let us fight together for every one of us to have the right to live, not just to survive.

Networking and experience sharing among the various groups at the (trans)national level were the central themes at the refugee-led conferences in Hanover (2015) and Hamburg (2016). The Hamburg International Conference of Refugees and Migrants was co-organized by refugees and supporters in Hamburg with the goal and ambition to "foster a powerful network of refugees and migrants and to create a platform for reflection and learning".[14] The framing was a way to prompt the formation of tighter and broader transversal political alliances and to encourage and strengthen the formation of new alliance constellations that could also act at the European level. The idea was to support demands at the transnational level, which groups, such as the CISPM (International Coalition of Sans-Papiers, Migrants and

[14] See http://refugeeconference.blogsport.eu/files/2016/02/program-overview_final_correct.pdf

Refugees), have promoted actively for many years. This requires mutual knowledge about and support of the various national and local refugee mobilizations and agreement on a political agenda that can bring forward the demands of the refugees and migrants to the European level. An example is the transnational March for Freedom to Brussels. It started before the 2014 European Union Parliament elections, and hundreds of non-status refugees, migrants and supporters crossed major geographical border nodes in the face of the European border policy. Among the many groups represented were the Berlin Refugee Movement and the LiHH. Symbolic actions marked the main stops of the march, which ended with a week of actions in Brussels. The Action Week culminated on 26 June in a large demonstration against Europe's restrictive asylum and migration policies (Nigg 2015). The slogans in Brussels emphasized the need to unite different, individual struggles across sectional national divides, addressing a common situation of exploitation and precarity in terms of the right to stay and freedom to move and the right to work and achieve decent living conditions.

The 2016 Hamburg refugee conference was another step towards the formation of a European refugee movement platform, although it also revealed that still many issues ought to be addressed at the national and local levels, in order to then be able to organize and consolidate the struggle at the transnational level. The issues of transversal alliances, solidarity and internal diversity emerged as challenges that need to be discussed and reflected upon together and at different stages by refugee activists and supporters likewise. Gender, gender minorities' and queer issues are among the problems that need to be equitably implemented in the refugee movements' claims for rights and recognition. Refugee leaders are not only predominately men but also all straight. These issues partially surfaced at the Hamburg conference, when, under the slogan "women's space is everywhere", the women occupied the theater central stage to protest the marginalization of their workshop and of their role (see, e.g. Schipkowski 2016). The importance of these questions urges undoubtedly for greater visibility and thorough discussions from refugees and supporters, to better address the intersections of multiple diversities (e.g. gender, sexuality, religion, ethnicity) within the movement.

Conclusions

Our globalized world harbors fundamental and growing contradictions at its core that foster socio-economic inequalities, precarity and conflicts. Forced migration is currently one of the most symptomatic effects. Responses to structural crises within the capitalist system oscillate between opposing, often self-contradicting and short-sighted policy measures: opening/confining, including/excluding, merging/dividing, moving/securing. Today's refugee movements are the reaction against the conditions of exclusion, marginalization and exploitation generated by societies that show increasing adverseness towards diversity. Social movements and unrest arise in a context of negated rights, lack of recognition, inequality and marginalization that affect several groups in society, not only refugees and migrants. The development of refugee-led movements in Germany shows the increasing efforts made by non-status refugees to organize, find autonomous leaders, create alliances and experiment with democratic and participatory forms of organization as well strategies that engage other groups in society. Yet, despite the quest to help generate a political and social transformation, the contemporary refugee movements rarely achieve consolidation, continuity and political and social gains. As the Hamburg and Berlin experiences illustrate, some of the reasons are lack of a clear strategic direction, coherence and continuity in the different phases of mobilization, the need to mobilize and maintain position. In particular, grassroots movements seem, at least at their creation, to benefit from the "momentum" and public support achieved through mobilization at the local level. However, they are eventually subjugated by internal differences created through the "divide and rule" tactics of those structures that were the initial trigger for the creation of the movement. Progress in the struggle entails building upon a critical consciousness based on mutual learning from the movements' positive achievements and from their failures and on the groups' abilities to connect and understand the power relationships that produce and reproduce inequality and marginalization at local, national and European level, as well as in their midst.

Appendix

Table 6.1 The Lampedusa in Hamburg (LiHH) main actions and messages (2013–2014)

Date	Action	Messages
3 May 2013	Manifestation at *Kirchentag*/Church Day	We are here and we do not go back
22 May 2013	March on the *Rathaus*/City Hall	We did not survive the NATO war in Libya to die on the streets of Hamburg Demand to speak to the SPD mayor Olaf Scholz
2 June 2013	Sanctuary at St. Pauli Church	
8 June 2013	Demonstration and solidarity party	Self-determination and freedom for the people of the world! No to NATO fascism
18 June 2013	Demonstration and manifestation in front of French consulate	France's involvement in the NATO war in Libya
17 Aug 2013	Demonstration	The NATO war in Libya has caused our flight We demand our rights §23 We fight for our right to stay Unite against colonial injustice
11 Sept–16 Oct 2013	Six weekly demonstrations	Lampedusa in Hamburg—We stay here!
9 Oct 2013	One of the weekly demonstrations: Remembrance of the shipwreck on the Lampedusa shores	In the name of democracy and human rights, stop this hypocrisy We remember the victims of Lampedusa
2 Nov 2013	Big demonstration	Solidarity with Lampedusa in Hamburg—We demand a right to stay according to § 23 Residence Act!
12 Dec 2013	*Schulstreik*/school strike	Right to stay for everybody Still loving *Bleiberecht* Bring politics class on the street Abolish *Residenzpflicht* Deportation is torture Deportation is murder
21 Dec 2013	Demo at Steindamm 2, LiHH Infotent	We fight for our rights Our families suffer The NATO war in Libya has detroyed our existence Solidarity without Borders

(*continued*)

Table 6.1 (continued)

Date	Action	Messages
1 Feb 2014	First seminar	Why do people flee from their countries? We are here because you destroyed our countries
8 Feb 2014	Second seminar	The EU war-politics against refugees: The silent death in *Lager*
1 Mar 2014	Big demonstration and political/cultural parade	Parade for our rights We are here to stay!
30 Apr 2014	Manifestation	A day for the "illegal" workers Better to die fighting for freedom than to be a prisoner the whole life
1 May 2014	Refugee Welcome Center, and LiHH Haus	Refugee Welcome; Squatting of empty school in Laeiszstrasse, St. Pauli
31 May 2014	Demonstration	We demand our working papers! How long? Not long! Stop killing us slowly We are not here to die, we demand our rights now
5 June 2014	Peaceful, silent sit-in in front of the Rathaus	
5 July 2014	Demonstration	Recognition of the LiHH now! Working papers
10/11 Oct 2014	Emancipation days	Let us break the silence!
13 Dec 2014	Demonstration	Selbstorganisierte Kämpfe stärken! Lagersystem abschaffen! Recht auf Wohnen für alle!

Selbstorganisierte Kämpfe stärken! (Stengthen self-organized struggles)
Lagersystem abschaffen! (Eliminate the system of camps)
Recht auf Wohnen für alle! (Right to live for everybody)

References

Agier, M. (2012). *Managing the undesirables: Refugee camps and humanitarian government*. Cambridge: Polity Press.

Arendt, H. (1951). *The origin of totalitarianism*. New York: Schocken Books.

Bader, I., & Bialluch, M. (2009). Gentrification and the creative class in Berlin-Kreuzberg. In L. L. Porter & K. Shaw (Eds.), *Whose urban renaissance? An international comparison of urban regeneration strategies* (pp. 93–102). New York: Routledge.

Balibar, E. (1997). What we owe to the sans-papiers. *European Institute for Progressive and Cultural Politics.* http://eipcp.net/transversal/0313/balibar/en

Bhimji, F. (2016). Visibilities and the politics of space: Refugee activism in Berlin. *Journal of Immigrant & Refugee Studies, 14,* 432–450.

Birke, P. (2016). Right to the city – And beyond: The topographies of urban social movements in Hamburg. In M. Mayer, C. Thörn, & A. Thörn (Eds.), *Urban uprisings. Challenging neoliberal urbanism in Europe, Studies in European political sociology* (pp. 203–232). London: Palgrave Macmillan.

Bloch, A., Sigona, N., & Zetter, R. (2012). *Sans-papiers: The social and economic lives of young undocumented migrants.* London: Pluto Press.

Butler, J. (2015). *Notes towards a performative theory of assembly.* Cambridge: Harvard University Press.

Davies, A. D., & Featherstone, D. (2013). Networking resistances: The contested spatialities of transnational social movement organizing. In W. Nicholls, B. Miller, & J. Beaumont (Eds.), *Spaces of contention. Spatialities and social movements* (pp. 239–260). Surrey: Ashgate.

De Genova, N. (2015). Border struggles in the migrant metropolis. *The Journal of Nordic Migration Research, 5,* 3–10.

Desai, M. (2013). The possibilities and perils for scholar-activists and activist-scholars. Reflections on the feminist dialogues. In J. S. Juris & A. Khasnabish (Eds.), *Insurgent transnational activism.* Durham/London: Duke University Press.

Flesher, F., & Cox, L. (2013). *Understanding European movements: New social movements, global justice struggles, anti-austerity protest.* London: Routledge.

Harreld, D. J. (Ed.). (2015). *A companion to the Hanseatic League.* Leiden/Boston: Brill.

Holm, A. (2013). Berlin's gentrification mainstream. In B. Grell, M. Bernt, & A. Holm (Eds.), *The Berlin reader. A compendium on urban change and activism* (pp. 171–187). Berlin: Transcript Verlag Editors.

Holton, J., & Appadurai, A. (1998). *Cities and citizenship.* Durham: Duke University Press.

International Refugee Center. (2015). *Movement: A heroes magazine,* Berlin. https://www.yumpu.com/en/document/view/36996214/movement-1

Isin, E., & Nielsen, G. M. (Eds.). (2008). *Acts of citizenship.* New York: Zed Books.

Jakob, C. (2016). *Die Bleibenden – Wie Flüchtlinge Deutschland seit 20 Jahren verändern.* Berlin: Ch. Links Verlag.

Karawane Für die Rechte der Flüchtlinge und MigrantInnen. (2011). *Contribution to the Second Assembly of the International Migrants Alliance.*

Katsiaficas, G. (2006). *The subversion of politics: European autonomous social movements and the decolonization of everyday life.* Edinburgh: AK Press.

Landry, O. (2015). "Wir sind alle Oranienplatz"! Space for refugees and social justice in Berlin. *Seminar: A Journal of Germanic Studies, 51,* 398–413.
Langa, N. (2015). About the refugee movement in Kreuzberg/Berlin. *Movements: Journal for Critical Migration and Border Regime Studies, 1.* http://movements-journal.org/issues/02.kaempfe/08.langa--refugee-movement-kreuzberg-berlin.html. Last viewed 03 Dec 2017.
Meret, S., & Della Corte, E. (2014, January 22). Between exit and voice: Refugees' stories from Lampedusa to Hamburg. *OpenDemocracy.* http://www.opendemocracy.net/can-europe-make-it/susi-meret-elisabetta-della-corte/between-exit-and-voice-refugees-stories-from-la
Monforte, P. (2014). *Europeanizing contention: The protest against "Fortress Europe" in France and Germany.* New York/Oxford: Berghahn Books.
Monforte, P., & Dufour, P. (2013). Comparing the protests of undocumented migrants beyond contexts: Collective action and acts of emancipation. *European Political Science Review, 5,* 83–104.
Nigg, H. (2015). Sans-papiers on their March for Freedom 2014: How refugees and undocumented migrants challenge Fortress Europe. *Interface: A Journal for and About Social Movements, 7,* 263–288.
Nyers, P. (2008). No one is illegal between city and nation. In E. Isin & G. M. Nielsen (Eds.), *Acts of citizenship.* New York: Zed Books.
Sassen, S. (1991). *The global city: New York, London, Tokyo.* Princeton: Princeton University Press.
Schipkowski, K. (2016, February 27). Frauen ergreifen das Wort. *TAZ.* http://taz.de/Eklat-bei-Fluechtlingskonferenz-Hamburg/!5282015/
Stehle, M. (2006). Narrating the ghetto, narrating Europe: From Berlin, Kreuzberg to the banlieues of Paris. *Westminster Papers in Communication and Culture, 3,* 48–70.

Interviews

Ali Ahmet, conversations in November 2017.
Asuquo Udo, interviews in Hamburg in February 2014 and April 2015.
Napuli Paul Langa, interview in Rome, May 2017; conversations in Aalborg, March 2017.

Internet Sites

Berlin Besetzt http://berlin-besetzt.de/#!id=687
Initiativen Esso Häuser. Wir sind Kein Objekt, Hamburg http://www.initiative-esso-haeuser.de/index.html

International Conference of Refugees and Migrants, Hamburg, February 2016. http://refugeeconference.blogsport.eu/files/2016/02/program-overview_final_correct.pdf

Kotti & Co, Berlin https://kottiundco.net/english

Lampedusa in Hamburg http://lampedusa-in-hamburg.org/

Napuli speaks at the UN conference on Migration https://vimeo.com/80632864

Oranienplatz refugees' site, Berlin https://oplatz.net/

Pressekonferenz der Flüchtlinge in der Ohlauer Straße, 27.06.2014 https://www.youtube.com/watch?v=yilF-UWoICY

Recht auf Stadt – Never Mind the Papers, Hamburg https://nevermindthepapers.noblogs.org/about/

Recht auf Stadt, Hamburg http://rechtaufstadt.net/about.html

Rote Flora, Hamburg https://rote-flora.de/

The Refugee Radio Network, Hamburg http://www.refugeeradionetwork.net/projekt.html

World Refugee Let Fear Go Tour, Berlin https://www.facebook.com/wrlfg/

CHAPTER 7

The Anti-discrimination Activism in a Backlash Context: A Panorama of the French Situation

Etienne Pingaud

This chapter explores the challenges for anti-discrimination activism in France in a backlash context. It aims to understand the shift in French discrimination policies during the past decades and the implications of the strong conservative countermovement. The chapter focuses on LGBT rights activists/activism. It looks at the transformations of daily activism, the practical tools and concrete work and on the way activists perceive their activism. The question is what these political and ideological changes mean for activists involved in anti-discrimination movements. On the one hand, the struggle against discrimination has become mainstream; on the other hand, it has been made more difficult by the intellectual and ideological "backlash" that emerged in France in the 2000s.

E. Pingaud (✉)
Université de Paris 8-Saint-Denis, Saint-Denis, France

© The Author(s) 2019
B. Siim et al. (eds.), *Citizens' Activism and Solidarity Movements*, Palgrave Studies in European Political Sociology, https://doi.org/10.1007/978-3-319-76183-1_7

The Common Threat: The Strong Conservative Countermovement

The 2017 French presidential election is an illustration of the recent evolution in the issue of discrimination; Marine Le Pen, who was present in the second round, managed to gain more than 21% of the first-round votes. François Fillon, the traditional right-wing candidate and for a long time main favorite in the race, came third with 20%. Both are part of a strong conservative ideological backlash, and both have argued that some legal discrimination can be positive, thus giving political legitimacy to it. Marine Le Pen claims that there are categories of foreigners who should not benefit from the French welfare state. For example, illegal immigrants should be excluded from the system that allows them to be admitted in hospitals and medical centers. François Fillon promoted activists of the movement called Sens Commun (a conservative organization that opposes same-sex marriage) to strategic positions in his campaign staff and gave them a key role in the organization of meetings and events.[1]

The electoral results reveal the context in which anti-discrimination activists must now operate. They are facing a new challenge: the rise of a powerful conservative ideological trend. The main leaders of this French backlash keep targeting anti-racism and LGBT rights as symbols of the weakness of modern societies governed by "good feelings" (bon sentiment). Popular support for these goals is currently declining, and political leaders and activists promoting legal discrimination have managed to gather thousands of people.

However, new legal instruments against discrimination have been installed in the past two decades. The French state has defined discrimination as a specific and official problem that must be solved, and state institutions may be the first activists to denounce governmental measures or projects. As an example, by denouncing the living conditions of migrants in the Calais Camp, the "Defenseur des droits" obtained significant improvements. These changes transform the opportunities for anti-discrimination organizations and activists. They increasingly use legal and juridical resources and less political classic repertoires like demonstrations or sit-ins in their actions.

---

[1] After his defeat, he publicly regretted giving Sens Commun a leading role.

In order to observe and understand how these developments affect activism against discrimination, the French team[2] decided to investigate people involved in these movements. The focus is on the transformations of daily activism, on the practical tools and concrete work as well as on the way activists perceive it. Our method is a crossing between sociology of social movements and cultural anthropology's "non-directive" or participant observation approach (Mathieu 2011; Olivier de Sardan 1995). We organized two focus group discussions of activists in LGBT rights and anti-racist organizations.

In the current context of a strong intellectual backlash in France, all organizations fighting for equal rights also have to fight against the new visibility of these opinions. More than ever, they have to prove the legitimacy of their actions. All the activists we met during the fieldwork told us about these difficulties. All of them have to look for new resources, new tools and new media to promote their ideas and see their struggle as harder than before. The LGBT group is at the center of the following discussion.

THE ROLE OF PUBLIC POLICIES ON THE ACTIVISM AGAINST DISCRIMINATION

Considering the evolution of anti-discrimination activism, it is relevant to notice that French state has made important legal changes in the past decades. Many institutional actors focus on the issue of discrimination and have instruments to stop or reduce it. Several laws concerning ethnic discrimination, gender and sexual orientation have been passed.

For activists, this situation marks a real turning point. On the one hand, the fight against discrimination has become a central institutional issue on which numerous new state actors—judges, teachers, local and national administrative leaders and employees—are now working. This can be seen as the result of all the activists' work. Anti-discrimination is now a mainstream and consensual topic, but it is less political than before and the fight against discrimination is moderate and focuses on individual cases. In comparison, most activists emphasize the political system that produces discrimination. However, the state instruments offer new opportunities for activists. The laws give them the possibility to claim for the application of justice. Specialized justice courts have become a new central place to defend people exposed to discrimination.

---

[2] The French team was made up of two researchers: Annie Benveniste and Etienne Pingaud.

The "Discrimination" Shift

During the late 1990s, several political initiatives inequalities in representation were implemented across different social fields: academics, social movements, NGOs and even factions of political parties joined to demand better official representation of minorities. The baseline of their action was the supposed failure of the French model of integration of immigrants (the French "republican model", which is usually contrasted with the Anglo-Saxon assimilation model, cf. Schnapper 1992[3]). In the classic French conception, the main principle is invisibility of specific identities (below the national identity). Unlike in many other countries, no minority, not even religious minorities, can be recognized by the state. Consequently, any official policy based on *affirmative action*, in which identification of minorities is central, is impossible. Increasingly, however, new claims and new kinds of association, often led by "second generation" immigrants, have reinforced political expression of minority identities (Guenif-Souilamas 2000). Various kinds of demands have emerged, for instance, official recognition of memories of immigration, slavery or colonization, minority quotas in public TV staff and increased diversity in political parties' leadership.

Increased public visibility of minorities has contributed to the paradigm shift in the late 1990s to the early 2000s. The activists defending them have benefited from of two favorable events: the victory of the left coalition in the 1997 French Parliament elections and the transposition of EU's "race equality directive" into French law in 2003[4] (Simon 2004; Guiraudon 2004). First, several members of the leftist Lionel Jospin's government, helped by counselors and administrative staff, played a central role in establishing a new conception of policies about racism.[5] Inspired by the first wave of academic work and opinion polls on discrimination, they sought ways to break the classic French conception. They gave birth to the first official anti-discrimination instruments and thus introduced the concept of discrimination to French policies (Chappe 2011). This recognition marks a real shift in France. It implies that the state officially recognizes inequalities linked to certain "properties" like ethnic origin and skin color and LGBT and that some groups in the population therefore do not have the same opportunities for social

---

[3] The classic philosophical debates about insertion, the role of cultures and multiculturalism came later in France than in many other countries due to this singular view of the phenomenon.

[4] http://europa.eu/rapid/press-release_MEMO-07-257_en.htm?locale=en

[5] For example, Martine Aubry, Minister of Work and Social issues 1997–2002.

mobility. In other words, it is no longer only "racism" and hate speech that can be taken to court but all everyday actions that include discrimination, hiring, housing, treatment by institutions and even access to nightclubs. In addition, people in positions of power can be sued for discrimination.

Finally, the adoption of EU's so-called race directive [Directive Race] definitely changed the French conception. The history of the directive has already been told several times (Guiraudon 2004; Chappe 2011). It was quickly adopted after Jorg Haider's FPO joined the Austrian government in 2000,[6] and it was incorporated in French law the following year. The directive officially recognizes the principle of "indirect discrimination" against people of "specific race or ethnic origin" and LGBT. It requires member countries to establish specific anti-discrimination authorities. The race directive became the legal basis of a new official recognition of the phenomenon.

A MAIN INSTRUMENT: THE EQUAL OPPORTUNITIES AND ANTI-DISCRIMINATION COMMISSION[7] (HALDE)

To execute the recommendations and obligations in the directive, the government created the Equal Opportunities and Anti-Discrimination Commission, born in 2005. HALDE is an independent administrative authority, which has the right to judge all discrimination, direct or indirect, that is prohibited by law or an international agreement to which France is a signatory. Its 12 members are appointed by the President, the Senate, the National Assembly, the Council of State and two other national bodies. It was conceived from the beginning as a judicial instrument, and not a political resource. HALDE handles individual cases according to the EU directive. The applied definition of discrimination must be as close as possible to the EU standard to avoid debates of qualification (Chappe 2011). The success of the new authority is obvious and immediate. It provokes real change by allowing victims of discrimination to sue and obtain damages, and the number of cases has increased every year since HALDE was established: 1410 in 2005, 4058 in 2006, 6222 in 2007 and so on. Most of the cases concern discrimination based on ethnic origin and in the professional sphere, that is, employment, career promotions and so on (HALDE 2008).

---

[6] The FPO received 27% of the votes in the 1999 Austrian elections, and a government coalition of the right-wing OVP and FPO was formed. Haider was not a member of this administration.

[7] In French: Haute autorité de lutte contre les discriminations et pour l'égalité.

In 2011, HALDE and the issue of discrimination, which has become a mission of the state, became integrated in a new constitutional function, in French the "Defenseur des droits" (Defender of rights). This means that in less than ten years, the topic of discrimination, which was unknown before the late 1990s, has become a constitutional issue.

In addition to the planned measures against racism and discrimination, the French state has established several programs in public institutions in recent years. The aim is to offer education and information about discrimination and to prevent that the state itself produces discrimination. As far as education and information, schools are obviously a central place for these programs. The second aim is more focused on public employees and agents to make sure their daily activities respect the mind of the struggle.

The role of the school as place of production and reproduction of social (Bourdieu and Passeron 1964), ethnic (Felouzis and Perroton 2009) and LGBT discrimination is well known and well documented by social sciences literature. However, the state sees the school as the key institution, as a "state antibody" against discrimination. Discrimination is a mandatory subject on all curricula[8] at all levels of French school, elementary as well as high school. Lessons on discrimination are directly planned, and the struggle against discriminations appears in many ways in regular school events (e.g., women's day, anti-racism day) or in school bylaws.

School policies have integrated as a key issue the education to combat discrimination. The School Ministry now provides official approval of "civil society" antibodies, especially associations. Approved associations are authorized to do interventions in classrooms to prevent discrimination and any related behavior. Many actions and initiatives are organized by these, for example, presentations, theater plays and testimonies, to show pupils and students the daily consequences of discriminations (Lorcerie 2009).

Concerning the second aim, many state agencies and institutions have their own anti-discrimination programs. They usually have two targets: clients and employees. At the first level, many local employment agencies (Pôle Emploi) offer information, help and advice about discrimination and explain how to react, including suing, to discrimination. The programs are made for a "working-class" audience, including immigrants and children of immigrants who are potential victims of any form of discrimination. These state institutions can be considered as real grassroots antibodies, playing the same role as the associations or teachers who do interventions in classrooms. At the second level,

---

[8] http://eduscol.education.fr/cid47746/prevention-des-discriminations.html

there are programs for state employees to prevent them from practicing explicit or implicit discriminations. Programs for state employees are not new, but before they were mainly aimed at teachers, street and social workers, to familiarize them with intercultural differences and aspects (cf. Escafré-Dublet 2008; Keyhani 2013). They now concern all types of discrimination and all public employees who have contact with clients.

Activists agree on using the new anti-discrimination resources provided by the state and think that the LGBT movement should take more cases to court. This is where all rights were won by same-sex couples in the USA. Although the French legal tradition is different, there are judicial tools that the activists have not exploited and they could be a great opportunity to make gains. In France, activists still do not use the law and the courts enough, although it is a good and sure way to obtain rights. The idea illustrates another gap between the LGBT movement and their opponents, namely, the fact that "La Manif pour tous" already works with a large panel of lawyers and legal specialists who can take the struggle against same-sex marriage (the so-called "anti-marriage" struggle—"le combat contre le marriage pour tout") to another level and develop arguments based on the texts and, often, on antiquated conceptions of the law, since anti-LGBT lawyers sometimes make arguments based on Roman law. There is a need to consider this legal approach, maybe in opposition with liberal conception of the movement really present among LGBT activists, but which proved to have more efficiency than politics or many fieldwork activities. The European Court of Human Rights has often made judgements in favor of gay and lesbian couples, and its Anglo-Saxon inspiration in its decisions should be seen as a great chance for all minority rights activism.

OUR EMPIRICAL MATERIAL: THE LGBT FOCUS GROUP

We decided to include this diversity in our fieldwork and analysis. Activists from different organizations, defending different conceptions of anti-discrimination activism and using different strategies to protest, were invited to join our focus groups and interviews. To the extent possible, we adopted a non-directive anthropological methodology in the interviews based on participant observation (e.g., Mathieu 2011; Olivier de Sardan 1995). We let the activists talk, in order to understand what they, in their own words, call discrimination, how they chose their strategies and leading issues, or what they consider good ways to counter hate speech.

To collect heuristic empirical data, we finally organized two focus groups, one for anti-racism activists and the other dedicated to LGBT issues, which will be the focus of the following discussion. This division has limits, but it also reflects the state of the anti-discrimination movement in France. In most of the cases, organizations fighting racism are not the same as the ones fighting homophobia. They may share common values and some activists may be involved in both causes, but anti-racists and LGBT rights defenders belong to different sectors in the "space of social movements" (Mathieu 2011). They may sometimes participate in the same demonstrations, but their daily work is mainly focused on a central issue. This is partly the result of the history of these organizations: most LGBT rights organizations were born in the 1980s and 1990s when AIDS ravaged the gay communities (Martel 1996). Moreover, in the French context, the concept of discrimination that includes the two issues has only been recently adopted by activists (cf. *infra*). The analogy between racism and homophobia was not a key point before.

About the Focus Groups

Both focus group panels were formed to gather activists from different trends and organizations. For the LGBT focus group interview, we interviewed members of the LGBT Centre of Paris, the French Inter-LGBT (which organizes the annual gay pride), FIERES, Acceptess-T (for transsexual rights) and the LGBT journalists' association. The anti-racist focus group consisted of members of MRAP, Ras l'Front, Collectif contre l'Islamophobie, Indigènes and La banlieue contre le racism.

Despite the differences between their respective issues, their opponents and collective-action repertoire (Tilly 2004), activists share common views on which we focus in this study. All of them deplore the new difficulty of being an anti-discrimination activist in the current political and intellectual context, and all identify the distance between political parties and organizations as one of the main transformations of these past years.

LGBT Rights and the Success of the "Anti-marriage" Movement[9]

As far as the anti-discrimination activists are concerned, it is important to notice that the LGBT movement has known the same form of disqualification from the new conservatives and new right intellectuals that presents it as a lobby serving the private interests of a minority, which is only popular

---

[9] The French term is "combat contre le mariage pour tout".

in socially oriented urban highly educated audiences. The LGBT struggle has never been as strong in France as the anti-racist struggle, partly because LGBT issues are only discussed in "extraordinary" cases as the votes of the civil union (called "PACS" 1999) or same-sex wedding (2013). In the 1970s, it was strongly linked to leftist organizations,[10] known as autonomous association and institutions. They are familiar with the classic debates of each minority in France about the necessity to defend a "gay" identity or, on the contrary, to refuse any kind of specific consideration (Martel 1999). However, in the 1980s, they had to face to the AIDS epidemic, which defined the terms of LGBT action for a while. The main organizations, like AIDES or Act-Up, demanded an end to discrimination in paramedical and medical treatments. A decade later, the topic of "homophobia" began to be invested by activists and associations, giving birth to new tools in the fight against anti-LGBT (e.g., SOS Homophobia). It was not until the 1990s when civil union began to be discussed that a new form of LGBT activism entered the political arena. It faced the growing movement of contestation led by Catholic and other religious groups who opposed a change of the family laws. Fourteen years later, the same configuration, but deeply amplified, was heard in debates about same-sex marriage. LGBT activists, even if they "won" the fight of influence on politics, were criticized by many people, including left-wing politicians, as a minority or sometimes community "lobby".

Many of the focus group as well as the individual interviews offered an opportunity to look back on the huge anti-gay rights movement in France in 2012–2014. Led by Catholic activists and organizations, this movement managed to organize demonstrations gathering around a million of people in the streets of Paris. An observer even called it a "conservative May 68" to emphasize the power of this protest (Brustier 2014). All the right-wing and far-right parties wanted to join the movement (except Marine Le Pen herself, who never clearly gave her opinion on this issue[11]). All participants in the focus group agreed that the period was marked by a surprising and visible homophobia, freed from all the debates and mobilizations that took place against same-sex marriage. Since the beginning of the controversies, following the election of socialist François Hollande,

---

[10] For example, the Homosexual Front of Revolutionary Action (FHAR), founded by a leftist activist, is very famous in France.

[11] Several leaders of Front National were present during the demonstrations, for instance, Marion Maréchal-Le Pen (Marine Le Pen's niece).

who promised to open marriage to same-sex couples, a strong opposition gained force, imposing its presence in the media and opening debates built upon previously unheard arguments to justify its positions. All participants, except two, said that they were astonished by the profusion and diversity of ways the opponents have managed to establish the legitimacy of discriminatory point of views ("many of us shared this feeling of total surprise, like a slap in the face"). For the two exceptions, their specific environments allowed prepared them for homophobia. One was a student in a Catholic school ("I was in a Catholic high school, I really felt it coming"); the other was transsexual, a particular condition that tends "to cumulate stigma and consequently attacks against us".

The strength of the "anti-marriage" movement against "same-sex marriage" was discussed for a long time, partly because it directly questions and reflects the weakness of the LGBT organizations, which won the adoption of the law but seemed to have lost the battle of ideas, numbers and dynamic of this period. It emphasizes that the struggle against homophobia in France is quite weak, split into many small associations or groups, and unable to resist the power of a movement like La Manif pour tous. All participants pointed to this gap, which is somewhat surprising because studies show that the majority of the French people support same-sex marriage. However, the leadership of La Manif pour tous is the expression of the decline of a homosexual activism that used to be very strong. The fact that many LGBT leaders and major organizations have left political activism shows that real conquests have been made in the past decades, but this has left an empty field when an unexpected situation arises and re-imposes the issue of sexual orientation into the public and political debates.

Meanwhile the LGBT movement seems to be too focused on gay pride, which affects the public perception of gays and lesbians ("we are often seen as the illustration of modernity, of neoliberalism, hedonism, individualism"). There is a lack of political conscience, which is one of the main conditions of the sudden rise of Islamophobia during the years 2012–2014. The main problem is that the opponents are really well organized, structured and united around the group who controls the representation and public relations of La manif pour tous ("We faced a real social movement, structured"). This particular aspect, even more than the violence of some slogans, has been a shock for the activists we met ("nobody could have planned the strength, the length and the professionalization of the movement"). During the first months of the fight, the opponents seemed to have one voice, giving the impression of an incredible human mass convinced of its own legitimacy to say the truth, enforced by the unexpected number of participants to all the activities they proposed. For example, in the demonstrations against same-sex marriage, the dress code defined by La Manif pour tous was strictly adopted and respected by participants: women and girls were dressed in pink, men and boys in blue. This makes a very powerful impression as a million people walk the Parisian streets, and it illustrates authentic unity, which is totally missing among the supporters of same-sex marriage. La Manif pour tous was able to organize and control the attitudes of the demonstrators.

This particular characteristic is a way to understand what the concrete needs are when the struggle is based on the ability to diffuse representations in public spaces and speeches. It emphasizes all the elements that LGBT organizations miss to oppose *"and say a strict no"* to this social movement. La Manif pour tous had plenty of funds and benefited from arguments and technologies developed abroad, especially in the USA ("There is an import of US methods"; "it's an international market of hate"). These financial resources and this ability to appropriate instruments that functioned elsewhere allowed the organization to establish a real professional staff serving the cause of anti-marriage. This is another resource that the supporters do not have, since they are mostly activists who invest their own time and funds ("It was really professionalized, with all these communication specialists, and real staff. We don't have that"). La Manif pour tous not only has the necessary funds to build a movement, it has a lot of people dedicated to the diffusion of their ideas, making it possible to design real media strategies to increase the movement. The central role of Frigide Barjot, the organization's spokesperson, was mentioned several times during the focus group interview. She is a perfect example of the communication skill that characterizes the anti-marriage movement. She claims to be a "fashion Catholic", gay friendly and known for her proximity with a lot of gay celebrities in Paris. She is a perfect figure to represent a movement does not want to be accused of homophobia. She epitomizes the professionalization of the mobilization; she is able to control the image it gives to others. In this perspective, it becomes clear for the LGBT activists that opposing the movement and preventing homophobia by large campaigns would require the ability to gather similar resources ("we have nothing, not even people"). Meanwhile, the opponents will still be stronger than the defenders of LGBT rights.

One of the activists, Clemence, mentions that the anti-gay rights movement, as surprising it has been, is not a new thing in French debates.

Strong demonstrations, with a solid homophobic component, were organized in various towns in the late 1990s, to protest against the Civil Pact of Solidarity, the first type of union allowed for gays and lesbian couples, which was instituted by the left government led by Lionel Jospin: "They already had the experience of PACS and CUCS.[12] They knew that homophobic speech was not accepted in French society. So they developed other arguments". The leaders and spokespersons of La Manif pour tous learned their lesson and came up with new and less conservative justifications. They often use PACS to oppose same-sex marriage, claiming that homosexual couples already have rights that are similar to heterosexual couples' rights, and therefore there is no need to question the centuries-old traditional union between a woman and a man.

With such historical, political, rhetorical and of course financial resources, the movement kept growing during the time of the controversies, reaching the historical level of the largest demonstrations in French history. Its strength allowed it to take control, from day one, of the agenda, the controversial issues and the media sphere. The pro-marriage camp was unable to organize so quickly, ("We had no organization, nothing at all"), and it took it a long time to mobilize real opposition. In sum, the anti-marriage movement was in a position to impose the temporalities of the struggle as well as the legitimate points of debates. Consequently, the activists of the panel we interviewed missed time to prepare the debates and all the instruments of pedagogy that could have stopped the omnipresence of La Manif pour tous in the media ("the debate was confiscated, we could not debate, we did not have the pedagogy"; "They imposed the debate on us"). It is partly this logic that made the arguments of the anti-marriage way more clear and heard than the others. Their timely engagement and strong organization allowed them to present themselves as non-homophobic, which was a key point in the controversial movement. It took too much time for the activists of the panel before they reacted and made the population understand why the opponents were homophobic.

The focus group discussants did not agree on how to characterize the positions and rhetorical aspects of La Manif pour tous. Most of them found that the main problem was that the spokespersons and leaders largely avoided homophobic speech and similar activities within their own activi-

---

[12] CUCS was one of the first propositions in the 1990s to propose rights for same-sex couples. It later became a model for PACS, the new proposition that was finally adopted in 1999.

ties. The debate strategically focused on the major points and issues like assisted reproductive technology or surrogacy to link them to the marriage topic ("they never talk about homosexuality, but always ART or surrogacy"). It was easy for them to denounce harsh slogans and hateful statements made in the demonstrations ("the CUCS and PACS debates taught them how not to be homophobic"; "the speeches have clearly changed in the past years"). It was therefore difficult to counter the most prominent figures of the struggle by emphasizing hate speech against gays and lesbians. However, other participants in the focus group categorize this situation as one of the biggest failures of the LGBT movement in terms of supporting same-sex marriage. Leaving the control of the arguments to the opponents, the activists did not take the time to develop easy arguments to show all the forms of homophobia that are present in La Manif pour tous texts and speeches. Another activist, Delphine, for example, considers that the only claim against legal discriminations based on sexual orientation is a demonstration of *homophobia, lesbophobia and transphobia*, a claim so far not enough used in the struggles to oppose the anti-marriage mobilized.

However, all focus group participants find that the movement as such has been a pretext for a strong liberation of hate concerning same-sex couples, lesbians, gay, bi and trans. The terms used to describe the situation vary ("homophobia without complexes", "freedom of homophobia", "return of the repressed"), but in all the interventions, the focus group participants make clear that throughout the debates they encountered an unknown climate of homophobia that far exceeded earlier challenges to LGBT rights. One example is Mathieu who recalls a physical attack against a young Parisian gay man, Wilfried. A picture of him after the attack went viral on social networks, and Mathieu says that "everybody knew the attack was going to happen", implying that the conditions of physical danger for gays and lesbians were in place. The repeated presence of LGBT issues in news features, increased mobilization of actions and activities, the progressive loss of control of La Manif pour tous to the more radical anti-marriage activists—all these elements made homosexuality a central issue in the period—with many speeches and ideas circulating, even the most hateful. The ordinary repression of comments, remarks and judgments about homophobia seems to have stopped in a period in which the considerations of homosexuality can become mere "opinions" on a news topic, possibly explaining this unexpected liberation of homophobia in several sectors of French society.

Being Political Again?

The transformations of the state have led to a significant change in the repertoires used by the activists. The skills needed are not the same anymore: being able to sue the perpetrators of discrimination is now as important as being able to make people show up for protest rallies or demonstrations. Most of the activists we discussed with emphasized the limits of these changes: activism is more focused on individual cases of discriminations. They find that there is a need to be political again and to defend a global cause against discrimination, beyond the individual experiences of the victims.

For the anti-racist activists we met, the political fight has to be linked with a new intellectual conception of discrimination. Four of the focus group participants agreed on the necessity to consider new theoretical frameworks as "postcolonial studies", seeing in them an interesting perspective on racism. In the French context, being postcolonial anti-racists would mean to emphasize all aspects of ordinary racism resulting from French colonialism (Bancel et al. 2005). The state should be denounced, for example, for the treatment of immigrants, which is still based on colonial perceptions of the others: a French "civilized" way of life is considered superior, and all other cultures are seen as threats to it.

The LGBT rights activists proposed a large variety of concrete actions during the focus group, most of which had so far not been used enough by the LGBT organizations. For Mathieu, one key point is the ability to keep track of homophobic acts and attacks, which means building statistics that document the development in homophobia in certain periods ("We should have real indicators that would allow the media to show that the rise in homophobia is authentic. Statistic measures that would be reliable and not contestable"). A certain form of quantification can be easily used by LGBT and pro-marriage activists as evidence of the negative effects of the mass demonstrations against the law. This work of census is done since several years by a big association named. For many years, SOS Homophobia,[13] a large organization that is closed to the authorities, has been conducting this kind of word. However, even though their work is appreciated ("They really do a great job"), there is a problem concerning the methodology,

---

[13] SOS Homophobia was founded in 1994 and provides psychological and sometimes material support to gay and lesbian victims of exclusion or homophobia. It is one of the most important groups in terms of size, number of people involved and available funds to start concrete initiatives. They were invited to the focus group but declined at the last minute.

which always misses large aspects of ordinary homophobia. For example, the acts that are recorded are based on sources that imply that the victims tell their stories, for instance in a report to the police or a confession to members of the association. The records need to include people who can't talk, who can't complain, but who are still victims of the climate of homophobia. Clemence states that very few transsexual people are willing to report direct and physical attacks ("Trans people never go to police stations, especially if they have not changed their official identity, they are afraid to be suspected").

But one of the main priorities emphasized by the participants is building unity around the cause of LGBT rights. The feeling of loss after the huge anti-marriage movement of 2012–2013 is closely linked to this inability to mobilize a united and strong LGBT voice. The dispersion of organization and lack of investment in all forms of political activities ("LGBT activism has quietly declined") have left the "community" without a major structure of representation, without resources to express an LGBT point of view that could be validated by a large part of the community. The problem is reinforced by the fact than La Manif pour tous has managed to install a common set of values to defend in public spaces, giving this specific impression of unity ("They had common values, it is clear, they know what values they want, a return to the good old days when everything was clear, even if that time never existed for real"). Common issues are missing in the LGBT movement, and to most participants, this is a paradox: The progress of LGBT rights during the past decades reduced the culture of activism in the community. There is no more urgent common fight like legalization of homosexuality before 1981 or the interpellation of the authorities in the 1980s and 1990s to establish real programs of prevention against AIDS and its huge consequences on the LGBT communities. Mathieu thinks that one of the goals the LGBT organizations should set is the transmission of the memory and the legacy of its specific history of lesbian and gay activism, to remember that the struggle for rights is a form of duty associated with the tough history of a community who suffered a lot due to discrimination and diseases. He suggests that the fights of the oldest factions of the movement should be known and regrets that the youngest don't even know the main initiatives of the LGBT movement of the 1970s and 1980s, for instance, the famous *Gai pied* newspaper, which played a central role in the defense of the community ("Young people don't even know what 'Gai pied' is and the role it played in the past. We should publish the different editions to make it known to everybody").

The question of the links with the established political organizations has been discussed for a long time, as it is seen as a key explanation of the decline of LGBT activism. The problem is that the LGBT movement has handed over its cause to the political sphere. As a result, it is impossible for LGBT communities to build a strong, independent political movement. Flora says, "We gave too much to politics", and Mathieu thinks a large part of the problem is that LGBT activists have "left to the LGBT initiative to the Socialist Party". All participants seem to be very critical of the manner the government led the debates that allowed the same-sex marriage bill to be voted in the Parliament. It made too many concessions to the opponents, particularly about opportunities for gay and lesbian couples to have children, including assistance reproductive technology and surrogacy. Politicians are seen as a problem because they are difficult to deal with but are necessary to obtain concrete rights. The participants do not trust them and make clear that they are a last recourse after different grassroots activities, which must be the center of their daily fight.

Finally, Clemence proposed a progressive shift in the arguments used by LGBT activists. For her, one problem is the conceptual level of the legal requirements, which can be advantageous but tend to put human considerations about LGBT people in the background. She thinks that the LGBT movement has insisted too much on "equality", which was the main slogan used to defend the principle of same-sex marriage. However, it would have been a good thing to also mention human factors, especially the specific vulnerabilities of LGBT people: higher suicide rates, widespread depression and frequent health problems ("We should have placed the human aspect in the center, not only equality … It is good to remember, because it is important, that suicide rates are very high in the LGBT community"). The goal is to break the widespread idea that most LGBT people are wealthy and healthy, to talk about the human difficulties they have to face and handle with.

Conclusion

This chapter shows how activism against racism and homophobia in France has changed during the two last decades. On the one hand, these transformations can be seen as a positive result of the general social changes, which means that people from ethnic minorities or people with LGBT orientations are in much better positions than before. On the other hand, activism for rights and equality is facing a new challenge: the rise of a powerful conservative ideological trend. The main leaders of this French backlash keep targeting anti-racism and LGBT rights as symbols of the weakness of modern societies governed by so-called good feelings (bons sentiments). Popular support for these goals is currently declining, and political leaders and activists promoting legal discrimination have managed to gather thousands of people. Marine Le Pen, candidate of the Front National, came second in the last presidential election with more votes than candidates of mainstream left- and right-wing parties. Four years earlier, almost a million people demonstrated in Paris against same-sex marriage.

In this political context, it is important that activists can find new resources in state institutions. The prevention of discrimination has been a state priority since the early 2000s. Agencies, laws and measures have been installed to counter all forms of discrimination. They illustrate the ability of activists to make their cause visible and, finally, consensual. However, this situation also reflects the leadership of one conception of discrimination: individual cases. Support for victims rather than the denouncement of daily, systematic racism or homophobia is now the center of the activism. The different activists we met, who are all involved in organizations fighting discrimination, would like to add more political content to their activism. Most of them are looking for ways to rebuild a political and more radical movement to stop discrimination.

REFERENCES

Bancel, N., Blanchard, P., & Lemaire, S. (2005). *La fracture coloniale*. Paris: La Découverte.
Bourdieu, P., & Passeron, J.-C. (1964). *Les héritiers*. Paris: Minuit.
Brustier, G. (2014). *Le mai 68 conservateur: que restera-t-il de la Manif pour tous?* Paris: Editions du Cerf.
Chappe, V.-A. (2011). Le cadrage juridique, une ressource politique? La création de la HALDE comme solution au problème de l'effectivité des normes anti-discrimination (1998–2005). *Politix, 94*, 107–130.
Escafré-Dublet, A. (2008). L'Etat et la culture des immigrés, 1974–1984. *Histoire@Politique, 4*, 15–15.
Felouzis, G., & Perroton, N. (2009). Grandir entre pairs à l'école. Ségrégation ethnique et reproduction sociale dans le système éducatif français. *Actes de la recherche en sciences sociales, 180*, 92–100.
Guenif-Souilamas, N. (2000). *Des beurettes*. Paris: Pluriel.
Guiraudon, V. (2004). Construire une politique europeenne de lutte contre les discriminations: l'histoire de la directive "race". *Sociétés contemporaines, 53*, 11–32.

Haute autorité de lutte contre les discriminations et pour l'égalité (2008), Rapport annuel 2008.
Keyhani, N. (2013). Former pour dépolitiser. L'administration des immigrés comme cible de l'action publique. *Gouvernement et action publique*, 4, 91–114.
Lorcerie, F. (2009). L'école, son territoire et l'ethnicité. *Revue Projet, 312,* 64–71.
Martel, F. (1996). *Le rose et le noir: les homosexuels en France depuis 1968.* Paris: Points.
Mathieu, L. (2011). *L'Espace des mouvements sociaux.* Bellecombe-en-Bauges: Editions du Croquant.
Olivier de Sardan, J. P. (1995). La politique du terrain. *Enquête*, vol.1 (online version)
Schnapper, D. (1992). *L'Europe des immigrés, essai sur les politiques d'immigration.* Paris: Francois Bourin.
Simon, P. (2004). Introduction au dossier: la construction des discriminations. *Sociétés contemporaines,* n°53, pp.5–10
Tilly, C. (2004). Les origines du répertoire d'action collective contemporaine en France et en Grande-Bretagne. *Vingtième Siècle. Revue d'histoire,* 4, 89–108.

Links

http://europa.eu/rapid/press-release_MEMO-07-257_en.htm?locale=en

CHAPTER 8

Racism, Post-democracy, and Economy That Kills: The Challenges of Civil Society Movements in Italy

Giovanna Campani

INTRODUCTION

The rise of the far right and, in general, of right-wing populist parties in Europe has provoked concern that liberal democracies may be threatened in their essence. "Authoritarianism"[1] may induce a shift toward "illiberal" democracy (Zakaria 1997),[2] which would affect minorities' and migrants'

---

[1] It refers to the forms of government that place the authority (of the state, of the leader) above citizens' freedom.
[2] In "Decline in democracy spreads across the globe as authoritarian leaders arise," Ari Shapiro and Larry Diamond comment: "Turkey is not the only country where democratic ideals are eroding. Democracy is retreating in Venezuela, where President Nicolas Maduro is consolidating power. In the Philippines, Rodrigo Duterte has jailed his political opponents. In Poland and Hungary, leaders are cracking down on the press and trying to control the judiciary" (NPR 2017).

G. Campani (✉)
Intercultural Education, Gender Anthropology and Intercultural Communication, City, UK

© The Author(s) 2019
B. Siim et al. (eds.), *Citizens' Activism and Solidarity Movements*,
Palgrave Studies in European Political Sociology,
https://doi.org/10.1007/978-3-319-76183-1_8

rights, gender issues (aborbtion, LGBT rights), reinforce racism and legitimate hate speech. In the Western experience, democracy and liberalism usually go hand in hand to the extent that "democracy" in popular usage has become shorthand for liberal democracy (Hamid 2014). The same core of "Western liberal values: human solidarity, openness toward those looking for a better future, diversity as an asset" (Kauffmann 2017: 10) would be threatened by populist insurgency.

The danger is concrete: mainstreaming of right-wing populist ideas—that is, the rejection of migrants and refugees, the refusal of multiculturalism in the name of a homogeneous "real" people, and a mono-cultural identity[3]—affects political majorities, government parties, and elected leaders. European examples are Jaroslaw Kaczynski, the head of Poland's ruling nationalist Law and Justice Party, and Prime Minister Viktor Orban of Hungary. Under their rule, Polish and Hungarian governments have assumed positions on migration and asylum that are clearly abandoning Western liberal values. As Kauffmann writes:

> For the first time since World War II, these values have come under attack in the West. Not from hostile foreign powers. Not from domestic fringe elements or extremist political movements, which we have come to see as a testimony to the pluralism of our democracies. This time, the assault is coming from within and from the top — from democratically elected leaders. Only a few of them. But enough to draw a line between two camps within the Western community, now divided by fundamental contradictions. (Kauffmann 2017: 10)

Among the "democratically elected leaders" assaulting the Western liberal values, Kauffmann mentions US President Donald Trump. His decision to rescind DACA, the Deferred Action for Childhood Arrivals program, allowing children of irregular migrants who were brought to the USA at an early age to stay in the country, is the last anti-liberal decision of the president. However, Trump's vision of migration reflects the mainstreaming of the right-wing populist ideas among the Republicans, who have become especially "hawkish." As Jan-Werner Mueller points out in an interview with Francis Wilkinson, "Trump did not win as the candidate of a third party committed to anti-establishment politics; rather, he became the leader of a very established party – with the blessing of very

---

[3] This idea seems to be the most successful. It is interesting that Alternative für Deutschland started as an anti-euro party and is presently focusing on migration and identity.

established figures such as Rudy Giuliani, Chris Christie and, especially, Newt Gingrich" (Wilkinson 2017). Trump's electoral victory was possible because of the "extreme partisanship" of the Republicans, whose positions are hard to distinguish from right-wing populism.

As a matter of fact, both in Europe and in the USA, right-wing populist ideas are not reserved for minority populist insurgents, generally excluded from power, but have become part of the European establishment's agenda, and they have been translated into government policies. Italy was one of the first European countries that experienced right-wing populism as a mainstream political force during the governments formed by Berlusconi[4] and his allies from the Northern League.

Italy might even be considered a sort of "laboratory of populism" that formed a "school," that is, established a model for "populist" leadership. It is not by chance that articles in different world journals compare Berlusconi and Donald Trump.[5] Being a laboratory for populism, Italy has been and is a laboratory for citizen mobilization against right-wing populism.

This chapter does not re-examine the long-lasting scientific debate about the concept of populism and the interpretations of the characters of the "populist" forces[6]; it looks at reactions to right-wing populism in government, using the Italian experience as an example, or, better, as a "prefiguration" of what would happen in other countries that elect populist governments at a later stage (e.g., now the USA). Considering the political opposition to right-wing populism, it describes the different positions of the parties and of the Italian "civil society," defined as the social relations, organizations, and actions that take place outside the government sector. The difference between civil society and civic society is, precisely, that the first is independent from the state and the institutional domain and the second concerns mainly local civic administrations and communities.[7]

---

[4] Berlusconi always defined himself as a "moderate," but he sought alliance with right-wing forces (like the neofascists). The Northern League was not originally characterized as a right-wing party, but it slowly drifted toward right-wing populist positions in matters of migration.

[5] See, for example, https://www.theguardian.com/world/2016/nov/21/if-berlusconi-is-like-trump-what-can-italy-teach-america.

[6] Political science has questioned and continues to question the macro-phenomenon of this "uncomfortable host of democracy," as Professor Marco Tarchi, one of the most acute Italian scholars on the topic, defined it. It is also well known that approaches may differ (Canovan 1981; Panizza 2005; Laclau 2007).

[7] We do not use the term "social movement," and we always speak of civil society organizations. This corresponds to the self-definition of the organizations that were contacted during

The fieldwork, which consists of individual interviews and focus groups, initially concerned organizations, associations, and groups fighting the xenophobic, racist, and populist ideas that construct the "others," especially migrants and refugees, as enemies (hate speech). However, discussions that arose during the interviews and the focus groups shifted our focus toward democracy, post-democracy, civic engagement, and political participation. The interviewees expressed the general opinion that true democracy and civic participation are prerequisites for achieving more inclusion for nationals and migrants, to promote antiracist values and to build a just, equal society. In practice, organizations fighting racism and xenophobia have also fought to improve democracy, while organizations created to defend and promote democracy have also taken part in the antiracist movement.

The fieldwork involved different types of civil society organizations. In the first research phase, interviews and focus groups concerned organizations opposing racism and/or struggling for migrants' and refugees' integration, for example, secular NGOs, trade unions, and religious organizations. Given the importance of the religious organizations in the anti-racist battle, we organized a specific focus group with them concerning intercultural and inter-religious dialogue. Given the importance of the issue of democracy, associations fighting for universal rights and for authentic democracy—encouraging a high level of participation—were involved. To hear the point of view of the parties, representatives of "progressive" political parties (Democratic Party, SEL [Sinistra Ecologia Libertà or Left Ecology and Freedom], Tsipras List) were also interviewed. Finally, the Five Star Movement was included in the research due to its strong engagement in democratic participation.

The fieldwork[8] was conducted between the end of 2012 and summer 2014. The period included the final months of Mario Monti's technocratic government,[9] which followed the fall of Berlusconi in November 2011,

the fieldwork. Many of them define themselves as civil society as opposed to the political establishment.

[8] Data are based on the research work implemented in the RAGE project—hate speech and "populist Othering" in Europe: through racism, age, gender looking glass (2013–2015)—financed by the Fundamental Rights and Citizenship Programme of the European Union. According to the project's methodology, qualitative interviews and focus groups were conducted with far-right extremists as well as with representatives of the forces opposing the "populist Othering" against minorities and migrants.

[9] The government was composed by "technicians," not by political actors. Monti's ministers were not members of political parties.

putting an end to the populist government experience, and the confrontation between the Tsipras Greek government and the European Union concerning austerity policies. This confrontation created a strong anti-European feeling in Italy. In the middle of the period, the Italian general elections in February 2013 marked the rise of Beppe Grillo's Five Star Movement.

Practically all interviewees expressed deep concern about what they called "the crisis of democracy." After having fought Berlusconi's populism and the Northern League's racism, civil society militants faced the "post-democratic" experience of Mario Monti's technocratic government (Crouch 2013), growing anti-EU popular sentiment and the rise of a new form of "progressive" populism—the Five Star Movement—whose declared aim is to undermine the political establishment in order to build new forms of democratic participation. The fieldwork is a snapshot of an important historical period when the democratic order is threatened by populism and post-democracy.

Let us repeat Colin Crouch's definition of post-democratic society from an interview in 2013: "A post-democratic society is one that continues to have and to use all the institutions of democracy, but in which they increasingly become a formal shell. The energy and innovative drive pass away from the democratic arena and into small circles of a politico-economic elite" (Crouch 2013).

The interviewees attributed the passage from a populist to a post-democratic situation to exogenous as well as endogenous factors: the world context—the neoliberal economic and societal patterns, the European context—the technocratic shift of the EU, and the specific Italian reality, characterized by a deep crisis of the political parties.

The interviewees expressed the dramatic awareness "that Italian democracy is in a sort of no-way-out situation where 'technocracy' [with reference to Mario Monti's technocratic government] *and* 'populism' face each other – as Scylla and Charybdis, the two horrible monsters who lived in the Straits of Messina – both ready to destroy democracy's frail ship."

The chapter is divided into six parts: the first describes the rise of civil society in opposition to Berlusconi's populist governments; the second considers the complex relationships between the civil society movements and the "mainstream" political parties, introducing the concepts of "econocracy" and "post-democracy"; the third, fourth, and fifth parts describe the organizations that have taken part in the fieldwork conducted between 2012 and 2014—active in anti-racism, migrants' integration, inter-religious dialogue, democracy, and the issues that have been debated; and finally, the sixth part presents the main outcomes of the fieldwork in terms of challenges for the civil society.

CRISIS OF DEMOCRACY AND CIVIL SOCIETY IN ITALY: OPPOSING POPULIST GOVERNMENTS

Italy experienced a long populist season under Silvio Berlusconi's center-right coalition governments, which were supported by the xenophobic Northern League. Berlusconi's conflicts of interest caused a democratic crisis in respect to media control, his attempts to curtail the autonomy of the legal system and to change the Italian Constitution. The Northern League's participation in the government gave rise to hate speech against migrants and repressive migratory policies.[10] Various forms of "resistance" to these multiple attacks on Italian democracy and human rights were auto-organized by what Italian scholars, journalists, and activists call "società civile"—"civil society."

The United Nations defines civil society as the "third sector" of society, along with government and business, comprising a large spectrum of non-governmental organizations.[11] However, more precise definitions make a distinction between "civic society" and "civil society." The former mainly refers to local government; the latter is "comprised of groups or organizations working in the interest of the citizens but operating outside of the governmental and for-profit sectors."[12] Civil society would then mean "voluntary action – undertaken by citizens not under the direction of any authority wielding the power of the state". This is the definition of voluntary action given by Lord Beveridge in his famous 1948 report of that name. Beveridge said that "the vigor and abundance of voluntary action – undertaken by citizens not under the direction of any authority wielding the power of the state – is one of the distinguishing marks of a free society!!"[13]

---

[10] Moreover, institutional racism was part of the Italian political experience between 2001 and 2006 and again between 2008 and 2011.
[11] http://www.un.org/en/sections/resources/civil-society/
[12] http://study.com/academy/lesson/what-is-a-civil-society-definition-examples.html
[13] The difference between civil and civic. Keynote speech to DTA Conference on 16 June 2008 by Laurence Demarco. http://www.senscot.net/view_art.php?viewid=7318.

"Civil society" refers to social relations outside the state or governmental control, that is, "nongovernmental organizations (NGOs) and associations that people belong to for social and political reasons: churches and church groups, community groups, youth groups, service organizations, interest groups, and academic institutions and organizations, for example. It also refers to the activities of these organizations."[14]

While civic society is not opposed to the state institutions, civil society functions independently from the state. In the case of Italy, civil society has clearly opposed the institutional political parties and the "political establishment," as the philosopher and political activist Paolo Flores D'Arcais (2011) describes[15]:

> When we speak of "civil society" today, in the sense of the struggles that have been self-organized for ten years in Italy against the regime (of Berlusconi), in controversy even with the acquiescent opposition parties, we are talking about something precise and recognizable: an anti-politics that really wants to radically innovate politics, bring it back to having a dignity that only existed at some crucial historical moments (Anti-Fascist Resistance, in a very special way), just because it is anti-establishment.

During the first Berlusconi government in 2001–2006, the "girotondi"—the "ring-a-ring-o'-roses"[16]—were one of the first examples of civil society activism (Tarchi, 2014). They developed independently of the existing political parties, which were seen as being too weak in their opposition to Berlusconi. The girotondi are a form of protest where the demonstrators hold hands and form chains around public buildings, for instance, the RAI (public television), in order to protect them from the reforms Berlusconi wanted to impose.

The girotondi movement had a short life. Berlusconi lost power in 2006, but he was re-elected in 2008. In 2009 it was Popolo Viola's—the Violet People—turn to organize large anti-Berlusconi protests (the demonstrators

---

[14] http://www.colorado.edu/conflict/peace/treatment/civilsoc.htm
[15] Paolo Flores D'Arcais is the director of the bimonthly journal *MicroMega*. "Flores has made his journal the organiser of the most uncompromising and effective front of hostility to Berlusconi in Italy, playing a political role unique in the EU for an intellectual publication of this kind. A year after the victory of the centre-right in 2001, it was from here that a wave of impressive mass protests against Berlusconi was launched, outside and against the passivity of the centre-left" (Anderson 2009: 16).
[16] See https://www.lrb.co.uk/v31/n05/perry-anderson/an-invertebrate-left.

wore violet scarves, shirts, hats, etc.). The movement was able to use social media networks, which created new possibilities for political mobilizations and participation from the bottom and gathered two million people to demonstrate against Silvio Berlusconi in November 2010.[17]

Like the girotondi movement, Popolo Viola was short-lived, but the civil action continued and even became more structured with the birth of associations like Libertà e Giustizia (Freedom and Justice), which was founded in 2002.[18] This association aimed precisely to be the junction between the best expressions of civil society and the official space of politics. Another association that played an important role, given the accusations that Berlusconi had contacts with the mafia, was Libera (FREE).[19] It was founded in March 1995 and aimed to support civil society in the fight against the mafia and promote the state of right. In addition, a myriad of organizations and NGOs, fighting racism while supporting migrants and refugees, maintained a high level of citizens' mobilization until Berlusconi's fall in 2011.

The militants who were interviewed and participated in the focus groups defined their organizations as democratic or democracy's "antibodies," which is an expression broadly used in Italian political speech (Rodota 2011, 2017). During a focus group, a militant of Libertà e Giustizia (Freedom and Justice) commented:

> We had to do something .... How was it possible that in spite of an Italian law that prohibits a person from being elected if he controls too many media (journals and televisions),[20] Berlusconi continued to stay in power and to be elected. Obviously the people who voted for Berlusconi didn't care about this law. Wouldn't this mean that the Italian democracy didn't possess the necessary antibodies and that, in the absence of checks and balances (e.g., independent media), Italy was going to shift from democracy to a sort of "populist" regime? We had to be these antibodies ...

---

[17] Popolo Viola denounced the sexist practices of Berlusconi that emerged in the "Ruby" affair (sex with an underage girl), protesting against the gender stereotypes that Berlusconi's sexism had produced in Italy through his televisions. They mobilized when important referenda (on public water, nuclear energy, and justice reform) were approaching. The movement also advocated for individual rights of LGBT persons and for homosexual marriage.

[18] http://www.libertaegiustizia.it/chi-siamo/. The name refers to a political movement "Justice and Freedom," which was established during fascism by two exiled partisans (the Rosselli brothers), who were murdered in France.

[19] http://www.libera.it/flex/cm/pages/ServeBLOB.php/L/IT/IDPagina/41

[20] This made him "unelectable."

The notion of political antibodies has been developed in political science literature that considers its pertinence in dealing with institutions, organizations, and movements that react against a weakening in democracy in respect to two main aspects: the first one is the "people's freedom as non-domination" or the immunity against the arbitrary interference of power (Allen and Regan 1998: 52), and the second one is discrimination of minorities—which includes, of course, racism against migrants, Islamophobia, and anti-Semitism. Political parties, representing citizens in the democratic arena, are the main antibodies that protect democracy; however, when they seem to not fulfill their role, civil society organizations—associations, NGOs, spontaneously formed citizens' groups—may intervene. This is precisely what happened in Italian civil society since the season of center-right populist governments, headed by Berlusconi and supported by the openly xenophobic Northern League.

The Crisis of the Parties, the Dangers of the "Econocracy," and the Post-democratic Society

The complex relations between the political parties and civil society's mobilizations are a main character of the Italian specificity in respect to the issue of democracy. While small leftist parties, namely, Rifondazione Comunista (Communist Refoundation), SEL, Sinistra Ecologia e Libertà (Left Ecology Freedom),[21] took part in the civil society demonstrations, the main left political force—the Democratic Party—was generally absent.

According to some eminent scholars (e.g., Gustavo Zagrebelsky, 2011), the Italian democratic crisis might be interpreted as a crisis of the political parties and their leaders rather than of the institutions. The roots of this crisis date back to 1995 when the traditional political system collapsed as corruption and scandals destroyed the main political parties. The new political parties, like Berlusconi's Forza Italia (Go Italy), did not comply with the constitutional mandate. The Italian Constitution establishes a central role for political parties in the determination of the democratic regime. Political parties are, in the understanding of the constituent fathers and in the history of the first decades after 1948, the principal intermediate actors between the individual and the State. They are democratic protectors of the liberties granted by the Constitution. These aims didn't

---

[21] SEL's leader, Nichi Vendola, is very active on minorities' rights (he is openly homosexual) and in the anti-racist battle.

belong to the "personal" party created by Silvio Berlusconi or to parties like the Northern League, which did not accept the Italian Constitution (the Northern League fought for the independence of the North).

The overall issue of "anti-politics"—as rejection of political establishment—which is widely debated in Italy, is embedded in this crisis. Zagrebelsky (2011), as a member of Libertà e Giustizia, claims that parties have to be supported in order to fully exercise their role as representatives of values, ideals, and legitimate interests. As mentioned, Libertà e Giustizia wants to be "the missing link among the best ferments in society and the official space of politics." However, not all civil society mobilizations subscribe to this relatively "moderate" approach to the political parties.

On 4 October 2009, the "anti-politics that really wants to radically innovate politics"—in Flores D'Arcais terms—seemed to find its true expression when comedian Beppe Grillo, whose blog, over the years, had gained more and more followers, and web designer Gianroberto Casaleggio founded the Five Star Movement, a "movement of free citizens." The Five Star Movement advocated direct democracy, internet-based deliberative processes, environmentalism, and the end of "professional politicians": in respect to politics, it presented himself as clearly anti-establishment. The strength of the Five Star Movement was its network of genuinely motivated citizens, who mobilize consensus by championing popular causes like anti-nuclear campaigns, direct political participation, renewable energy reform, and the end of conflicts of interest between the public and the private sectors.

However, the rise of the Five Star Movement, which received 25% of the votes in the general elections of February 2013, was a consequence of Italian citizens' rejection of the Mario Monti's technocratic government, which had imposed austerity policies following an EU mandate. The Monti government was supported by the entire political class, except the Northern League and the Five Star Movement, which were anti-austerity and eurosceptic.

The Five Star Movement captured the citizens' disgust with the political class and the Mario Monti's government, which embodied the economic establishment at the European level passing the costs of the crisis on to the middle class.

Berlusconi's fall in 2011 marked the end of a populist government experience and opened the door to another, even greater threat to democracy: the technocratic rule of economic orthodoxy. Appointed by

President Napolitano, without any popular vote, Prime Minister Mario Monti (2011–2013) imposed an austerity policy—a European agenda dictated by Germany, the leading EU country. Italy, like other member states, found itself in a difficult economic position with public deficit, made inevitable by the constraints imposed by the euro and by the impact of the global financial crisis. Deficit reduction became the main and essentially short-term policy of Germany (Gould 2013) and its Northern allies like Holland.

The Italian population strongly rejected the austerity measures. When the "proconsul of Germany,"[22] as Paul Krugman described Mario Monti, presented his own list in the 2013 elections, he received less than 10% of the votes, while the eurosceptic and anti-austerity Five Star Movement received 25%. Paul Krugman made an ironic comment about the results of the Italian elections in 2013:

> When Mario Monti stepped down as Italy's prime minister, *The Economist* opined that "The coming election campaign will be, above all, a test of the maturity and realism of Italian voters." The mature, realistic action, presumably, would have been to return Mr. Monti — who was essentially imposed on Italy by its creditors — to office, this time with an actual democratic mandate. Well, it's not looking good. Mr. Monti's party appears likely to come in fourth; not only is he running well behind the essentially comical Silvio Berlusconi, he's running behind an actual comedian, Beppe Grillo, whose lack of a coherent platform hasn't stopped him from becoming a powerful political force. (Krugman 2013)

Mario Monti's government was an expression of what can be called post-democracy and "econocracy." We have already defined post-democracy, a theory developed by Colin Crouch in the early 1980s. We can now introduce a new concept, "econocracy," recently developed by three British economists:

> The econocracy extends beyond a fixation with the economy's success. It is built on a particular vision of the economy that over time has been bought

---

[22] "For Mr. Monti was, in effect, the proconsul installed by Germany to enforce fiscal austerity on an already ailing economy; willingness to pursue austerity without limit is what defines respectability in European policy circles. This would be fine if austerity policies actually worked — – but they don't. And far from seeming either mature or realistic, the advocates of austerity are sounding increasingly petulant and delusional" (Krugman 2013).

into by politicians, businesspeople and the general public. Within an econocracy, economic discussion and decision making has become a technocratic rather than a political and social process. We increasingly view the economy as something separate from wider society and, in many cases, outside the sphere of democratic debate. The philosophy of econocracy is lo leave decisions about the economy to those who supposedly know best. (Earle et al. 2017: 8)

The fact that the Monti government's discourse on migration assumed a less repressive and more inclusive approach than Berlusconi's represents a small positive outcome in the context of the economic devastation produced by austerity policies. In respect to migration, Monti's government sought an agreement with the Vatican and put a member of the Santo Egidio Community in charge of migration (see below). Laws and practices did not change accordingly, however. The austerity policies resulted in a drastic reduction of the budget for the weakest parts of the population, including migrants and refugees. Moreover, the Northern League embraced far-right populism after being excluded from government; it strengthened the anti-immigrant discourse and put constant pressure on the government.

The fall of Monti's "econocracy" in the 2013 elections was brutal. As mentioned, the Five Star Movement was the great winner with 25% of the votes, almost the same as the Democratic Party, and Monti's list received less than 10%.

Under the Letta and Renzi governments, which were coalitions between the majoritarian Democratic Party and a small centrist party, mainstream politics did not respond to the disappointment/disgust with the political class or to the economic crisis. As already pointed out, during our fieldwork, which was supposed to focus on xenophobia, racism, hate speech, and right-wing populists ideas, the economic crisis and the political crisis (i.e., the rejection of the parties and the political establishment and disappointment with the EU) ended up dominating the debates.

Civil Society Actions: Anti-racism and Migrants' Integration

In the introduction we described the three types of civil society organizations that were involved in the fieldwork research. Here we detail their main characteristics.

The secular anti-racist organizations and the NGOs of the so-called "private social" sector, which are active in migrants' protection and integration, are ARCI,[23] Lunaria, and the trade union CGIL (Confederazione Generale del Lavoro). ARCI (Associazione Ricreativa Culturale Italiana) is a social and cultural promotion organization that coordinates networks of different associations and realities. ARCI was born out of the democratic culture of the Italian left and turned to anti-racism when Italy became an immigration country. Anti-racism is now considered as necessarily part of ARCI's progressive and anti-fascist culture (Delanty et al. 2008). In the interviews, the representatives of the ARCI stated:

> The ARCI has been active since 1957 in the social-cultural field ... its initiatives are aiming at promoting active citizenship and democratic participation processes for all people; with special attention to people who have fewer social opportunities in order to promote their autonomy, emancipation, equal dignity and their social inclusion. Migrants are, of course, among them.

Lunaria is a nonprofit association for social promotion, secular, independent, and autonomous from political parties, established in 1992. The general aims of Lunaria are peace, social and economic justice, equality and guarantee of the rights of citizenship, democracy, and grassroots participation, and in recent years, anti-racism and intercultural dialogue have become its main focus. Every year, Lunaria edits *Chronicles of Ordinary Racism*, a white paper on racism in Italy. They also offer programs for training for young people by volunteering in work camps.

The role of the organizations of the so-called "private social" sector is crucial in the field of legal assistance during the amnesties, or regularization processes that have allowed irregular migrants to obtain residence and work permit in Italy. They also assist immigrants with residence and work permit procedures, family reunification, and access to all public and private services.

While the "private social" organizations have played and continue to play a leading role in assisting immigrants in Italy, immigrants have also developed their own associations, mainly along ethnic or national lines,

---

[23] ARCI also has a sector dedicated to the rights of the gays and lesbians. The issue of LGBT persons is at the core of many anti-discrimination movements like the ARCIGay. See more at: http://www.arcigay.it/chi-siamo/info/#sthash.JaGlQVQ5.dpuf.

relying upon their own resources.[24] Migration in Italy dates back to the 1980s, and since then migrants have created their own associations, based on their national (Albanian, Senegalese, Romanian, etc.) and ethnic origin (e.g., African associations), or common interests (e.g., women's associations). In the field of integration and in general defense of the migrants' rights, they are, however, weaker than the trade unions, the church bodies, or the secular NGOs (as ARCI). Many migrants are active in this other type of organizations. This is due to the specific Italian integration policies that never promoted multiculturalism but rather a sort of intercultural dialogue framed by the existing civic and civil society organizations. In spite of their weaknesses, the immigrants' associations contribute to the process of migrants' political participation. We interviewed representatives of migrants' associations from the North African countries, Senegal, Somalia, and Eritrea, as well as migrant women's associations.

In the interviews and the focus groups, the participants expressed deep disgust with the EU's inaction in light of the Mediterranean tragedy of the migrants and refugees, and they denounced the role of populism. A member of the trade union CGIL stated: "Caught between the European Union's commitment to humanitarian values and growing voter anti-immigrant sentiment, Europe has reached an impasse on migration that risks fatal consequences. Thousands of migrants have died trying to cross the Mediterranean from Africa to Europe. More will die unless Europe can find a way out of its migration paralysis."

The Religious Organizations Defending the Migrants

Also religious organizations, especially organizations that are close to the Catholic Church, like *CARITAS*, the Comunità di Sant'Egidio in Rome, and the Centro La Pira in Florence, support migrants and refugees in the reception and integration processes.

Through the widespread assistance offered by *CARITAS*, the Catholic Church has been a main actor in the response to the increasing volume and frequency of incoming migrants. The Italian state has traditionally delegated many welfare activities to organizations and NGOs.

---

[24] We interviewed representatives of immigrant associations who have experienced the entire migration process, the crossing of the desert, then the Mediterranean in rotten boats, and so on.

Many of them, for example, *CARITAS*, are linked to the Catholic Church; others are secular.[25]

The Comunità di Sant'Egidio (Sant'Egidio Community) has played a vital role in welcoming migrants, promoting integration, and addressing racism. It was founded in 1968 in the spirit and under the auspices of the reforms adopted during the Second Vatican Council and has, since its establishment, hosted and welcomed those foreigners as well as nationals in need. The association is active in the intercultural and inter-faith dialogue and has promoted integration of migrants and ethnic minorities (Roma and Sinti) as well as inter-religious dialogue, especially with Muslims. Outside Italy, Sant'Egidio played an active role as conflict negotiator in Madagascar and, recently, in Central African Republic.

The Valdense community and the Jewish community, which are historically among the most persecuted groups in Italy, also promote intercultural dialogue, especially with Muslims. As historically victims of marginalization and discrimination, they recognize the signals of growing intolerance that can lead to tragedies. The two communities consider the powerful investments they make in educating their members to open mind and dialogue the best instrument against the diffusion of racism. The Valdense community is very active in the reception of migrants, while the Jewish community is more active in interreligious dialogue.

The Valdense church has developed very interesting intercultural experiences with migrants. As the pastor (who is a woman) told us in a focus group:

> The liturgy has been adapted and changed, by introducing a different understanding of body language in respect of the liturgy often used by the immigrants. Far from being a pure symbolic adaptation and inter-relation there is also an intercultural debate concerning issues and aspects (homosexual marriage and polygamy, the role for women) that are regulated in a different way in the national and non-national community. To give an example, homosexual marriage and a leading and active role of women is largely accepted in the national (Italian) community, but the same aspects are not accepted by communities coming from Latin America or Africa. Similarly and symmetrically, the Italian Valdense church does not accept polygamy, but the practice is well established in non-national communities. Such differences have to some extent led to debate but also a mutual recognition of practices that are alien to some of the members.

---

[25] In addition to helping migrants with food and shelter, *CARITAS* has a research center in Rome, whose reports and studies on immigration are among the most accurate in the country.

The representatives of the Catholic, Valdense, and Jewish community insist on the point that, for the majority of the migrants, religion is an important aspect of their identity. Consequently, the religious communities (and related associations) play a unique role as a welcoming community that does not force newcomers into cultural, social, political, and economic marginalization.

During our fieldwork, representatives of the Catholic organizations and NGOs referred on many occasions to Pope Francis' position on migrants and to his harsh criticism and rejection of the present world order. "Now, as the European Union and the European countries are ignoring desperate people dying in the Mediterranean – a real shame – we have finally heard the voice of Papa Francesco!!! It was time! Finally!," said a militant of the La Pira Center. In July 2013, on the island of Lampedusa, Pope Francis denounced with harsh words the "indifference" toward the destiny of migrants who risk their life in the Mediterranean.[26]

Catholic militants and others increasingly see Pope Francis as the Pope of the "excluded," of the "forgotten" of our societies. He is critical of capitalism, which produces inequalities and becomes a religion of money with its focus on profit. The Pope attributes great importance to popular movements to counter this economic system.

The first meeting between Pope Francis[27] and the popular movements, which took place in October 2014, represents a significant moment. After having criticized the capitalist system in the *Apostolic Evangelii Gaudium* and in encyclical *Lumen Fidei*, Pope Francis addressed the popular movements as follows:

> Grassroots movements express the urgent need to revitalize our democracies, so often hijacked by innumerable factors. It is impossible to imagine a future for society without the active participation of great majorities as protagonists, and such proactive participation overflows the logical procedures of formal democracy. Moving towards a world of lasting peace and justice calls us to go beyond paternalistic forms of assistance; it calls us to create new forms of participation that include popular movements and invigorate local, national and international governing structures with that torrent of moral energy that springs from including the excluded in the

[26] In April 2016, he went to the Lesbos island where thousands of migrants live, and he returned to Rome with three Syrian families.
[27] Pope Francis' actions are in accordance with the Second Vatican Council, which also marked a turning point as it changed the old hierarchy of the Catholic Church and its loyalty to the ruling classes.

building of a common destiny. And all this with a constructive spirit, without resentment, with love.

I accompany you wholeheartedly on this journey. From our hearts let us say together: No family without housing, no farmworker without land, no worker without rights, no one without the dignity that work provides.

Dear brothers and sisters, carry on with your struggle. You do us all good, like a blessing for humanity. Here are some rosaries made by Latin American artisans, waste collectors and grassroots workers, which I leave you as a memento, as a present and with my blessing.[28]

Pope Francis has described our economic system as "an economy that kills" that has to be fought:

Putting money in the center of everything we end up seeing people as waste. A system in which war has become, in large parts, a structural element and indispensable. A system to fight with courage and intelligence, with tenacity but without fanaticism, with passion but without violence, by addressing conflicts without being caught and always trying to resolve tensions to reach a higher plane of unity, peace and justice.

Defending Democracy: Direct Democracy, Participative Democracy, and Deliberative Democracy

Libertà e Giustizia and Libera defend democracy and the human rights values enshrined in the Italian Constitution. The main activities of Libertà e Giustizia consist of periodic organization of public meetings to inform and to argue in favor of the spirit of the Italian Constitution, which the Berlusconi as well as the Renzi government has attempted to modify. As one militant declares:

The educative and campaigning activities put in place in defense of the Constitution represent a concrete instrument to preserve the equilibrium of rights and duties, individual freedom and solidarity, equality and sense of justice that is maintained in the first part of the Italian Constitution. These activities are also important in respect to migration ... These actions, of course, develop awareness about discrimination and racism in the Italian population and promote migrants' integration.

---

[28] https://w2.vatican.va/content/francesco/it/speeches/2014/october/documents/papa-francesco_20141028_incontro-mondiale-movimenti-popolari.html, http://w2.vatican.va/content/francesco/en/speeches/2014/october/documents/papa-francesco_20141028_incontro-mondiale-movimenti-popolari.html

Democracy is also at the core of the activities organized by Libera, founded by a priest, Don Ciotti, with the aim to fight the mafias (all the mafias). Even if the founder belongs to the Catholic Church, the organization is completely secular

> We organize initiatives with schools and marginalized sectors in order to develop a sense of legality, which is the basis of democracy; we do job camps for young people, volunteering services, economic programs to help establish small enterprises with shared capital to give young people a chance to find jobs that are not linked to illegal activities and thus reduce the mafia's influence nationally and worldwide. All these activities have also an impact on discrimination and racism issues, especially in the Southern part of the country.

The regional representatives who participated in interviews and focus groups insisted on the importance of the educational laboratories where young or unemployed people from the regions mostly affected by the mafia's influence and by corruption practices attend legal training in order to learn the principles of a correct public administration.

The representatives of these two organizations share the opinion that the crisis of democracy (which, inter alia, encompasses representation, rule of law, trust in institutions, and public authorities) is caused by the dominant neoliberalism and the crisis of political representation, that is, politicians no longer work for ideals. They share also the opinion that the EU with its current technocratic approach is part of the problem and not the solution.

During the focus groups, the representatives of Libertà e Giustizia and Libera developed a dialogue with representatives of the Five Star Movement about democracy. The Five Star Movement is stigmatized as "populist" by the majority of politicians and scholars because of its anti-establishment positions and Beppe Grillo's political communication style. This is not, of course, the point of view of the members and sympathizers. The Nobel Laureate actor and writer, Dario Fo, supporter of the Grillo's movement, stated: "The populist acts in favor of the people; there is an overlap between populism and demagogy in the mainstream press and academic literature."

The Five Star Movement representatives who took part in the focus groups also rejected the accusation of populism. They defined themselves as "antibodies" of democracy (see above):

Our action should be identified as a democratic safeguarding body against the power of economic elites and traditional professionals of politics .... The Five Star Movement is the response to the citizens' need for political participation and civic engagement; it allows ordinary people to interact with politics and its aspirations without delegating it to professional politicians; it represents a laboratory where we experiment with innovative and alternative methods and forms of democracy .... Political engagement through on-line debate and decisions, transparency in the selection of candidates, discussions and information on the content of the program are some of the pillars on which the Five Star Movement bases its intent to renovate politics and democracy.

The issue that emerges here is the need for new forms of democratic participation in order to oppose right-wing populism.

The Five Star Movement is the concrete response to the spread of right-wing populism, which in Italy is represented by the Northern League. To some extent, the Five Star Movement has managed to convert people's discomfort with, and hate and anger towards political (and non-political) leaders into a political initiative (the Movement itself), thus limiting the space for more extreme alternatives. Therefore, it acted, unintentionally, as an antibody against the spread of the racist behavior and hate speech that characterize right-wing populism.

The processes of participation from the bottom that the Five Star Movement has implemented have provoked a debate on the web as a political instrument for direct democracy[29] and internet-based deliberative processes (Gagliardone 2013).

This is not the place to develop the scientific debate about direct democracy, deliberative democracy, and participatory democracy (della Porta et al. 2017); we will limit ourselves to some elements of the issue.

Direct democracy is a complex idea: it refers to the fact that the people should decide and not delegate and that the number of people who actually would take decisions should be extended in respect to representative democracy (where the elected members of the Parliament decide). The web offers an instrument in this respect and facilitates deliberative processes. Another concept in direct democracy is the involvement of citizens

---

[29] However, if the web was extremely important for the rise of the Five Star Movement, its success is due to a double strategy, including the web and Grillo's numerous speeches in town squares all over Italy.

in the entire decision-making process: they should not only say yes or no at the end. This is the deliberative democracy designed by Jürgen Habermas and John Rawls.[30]

The ideal process would be to combine participatory democracy, whereby citizens invest their time and knowledge to participate in informed decision-making on laws and policy, with deliberative democracy, "based on horizontal communication flows, multiple producers of content, many occasions for interaction, confrontation on the basis of rational arguments and a propensity to listen to the other side. In this sense, deliberative democracy is discursive" (della Porta 2011: 83). According to della Porta, deliberative and participative democracy goes beyond the idea of a public sphere in favor of a broader consideration of an alternative public sphere in which the mechanisms of deliberation come into effect (della Porta and Tarrow 2005). "Social movements move precisely in these alternative public spheres, which allow citizens to experience new forms of participation, within an inclusive political logic" (Luengo 2016: 3).

The Five Star Movement has, in fact, introduced innovative deliberative processes, for example, online voting on bills presented by the members of Parliament. This deliberative process would give laws legitimacy.[31]

In its search for new forms of direct democracy, the Five Star Movement has clearly chosen the parliamentarian over the extra-parliamentarian path. As a militant said in an interview: "Irrespective of the attacks adopted by the Five Star Movement against financial elites, mainstream parties and masonry lobbies, the movement itself through the introduction of an alternative method of doing politics (often presented in a very confrontational way) can be interpreted as a national antibody (operating in the politics field) that Italian society created and that de facto limited the impact that nationalist, far right, extreme movements might have had."

---

[30] "Two of the early influences on deliberative democratic theory are the philosophers John Rawls and Jürgen Habermas. Rawls advocated the use of reason in securing the framework for a just political society. For Rawls, reason curtails self-interest to justify the structure of a political society that is fair for all participants in that society and secures equal rights for all members of that society. These conditions secure the possibility for fair citizen participation in the future. Habermas claimed that fair procedures and clear communication can produce *legitimate* and *consensual* decisions by citizens. These fair procedures governing the deliberative process are what *legitimates* the outcomes." https://www.britannica.com/topic/deliberative-democracy.

[31] https://www.quora.com/What-is-the-difference-between-the-deliberative-and-participatory-models-of-democracy

The Outcomes: Challenges—Post-democracy, Totalitarianism, and Neoliberal Economy

An attempt at synthesizing the rich debates that have emerged during the fieldwork should start from the fact that the shift toward a post-democratic world (Crouch 2003) that is marked by the power of economy over policy—or the rise of an "econocracy" (Earle et al. 2017)—have emerged as a core issue that is impossible to separate from racism and populism.

The Tsipras government and the Five Star Movement—as expressions of citizens' participation—represent a reaction to the fear of a post-democratic order. The Tsipras government especially, raised some hopes for a change in the technocratic management of the EU crisis. The hopes were dashed by the inflexibility of the EU approach to the debt crisis, but the support for political forces proposing another path didn't fade.

The Five Stars Movement represent one of the European forces that are critical in front of the present EU Management. The militants that have been interviewed described the present form of the EU as post-democratic. A representative of the Five Star Movement said: "The European Union is governed by a pair of hegemonic nations that impose their will on the other subordinated nations via a caste of appointed bureaucrats. There is no democratically legitimized federal power. The EU is not an answer to the crucial relationship between national states and globalization, citizenship and cosmopolitanism."

The failure of the EU appears both in the austerity policies imposed on the debt-ridden countries and in the migration policies where an impasse has been reached, while thousands die trying to cross the Mediterranean from Africa to Europe.

The common refrain that the militants repeated was that a solid democracy is a vital element in addressing and responding to racism, discrimination, and hate speech. The analytical frame that can be deduced from the interviews and the focus groups is the recognition that Italy is experiencing a deep democratic crisis, which encompasses representation, rule of law, and trust in institutions, parties, and public authorities. Some of the causes are endogenous (the collapse of the Italian party system provoked rising "anti-political" sentiment); some are global, for example, the dominant neoliberal model and the rise of a post-democratic world (Crouch 2003). A representative of Libera used very strong words to describe the present world order. He first quoted Pope Francesco Bergoglio's apostolic exhortation, Evangelii Gaudium ("The Joy of the Gospel") issued on 26 November 2013:

Just as the commandment *"Thou shalt not kill"* sets a clear limit in order to safeguard the value of human life, today we also have to say *"thou shalt not"* to an economy of exclusion and inequality. *Such an economy kills.* How can it be that it is not a news item when an elderly homeless person dies of exposure, but it is news when the stock market loses two points? This is a case of exclusion. Can we continue to stand by when food is thrown away while people are starving? This is a case of inequality. Today everything comes under the laws of competition and the survival of the fittest, where the powerful feed upon the powerless. As a consequence, masses of people find themselves excluded and marginalized: without work, without possibilities, without any means of escape ...[32]

The militant then referred to Hannah Arendt's analysis of totalitarianism, quoting the following sentence:

The greater the bureaucratization of public life, the greater will be the attraction of violence. In a fully developed bureaucracy there is nobody left with whom one could argue, to whom one could present grievances, on whom the pressures of power could be exerted. Bureaucracy is the form of government in which everybody is deprived of political freedom, of the power to act; for the rule by *Nobody* is not no-rule, and where all are equally powerless we have a tyranny without a tyrant. (Arendt 1969)

The challenge for civil society is how to respond to the widespread sense of mistrust and incertitude toward the future and how to convert feelings like hate, depression, addiction (to media power, to mainstream narratives, to stereotypes, and to the current social and cultural situation), and impotence into positive processes of civic engagement, solidarity, participation, care of common goods, and political activism.

In order to activate this change, it is necessary to revitalize civic engagement, political passion, and sense of belonging. This should start in schools, universities, and all the places where civil society meets. A militant of Libertà e Giustizia reported the experience of the social movement for the protection of common goods—movimento per i beni comuni—(such as public water systems, the environment, etc.) as one example of this revitalization. He has a direct knowledge of the movement, being the president of the local committee in Florence. The civic initiatives that have been developed to protect public goods (like water) and their use from

---

[32] https://www.ncronline.org/blogs/francis-chronicles/popes-quotes-economy-kills

privatization finally led to a national referendum, whose symbolic meaning and political action were based on the idea (that might also be defined as "philosophy") of "common goods." The intention was to introduce conceptual criticism of a way of governance and thinking that neglects solidarity and reciprocity among citizens, which limits the effort of politics to include people and promote equality, and which marginalizes values in favor of economic interests of financial elites. The referendum battle against the privatization of the water as a common good has been won. However the public authorities have given little attention to the referendum's result and forms of privatization of the water have continued.

All interviewees have insisted on the importance to revitalize community-based feelings. Actions should emphasize valorization of small communities where individual citizens could have a voice in dialogue with the "other," thus establishing relationships among citizens and peers rather than "Othering" relationships of discrimination and exclusion.

According to the militant of Libertà e Giustizia, who is also president of the local committee for common goods (and a teacher of history and philosophy at the high school), the young generation needs a deeper and stronger sense of community where interpersonal relationships are built and developed in a non-competitive way. The sense of community can reverse the hopeless character of the current democratic societies where the sense of future, engagement, effort, personal investment, and clash of or debate on values are de facto abandoned.

Conclusions

Since 2014, when the fieldwork described in the chapter was done, the economic, political, and social context has changed profoundly in Europe and in Italy. In 2015, the migratory and refugee crisis transformed the debate on migration inside the EU, splitting the continent between countries open to the reception of refugees and countries that build walls.

In respect to economic and political issues, the Tsipras government's submission to the troika's decisions, showing that no alternative to the present economic policies was possible, Brexit and a modest economic reprisal have induced the majority of the Italian population to a less critical attitude towards the EU's economic policies in the frame of the European project as a whole, after years when euroscepticism dominated all opinion polls.

The general ideas that emerge from our interviews and focus groups in 2014 are, however, valid today: they express a concern about democracy that goes beyond the populist threat. Behind the concern about democracy, a theoretical frame comes into focus: the impact of neoliberalism (provoking growing inequalities) and the rise of the post-democratic world. If right-wing populists are successful in spreading racist ideas, the cause also lies in the mainstream parties' incapacity to offer a global alternative vision for our multicultural societies, develop intercultural dialogue, and combine cultural respect with social justice for all citizens. The importance of a critical intercultural dialogue was underlined by almost all participants: "No one has monopoly on the truth," as both representatives of the Valdense church, the Jewish community and the Catholic organisation declared. A representative of the trade union CGIL said: "The two pillars of migrants' integration are intercultural dialogue and social justice for everybody in order to avoid wars among the poor, as the lowers classes consider migrants as competitors."

"On the contrary, mainstream parties – including traditional social-democracy or 'the left' (e.g., Italian Democratic Party) – have completely submitted to neo-liberal dogmas and are destroying the welfare state." He added. "The EU's technocratic approach to the economic crisis, imposing the troika on debt-ridden countries, is a sign of adaptation to economic neo-liberal dogmas and of the prefiguration of a post-democratic order. Consequently, it is difficult to separate anti-racist battles from a broader engagement for democracy and social justice."

The proposals for action emerging from the interviews and the focus groups consider it necessary to go beyond the processes of formal democracy. It is necessary to commit to re-establishing places and spaces where a different sense of community and living together can be experienced (first) and then lived and promoted for young generations (especially) and for everyone who does not approve a competitive, exclusive (rather than inclusive), discriminative society and politics that increasingly privilege individual, opportunistic, "Othering" approaches.

This seems to be the best way to fight racism, discrimination, and hate speech. This model would address the exclusion of the "others" whose identity would be incorporated in the solidaristic community and the depression of a young generation with limited hopes for the future. Two paths to reaching this goal appeared: the representatives of the Five Star Movement, Libertà e Giustizia, and of course the political parties were in favor of adopting an ordinary method of engagement within the institution and through the institutions (and the traditional procedures, not least the political representation mechanism). The representatives of Libera, the religious organizations, and the Centro La Pira highlighted the need for "epistemic communities alien to the traditional ones as pioneering experiments to prophetically indicate and go along alternative paths" that means communities expressing a new worldview, projecting in a future whose characters are not yet very clear, but that are alternative to the ones of the present world order. In the words of the representative of Libera:

> At the end of the Roman Empire, when the old world was collapsing, some found refuge in the monasteries to preserve a part of the old world and to project a new one; in the same way, now, we have to build communities, groups, networks that – outside the system – start slowly to build something new.

References

Allen, A. L., & Regan, M. C., Jr. (1998). *Debating democracy's discontent: Essays on American politics, law and public philosophy.* New York: Oxford University Press.
Anderson, P. (2009). An invertebrated left. *London Review of Books, 31,* 12–18.
Arendt, H. (1969, February 27). On violence. *The New York Book Review.* http://www.nybooks.com/articles/2013/07/11/hannah-arendt-reflections-violence/
Beveridge, W. (1948). *Voluntary action: A report on methods of social advance.* London: Allen & Unwin.
Canovan, M. (1981). *Populism.* London: Junction Books.
Crouch, C. (2003). *Post-democrazia.* Roma/Bari: Laterza.
Crouch, C. (2013, February 5). Five minutes with Colin Crouch. *British Politics and Policy.* http://blogs.lse.ac.uk/politicsandpolicy/five-minutes-with-colin-crouch/
Delanty, G., Wodak, R., & Jones, P. (Eds.). (2008). *Identity, belonging and migration.* Oxford: Oxford University Press.
della Porta, D. (2011). *Democrazie.* Bologna: Il Mulino.
della Porta, D., & Tarrow, S. (2005). *Transnational protest and global activism.* New York: Rowman and Littlefield.
della Porta, D., O'Connor, F., Portos, M., & Subirarts Rivas, A. (2017). *Social movements and referendum from below: Direct democracy in the neoliberal crisis.* Bristol: Policy Press at the University of Bristol.

Earle, J., Moran, C., & Ward-Perkins, Z. (2017). *The econocracy: The perils of leaving economics to the experts.* London: Penguin Books.
Flores D'Arcais, P. (2011, May 10). Societa' civile e razza padrona. *Il Fatto Quotidiano.*
Gagliardone, I. (2013). A new Italy and the myth of the web. http://www.huffingtonpost.com/iginio-gagliardone/a-new-italy-and-the-myth_b_2906173.html
Gould, B. (2013). *Myths, politicians and money: The truth behind the free market.* Basingstoke: Palgrave Macmillan.
Hamid, S. (2014, May 14). The future of democracy in the Middle East: Islamist and illiberal. *The Atlantic.*
Kauffmann, S. (2017, September 22). The West's schism over liberal values. *New York Times.*
Krugman, P. (2013, February 24). Austerity, Italian style. *New York Times.* https://www.nytimes.com/2017/09/22/opinion/west-liberal-values.html?ref=collection%2Ftimestopic%2FKauffmann%2C%20Sylvie&action=click&contentCollection=opinion&region=stream&module=stream_unit&version=latest&contentPlacement=1&pgtype=collection&_r=0
Laclau, E. (2007). *On populist reason.* New York: Verso.
Luengo, O. S. (Ed.). (2016). *Political communication in times of crisis.* Berlin: Logos Verlag.
NPR. (2017, August 3). Decline in democracy spreads across the globe as authoritarian leaders arise, Ari Shapiro (host) and Larry Diamond. http://www.npr.org/2017/08/03/541432445/decline-in-democracy-spreads-across-the-globe-as-authoritarian-leaders-rise
Panizza, F. (2005). *Populism and the mirror of democracy.* New York: Verso.
Rodota, S. (2011). *Elogio del moralismo.* Bari: Laterza.
Rodota, S. (2017). *Diritto d'amore.* Bari: Laterza.
Tarchi, M. (2014). *Italia populista. Dalqualunquismo a Beppe Grillo.* Bologna: Il Mulino.
Wilkinson, F. (2017, February 16). Why Donald Trump really is a populist. Billionaire appointees. Tax cuts for the rich. None of that matters. https://www.bloomberg.com/view/articles/2017-02-16/why-donald-trump-really-is-a-populist
Zagrebelsky, G. (2011, December 12). La democrazia senza i partiti. *La Repubblica.*
Zakaria, F. (1997, November/December). The rise of illiberal democracy. *Foreign Affairs.* https://www.foreignaffairs.com/articles/1997-11-01/rise-illiberal-democracy

Links

http://study.com/academy/lesson/what-is-a-civil-society-definition-examples.html
http://www.colorado.edu/conflict/peace/treatment/civilsoc.htm
http://www.huffingtonpost.com/iginio-gagliardone/a-new-italy-and-the-myth_b_2906173.html
http://www.ilfattoquotidiano.it/2011/10/05/societa-civile-e-razza-padrona/162159/
http://www.libera.it/flex/cm/pages/ServeBLOB.php/L/IT/IDPagina/41
http://www.libertaegiustizia.it/chi-siamo/
http://www.npr.org/2017/08/03/541432445/decline-in-democracy-spreads-across-the-globe-as-authoritarian-leaders-rise
http://www.senscot.net/view_art.php?viewid=7318
https://w2.vatican.va/content/francesco/it/speeches/2014/october/documents/papa-francesco_20141028_incontro-mondiale-movimenti-popolari.html
https://www.ncronline.org/blogs/francis-chronicles/popes-quotes-economy-kills

CHAPTER 9

Being a Citizen in Times of Mainstreaming of Populism: Building Post-communist Contestatory and Solidary Citizenship

Anna Krasteva with Evelina Staykova and Ildiko Otova

"I feel that I can change the world,"[1] a volunteer said. Such unqualified confidence seems paradoxical: how can volunteer work with refugee children—rendered invisible in the public space by the hegemonic securitarian and anti-refugee discourses—change society, politics, and "the world"? However, it deftly captures the emergence of a new type of citizenship and its transformative power.

> To act … means to take an initiative, to begin (as the Greek word *archein*, 'to begin,' 'to lead,' and eventually 'to rule'), to set something into motion. Because they are *initium*, newcomers and beginners … take initiative, are

[1] Interview with a volunteer working with refugee children.

A. Krasteva (✉)
Department of Political Sciences, New Bulgarian University, Sofia, Bulgaria

E. Staykova • I. Otova
CERMES, Department of Political Sciences, New Bulgarian University, Sofia, Bulgaria

© The Author(s) 2019
B. Siim et al. (eds.), *Citizens' Activism and Solidarity Movements*, Palgrave Studies in European Political Sociology, https://doi.org/10.1007/978-3-319-76183-1_9

prompted into action. This beginning is not the same as the beginning of the world; it is not the beginning of something but of somebody, who is a beginner himself. (Arendt 1998: 177)

For Hannah Arendt, acting blends together agency, initiative, beginning, change—of the world and of the active Self. This conceptual blend underlies our concept of citizenship as commitment, participation, and transformation.

Donatella della Porta's four core questions about the analysis of social activism are relevant to this study: the relationships between structural change and transformation in terms of social conflict; the role of cultural representations in social conflict; the process through which values, interests, and ideas become collective action; and the impact of context on social movements' chances of success (della Porta and Diani 2006: 16). However, the present analysis focuses on two other issues. One: is civic activism capable of, not merely opposing, but overturning, the populist surge, through innovating citizenship and revitalizing democracy? Two: how can civic agency "emancipate" itself, theory-wise, from the exogenously formulated and implemented project for creating a post-communist civil society?

Post-communist civic agency is conceptualized through the theoretical perspectives of Donatella della Porta's diffusion model (2015), the acts of citizenship (Isin and Nielsen 2008), and A. Krasteva's contestatory citizenship (Krasteva 2016a). The authors' preferences for theorizing civic resistance and responses to post-communist far-right populism through the conceptual lenses of *citizenship* are substantiated by four reasons. During communism, citizenship was understood as status and belonging, as integration into the state; one of the democratic innovations of post-communism was citizenship as "a consciously assumed responsibility" (Carter 2001: 10), as participation, activism, and contestation. The second reason is the development of the concept as a heuristic tool for understanding and explaining the diversification of civic mobilizations. Anna Krasteva has elaborated the concepts of e-citizenship, green, contestatory, and creative citizenship (Krasteva 2013, 2016a, b); this article aims to elaborate solidary citizenship. The third reason is that citizenship expresses the transition from NGOs to "acts of citizenship" (Isin and Nielsen 2008), from the engineered project of building a civil society to the emergence of new forms of civic agency. Post-communism has been criticized for its lacking political imagination; its beginning has been conceptualized as an end: "the end of history" (Fukuyama 2006). "Citizenship remains a significant site through which to develop a critique of the pessimism about political possibilities" (Isin and

Nyers 2014: 9). It is precisely the active and positive potential of citizenship in generating change and change-bearers that served as our fourth reason for selecting this concept for the analysis of post-communist activism.

Actors take the center of our stage. This theoretical decision in turn determines our methodology: civic activists will speak in their own voices. The theoretical value of civic voices consists of both their authenticity and their openness to multiple interpretations. The authors offer their interpretations, and readers can argue or elaborate their own readings of the narratives here. This article summarizes observations and problematizations of long-term research exploring various waves of civic mobilizations and the emergence of a post-communist citizenship (Krasteva 2009, 2013, 2016a, b). It includes structured and semi-structured interviews with human rights advocates and pro-diversity civic actors, participant observation of civic activism. The empirical work is focused on Bulgarian civic activism; the conclusions have a broader validity.

The article is structured in four parts. The first part analyzes the transition from the project of democratic engineering of civil society to the emergence of civic contestatory agency. We examine the main steps of this transition: the professionalization of civic activism through NGOs, the greening of the contestatory Self, and the mass anti-oligarchy protests. The second part examines the disclosure of agent through action and speech, and identifies the key figures of civic agency and the clusters of narratives which propose the discourse about solidarity and rights in opposition to the mainstreaming of populism. The third part regards citizenship as politics of transformation and examines the possibility of a neo-post-transformation: a positive overturning of the negative trend in the mainstreaming of national populism. The final part maps post-communist citizenships and compares the three types of citizenship—green, Occupy, and solidary—in three respects: the adversaries whose hegemony they attack, the audibility of their claims, and the temporalities of mobilizations.

From the Democratic Engineering Project of Building a Civil Society to the Creation of Post-communist Citizenship

Civil Society Without Citizenship

It was Ralf Dahrendorf (1990) who mapped out the agenda of the post-communist democratization. The implementation of the three objectives—creating the institutions of parliamentary democracy, transition from planned to market economy, and building civil society—has different temporalities: six months, six years, and six decades. This ironic symmetry highlights the fact that constructing a strong and vibrant civil society is the most challenging and long-term task of the triple post-communist democratization. Civil society was conceived "as a training ground that 'grooms' citizens, preparing them for civic participation and political engagement" (Dahlgren 2006: 272). The role of NGOs has been crucial for building a democratic culture at the beginning of the post-communist transition. The NGO-ization of civil society is the result of a Western project for building democracy and civil society through funding and forming civic activists. This *first generation* of civic actors could be recapitulated in two trends. The NGOs promoted the European standards and discourses of human rights and anti-discrimination and contributed to the emergence of a pluralistic multi-voice public agora. In this regard, their contribution was positive and tangible. The second trend refers to the type of agency they created: the professional civic activist. This is a more ambiguous result. "The citizen – not a profession, but a commitment" (Krasteva 2009) summarizes Anna Krasteva's criticism. The profile of the NGO expert focused on fundraising and project management is closer to think tanks and business skills than to the spontaneity of civic agency. The NGO-ization failed to take into account how people become civic agents and how they make themselves into citizens. We define this ambiguous result of the NGO-ization of civic agency with the paradoxical formula "civil society without citizenship."

The formation of another type of civic actor—the "amateur," able and willing to experiment, to search, to propose new, "rough" ideas, to make mistakes, to act, to innovate (Krasteva 2009)—will be the result of the *second generation* of civic mobilizations which will be analyzed through the greening of citizenship and the Occupy mobilizations.

Green Citizenship

Which issues are worthy of civic activism? Young people[2] in post-communist Bulgaria have a definitive answer. Green values and ideas inspire them more than any other cause or challenge. Poverty, discrimination, and inequalities do not have the mobilizing potential of mountains,

---

[2] Green values are shared by representatives of all generations; but young people are the most numerous and committed activists in environmental activism.

forests, and wild nature. Blogger and journalist Svetla Encheva[3] has mocked this asymmetry in her polemic post "If Averik had been a mountain or a dog": immigrant Averik would have attracted more civic sympathy if, rather than a pregnant woman in love whose residence documents have expired, she had been a mountain or a dog. Environmental issues are virtually the only ones capable of engaging the attention of young Bulgarians—who are often apolitical—and of mobilizing and stirring them (Krasteva 2009: 90; Otova 2013; Люцканова 2011). Here, we have an explicit adversary: post-communist capitalism has even less consideration for nature than it does for people[4]; the business lobbies behind both the parties in power and the opposition have captured the state. Eco-mobilizations are the activism of a generation that does not identify itself in terms of communism/anticommunism opposition. The struggle for preserving the *purity of the environment* is a struggle against the *pollution of politics* (Krasteva 2016a).

Green mobilizations present a vital laboratory for post-communist activism. Four aspects of this civic workshop are particularly relevant to our study. The first one concerns values: green activists are among the first and key carriers of post-materialist values such as "less is more," which are unpopular in post-communist societies; they express and catalyze the greening of the Self, "of future responsibility towards others" (Isin and Nielsen 2008: 4), and exhibit a high capacity for being "engines of change, primarily in relation to values system" (della Porta and Diani 2006: 23). The audibility of green claims is the second characteristic: green mobilizations involve relatively few participants, yet their demands reverberate across public space and trigger reactions—usually critical—from both the media and politicians. "Bottom-up globalization" (della Porta and Mattoni 2014) is the third aspect: green mobilizations are the most globalized in the sense that among all other protests, they stand the closest to the transborder inspiration for a radical participatory democracy and deliberative and participatory democratic practices (della Porta and Mattoni 2014: 5; Krasteva 2016a). The fourth aspect is the most important one: green mobilizations are the first in post-communist activism to innovatively create citizenship in the two directions theorized in acts of citizenship of E. Isin and G. Nielsen—deeds and a new type of

---

[3] Svetla Encheva, "If Averik had been a mountain or a dog," 14 April 2010: http://svetlaen.blogspot.bg/2010/04/blog-post_14.html.
[4] One of the Bulgarian eco-coalitions is tellingly called *For Bulgaria to still have nature*.

actors: "citizenship is examined as an act or deed that produces new subjects" (Isin and Nielsen 2008: 6).

Contestatory Citizenship

The 2013 Bulgarian summer of protests started on the day when an oligarch with a particularly negative reputation was appointed director of the governmental agency for national security. Tens of thousands of people gathered in downtown Sofia, and the protests lasted a whole year (Krasteva 2016a). In this Bulgarian Occupy, oligarchization (von Beyme 2015) had a concrete face, but those protests also had a more global goal. "The problem isn't with people; it's with the system",[5] and "We've had enough of hierarchy. We want direct democracy": those slogans from the June 2013 protests in Sofia summarize the high ambitions to reject the existing model and to invent a new one. The Occupy mobilizations in post-communist Bulgaria have had a great impact in two directions: taking the floor, having a say in Bulgarian political agenda, and affirming contestation as the other face of democracy: "Democracy develops within the permanent contestation of power and social movements are the most relevant for 'expressive democracy' – the *prise de parole* of society" (Rosanvallon 2006: 26).

The protests of both international and Bulgarian Indignados have been severely criticized; two of these criticisms are relevant to our study: the absence of an alternative project and the lack of genuine political change. According to Chantal Mouffe, "the Occupy and similar movements are strategically ineffective since they are not able to develop a counter-hegemonic political project that truly challenges the existing order" (Decreuse et al. 2014: 16; Mouffe 2013). Valentina Georgieva pessimistically summarizes the failure of Bulgarian protests to yield results, instead becoming tamed by the elites: "The same elites took the power and reproduced the old model of democracy with a limited civic participation" (Георгиева 2016: 259). Analyzing the protests through the lens of evolving civic agency, Anna Krasteva reached the opposite conclusions: the protests may not have achieved their goals or provided a new democratic model, but they have been a laboratory for citizenship through contestation. Their impact is so crucial that A. Krasteva (2016a) defines it as a "second democratic revolution." It did not transform society but trans-

---

[5] Bulgarian Indignados speak the language of all Indignados: "It's time to change things, time to build a better society together" (Manifesto of Spanish Indignados).

formed civic agency. In the first post-communist revolution of the elites, citizens were assigned the role of attending the democratization process; they were second-class actors. In the second, it is the citizens who experiment, innovate, and re-found democracy. The keyword is experimentation: in Occupy mobilizations, we see more aspirations than results, more proposals for radical change than proposals for policies. Occupy is the watershed marking the transition from party politics to contestatory democracy: contestability is more important than consent (Pettit 1997; Braithwaite 2007; Krasteva 2016a).

"The Disclosure of the Agent in Speech and Action"

We must see the truth, no matter how unpleasant: our society generates racism and Nazism because it needs them; they're a tried-and-true mechanism for division and political manipulation ... it needs them to preserve the status quo, the hegemony, money, power .... This was how Hitler rose to power too: in times of a crisis, displacing class and social antagonisms. Nazi ideas serve to maintain and justify inequality, to thwart the effective unification of people toward a better society. A society like ours, where these trends are a fact, is a grim society, it's dangerous. This is what we must fight against.[6]

This is how an anti-racist activist introduces the complicated political context giving birth to and opposed by solidary and contestatory citizenship.

"The new always appears in the guise of a miracle. The fact that man is capable of action means that the unexpected can be expected from him, that he is able to perform what is infinitely improbable" (Arendt 1998: 178). The mainstreaming of Othering and Bordering discourses and the hegemonizing of national populism (Krasteva 2016b; Krasteva and Vladisavljević 2017) aim to take away the audibility of alternative discourses. Civic actors who oppose the "grim" and "dangerous" in society make Hannah Arendt's miracle come true. This section is dedicated to them: the miracle of civic resistance and its makers.

"The disclosure of the agent in speech and action" introduced by Arendt (1998: 175) is the entry point to the core of our study: solidary citizenship. "Speech and action ... are the modes in which human beings appear to each other, not indeed as physical objects, but *qua* men" (Arendt 1998: 176). The constitutive function of action and

[6] Interview with an anti-racist activist.

speech gets instantiated only in an intersubjective environment of togetherness: "This revelatory quality of speech and action comes to the fore where people are with others and neither for nor against them – that is, in sheer human togetherness" (Arendt 1998: 180). It is this intersubjective environment (in which Arendt elaborates the agent-action-speech triad) that is the leading factor in conceptualizing civic actors. We will analyze them in two perspectives: the figures of civic agency and the clusters of narratives of solidary speech. Arendt's notion of the agent in action and speech provides the philosophical bridge to the political science concept of solidary citizenship, where acts are foundational for constituting civic actors through their demands and struggle for human rights, and speech underlies the symbolic battles against the hegemonization of the discourses of Bordering/Othering and the (in)ability to transform public space through the alternative discourses of solidarity, human rights, and inclusion.

The Figures of Civic Agency

The Anti-racist Activist

She crossed the border from the "informed citizen" to the "engaged" citizen (Riesman 2001) on a portentous day. It was a day when extremists assaulted peaceful activists going to a rally in support of refugee rights. Then Natalia[7] entered activism with a flying start, becoming one of the founders and most active representatives of HoRa[8]:

> Ever since I can remember, I've been dealing with these issues, watching racism in intimate detail .... My strongest motivation for HoRa was the feeling that we've reached the last straw. ... the group was founded after a brutal assault, in broad daylight, against peaceful activists .... We realized it could've been any of us. My general motivation is the acute awareness that neo-Nazism threatens me, my friends, everyone: the entire society. But it's not just a self-defense instinct; it's also the sense of justice, of solidarity. For me, it's also a sense of continuity: so many people have died to stop Hitler .... So I feel responsible to the next generations.[9]

---

[7] All names have been changed.
[8] A civic anti-racist initiative.
[9] Interview with an anti-racist activist.

This interview sounds like a manifesto and conveys vivid messages: extremism threatens not only vulnerable groups such as refugees but "everyone, the entire society"; civic mobilization is not defensive, aiming at protecting oneself, but proactive, promoting the values of justice and solidarity; despite emerging ad hoc, in response to a specific occasion, civic activism bears the historical memory of Nazism. This bouquet of messages outlines the political platform of solidary citizenship. Perhaps the most vivid message is that of feeling "responsible to the next generations." The leap from the ephemeral temporality of small ad hoc civic initiatives to the historical *longue duree*, ethically perceived as a duty to the future generations, defines civic activists as actors of the politics of transformation. Natalia perceives anti-racist activism as an opposition to Nazism in all its embodiments. In Sofia, the symbolic peak of Nazism is the annual Lukov March, when far-right members of various organizations hold a procession with torches in the center of the capital to commemorate their fascist ideas. Natalia was among the originators of an Anti-Lukov March: "in 2013, we held the first counter-protest against the neo-Nazi Lukov March, in the form of a symbolic vigil for the victims of Nazism and fascism, at the memorial of Bulgarian Holocaust victims."[10]

Hannah Arendt's *vita activa* carries the connotations of "unquiet" (Arendt 1998: 15). To Natalia, activism means active unquiet, implacability, resolution, and opposition. She embodies the *activist as a fighter*: a powerful actor of contestatory citizenship. Her world draws stark lines between foes and friends (Carl Schmitt 2007). The adversaries are given explicit names and structured into different categories. The first one consists of fascists and neo-Nazis: from those who carry the torches during the Lukov Marches to those who beat up peaceful activists in city trams. The second group is those post-communist politicians, leaders, and institutions, who, having rejected communism, have been uncritically praising everything that opposes it—including fascism:

> ... they have been paying their respect to the victims of communism, but some of those were fascists and anti-Semites. It's dangerous because it legitimizes fascism. In a history textbook for the 6th grade, the lesson for World War Two defines Bulgarian Legionaries as a patriotic organization. And then, on the side, you have the logo of BNU[11] as their successors – but BNU are a neo-Nazi organization.[12]

---

[10] Interview with Natalia.
[11] Bulgarian National Union: a far-right organization.
[12] Interview with Natalia.

Another group of adversaries is the segment of the political elite that offers a political pardon to extremism.

> For three years, there hasn't been a verdict in the 2010 trial.[13] I was at the trial. So were Angel Dzhambazki,[14] Dimitar 'the Homeless' Lazarov, and one of the assailants. They've been trying to exonerate those thugs by involving them in politics, putting them on the voting lists for district delegates. The law must stipulate that such people cannot enter those lists, and it must be enforced.[15]

Friends have been defined as well. Unlike adversaries, who are characterized by particularities, such as a specific extremist ideology, affiliation, and activities, friends are defined universally, as carriers of lofty humanistic values: "In HoRa, we're unified by the idea that it is a most human choice to be against racism."[16] The very name of the group sounds like a slogan: **Ho**rata sreshtu **ra**sizma (People against Racism) = HoRa (PeoPle).

Curiously, this universalist conception of friends sees Others as a cause, not as individuals. They will be transformed into individuals and genuine friends by the figure of the pro-diversity activist.

The Social Entrepreneur

She never imagined that one day people would point to her as an example of a successful social entrepreneur. Business is not her world; her fundamental values are sharing and solidarity. Her civic activism started during her university years: "... I saw an invitation on Facebook, about some civic monitoring. I applied and was interviewed on the following day, and they accepted me. That was my first contact with volunteer work, with the civil sector, with activism. Right during the interview, I realized that these people and I speak a language I've never spoken with anyone else. I felt part of them."[17] She was interested in a plethora of issues and did not have a predefined target for her volunteer work, but it was the latter that introduced her to a core issue in her activism: refugees and migrants: "... that was my first encounter with refugees, with the idea that people who have applied for asylum have been detained instead of going to free-access facilities. It was a grave violation of human rights .... And it somehow moti-

---

[13] The lawsuit about the assault against the peaceful activists.
[14] A leader of VMRO (IMRO), a Bulgarian nationalist party.
[15] Interview with Natalia.
[16] Interview with Natalia.
[17] Interview with Svetlana.

vated me."[18] She did not intend to turn volunteering into a profession, but—as easily and naturally as everything else that happens to her—it became one: "everywhere I've been, I've started as a volunteer and then I've been offered a paid position. It was the same with X, this volunteering platform: at first I was a volunteer, but as soon as they got their first funding, they invited me, promoted me twice in the first months, and from a coordinator, I suddenly rose to chair of the board."[19] Nowadays, Svetlana is widely renowned. What distinguishes her case is not her rise from volunteering to a professional career and recognition but in a sense the opposite: notwithstanding her rise and recognition, she radiates the same enthusiasm, spontaneity, joy, smiles, curiosity, and warmth as she did during her first steps. Hence the choice of her pseudonym ("Svetlana" means "Light One"): it captures the smiling lightness of her activism.

Social entrepreneurship also came easily—in the multicultural initiatives in which she involved migrants: "We do social entrepreneurship, which lets us be sustainable and independent of donors. … We're often presented as successful social entrepreneurs, for instance we organize multicultural catering and thus provide work to refugees and migrants who own restaurants. We also run culinary trainings or team building for businesses."[20]

If Natalia's cause is the struggle against racism and xenophobia, Svetlana's is the bridge: "… building bridges among people, on a purely human, basic level. Also, we've always made it a top priority to provide foreigners with a platform where they can speak for themselves, introduce themselves, be the center of attention."[21] Her interview did not focus on the numerous invitations she receives from prestigious international forums in order to present her social entrepreneurship but rather dwelt on her joy when she managed to make the immigrant owner of a small restaurant "open up." For a long time, he used to steer clear of Bulgarians, but Svetlana's skill in building intercultural bridges gradually helped him relax, and nowadays he is actively looking for forums and opportunities to speak up. Svetlana's pro-diversity narrative constructs the Other in the spirit of Emmanuel Levinas's ethics of Otherness: "The Other reveals himself in

---

[18] Interview with Svetlana.
[19] Interview with Svetlana.
[20] Interview with Svetlana.
[21] Interview with Svetlana.

his alterity not in a shock negating the I, but as a primordial phenomenon of gentleness" (Levinas 1969: 150).

Characteristically, Svetlana's narrative contains no adversaries, only friends. She personalizes and humanizes even those institutions criticized by all activists: she "translates" them into concrete experts, and then she introduces those experts to the target group of their job ("they used to know only a few refugees, never had the chance to meet them, and now thanks to our efforts, some of them have come to know the migrants"[22]).

Svetlana is something of an exception within social entrepreneurship, but she's the norm for pro-diversity activism. Her citizenship is not contestatory like Natalia's but solidary and multicultural. Her potential for transformations is similarly high and assumes three aspects: firstly, the model of social entrepreneurship that makes pro-diversity NGOs financially independent; secondly, the pro-diversity activism that builds bridges both to the Others (refugees and migrants) and to one's own (governmental institutions); and thirdly, the power of the utopian narrative that a world without enemies is possible, and Others are friends who have faces and voices (after Hannah Arendt).

The Human Rights Lawyer
Maria has been called a "wonderful lawyer"[23] in the field of human rights. She is the director of the law program of a prestigious human rights organization,[24] an internationally recognized expert, participant in European anti-discrimination networks. She was one of the main authors of the Protection Against Discrimination Act and a champion for its passing. Maria grows furious as she lists countless examples of discrepancies between Bulgarian and EU law, of the false dilemma between freedom of speech and hate speech:

> ... our magistrates become solidary with them by defending their right of expression. There is no such thing as the right of hate speech .... And the European Court has an unambiguous position. When someone like Volen Siderov makes a complaint in Strasbourg, not only does the court tell him, 'Your appeal is unfounded,' it also tells him, 'It is inadmissible. It abuses the

---
[22] Interview with Svetlana.
[23] Interview with a human rights journalist.
[24] Because of her public visibility, Maria's anonymity is relative, but we use a pseudonym as with our other interviewees. During her interview, Maria did not request complete anonymization of her statements, which she makes public on a regular basis.

right of appeal, because hate speech is a priori incompatible with the values and spirit of our conventions.' However, our supreme judges either have no idea about this or have reasons to protect these people.[25]

Maria's accomplishments are highly appreciated and recognized both at home and across Europe. She is typical and emblematic of an extremely positive phenomenon: young lawyers' involvement with the rights of vulnerable groups, including minorities and migrants. Human rights lawyers are among the most public and influential actors of both solidary and contestatory citizenship, greatly boosting its impact. The efficacy of their politics of transformation can be synthesized in the following directions: synchronizing Bulgarian legislation with lofty anti-discrimination and human rights regulations, a positive example of which is the Protection Against Discrimination Act; vigorous counteraction against the systemic deficits of Bulgarian justice through appealing and winning cases in the European Court of Human Rights; and the blending of legal practice and activist causes, which generates a powerful public resonance.

The Minority Activist
"The problems of 4,000 Bulgarian Jews are, how shall I put it, insignificant; it's Bulgarian society that has a problem, and we try to do something about it. Sometimes we succeed too. Take, say, the Bulgarian National Union: by cooperating with people from the responsible governmental agencies, we prevented the union from registering a political party in 2005."[26] This excerpt from Isaac's interview illustrates minority activism with its anti-racist struggle (focusing on anti-Semitism) as a key actor for consolidating both contestatory and solidary citizenship. Sartre said that if Jews did not exist, anti-Semites would have invented them (Sartre 1946: 14). Isaac knows that anti-Semites, with their "hater" efficacy in overproducing Others as enemies, pose a problem, not for a particular minority but for society as a whole. Fighting anti-Semitism is defined as a civic and political project of resolute opposition to all manifestations of extremism: online and off-line hate speech,[27] extremist organizations, and campaigns. This endeavor requires broad coalitions, and when civic activists and governmental institutions manage to form them, the results soon follow, such

---
[25] Interview with Maria.
[26] Interview with Isaac.
[27] We analyze it in the next section.

as the BNU case: an institutional barrier was created, preventing the entry of a new extremist party into politics.

The Human Rights Blogger

"I decided to start a blog and had to choose a cause for myself."[28] Valentina entered activism via the Internet. She decided to stay and diversified her virtual agoras: the blog established her as a key online human rights activist; she left her prestigious job to become a journalist in an electronic human rights media; there is barely any human rights group across the social networks where she is not among the most active authors.

Valentina entered activism via the Internet but did not remain confined to it. From street protests against state capture to anti-racist rallies, she has been on the square with her mild smile and her activist resolution, her camera and journalistic spirit, with which she brings protests to social networks and online media. Valentina is one of the first Bulgarian actors of e-citizenship, defined by Anna Krasteva with the Internet-Indignation-Imagination triad (Krasteva 2013). Indignation at racism, extremism, and violence becomes balanced by the imagination of the politics of friendships, of the possibility of a world of solidarity with the most vulnerable, discriminated, marginalized people: Roma, immigrants, refugees, and LGBT. Valentina sees them as her friends in all senses of the word: from Facebook to the existential one.

The Immigrant Activist

We met at a radio station during a debate about the Syrian crisis when it had just started. Ever since, Emelie has been one of the most widely known and respected figures of the Syrian community in Bulgaria, tirelessly carrying out a wide palette of activities. Since the first days of the refugee crisis, she was in the fore of humanitarian aid. When the crisis abated in Bulgaria, Emelie transferred her humanitarian activity to the refugee camps in Greece. Of course, she has not forgotten the camps in Bulgaria, and as we finalize this text in the scorching heat of summer, she is with the refugees in the largest camp near the border.

Emelie's enemies differ from those we have discussed so far: they are led by Bashar al-Assad, dictator and persecutor of his own people. Emelie speaks Bulgarian fluently, and while her humanitarian work was in full swing, she received a Bulgarian passport: an illustration of multicultural

---

[28] Interview with Valentina.

citizenship (Kymlicka 1996) and the capacity of immigrants in Bulgaria to be among the pioneers and activists of solidary citizenship. Solidary citizenship is the keyword here; Emelie's activity—along with that of the immigrant community—is humanitarian, not contestatory. It does not demand rights but provides aid.

Neo-post-transformation, or How to Create Solidarity Citizenship with Words

Michael Minkenberg constructed the notion of *transformation of the transformation* in order to diagnose the manner in which far-right radical parties have reversed the post-communist transformation by shifting it away from the liberal democratic order (Minkenberg 2015). We would rename this negative transformation stemming from the mainstreaming of national populism as *post-transformation*. The research question in this chapter is the opposite: can the populist post-transformation be turned around by revitalizing the civic democratic potential, and does solidary citizenship have the capacity to enact this change, which we would call *neo-post-transformation*[29]?

> In Bulgaria, there are few civic activists, few people willing to lend their name to a cause, few people prepared to dedicate some of their leisure time to a social cause, few people ready to go out in the streets in the name of an idea, and I think this is the main reason for the fragility of Bulgarian democracy. … Each cause that has attracted a significant number of people has succeeded. So the problem is lack of support.[30]

This critical diagnosis of civic activism comes from a human rights blogger; an anti-racist activist explains its origins: "Anti-Nazi and anti-fascist formations have never united. They split into right-wing and left-wing ones. However, Nazis unite, no matter their differences."[31] The human rights blogger outlines the dilemma of civic activism: a proper change requires a critical mass of involved citizens, which is difficult to gather in the situation of a populist wave.

---

[29] This term has been inspired by the history of art, where *post* is sometimes followed by *neo*: for example, neo-Impressionism and neo-Dadaism (von Beyme 2015: 23).
[30] Interview with a human right blogger.
[31] Interview with an anti-racist activist.

We will analyze the counter-populist strategy of contestatory and solidary citizenship through the discourses produced and reinforced by civic activists in public space. Civic activists will speak in their own voices again, yet here they will sound more forceful for two reasons: the formation of clusters and performativity. *How to Do Things with Words* (Austin 1975) is a lesson that has been perfectly learned by each influential extremist populism, which generates xenophobia, exclusive attitudes, and politics of Othering by hate speech. We will analyze how the lesson of performativity has been learned by solidary speech by examining four narrative clusters crucial for the civic deconstruction of politics, policies, and practices of discrimination: deconstruction of the hegemonization of discrimination; the justice system, discrimination instead of justice; discrimination practices of anti-discrimination institutions; and civic visibilization of extremism versus institutional invisibilization. We should note that we analyze the discourses of civic activists on institutions, not the institutions per se. These discourses are often critical, even very critical.

Deconstruction of the Hegemonization of Discrimination

The discursive strategy of activist speech in the first group of narrative clusters expands in two directions: the mapping of scapegoats and a critical assessment of the civic capacity for protecting vulnerable groups.

The map of scapegoats is delineated by determining which social groups suffer most discrimination. This map is so densely populated by both classic minorities and the new immigrants that we may speak of a hegemonization of discrimination:

> I don't think there's such a thing as "most discriminated." All kinds of discrimination are terrible. Roma people have been turned into a sub-class. Many Roma become the subject of multi-layered discrimination: as Roma, as marginalized laborers, as the poorest stratum. Hatred of Turks is very visible but also very normalized. For instance, barely anyone explains to children that contemporary Turks have very little in common with the Ottoman Empire. Hatred of people of color and migrants also gets swept under the rug. Most people of color in Bulgaria have been assaulted by skinheads but nobody talks about it.[32]

---

[32] Interview with an anti-racist activist.

The other discursive aspect is the critical assessment of insensitivity toward vulnerable groups, of perceiving discrimination as a concrete problem affecting a specific group but not as a systemic problem of society as a whole: "When gypsies get assaulted – it's nothing, they're marginalized; when left-wing people get assaulted – it's nothing, they're evil; when Jews get assaulted – it's nothing, they're arrogant; when LGBT get assaulted – there's some talk, but nobody sympathizes with them, etc."[33]

The Justice System: Discrimination Instead of Justice?
"On a sidetrack"[34] is how a human rights journalist summarized the key problem of the Bulgarian justice system: the legislation is good because it has been transposed from EU and also because of the competent dedication of human rights lawyers, but it does not work: "… the Deputy Chief Prosecutor says, "I understand, colleagues, but we ask that our prosecutors receive training; they do not know or understand this article,[35] do not know how to administer it, cannot identify the crime.""[36] This lack of understanding or implementing is systematic, and the border between the two is rather fluid: "The authorities don't recognize such crimes or look the other way, treat them as acts of hooliganism, domestic violence, an accident, and not as hate crimes – or in certain cases, when there's been a planned assault, as organized crime."[37]

Unadministered anti-discrimination legislation is the first sub-cluster in the criticisms of our legal system. The interviews teem with examples; we will mention only two more. Volen Siderov's virulent anti-Semitism had been interpreted by a certain prosecutor as "'problematization' on the Jewish issue in Bulgaria. We wonder what this issue is; is Holocaust denial problematization?"[38]

The extremist party Ataka's brochure "Gypsy Violence: a Threat to the State"[39] "overflows with qualifiers such as 'monsters, animals, semi-

---

[33] Interview with an anti-racist activist.
[34] Tatyana Vaksber, 26 April 2012. "Waiting for the train on a sidetrack" (in Bulgarian): http://www.bghelsinki.org/bg/publikacii/obektiv/tatiana-vaksberg/2012-04/da-chakash-vlaka-na-gluh-kolovoz/.
[35] Concerning Holocaust denial.
[36] Interview with a human rights journalist.
[37] Interview with an anti-racist activist.
[38] Interview with a minority activist.
[39] Multiple NGOs have notified the Prosecutor's Office about this brochure. Interview with an anti-racist activist, representative of ENAR.

humans.' A prosecutor said those weren't evaluative statements but facts, and the Prosecutor's Office refused to file a suit."[40] Civic activists see this stance not as poor understanding, passivity, and inaction but as an active policy of legitimizing populist extremism.

The other sub-cluster of criticisms concerns the legal system's resistance to positive change. The European Court of Human Rights can correct but cannot change Bulgarian justice: its decisions affect neither the official assessment of Bulgarian judges nor the system as a whole:

> Bulgaria has a systematic problem of failing to implement the rulings of the Strasbourg court. There aren't even measures to bring these rulings to all magistrates, as a form of prevention so that similar things don't happen again. Such questions – whether a magistrate has contributed to the Bulgarian state receiving a guilty verdict from Strasbourg – are being utterly ignored; they play no role in the external assessment of the magistrate, just like human rights. It's a huge issue, because the system effectively says, "Human rights are irrelevant."[41]

Discrimination Practices of Anti-discrimination Institutions
Discourses in this cluster range from criticisms of inaction ("The Commission for Protection against Discrimination[42] seems to have gone AWOL: for 60 trials, they've issued only two rulings."[43]) to indignation at the deliberate violation of the law and the emergence of a Kafkaesque world of lawlessness, which can be challenged only by European courts:

> We had a suit at the Commission for Protection against Discrimination, because S.K. had been kept in solitary confinement ... for almost a year, while the law stipulates that the maximum detention period in solitary confinement is 15 days. Also, an order must be issued for placing the person in solitary confinement, the person has the right to appeal and be given a hearing in advance ... S.K. didn't have such an order ... we made a lot of attempts to appeal, but our appeals were declared absolutely inadmissible, with no opportunity for defense. It was a desperate situation. ... The Commission ruled that there hadn't been any discrimination. ... they didn't have any meaningful arguments. Ultimately, S.K. was let out, because we got a ruling from the Grand Chamber of the European Court of Justice in Luxembourg,

---

[40] Interview with human rights lawyer I.
[41] Interview with human rights lawyer I.
[42] We analyze the civic activists' perceptions of institutions, not the institutions per se.
[43] Interview with an anti-racist activist, representative of ENAR.

but the credit goes to the court in Luxembourg, not to the Bulgarian commission. I'm very critical of the work of the commission.[44]

Civic Visibilization of Extremism Versus Institutional Invisibilization
The systematic inability and unwillingness of Bulgarian institutions to recognize, name, and counteract extremism have spurred civic activists into action. We will summarize this action in three strategies: civic mobilization, mapping of extremism, and prevention.

The already cited instance of hooded boys attacking peaceful activists is emblematic. The Minister of Internal Affairs invisibilized extremism by calling the aggression a "scuffle between various extremist organizations, left-wing and right-wing."[45] This blurring of the boundary between assailants and activists inflamed the latter, who decided to turn the spotlight on extremism and created the anti-racist civic initiative HoRa.

The mapping of extremism, the methodical monitoring of various extremist groups along with their "specialization" and intense collaboration, has been done by certain activists and NGOs:

The same people moving around these [extremist] circles, some 5–6,000 people. They can mobilize through soccer fans, local patriotic associations or in another way. ... What we'd call "active" participants is also relative. I mean the people on the Internet; how many of these will go out in the streets depends mostly on their payment. This is a serious issue, and it gets serious payments. Also, formal structures – political parties like the Internal Macedonian Revolutionary Organization – and informal ones, such as National Resistance, interact all the time. For instance, Angel Dzhambazki, IMRO's deputy chairman, provides constant political support for the initiatives of National Resistance. He'd appear in front of the Court of Justice when a homicide trial is taking place and, being a public figure, he'd attract media, create moods. Conversely, when formal actors need someone to do a job they feel uncomfortable with, they'll use the services of those guys. They don't have a specific political platform, they only have hatred.[46]

Unlike the first strategy, which sets civic activism as a response to the institutional insensitivity to extremism, the second mapping strategy is open to collaboration with institutions: activists and NGOs are ready to involve

---
[44] Interview with human rights lawyer II.
[45] http://stopnazi-bg.blogspot.com/2010_06_01_archive.html.
[46] Interview with a minority activist.

them in order to create effective countermeasures, cf. the above example of preventing the registration of a new extremist party.[47]

It is vital to note that the civic monitoring of extremism does not have only mapping functions but also aims at prevention: "We had a case when they overlooked the fact that a boy was an active Nazi, and then this boy killed one of his classmates .... If someone had paid attention to this child – because he was a child – during his deviant behavior, perhaps the second boy would've still been alive, and the first wouldn't have to spend 15 years in prison, wrecking his whole life."[48]

POLITICS OF TRANSFORMATION

"If people invest themselves in claiming rights, they are producing not only new ways of being subjects with rights but also new ways of becoming subjects with responsibilities, since claiming rights certainly involves 'responsibilizing' selves" (Isin and Nielsen 2008: 1). The idea of citizenship as producing both acts and subjects (Isin and Nielsen 2008: 6) is crucial also for our understanding of citizenship as politics of transformation.

"These issues are utterly outside the spotlight, they're among the least important ones in the public debate."[49] Activists are acutely aware they will not change the overall political agenda, but they have a cause and a mission—to be the voice of those who have no voice: "The mission of our organisation is to actively protect the rights of disadvantaged groups – mostly refugees, immigrants and foreigners seeking asylum – thus becoming the public voice of those who haven't got a voice, promoting justice and truth applied with kindness and compassion."[50]

An activist describes the first people who introduced him to activism as "people who care about processes and social issues; they've found a proactive way to make an impact ..."[51] It is this activity—*prise de parole*, the introduction of alternative topics, protection of human rights, opposing extremism—that we define as politics of transformation. We will elaborate on its key dimensions: countering populism, or neo-post-transformation; politics of courage vs. politics of fear; and transformation as self-transformation.

---

[47] Interview with a minority activist.
[48] Interview with a minority activist.
[49] Interview with human rights lawyer II.
[50] Interview with human rights lawyer III.
[51] Interview with a pro-diversity activist.

Countering Extremism or Neo-post-transformation

We consider the very change in the media environment a success. Up until a few years ago, Nazis were called nationalists and patriots. Now they're called neo-Nazis, neofascists, racists. Some of our street actions have been successes too. ... Winning the trust of eminent intellectuals and having them participate in anti-racist videos is a success. The involvement of new people in the rallies against the Lukov March and the broadening debate about its neo-Nazi character is a success. Yet it makes little sense to talk about successes. Our goal is not to build up our CV or prove ourselves, it's to change the situation. To ... create a wave, help new activities and groups emerge.[52]

Solidary citizenship does not have the power to overturn the rise and mainstreaming of national populism, but its contributions are twofold: genuine activities and results in countering extremism and the political project for a unification, a "wave" aiming at neo-post-transformation.

Politics of Courage Versus Politics of Fear

It is important to state that neo-Nazis today, just like before, rely on terror. Be it street beatings, threats, insults – it's always some kind of violence. Everyone who gets involved with anti-Nazism has to be ready to face their aggression. However, being scared means that terror has won; that's what they want, that's why they do it. After all, they're weaker because, all things considered, they're the minority. They oppose left-wing folks, liberals, democrats, foreigners and everyone they call a 'national traitor,' LGBT, intellectuals, the minorities. ... They attack any religion or kind of Christianity that doesn't fit their Nazi interpretation of religion, they attack young people from subcultures, people with disabilities, tramps and other destitute people, or more successful people such as 'Jewish capitalists,' they call students and activists 'Sorosoids,' and ultimately, they attack everyone who doesn't fit their idea of a 'wholesome white man.' ... Tomorrow, for some invented reason of theirs, anyone may fall within the 'subhuman' category. What we must realize is that we can't let a bunch of squalling aggressors force their notion of 'patriotism' or 'Bulgarianness' onto us.... We mustn't let them be used by politicians to displace the social conflict, inequality issues and problems of the current system with interethnic hatred, a favorite tool of each power regime.

---

[52] Interview with an anti-racist activist.

Civic activism defines itself through a few ambitious political goals. The first is the struggle between interpretations of the key political conflict and the determination to counter manipulative ethnicizing and Othering with the social issue of inequality and the political problems of "the system." "Transforming the fear into moral indignation and anger" (della Porta and Diani 2006: 24), channeled and catalyzed by civic alchemy into protest energy, is the next political goal. The last one is countering the politics of fear, of overproducing adversaries, of violence and extremism with the politics of civic courage, the power of resistance.

Transformation as Self-Transformation

> I can give the example of my brother, who, when he saw a black soccer player on TV, used to say, "monkey, go back to Africa," or something like that, while in fact he didn't know any such people ... he had a very bad attitude to Muslims too, but started joining our multi-culti kitchen events – because of the food – and eventually I introduced him to a Pakistani who teaches cricket, and my brother started playing cricket ... And one day he called me to say he had a new friend from Afghanistan and really wanted me to meet him. That's when I knew we've totally done our job. Today, my brother left for Vietnam. He's become so open for other cultures, and I'm so happy, and I know it's happened to others too.[53]

This example is illustrative of transversalism, when change and transformation happen not through confrontation but through meetings, new intercultural experiences, and experimentations, transforming the Others into friends.

The politics of transformation is targeted, not only at "the system" but at every individual citizen. Every woman and man won for the cause of tolerance, and dialog is a genuine, small victory: the politics of transformation needs transformers.

CONCLUSION, OR MAPPING POST-COMMUNIST CITIZENSHIPS

Valentina and many civic activists take part in various mobilizations and embody various kinds of citizenship. Transforming citizenship from belonging and adherence to the state during communism to a larger, more dynamic understanding embracing participation, activism, and engage-

---

[53] Interview with a pro-diversity activist.

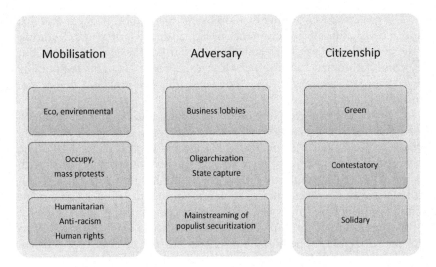

Fig. 9.1 A comparison of three types of citizenship

ment is a significant post-communist development, one of the rare instances of experimenting and revitalizing democracy. For the purposes of this conclusion, we will compare the analyzed types of citizenship—green, Occupy, and solidary—in three respects: the adversaries whose hegemony they attack, the audibility of their claims, and the temporalities[54] of their mobilizations (Fig. 9.1).

The adversaries of eco-mobilizations are powerful business lobbies, which break the rules of nature conservation, aided by corrupted institutions. Mass protests target the same adversary but on a higher level—the corruption networks of political, media, and business elites, oligarchization, state capture. Human rights and anti-racist activism opposes a different adversary: far-right nationalist parties and organizations and hate speech regardless of its source—extremist or mainstream politicians.

As far as the audibility of claims is concerned, there are two distinct poles: high audibility for green and Occupy activists versus marginalization and ridicule of human rights voices.

---

[54] For the temporalities of civic activism, see M. Castells' definition of the temporality of Occupy as a "timeless time" (Castells 2012: 223) and Anna Krasteva's idea of protest as a civic takeover of the political temporality (Krasteva 2016a: 180).

The civic takeover of time by mobilizations is one of the most invisible and most significant achievements of citizenship. During mobilizations, "the political time is not determined by the authorities or the markets, but by contestation and the citizens" (Krasteva 2016a: 21). This temporality lies "between 'no longer' and 'not yet,' after the past and before the future" (Isin and Nyers 2014: 6).

"The meaning of every mobilization is split: aside from specific literal demands, each mobilization represents the revolutionary process as a whole" (Laclau and Mouffe 2001: 11; Decreuse et al. 2014: 140). The conceptual toolkit of this study replaces "the revolutionary process" with contestatory citizenship but retains the symbolic dimension of activism when activism becomes a point of identification in itself. It is this dimension upon which we build the coordinate system for mapping the types of post-communist citizenship. The vertical axis spans from contestatory to solidary citizenship. The horizontal axis situates the adversaries of activism between the two poles of state capture and anti-racism (Fig. 9.2).

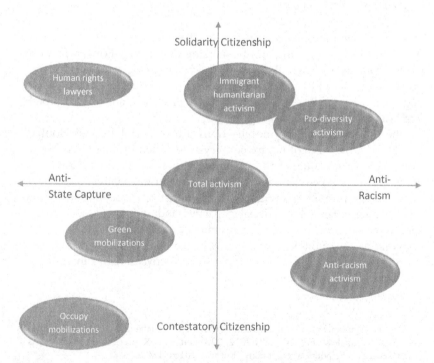

Fig. 9.2 Mapping post-communist mobilizations and citizenships

Two types of mobilizations occupy the lower left part of the diagram, the anti-state capture contestatory citizenship: Occupy and green. "Gramsci argues that one does not change the terrain of struggle oneself, but that it is to a large extent determined by the adversary. What Occupy and similar movements do is to try to reverse the order: not to chase the adversary in the latter's place, but to occupy a proper place" (Decreuse et al. 2014: 144). In the case of Bulgaria, innovating the place for civic activism is more characteristic for green mobilizations. Due to the presence of a particular face emblematic of oligarchy, the struggle of Occupy is focused on the concrete faces of state capture, along with the system that makes them possible.

Human rights lawyers occupy the area marked by solidary citizenship and anti-state capture: they defend the rights of the most vulnerable groups, often bringing lawsuits to the European Court of Human Rights due to the systematic inability of Bulgarian anti-discrimination institutions and the justice system to counteract discrimination.

In a political situation of growing "racist, anti-Turkish, Islamophobic, anti-Semitist, homophobic and far-right trends, it's crucial to create more self-organizing civic groups – for the people by the people, groups with an anti-racist and anti-fascist orientation. Groups outside of the state structures and the established NGOs and schemes; groups of genuine champions of a cause."[55] An anti-racist activist captures the pathos of the lower right part of the diagram, where civic activism unifies anti-racism and contestatory citizenship. Anti-racist activism has adopted Thomas Mann's maxim that tolerance becomes a crime when applied to evil; hence its combative nature: "We must fight for a better new world, in various ways. Anti-racism is only one of the ways and aspects of this better world."[56] This illustrates that anti-racism is mostly a struggle and counteraction; therefore it straddles the axis of adversaries.

The axis of friends—solidary citizenship—in the upper right corner is straddled by humanitarian as well as pro-diversity activism, which builds the intercultural bridges of the politics of friendship. Solidary citizenship uplifts civic activism to the intersubjective imperative of E. Levinas, where our responsibility toward others makes our own existence meaningful: "Our responsibility for the Other *founds* our subjective being-in-the world by giving it a meaningful direction and orientation" (Levinas 1969: 22).

---

[55] Interview with an anti-racist activist.
[56] Interview with an anti-racist activist.

Valentina is the total activist: she is active in both writing and protesting; her battles with racism, xenophobia, and extremism quite naturally intertwine with her friendships with the targeted victims: from refugees to LGBT. She was one of the first and most regular attendants of Occupy mobilizations. Valentina is a genuine activist and a wonderful human being, and she embodies the human rights advocacy which wages a war on all fronts of the antagonistic field ranging from the mainstreaming of national populism to state capture. This type of total activists occupies the center of the citizenship map. They create both citizenship and themselves-as-citizens. Total activists demonstrate the close bond between solidary and contestatory citizenship inasmuch as they perceive the former not merely as caring for the more vulnerable groups but as a drive to change the system which systematically (re)creates these groups. Total activism combines the agonistic and the creative; the actor's pleasure in creation through the act is intense: "… every doer, in so far as he does, takes delight in doing; … since in action the being of the doer is somehow intensified, delight necessarily follows" (Arendt 1998: 176).

None of these types of citizenship have achieved their goal, be it de-oligarchization or transformation. The neo-post-transformation did not happen, the civic activism does not succeed to reverse the far-right wave. The symbolic efficacy of mobilizations has not yet transformed into institutional efficacy (Mouffe 2013; Decreuse et al. 2014); state capture and mainstreaming of populism are still the main game in town. The battle is uneven but it hasn't been lost: Natalia's "responsibility to the next generations" connects ad hoc civic action to the historical perspective and puts citizenship on the pedestal where the political and the ethical resonate and reinforce each other.

"Politics of citizenship or politics *for* citizenship […] not only takes passion and perspective, but it also takes time. The space between 'no longer' and 'not yet' may sound like a small space but it is an enduring time" (Isin and Nyers 2014: 10). The fundamental contribution of civic mobilizations has been the political appraisal of the time between "no longer" and "not yet": it is not merely void or lost by elites for the project of democracy; it has been creatively filled up by alternative visions, multi-voice agoras, diversification, and consolidation of post-communist citizenships.

List of Interviews

1. Volunteer working with refugee children. 13 July (2017). Interviewer: Anna Krasteva.
2. Anti-racist activist, representative of HoRa, and Anti-Lukov March. 23 July 2013. Pseudonym in the text: Natalia. Interviewer: Vanya Ivanova.
3. Pro-diversity activist, representative of multi-culti NGO. 20 January 2017. Pseudonym: Svetlana. Interviewer: Anna Krasteva.
4. Human rights lawyer I. 22 April 2013. Pseudonym: Maria. Interviewer: Denitza Kamenova.
5. Minority activist. 7 August 2013. Pseudonym: Isaac. Interviewer: Ildiko Otova.
6. Human rights blogger. 11 March 11. Pseudonym: Valentina. Interviewer: Anna Krasteva.
7. Educational innovator. 25 January 2017. Pseudonym: Anton. Interviewer: Vanya Ivanova.
8. Minority rights activist. 12 August 2016. Interviewers: Anna Krasteva and Evelina Staykova.
9. Civic activist. 26 June 2013. Interviewer: Vanya Ivanova.
10. Human rights journalist. 23 July 2013. Interviewer: Anna Krasteva.
11. Numerous talks with an immigrant activist, 2013–2017. Pseudonym: Emily. Interviewers: Anna Krasteva, Ildiko Otova, and Evelina Staykova.
12. Anti-racism activist, national coordinator of European Network Against Racism (ENAR). 5 June 2013. Interviewers: Evelina Staykova and Vanya Ivanova.
13. Human rights lawyer II. 13 July 2013. Interviewer: Vanya Ivanova.
14. Human rights lawyer III. 6 June 2013. Interviewer: Vanya Ivanova.

References

Георгиева, Валентина. (2016). *Множества на несъгласните. Антропология на протестните движения в България (2009–2013)*. София: СУ Кл. Охридски.

Люцканова, Мила. (2011). „Нови, млади, „зелени". Онлайн измерения в развитието на зелената идея." В *Нови медии–нови мобилизации*, съст. Ивайло Дичев и Орлин Спасов. София. Отворено общество.

Arendt, H. (1998). *The human condition.* Chicago/London: University of Chicago Press.

Austin, J. L. (1975). *How to do things with words.* Harvard: Harvard University Press.
Braithwaite, J. (2007). Contestatory citizenship; Deliberative denizenship. In M. Smith, R. Goodin, & G. Geoffrey (Eds.), *Common minds: Themes from the philosophy of Philip Pettit* (pp. 161–181). Oxford: Clarendon Press.
Carter, A. (2001). *The political theory of global citizenship.* London: Routledge.
Castells, M. (2012). *Networks of outrage and hope. Social movements in the internet age.* Cambridge: Polity Press.
Dahlgren, P. (2006). Doing citizenship: The cultural origin of civic agency in the public sphere. *European Journal of Cultural Studies, 9,* 267–286. https://doi.org/10.1177/1367549406066073.
Dahrendorf, R. (1990). *Reflections on the revolution in Europe: In a letter intended to have been sent to a gentleman in Warsaw.* London: Chatto and Windus.
Decreuse, T., Lievens, M., & Braeckman, A. (2014). Building collective identities: How new social movements try to overcome post-politics. *Parallax, 20,* 136. https://doi.org/10.1080/13534645.2014.896560.
della Porta, D. (2015). *Social movements in times of austerity.* Cambridge: Polity Press.
della Porta, D., & Diani, M. (2006). *Social movements. Introduction.* Oxford: Blackwell.
della Porta, D., & Mattoni, A. (Eds.). (2014). *Spreading protest. Social movements in times of crisis.* Colchester: ECPR Press.
Fukuyama, F. (2006). *The end of history and the last man.* New York: Free Press.
Isin, E., & Nielsen, G. (Eds.). (2008). *Acts of citizenship.* London/New York: Zed books.
Isin, E., & Nyers, P. (2014). Introduction: Globalizing citizenship studies. In E. Isin & P. Nyers (Eds.), *Routledge handbook of global citizenship studies* (pp. 1–11). London/New York: Routledge.
Krasteva, A. (2009). Being a citizen – Not a profession, but a commitment. In K. Hristova-Valtcheva (Ed.), *New actors in a new environment: Accession to the EU, civil society and multi-level governance* (pp. 35–43). Sofia: BECSA.
Krasteva, A. (Ed.). (2013). *E-citoyennetés.* Paris: Harmattan.
Krasteva, A. (2016a). Occupy Bulgaria or the emergence of the post-communist contestatory citizenship. *Southeastern Europe, 40,* 158–187.
Krasteva, A. (2016b). The post-communist rise of national populism: Bulgarian paradoxes. In G. Lazaridis, G. Campani, & A. B eneviste (Eds.), *The rise of the far right in Europe: Populist shifts and 'othering'.* Basingstoke: Palgrave Macmillan.
Krasteva, A., & Vladisavljević, N. (2017). Securitisation versus citizenship: Populist and authoritarian misuses of security threats and civic responses in the Balkan states. *Global Campus of Human Rights Journal,* 1.2. https://globalcampus.eiuc.org/handle/20.500.11825/423
Kymlicka, W. (1996). *Multicultural citizenship: A liberal theory of minority rights.* Oxford: Clarendon Press.

Laclau, E., & Mouffe, C. (2001). *Hegemony and socialist strategy. Towards a radical democratic politics.* London/New York: Verso.
Levinas, E. (1969). *Totality and infinity.* Pittsburg: Duquesne University Press.
Minkenberg, M. (2015). *Transforming the transformation? The East European radical right in the political process.* New York: Routledge.
Mouffe, C. (2013). *Agonistics. Thinking the world politically.* London/New York: Verso.
Otova, I. (2013). Le mouvemeent ecologiste en Bulgarie. In A. Krasteva (Ed.), *E-citoyennetés* (pp. 147–162). Paris: Harmattan.
Pettit, P. (1997). *Republicanism: A theory of freedom and government.* Oxford: Oxford University Press.
Riesman, D. (2001). *The lonely crowd. The study of the changing American character.* New Haven: Yale University Press. Revised version.
Rosanvallon, P. (2006). *La contre-democratie a l'age de la defiance.* Paris: Seuil.
Sartre, J.-P. (1946). *Réflexions sur la question juive.* Paris: Gallimard.
Schmitt, C. (2007). *The concept of the political.* Chicago: University of Chicago Press.
von Beyme, K. (2015). Transforming transformation theory. The East European radical right in the political process. In M. Minkenberg (Ed.), *Transforming the transformation? The East European radical right in the political process.* New York: Routledge.

CHAPTER 10

Feminist Movements' Acts of Citizenship: Experiences from Post-Socialist Slovenia

Mojca Pajnik

This chapter starts from the thesis that social movements are not just about individual actions of protest but rather opportunities to create new ways of being in the world and practice worldly relations (Arendt 1958/1996). Movements redefine political and media agendas, they change the focus of debates, have the aspiration and the potential to change politics, and in this context we argue that they should be treated as "key actors of social change" (Crossley 2002). This chapter reflects on the differences and similarities between the "older" civil society movements from the 1980s that developed in statist/national frameworks and the "new" social movements that operate transnationally and analyzes the contemporary struggle of feminist movements in post-socialist Slovenia. As a part of the 1980s' civil society movements in the Slovenian and larger Yugoslav context, the feminist movement significantly influenced the institutionalization of gender equality politics. In the 1990s when feminist groups consolidated into non-governmental organizations, gender issues gradually became integrated in official politics. The latter trend acceler-

M. Pajnik (✉)
Faculty of Social Sciences, University of Ljubljana, and the Peace Institute, Ljubljana, Slovenia

© The Author(s) 2019
B. Siim et al. (eds.), *Citizens' Activism and Solidarity Movements*, Palgrave Studies in European Political Sociology, https://doi.org/10.1007/978-3-319-76183-1_10

ated as Slovenia joined the EU in 2004, and as noted by Burcar (2012), the new gender mainstreaming policies do not really tackle structural inequalities. Rather, institutionalized discrimination at the national and EU level is manifested in, for example, restrictive migration policies, downsizing of social provisions, and restricted access to welfare rights, which all adds to the gender, ethnic, sexual, and class divide.

In this chapter, we discuss current feminist alternatives to patriarchy, neoliberalism, and racism as articulated by feminist civil society actors and feminist initiatives borne of the citizens' uprising in 2012–2013 in Slovenia.[1] We aim to conceptualize the meanings of the recent feminist "acts of citizenship" for the democratization of societies (Isin and Nielsen 2008) in the Slovenian context. Like Isin and Nielsen (2008, p. 4), we understand acts of citizenship as creating the sense of the possible and of citizenship that is "yet to come". Acts of citizenship ask questions about responsibility towards others, they are "fundamental ways of being with others" (p. 19), and they renew people's openness to the world and enable them to disrupt the everyday routine.

The chapter explores actors and initiatives in Slovenia empirically based on focus group discussions with protagonists of feminist movements (conducted in fall 2014) and on participant observation at events. We examine the pertinent issues in these movements, their ideas as well as concrete actions and strategies of resistance. We follow Isin and Nielsen (2008, p. 24), who propose that theorizing acts of citizenship means focusing on "an assemblage of acts, actions and actors in historically and geographically concrete situations, creating a scene or state of affairs". By way of contrasting and connecting contemporary and "older" civil society feminist actors, we explore their ideologies and operational strategies. The movements' resistance is analyzed based on their perceptions of democracy, meanings of anti-racial struggles, tactics of civil disobedience, and operational strategies, that is, how they are connected and what tactics they use in struggle. We first explore the meanings of movements with focus on definitions that align with their democratization and citizenship

---

[1] The uprising started in the northeastern town Maribor in autumn 2012 and soon spread to cities throughout Slovenia. Thousands of protestors expressed dissatisfaction with local and national authorities, the corrupt political and economic elites who were responsible for the poor conditions in the country. In local communities and on the streets, a diversity of groups and initiatives responded to the forced austerity measures and malfunctioning of the contemporary political system. These were the largest protests in Slovenia since its independence in 1991.

potential and their activities. Next, we contextualize the analysis by discussing the anatomy of past and recent feminist struggle in Slovenia to shed light on the differences and similarities between feminist actors. In the methodological section, we explain the sample and introduce the movements whose opinions and actions we analyze in subsequent sections. We discuss the empirical material (focus group transcripts and observation of specific actions) in the intersection between ideological and operational struggles.

On the Meaning of Movements

In the late 1990s, we saw a revival of global activism, a proliferation of social movement actors that resist the superiority of transnational corporations, trends of commercialization, commodification of politics and culture, and the weakening of the public sphere. As pointed out by Touraine (2002, p. 95), movements are "absolutely necessary" in the efforts for democratization, which enhances participation of citizens and civil society. New social movements include movements for gender equality, migrants' movements, student movements, environmental initiatives, and so on, which change dominant political and social patterns by practicing "new forms of thinking and acting" (Crossley 2002, p. 5). Movements are not just about individual acts of protest; rather, they redefine political and media agendas and change the focus of debate and politics. In this context, they are key actors of social change (ibid, p. 8), a definition that reflects the above-mentioned theorization of acts of citizenship.

Despite their differences, social movements share the circumstance of placing themselves outside the principles of the market and ideology of the free market. Social movements are by definition protest movements—they protest against, often, illegitimate domination and the use of resources/power in society (Touraine 1987, p. 221). By politicizing the private, they transcend traditional divisions of public and private, strive for realization of solidarity, participation, and for direct democracy (Melucci 1996). Many are indifferent towards the political system and are not interested in gaining political power; others dive into mainstream politics, aspire for democratization of the system and the life-world in questioning the legitimacy of existing power holders.

As defined by Tarrow (2011, p. 6), social movements are "a form of political confrontation with elites, authorities and opponents that involve mounting, coordination and sustaining ... against powerful opponents".

Melucci (1996, pp. 29–30) sees social movement as a form of collective action that (a) generates solidarity, (b) manifests a conflict, and (c) initiates a violation of established restrictions that determine compatibility with the social system. In defining movements, existing discussions focus partially on the conception of a conflict. Like Melucci, Tarrow (2011) considers conflict as a constituent element of the movement; a conflict is a condition for the functioning of the movement, and the movement is necessarily in direct confrontation with the elites.

There is some disagreement as to whether movements prejudge their opponents, but it is agreed that they change the dominant social patterns by practicing "parallel worlds" as new forms of thought and action. Therefore, a movement is not just an individual protest action but can, in Arendtian (1958/1996) terms, be viewed as generating new ways of being in the world. The bare act of protest is, as a manifestation of the movement, of secondary importance in comparison with generating debates on public affairs. According to Habermas' early work (1963/1972), new social movements constitute the public and regenerate the vitality of the normative structure of society. They resist the colonization of the life-world by questioning the legitimacy of existing power actors and rationalize the debate about the present and the future. We can agree that movements not only focus on expressing a conflict but also push the conflict beyond the established boundaries of the system of social relations. In other words, movements violate the rules of the game, question the legitimacy of the authorities, and offer alternative guidelines for a political future (e.g. solidarity, social policies, inclusion of marginalized groups, etc.).

Diani's (1992) concept of social movements, which has recently been elaborated as a "network approach" to social movements (Diani and Mische 2015), is valuable in terms of defining trends in movements. A social movement is a non-hierarchical informal network of individuals and/or organizations that share a specific collective identity and position in a political and/or cultural conflict. The movement is fluid, not limited to formal frameworks, enabling individuals to identify with collective efforts while maintaining their own distinctive identity and position. Importantly, Mattoni and Trere (2014, pp. 257–258) distinguish between social groups participating in movements, which often "lack formal hierarchies, adopt decision-making processes based on participation and value the first-person commitments of activists", and social movement organizations, "which tend to have formal hierarchies, employ decision-making processes based on delegation ..." and have stricter organizational routines regulating their daily life. Our analysis includes both forms of movement organizing, that is, the more formal and institutionalized and the more horizontal, self-managing, and prefigurative (della Porta 2009, pp. 74–78).

Here we defend the view that social movements should be considered a manifestation of the public, a "nomadic public" (Pajnik 2007) that acts to change public space, or as "antagonism", for example, the labor movement or the proletarian counter-public (*Gegenöffentlichkeit*) conceptualized by Negt and Kluge (1972/1993). We question the thesis about the alleged invalidity of the "old" theories for the theorization of movements today. To illustrate, Cohen and Arato (1994) do not thematize social trends in opposition to civil society, which is the prevailing practice, but rather along with it. Our approach is similar in the sense that we analyze both recent and older feminist initiatives. As far as the public dimension of movements, Fraser (1992, p. 123) introduced the concept "subaltern counter-publics", which points to a multitude of publics and defines the public(s) in plural. Unlike early conceptions of (proletarian) oppression, which were created in a class conflict, alternatives to understanding the public as dynamics of citizens' movements are found among authors who do not treat the public solely in relation to power but try to rehabilitate it as a category of political action on its own (e.g. Warner 2002). According to these rehabilitations, or, as they are also called, alternative, non-dominant, rebellious, discursive, and so forth, the public is interpreted as fields that resist forces of dominant discourses and practices (Bourdieu 1998; Touraine 2002).

Over the last ten years, Europe has seen a proliferation of so-called anti-austerity movements that in conflict with the elites focus mainly on problematizing the deterioration of democratic institutions and pay attention to long-term structural transformation. In this context, della Porta has recently opted for "bringing capitalism, classes and political economy back into protest analysis" (della Porta 2015, p. 4). The 2012–2013 uprising in Slovenia, which first included diverse masses of protestors, including the young, public officials, and social movements as a "constant" and a "motor", indeed started as a critique of some capitalism trends. The critique included the public-private partnership that subjects public goods to private capital, the state-centered capitalism that impoverishes local communities, the corruption of local-regional and state elites, and the rising impoverishment of citizens (Zavratnik and Šori 2016, p. 15, 18).

However, the existing analysis refuses to simply label the uprising as anti-systemic or anti-capitalist (or anti-austerity for that matter) because many of the required changes opted for modification or "humanization" of the existing system rather than its elimination (Zavratnik and Šori 2016, p. 18). Other studies are also critical of the all-encompassing labelling of the uprising, arguing that we cannot speak about a unified or a homogeneous civil society of uprising movement (Ribać 2016; Pajnik and Zavratnik 2016). Thus, rather than labelling the feminist movement as anti-austerity movement, our analysis aims to understand one segment of the uprising, that is, feminist initiatives, by way of examining conflicts, antagonisms, and similarities between the initiatives. Consequently, it is not only important for our approach to recognize the general critique of the uprising movements against the structural transformation of society by capitalism, but it is equally important, if we are to theorize acts of citizenship, to understand the historical and the geographical background of the analyzed movements (Isin and Nielsen 2008, p. 24). The next section briefly therefore describes the history of Slovenian feminist movements.

A Brief History of Feminist Movements in Slovenia

The women's/feminist movement in Slovenia has the longest tradition among the civil society initiatives in the country. The first-wave movement, which lasted from the second half of the nineteenth century until the first decades of the twentieth century, was closely related to the national liberation movement. As elsewhere in Europe and globally, women fought for the right to vote, equal pay, pension insurance for all workers, abolition of discrimination in the private sphere (e.g. celibacy for female teachers), the right to abortion, equality of children born in and out of wedlock, and so on, and they fought to raise the educational level of women and for gender equality in politics (Jogan 2001). Women were legally given the right to vote in 1942, and in 1946, voting became a constitutional right in the Federative People's Republic of Yugoslavia (FLRJ). The constitution of the FLRJ also recognized equality of women and men in marriage; it legalized divorce and put children born in and out the wedlock on equal legal footing. Abortion became a constitutional right in 1974 (Jogan 2001).

The feminist movement in the late 1970s consisted of diverse feminist groups and voices, and there was a strong relation between theory and activism, unlike some Western European feminist movements, which separated theory and practice. In the 1980s and 1990s, feminist action was not part of national and nationalistic movement. However, the first wave of feminist action was an integral part of the national emancipation strategy in Slovenia (Jalušič 2002, p. 18). In this period, the feminist movement contributed visibly to the foundations of gender equality politics in Slovenia (Jalušič 2002; Humer 2007). The crucial event, which brought together feminist organizations and the majority of political parties, was the conservative parties' attempt to abolish Article 55 of the Slovenian Constitution, which protects the right to abortion. In addition to preserving Article 55, the feminist movement contributed to the formation of state institutions, such as the Committee for Women's Politics and the Office for Women's Politics (Humer 2007). The 1980s were also a vibrant decade marked by initiatives for rights of LGBT people in Slovenia and the establishment of the first gay and lesbian organizations (Magnus in 1984 and Lesbian Lilith in 1987).

The 1990s gave rise to a new phenomenon: the so-called period of NGO-ization of feminist and LGBT movements in Slovenia, especially in terms of institutionalization, formalization, and professionalization (Jalušič 2002; Dobnikar 2009). Over the next 15 years, the feminist NGOs' main focus area has been violence against women, engaging actors who develop anti-violence programs and campaigns, activities to stop trafficking of women and children, and equal pay, the right to abortion, and so on. LGBT organizations, which engage various groups, recently also transgender people, visibly focused on equality of same-sex partnership. In the early twenty-first century, NGOs maintained their focus in these areas while the increasingly visible and vocal third-wave feminism started to develop, at the intersection of queer politics, critique of economic-political structures, relating gender topics to other inequalities. These movements gained prominent visibility in the 2012–2013 uprising, which rekindled the spirit of the social movements from previous times, however in a new context of the social crisis and social and political disintegration, and with novel ideas. New groups, networks, and cooperation emerged, demanding responsible politics, social justice, fairness, and anti-discrimination.

Methodology and Sample

The aim of our empirical study is to explore the diffusion of "acts of citizenship" (Isin and Nielsen 2008) performed by feminist movements. We focus on the uprising, taking into consideration differences/similarities of struggle between contemporary and established movements and initiatives. Our analysis is two-pronged: We explore the movements' ideologies as well as their concrete tactics of struggle. This approach follows Melucci's (1996) understanding of movements at the crossroads of their ideas/"thinking", the ideological repertoire, and the way they operate and organize their activities in practice. In order to capture the different ideas and contrasts between various actors, we conducted two focus groups, in the fall of 2014, with actors who work with gender, feminism, and LGBT. The selection criterion was public visibility before and during the uprising in 2012–2013.

The first focus group included participants from Cultural Informational and Counselling Centre Legebitra, Central and Eastern European Network for Gender Issues, Feminist and Queer Festival Red Dawns, Lesbian Feminist University (LFU), and Feminist Action (FemA). The second focus group included an activist from Kombinat (a female choir), a representative of Legebitra, and an activist from the Revolting Women Social Workers and the Red Dawns festival. On two occasions, activists from the same initiatives participated in both focus groups, which gave us information from different actors from different generations (the focus groups included activists of both different and similar generations). Following the definitions of formalized and loose/non-hierarchical movements (Diani 1992; Mattoni and Trere 2014), our focus groups included feminist and LGBT activists from more established initiatives and from newer groups that denounce any structural organization of own operation. Ten focus group partners participated in the research. One focus group lasted for two hours and one for three; the analysis is based on verbatim transcripts of the conversations. In addition, the chapter explores material that is related to anti-racist and anti-sexist events that took place in spring and fall 2014, at the time of our research: the conference Women 20 years after Beijing and a feminist march.

A brief overview of the background of our focus group partners' initiatives shows a variety of experiences and focuses. Cultural Informational and Counselling Centre Legebitra's main aim is to empower individuals in relation to sexual orientation and to foster changes of the social system to enable a free and sovereign life regardless of sexual orientation. Legebitra was established as an NGO in 1998 and activities include activism, workshops, and training in human rights, LGBT rights, and discrimination, including lobbying. The main aim of the Central and Eastern European Network for Gender Issues is to put pressure on social democratic parties, which were formed during the transition period, to understand gender equality as the main democratic issue. The Network was established in 1994 under the auspices of the European Forum for Democracy and Solidarity, and its activities include training for advocacy and lobbying and efforts to implement gender equality in the legal frameworks of political parties and in individual countries.

Other initiatives are more recent. The feminist group Feminist Action (FemA) was formed during the uprising in 2013 as a group of feminist intellectuals aiming to incorporate the gender perspective in politics. Its main activities were related to the proposal to amend the Confiscation of Proceeds of Crime Act and to publicly problematize the situation of self-employed women in culture and put pressure on the Ministry of Culture. The Revolting Women Social Workers who joined as a group in 2012 during the uprising has a horizontal organization, that is, it has no leader, no face, and no single person can make decisions for the whole group. All actions are dedicated to combat issues they see as restrictive and oppressive regardless of whether the action is legal or not.

Lesbian Feminist University (LFU) was formed in 2010, and its main idea is to provide a safe space for theoretical and artistic activities on the platform of lesbian feminism, using methods of informal education. They tackle questions related to young women/lesbians, poverty, precarity; they organize workshops, lesbian cinema club, and other activities to promote gender equality. The main aim of the female choir Kombinat, which has attracted public attention since its establishment in 2008, is to maintain the tradition of anti-fascist resistance in the form of songs and some accompanying activities. Resistance is understood in a wider sense as national liberation resistance and as the emancipation of various marginalized groups, particularly women, but also refugees, workers, Roma, and so on. The choir says that its aim is to "use the red chalk to write a story of rebellion. Not on the walls, but on the eardrums". Their repertoire wants to maintain the music tradition of "upright posture".

In line with the social movement literature that emphasizes both the ideological and operational dimension of movements, the analysis below is twofold. First, we explore the movements' thinking, ideas, ideologies, and their understanding of racism. Second, we analyze how the movements operate, what direct actions they pursue, and how they ally with other movements. The analysis discusses differences and similarities of movements at both levels.

Movements' Thinking and Ideological Frameworks

Democracy: (Im)Possibilities of a Contested Concept

In our fieldwork we applied the RAGE project questionnaire for interviews and/or focus groups. Below, we discuss and analyze the topics that were most important for our focus group partners and reflect their understandings of the political system, democracy, anti-discrimination, and anti-racism.

Our focus group partners elaborated on their pro-feminist and anti-racist/anti-discrimination activities as acts that relate to the "renewal" of democracy. In general, they were critical of the contemporary state of democracy. However, we found some generational differences as older participants from more established initiatives focused more in their reflection on the critique of the present state of democracy, while younger generations were more prone to elaborate how they themselves view democracy through their own action. A participant who was active in the feminist movement of the 1980s and was recently active in FemA reflected that democracy has become "a very problematic notion". "Democracy that was a sort of password we used when we wanted to say something meaningful is totally non-functional today. ... It has become clear that what is behind democracy today is a total propaganda machine. ... Democracy, what we expected it to be, does not exist; it only functions as a word for misleading us". A representative from Legebitra added, "Democracy has become a swear word because representatives of democracy made this out of it. So I would not speak of a democratic struggle but of a struggle to reform this democratic system".

On the notion of democracy, a member of Kombinat reflected that what we currently experience in Slovenia is "the abuse of democracy". She referred to corruption, corrupt politicians, and the economic elite who should be stopped, fought against collectively for a kind of catharsis and "a renewal of democracy". Kombinat was established on anti-fascist and anti-racist ideology, and our focus group partner explains that she and other members find it easier to associate themselves with the label of anti-fascism and anarchism or the Liberation Front ideals.[2] She also reflects

---

[2] The Liberation Front of the Slovene Nation, originally named the Anti-Imperialist Front, was the main anti-fascist Slovene civil resistance and political organization and was active during WW 2. Its military arm was the Slovene Partisans.

that people under 40, unlike older generations, do not associate their lives with the distinctions between the left and the right, except in elections when they choose their favorites between "the horses that pull and the donkeys that are dying". Or, in the words of a representative of Legebitra, "I do not believe in the left in Slovenia. I think everyone is right-wing".

A young activist from the Revolting Women Social Workers, whose struggle is also related to other anarchist groups, focuses in her narrative on "alternative" conceptualizations of democracy rather than lament the disappearance of democracy. She also relates democracy with her experiences in the 15o movement (global protests inspired by the Arab Spring) in Slovenia "where there were a lot of experiments with decision-making, with ways of being together, and I thought this was essential for democracy". Unlike other interviewees, she adds that she has never voted, she finds elections "alienating", and she feels that elections are "a great violence over my body". She feels close to the "Zapatistas' understanding of the world" where there is multiplicity of different worlds, and each group, community, and individual organize as they wish, and they all explain their own needs the way they feel without imposing something on the neighbor or another community. She stresses the importance of a "self-organizing, horizontal level of decision-making without the established leadership or authority that tells you what to do".

A young representative from Legebitra similarly says she intimately understands democracy as participatory democracy where everyone who is affected by a certain topic has the opportunity to speak their mind and decisions are formed jointly. "This is the way I see democracy: not as elections, assemblies and not as public opinion polls". However, she reflects the (im)possibilities of practicing democratic ideals in Legebitra, which is an NGO, in contrast to the Revolting Women Social Workers. Addressing the needs of those who use the services of Legebitra, and being a formal association with a certain structure and financial scheme, Legebitra for our focus group interviewee is "not exactly an embodiment of democracy" or of her own vision of democracy. "It is illusory to expect that Legebitra would practice participatory democracy … Still, it is democratic, surely". As an example of participatory democracy, she mentions the self-organizational group for transgender persons that works under the umbrella of Legebitra.

From a more theoretical point of view, we could interpret some of these accounts together with ideas of participatory democracy developed by some feminist authors in the context of "feminist ethics of justice" (e.g. in the works of Iris M. Young, Seyla Benhabib, Carol Gilligan). Legebitra's activists, for example, seem to deal with judgements through a measure of rights, rooted in respect for the legal system. Contrary are narrations by the Revolting Women Social Workers who, following Zapatista's, adopt a more revolutionary, political, and militant discourse in describing their operation.

Critique of Racism and Its Relation to Social Stratification

A considerable part of the discussion was devoted to the issue of racism. We were interested in the actors' opinions on racism, how they understand its manifestations and how it relates to gender. If they disagreed on the meanings and problems with democracy today, they were more "orchestrated" in their critical reflections on racism. The interviewee from Central and Eastern European Network for Gender Issues in general sees the contemporary social and political system as "deeply racist, although one does not recognize this. But it is visible, in how it functions in everyday life, how it fragments groups that are un-popular, for whatever reason; how it treats Roma, other groups, women, how it produces hate speech against women, political violence against women".

Several of focus group partners relate racism to discrimination and inequalities in societies, locally and globally. A representative of Legebitra says that claiming that the only true family is a union of a mother and a father who live with their children, stressing heteronormativity as a norm and insisting this is the only genuine norm is racism. In terms of cultural differences, sexual orientation, and identity, claiming that one culture or one sexual orientation is the ultimate is also racism. The interviewee reflects critically on the notion of "the other", arguing that it always implies a certain norm against which "the other" is then judged. "One is not 'the other', the different, we all are different". "All these well-intentioned persons say: 'Yes, we accept those who are different. We tolerate those who are different. By saying this you actually create differences'".

The other representative of Legebitra similarly mentions that he uses racism to speak of different forms of discrimination. "Sometimes, a misogynist reaction is racist". He mentions the re-Catholization of Slovenian society as a problem that in the last 30 years has given rise to conservative and right-wing political parties. He adds that in the Slovenian context, racist othering refers to everyone who is not "a heterosexual white male, young or middle-aged, healthy, of Slovenian nationality and citizenship and a Catholic".

The interviewee from the Red Dawns stresses the problem that racism, ethno-nationalism, and other "tactics of othering and exclusion" have become normalized in our societies. These discourses have become omnipresent and "it becomes scary when you see what you actually fight". She feels that the media have added to this development and that these phenomena did not become normal but have always been "racism, ethnocentrism, heteronormativity, they have always been treated as normal. ... There was always something that produced the abnormalities, the deviations from the norm. Normal in our societies has always been a man, heterosexual, upper class and white". Several interviewees agree that lately most targeted groups of othering have been the poor, especially poor women, poor migrant women, and single people. An interviewee from the Revolting Women Social Workers adds othering of people who have been institutionalized. "Many end up there for having social and economic problems, they cannot pay their bills, lose their job, their apartment, live with a violent partner etc. Many have nowhere to go to and they end up in institutions, even for life".

The representative from the Central and Eastern European Network for Gender Issues mentions LGBT people, the erased, and Roma as frequent targets of "right-wing populism" that is "hiding under the vocabulary of human rights". An activist from the Red Dawns similarly observes that in Slovenia "other concepts are used so that racism can be covered up". Several of our interview partners agreed that right-wing populism is problematic when it uses terminology that is generally more used by the left political sphere.

In general, our interviewees' accounts of racism were similar in the sense that they critically view racism in relation to larger social stratification processes that mostly affect marginalized groups. We observed that discourses on racism generally recognize the shift towards what Balibar (1988) has called the culturalization of racism or "racism without races" to describe exclusion that is not only based on race but also on other personal circumstances such as gender, sexuality, religion, and so on. In addition, some accounts adopt what Pitcher (2012) would call the explanation of racism by capitalism critique. Generally, we found in our analysis that critical accounts of contemporary racism are what movements and activists have in common and they all relate their struggle along the lines of anti-racism.

Movements' Networking and Action

Our empirical analysis also explored connections or possible dissociations between movements in order to assess the differences/similarities between feminist movements. We "tested" the so-called network approach to social movements (Diani and Mische 2015), which points to differences between more fluid and more hierarchical initiatives (Mattoni and Trere 2014).

Networking with Allies

As one part of focus group discussion, we wanted to know if and to what extent movements cooperate with other actors nationally and transnationally. Despite generational differences between movements, they all participate in local and transnational networking. The specificities of their networking strategies reflect the thematic foci of their work, meaning that they associate with similar initiatives and groups, and their networking and organization practices reflect their ideologies discussed above.

Kombinat has connections with other self-organized choirs in the former Yugoslavia. Their bond is their will to self-organize and express rebellion through songs. Our focus group partner reflects that Kombinat has been self-organizing for seven years, sticking together, networking, experimenting with finances and locations, and that it is very different for them than for established choirs that receive public funding. The Red Dawns also network both in and outside of Slovenia. They have organized some "half-guerrilla actions", attended protests in cooperation with the Revolting Women Social Workers and the Lesbian Feminist University. They have worked with the anarchist group gathered around Infoshop; and they have cooperated with NGOs such as the Association Against Violent Communication and the SOS telephone line on actions related to violence against women (established in the 1990s in the NGO-ization period of the movement). Our interviewee explains that they also work regionally and have partners in other EU states. In the Balkan region, there is a network feminist-queer festivals with focus on certain topics, and they "experiment with methods, ways of doing things, in a non-hierarchical way, bottom-up".

Legebitra, which is formally an NGO, is member of several international associations, like IGLYO and ILGA Europe, and co-founder of an informal international network of LGBT associations from the Balkan region, East Europe, and Scandinavia. Unlike most other initiatives from our sample, Legebitra is funded by the state and cooperates with several NGOs and governmental institutions on various human rights and anti-discrimination issues. Legebitra is active in the campaign "For all families", which demands rights for same-sex families, and has formed a network of 13 organizations, including three leftist political parties. They work with governmental institutions when its members are invited as experts to various professional bodies.

The Revolting Women Social Workers network with Infoshop, Social Center Rog, have organized a rally against sexism with an autonomous feminist coalition, including the Red Dawns, the Lesbian Feminist University, and a new feminist choir, Zborke. Unlike Legebitra, the interviewee explains that the Revolting Women Social Workers do not cooperate with formal institutions, "because we like being autonomous so that we can attack anybody at any time, whenever we feel there is a need, and this would not be possible if we were financed by someone". The Revolting Women Social Workers prefer non-hierarchical organization, practicing direct democracy and form alliances with anarchist groups. Like the Red Dawns, they did not join FemA, which managed to bring together several movements during the uprising in the demands against political and systemic corruption, clientelism, nepotism, and for restoration of property that was taken away unlawfully. The interviewee from FemA says they never explicitly said why they did not want to cooperate, but they allegedly feared the domination of the All-Slovenian Uprising Movement, which goes along with their ideal of non-hierarchical organization of struggle.

The movements use different strategies when they seek allies for their causes. Groups with a longer history of operation generally form networks not only with sympathizers but also with established institutions aiming at institutional change. Other groups define their operation beyond and against any institutionalism. The different strategies and goals should not be used against movements but be viewed as a characteristic of movement's organizing that points to the plurality of voices and opinions.

Approaches in Fighting Racism and Gender Inequality

In addition to reflecting on racism at the general level, our fieldwork partners talked about their own anti-racist engagement, which, as found in the analysis, is related to the thematic and organizational foci of their movements and reflects their thinking and ideas. For example, the women's choir Kombinat fights racism through their songs; they select anti-fascist and anti-racist songs for their repertoire and include their own interventions in the songs, for instance, the recent "We are against suppressors, abusers, homophobes and racists".

The Red Dawns mainly engage critically against misogyny and ethno-nationalism and mainly in the Slovenian context. Our interviewee mentions workshops where they debate the effects of the intersections of gender, ethnicity, and age with migrant women. They organize educational seminars, readings, and film presentations and critically address issues related to gender and ethnicity as their anti-racist engagement. At the time of research, the Revolting Women Social Workers were active in mental health as one aspect of racism. Our interviewee explains that they work a lot with overcoming the situation where intellectual or physical ability determines who lives "outside" (of institutions); who can have children, a job, an apartment; who is able to move around freely; and so on.

Legebitra works with various NGOs and governmental bodies on anti-discrimination, anti-homophobia, and anti-racism projects. In contrast to other non-formal groups, they engage in direct work with state institutions and political parties, for example, the referendum on same-sex partnership. The interviewee from Central and Eastern European Network for Gender Issues mentions migration-related activities where they made contact with the asylum seekers. "The worst thing is that we have never succeeded in changing the state's attitude towards male and female asylum seekers. This relation is very bureaucratic, very much driven by the toughest European bureaucrats".

The difference between the movements' actions is that some use institutional means of struggle, while others practice anti-racism by organizing workshops, events, and screenings, and in whether the struggle is "legal" or breaches officially defined borders of legality/illegality. More formalized initiatives such as Legebitra and the Central and Eastern European Network for Gender Issues use recognized legal means of struggle, whereas the Red Dawns and the Revolting Women Social Workers engage in guerrilla-like actions to point out injustices and make authorities accountable for their actions. The interviewee from the Revolting Women Social Workers mentions the temporary occupation of the empty cinema Triglav in Ljubljana during the uprising. An assembly was organized to discuss the problem of empty places, the issue of property, and other topics. The occupation was initiated by activists and was then joined by several other people who became interested and participated in the debates about homelessness, needing a place to study, work, and so on. "This was an important experience. If you look at it, it was illegal since people still have proceedings in court. At the same time, the action gave food for thought to the community in the sense that what is written as legal is not necessarily legitimate. It is not necessary to comply with the rules, and not complying is not dangerous. It is not necessarily something that some anarchist and extremists do. Rather it is something that we can all do".

The interviewee from the Central and Eastern European Network for Gender Issues has many years of experience with institutional politics. She explains that the Women's lobby did not act directly against the law, but that the members breached the party indiscipline: "Every time the party went in a direction that we did not want it to go, we organized public actions. Several times the party had to change its point of view and move a bit towards where we wanted it to be. ... and party disobedience can have severe consequences. Because if you do it about three times and when they realize that you may be dangerous for their peace and action, they start isolating groups that act this way. ... Several groups have been isolated this way. Their leadership changed, the group was suppressed, something happened, or they simply vegetate".

To explain the similarities and differences between contemporary feminist movements, our analysis includes participant observation of anti-sexist events that took place during our research. The events were the Feminist riot, organized by the Revolting Women Social Workers (May 23, 2014), and the conference Women 20 years after Beijing,[3] organized by the Women's Lobby of Slovenia and the Ministry of Labor, Family, Social Affairs and Equal Opportunities (November 13–14, 2017). The riot took place in the streets of Ljubljana, and the conference was held at the congress center Brdo pri Kranju, where meetings at state and government level are organized.

The main idea of the conference was to discuss gender equality and the position of women in general, to find out what has been done and achieved in Slovenia and compared to 1995. The topics of debate among participants, mainly women from different professional backgrounds, age, sexual orientation, and gender identity, included the situation of women in Slovenia, and in Europe, in the last 20 years, and challenges for the future, with strong emphasis on young women and transgender persons as an overlooked but integral part of gender equality politics. Other topics were women and decision making, women and economy, women in private lives, violence against women, sexual and reproductive rights of women, and poverty. The conference ended with the adoption of the

---

[3] The reflection on the conference is based on observations by Živa Humer, who attended the conference (see Pajnik et al. 2014).

Feminist Manifesto 2014, which was first called Women's Manifesto, but in the joint discussion activists from Transfeminist Initiative TransAkcija Institute emphasized the importance of inclusion of all, and the term "feminist" was recognized as a broader and including transgender and queer persons. The Feminist Manifesto 2014 contains findings and requirements in the areas identified as important in Slovenia in order to achieve greater equality between women and men and is the basis for the action (http://www.zenskilobi.si/).

"Feminism to the streets – March against sexism!" was one of the slogans inviting people to join a feminist march, via Facebook, posters, and other communication means, where the Revolting Women Social Workers played a visible role. Women 20 years after Beijing was organized by an established women's initiative, while the march was initiated by recent feminist movements who prefer non-hierarchical and non-representative action. The conference ended with a manifesto pointing out the needs to improve gender policies, but the march adopted a different action strategy and language: "The march will appropriate the streets, flood the city, and give us the chance to say where the vulva pinches us! We shake the trends in society, spit over sexists and try to analyse the position of women in times of crisis, and we want at the same time to take back the streets. ... Sexism is a glue that holds together political elites, economic exploitation, the academic environment, the media, the church that hypocritically contributes to the retraditionalization of women's position in society and to the repatriarchization of society". Manifestos published on Facebook defined sexism: "Sexism is academic institutions that sustain men in managerial positions and push women towards less esteemed work in precarious positions. Sexism in church ideology that reduces us to the uterus and the career of the family ..., attacks the right to abortion and the right to decide over our own body. Sexism is the idea that we need the police to protect us as if we cannot protect ourselves, and by this it covers up that violence is a problem of a patriarchal society. Sexisms is inscribed in the economic exploitation as women are the first to get fired, receive less pay and do most of the unpaid work at home. ..."

Conclusion

We have analyzed contemporary feminist movements in post-socialist Slovenia with focus on similarities and differences between various movements. Our analysis, which is based on focus group discussions and participant observation at events, includes actors who work in informal networks and in NGOs and, expectedly, some of their viewpoints as well as modes of anti-racist and anti-sexist struggle differ. While some actors refuse to cooperate on anti-racism with the established bodies, others are engaged with political bodies who are in power and fight, for example, for legal changes. We have shown that most of the actors are aware of the empowerment potential in working with others, and in general, they express inclination towards intersectional engagement, that is, working across differences between movements. On the other hand, we have also pointed to some differences between movements, their ideas, understandings of action, and so on that might prevent collaboration. Still, discussions have shown that on several occasions movements do cooperate, nationally and transnationally.

The analysis has uncovered some interesting thinking about concepts like (anti)racism and democracy. The anti-racist struggle has been reflected in broad terms by movements that critically address gender differences, the rising ethno-nationalism and retraditionalization of society. Younger movements are more keen to reflect on anti-racism in combination with anti-capitalism; social stratification, rising poverty, and unemployment add to the hate against minority groups. Moreover, our focus group partners critically addressed democracy as a concept that has been emptied by the incapacities of the political establishment. Political actors distancing themselves from the citizens, elitism, and corrupt dealings between political and economic circles have devalued democracy, which needs to be "renewed" or "reformed". A new meaning should primarily capture in a satisfactory way the current processes of social and political disintegration. Social movements propose alternatives to improve life conditions for citizens and non-citizens alike and are key actors in struggles against the disintegration.

References

Arendt, H. (1958/1996). *Vita activa*. Ljubljana: Krtina.
Balibar, É. (1988). Is there a "neo-racism"? In É. Balibar & I. Wallerstein (Eds.), *Race, nation, class: Ambiguous identities* (pp. 17–28). Verso: London.
Bourdieu, P. (1998). *Acts of resistance: Against the myths of our time*. Cambridge: Polity Press.
Burcar, L. (2012). Tradicija in feminizem [Tradition and feminism]. *Borec, 64*, 233–236.
Cohen, J. L., & Arato, A. (1994). *Civil society and political theory*. Cambridge: MIT Press.

Crossley, N. (2002). *Making sense of social movements in a globalized world.* Houndmills: Palgrave.
della Porta, D. (2009). Consensus in movements. In D. della Porta (Ed.), *Democracy in social movements* (pp. 73–99). New York: Palgrave Macmillan.
della Porta, D. (2015). *Social movements in times of austerity: Bringing capitalism back into protest analysis.* Cambridge/Malden: Polity Press.
Diani, M. (1992). The concept of social movement. *The Sociological Review, 40,* 1–25.
Diani, M., & Mische, A. (2015). Network approaches and social movements. In D. della Porta & M. Diani (Eds.), *The Oxford handbook of social movements* (pp. 306–325). Oxford: Oxford University Press.
Dobnikar, M. (2009). Gibanje proti nasilju nad ženskami med feminizmom in socialnim delom [Movement against violence against women between feminism and social work]. *Dialogi, 45,* 98–111.
Fraser, N. (1992). Rethinking the public sphere: A contribution to the critique of actually existing democracy. In C. Calhoun (Ed.), *Habermas and the public sphere* (pp. 109–142). Cambridge, MA: MIT Press.
Habermas, J. (1963/1972). *Theorie und Praxis: Sozialphilosophische Studien.* Suhrkamp Verlag: Frankfurt am Main.
Humer, Ž. (2007). Europeanization and the equal opportunities policy in Slovenia. In K. Fábián (Ed.), *Globalization: Perspectives from Central and Eastern Europe* (pp. 305–326). Amsterdam: Elsevier.
Isin, E., & Nielsen, G. M. (Eds.). (2008). *Acts of citizenship.* London: Zed Book.
Jalušič, V. (2002). *Kako smo hodile v feministično gimnazijo* [How we attended feminist gymnasium]. Ljubljana: * cf.
Jogan, M. (2001). Žensko gibanje [Women's movement]. *Enciklopedija Slovenije,* zv. 15(WI-Ž), 318–324. Ljubljana: Mladinska knjiga.
Mattoni, A., & Trere, E. (2014). Media practices, mediation processes, and mediatization in the study of social movements. *Communication Theory, 24,* 252–271.
Melucci, A. (1996). *Challenging codes: Collective action in the information age.* Cambridge: Cambridge University Press.
Negt, O., & Kluge, A. (1972/1993). *Public sphere and experience: Toward an analysis of the bourgeois and proletarian public sphere.* Minneapolis: University of Minnesota Press.
Pajnik, M. (2007). Nomadska javnost [Nomadic public]. *Javnost–The Public, 14,* 39–53.
Pajnik, M., & Zavratnik, S. (2016). Uvodnik. Družbena gibanja in alternativna politika: Vstaje v Sloveniji 2012–2013 [Introduction. Social movements and alternative politics: Uprising in Slovenia]. *Družboslovne razprave, XXXII*(82), 7–11.

Pajnik, M., Humer, Ž., & Šori, I. (2014). *Social movements as populist "antibodies" in Slovenia*. WS3 Rage project report. Ljubljana: Peace Institute.
Pitcher, B. (2012). Race and capitalism redux. *Patterns and Prejudice, 46*(1), 1–15.
Ribać, M. (2016). Dinamika in duh vstajništva – Klasifikacija in nasprotja med protestnimi skupinami v Sloveniji [The dynamic and spirit of uprisings: Classification and differences of various protest groups in Slovenia]. *Družboslovne razprave, XXXII*(82), 33–49.
Tarrow, S. (2011). *Power in movement: Social movements and contentious politics*. Cambridge: Cambridge University Press.
Touraine, A. (1987). Social movements: Participation and protest. *Scandinavian Political Studies, 10,* 207–222.
Touraine, A. (2002). The importance of social movements. *Social Movement Studies, 1,* 89–95.
Warner, M. (2002). *Publics and counterpublics*. New York: Zone Books.
Zavratnik, S., & Šori, I. (2016). Od 'Nesimo jih vun k zamolku ulice: Diskusija o kriminalizaciji uporov in premiku k družbi nadzora [From "Let's throw them out" to silenced streets: A discussion on criminalization of the uprising and the shift towards a society of control]. *Družboslovne razprave, XXXII*(82), 13–32.

CHAPTER 11

Citizens' Activism for Reimagining and Reinventing Citizenship Countering Far-Right Populism

Anna Krasteva, Aino Saarinen, and Birte Siim

Citizenship is a Janus: status and participation, belonging and contestation, membership and practice, legal label and performance. Citizenship is "fixed" by law and policies, from one side, and is liquefied as a process by non-governmental actors, from another side. The two faces can "discipline or emancipate, enforce norms or open up new possibilities for their questioning and transformation" (Neveu 2014, p. 87). The two faces of Janus differ in multiple ways: the major instance, the type of definition, the key function, the variety of identity, and the forms of expressions—passive and active citizenship. The state is the central instance that defines citizenship in legal terms as a status. The citizens take the scene in the second

A. Krasteva (✉)
Department of Political Sciences, New Bulgarian University, Sofia, Bulgaria

A. Saarinen
Aleksanteri Institute, Helsinki, Finland

B. Siim
Department of Culture and Global Studies, Aalborg University, Aalborg, Denmark

© The Author(s) 2019
B. Siim et al. (eds.), *Citizens' Activism and Solidarity Movements*, Palgrave Studies in European Political Sociology, https://doi.org/10.1007/978-3-319-76183-1_11

interpretation and define citizenship as participation. The first reading is top-down, the second is bottom-up. Ordering is the major function of the institutional citizenship, while the activist face dynamizes citizenship. The first is more "generous"—the allegiance to a citizenship opens access to rights: "citizenship as an 'institution' mediates rights between the subjects of politics and the polity to which these subjects belong" (Isin and Nyers 2014, p. 1). The second is more problematic and is often expressed in struggles (Harrington 2014) for rights where contestation takes the scene: "Because contestation is at the heart of our definition, we believe that citizenship is fundamentally about political struggles over the capacity to constitute ourselves as a political subject" (Isin and Nyers 2014, p. 8). Citizenship as political subjectivity (Harrington 2014) also varies: from belonging and loyalty to contestation and activism.

The discontinuities, distances, and tensions between the two faces— "the gap between the legal and performative dimensions of citizenship" (Isin and Nyers 2014, p. 5)—have been extensively theorized and studied. The present book contributes to these debates both theoretically and empirically. The theoretical contribution is triple: critical interpretation of the "critical citizenship studies" and of their deconstructivist perspective in the epoch of transition from neo-liberal globalization to mainstreaming of national populism, citizens' activism and solidarity movements as a major challenger to the hegemonized sovereignist politics of citizenship, and reinvention and diversification of citizenships—contestatory, solidary, everyday, creative, and so on.[1]

The theoretical challenges have been studied and tested on a variety of empirical case studies, which can be clustered in three categories: rich spectrum of civic actors, mobilizations, and movements (pro-migrants, pro-Roma, pro-LGBT, feminists, etc.); different types of citizenship; and nine national case studies covering different facets of EU—from new comers like Bulgaria and Slovenia to the leaver UK, from the South (Italy) via Central Europe (Austria) to the North (Finland, Denmark) passing by the key pillars, Germany and France. The emphasis is on challenging and contesting the politics of citizenship through activism from and for the margins: the poorest of the poor, the Roma; the most excluded, the irregular migrants; the marginalized civic activists.

---

[1] Donatella della Porta assesses the book's findings on citizens' activism and solidarity movements through the theoretical lenses of social movements theory. We'll complement her excellent synthesis by privileging the citizenship perspective.

Re/De/Constructing Citizenship in Time of Strengthening Sovereignist Citizenship

The book engages in critical and constructive dialogue with critical citizenship studies. Three of their ideas are simultaneously relevant to our study and problematized in the book—namely, citizenship beyond state sovereignty, dethroning of the state, and liquefaction of citizenship.

Citizenship beyond state sovereignty (Mhurchu 2014) summarizes the critical perspective of the critical citizenship studies:

> The need to reject State sovereign time and space as the necessary starting point for questions about citizenship and embrace logic of alterity is linked to the ability to begin to liberate citizenship from status (someone) and bounded community (somewhere). Rather than starting with these and presupposing who is and who is not a citizen – for example, a rights-bearing subject rather than a subject who officially bears no rights – and/or where citizenship takes place – for example, among people of a similar culture, history, language, or ideology and along a particular scale which is local or global – citizenship can instead begin to be associated with certain sites of struggle and contestation which have the potential to constitute citizenship anew. (Mhurchu 2014, p. 124)

The radical deconstruction of the classic understanding of citizenship in this interpretation is substantiated by four epistemological procedures. The *dethroning of the state* as a key institution defining citizenship is the first most radical step of the deconstruction. Yasemin Soysal argues that citizenship has increasingly become an international institution that constrains nation-states to open up membership of their polity to non-nationals thanks to the "transnational discourse and structures celebrating human rights as a world-level organizing principle" (Soysal 1994, p. 3). The d*e-essentialization of the belonging* by detaching it from primordial identities—culture, language, and so on—continues the deconstruction at the level of identity. N. Sozuk's global citizenry (Sozuk 2014) illustrates the de-essentialized identity in a globalized world. *Rescaling citizenship*, challenging the monopoly of the national on behalf of alternative scales—local or global—makes it possible to destabilize the space-time of the nation-state. The new sites lead to new subjectivities, and the fourth step hospitably opens a theoretical space for new *non-authoritative actors* who can creatively reconstitute citizenship anew through contestation and struggles.

By redefining citizenship as *institution in flux* (Mezzadra 2011; Isin 2009; Mhurchu 2014), the critical approach liquefies it. This approach refuses state citizenship's "reified spatial frame (the modern territorial nation-state), specific subject (the autonomous citizen) and mode of political practice (claiming rights)" (McNevin 2012, p. 100). The liquefied world of citizenship in flux is inhabited not so much by fixed but by increasingly mobile individuals who can be linked to new sites of struggles and enable imagining of 'the spaces of citizenship to come' (McNevin 2012, p. 9). The liquefaction of citizenship is conceptualized as deterritorialization and blurs the distinction between citizens and non-citizens: "This is a world which is better understood in terms of fragmented temporal belonging and deterritorialized spatial belonging (where the boundaries between 'citizen' and 'non-citizen' are increasingly blurring) rather than in terms of statist linear progressive belonging and bounded territorialized spatial belonging (where 'citizens' remain clearly distinguishable from 'non-citizens')" (Mhurchu 2014, p. 120).

The merit of the critical citizenship studies deconstruction lies in their strong normativity, in the theoretical effort to open up conceptual space to accommodate multiple non-authoritative actors of citizenship, in the fundamental assumption—almost never explicated, conceptualized, demonstrated—of the alternativeness of non-state citizenship practices. Two types of actors understood literally the deconstructivist pathos of the anti-state-centered turn in citizenship studies, the normative appeal for legitimizing alternative actors and for counter-hegemonic imaginaries, namely, the refugees/migrants in Germany and elsewhere who raised the slogans "Open the borders", "Right to stay to everybody" and wrote a Refugee Manifesto in Denmark claiming the right to move free or stay and not to be forcefully confined to deportation camps, nor deported by force, and the civic activists who joined their protest in the name of mobility understood in a liberating and human rights perspective.

The authors in this book share the normative and liberating perspective of the anti-state deconstruction of citizenship, but problematize its analytical validity. We develop a different argumentation: the populist turn has deepened the discrepancy between the citizenship studies and the citizenship politics: the more the state produces exclusion through sovereignist citizenship, the more deconstructive, creative, and alternative the citizenship theorizations become. We substantiated our critical approach to the critical citizenship studies in three regards: the "revenge" of the state, the exclusionary intersectionality, and the reconquering of sovereignist citizenship through instrumentalization of various crises—migration, neoliberalism, and so on. These trends vary in expressions and intensity from a polity to a polity; the quotations from the case studies illustrate the political scenes and the civic mobilizations where they have been identified and highlighted.

Anna Krasteva formulated the idea of the *Neo-Post-Westphalian state* (Krasteva 2017a) as a new stage of reinvigorating and strengthening the nation-state. In the globalized era or the tripolar post-Westphalian order of Bertrand Badie—the international frame for liquefaction of citizenship—the nation-state is challenged from below, by regional, minority, and other identitarian movements, and from above, by carriers and exponents of globalization such as transnationalism (Badie 1995; Krasteva 2017a). The populism with its radical rejection of globalization catalyzes the renaissance or "revenge" of the state as the central institution for defining and defending the sovereign state in the neo-post-Westphalian order. Several expressions of the revenge of the state are analyzed, such as tightening of border and migration policies and the rapid transformation of Denmark from a liberal and open approach to immigration and asylum to the most restrictive in the Nordic context (Birte Siim and Susi Meret). Opposite to the liquefaction of citizenship concept, the deterritorialization of belongings, and the blurring of statuses, the authors of the book critically observe and analyze the hardening of citizenship politics, reterritorialization, and sharpening of the distinctions between citizens and non-citizens through detention camps and deportations.

The second line of the book's argumentation refers to the *hegemonization of the exclusionary intersectionality*: "The right-wing discourse of an "exclusionary intersectionality" (combining class, nationality, religion, gender, sexuality) forges these narratives into a common-sense perspective of difference and inequality, of belonging and non-belonging and thus exclusion. The radical right's strategy of "exclusive intersectionality" builds on a "chain of equivalence" (Laclau 2005), which results in "anti-immigration", "anti-Muslim" and "anti-gender" as "empty signifiers" (Laclau 1996, p. 36) for the new hegemonic project of exclusion, inequality and solidarity of nationals only, of the nativist and homogeneous "we"'" (Birgit Sauer). The exclusionary intersectionality is an expression of the shift towards culturalization of racism or "racism without races" by which Balibar (1988) conceptualizes exclusion not only based on race but on other personal circumstances such as gender, sexuality, religion, and so on (Mojca Pajnik). A Bulgarian activist stresses the social and political mainstreaming of this culturalized racism: "our society generates racism and Nazism because it needs them; they're a tried-and-true mechanism for division and political manipulation … it needs them to preserve the status quo, the hegemony, money, power …" (Anna Krasteva et al.). The exclusionary intersectionality is identified by civic activists as a major threat: a Slovenian feminist activist mentions that racist othering refers to everyone who is "other than a heterosexual white male, young or middle aged, healthy, of Slovenian nationality and citizenship and a catholic" (Mojca Pajnik). The re-Catholicization of Slovenian society and its political expression—more influential conservative and right-wing parties—contributes to the hegemonization of exclusionary intersectionality. An interviewee from the Red Dawn in Slovenia stresses the problem that "racism, ethnonationalism and other tactics of othering and exclusion have become normalized in our societies; they have become the discourses that are omnipresent and it becomes scary when you see what you actually fight" (Mojca Pajnik).

"If crises did not exist, populism/euroscepticism would have invented them" is A. Krasteva's (2017a, b) paraphrase of Sartre[2] for theorizing the turn from elites aimed at resolving crisis to elites profiting from and producing crisis. The populist elites flourish in times of crises and they transform crises into fears and fears into electorates. Populism needs crisis the same deep way as anti-Semitism needs Jews and masterfully manages the fears converting them into political support. Birgit Sauer studies this mechanism in Austria: "The dramatic economic and social changes and the crisis of neoliberalism since 2008 have marginalized working people, nurtured fears of social degradation, marginalization and insecurity of the working class and the lower middle-class and thus fostered the rise of the FPÖ. The FPÖ has been able to transform these fears into resentment and anger against migrants, and it has exploited the rising numbers of refugees arriving in Europe and Austria to mobilize intensively against immigrants".

The three groups of arguments frame the political context of citizens' activism, solidarity movements, and acts of citizenship in the era of mainstreaming of national populism and hegemonization of sovereignist politics. The hegemonized populism in a number of countries explains the paradox between innovative citizens' activism and lack of political impact

---

[2] If the Jews did not exist, anti-Semitism would have created them (Sartre 1946; Krasteva 2017).

of numerous civic mobilizations, between the differentiation and determination of civic actors and the difficulties in building a counter-hegemonic strategy. Susi Meret and Waldemar Diener observe that contemporary refugee movements in Germany rarely accomplish consolidation, continuity, and political and social achievements. Birgit Sauer makes a similar observation for Austria: "Despite the huge mobilization capacities at the turn of the century, when the FPÖ entered a government coalition with the Christian-conservatives, it seems that these anti-right organizations were unable to stop the wave of success of the FPÖ and right-wing radical groups and to counter their practices and policies of inequality and exclusion. The right-wing hegemony of exclusionary intersectionality makes it difficult for anti-discrimination groups to establish a counter-strategy".

Critically rethinking citizen's activism and citizenship politics in time of hegemonized national populism is a challenging ambition. We approached it inspired by Isin and Nyers' reading of Derrida's idea of "erasure" (Derrida 1998). "For Derrida, to write 'under erasure' is to write and delete simultaneously, to script and cross out, to present and bracket, create and destroy. Erasure allows one to posit something affirmatively and yet remain sceptical and question it as a problematic. Erasure brings both the concept and the deletion to the forefront in order to allow for some critical distance" (Isin and Nyers 2014, p. 6). The contribution of the book is in the constructive "erasure" of citizenship in populist time—of T. Marshall's classic conception, as well as the new critical citizenship studies. The theoretical efforts focus on the discrepancy and tensions between the two faces of citizenship: the more hardened through overbordering and sovereignist ideology is the institutional face, the more innovative, dynamic, and engaged the participatory one becomes.

The theoretical contributions can be summarized in two clusters. The first studies the innovation and diversification of new practices of citizenship with emphasis on four of them—solidary, contestatory, everyday, and creative citizenship—as dynamic democratic alternatives to the populist redesign of the institutional citizenship.

The second cluster examines the potential of citizens' activism for a counter-hegemonic strategy to the mainstreaming and hegemonization of populist discourses, politics, and policies. Actors take center stage and activism is analyzed through their perspectives. The methodology is actors-centered: focus groups, structured and semi-structured interviews with human rights advocates and pro-diversity civic actors, observation and participant observation of citizen's activism.

The book assembles a "broad cross-section of local, regional and national 'antibodies' from across a spectrum running from prominent to small organizational forms" (Don Flynn and Gabriella Lazaridis). The UK chapter makes an interesting methodological observation: through snowballed invitations, more than 20 people approached the researchers directly to request participation (Don Flynn and Gabriella Lazaridis). Several participants saw the focus groups as a site where their voices can be raised and heard. "The theoretical value of civic voices consists of both their authenticity and their openness to multiple interpretations. The authors offer their interpretations, and readers can argue or elaborate their own readings of the narratives here" (Anna Krasteva et al.).

The study does not aim to build a portrait of activists but rather to portray the diversity of activists (Anna Krasteva et al.). The study demonstrates that activists are not driven into their roles by a unified set of personal experiences and expectations, as the UK chapter summarizes. At one end of the spectrum, some have "just drifted into it"; at the other end, others have been activists from school. For this second group, activism is "like coming home" (Don Flynn and Gabriella Lazaridis).

Analyticity and normativity are interlinked biographically and theoretically. Several authors, for instance, those around the Hirundo drop-in center in Helsinki (Aino Saarinen et al.), are also activists, involved in a variety of activisms of solidarity, protests,[3] human rights, and so on. The analysis of citizen's activism is connected with the book's double message: citizen's activism is a major site for countering far-right populism and for reimagining and revitalizing democracy. "Every change is a form of liberation. My mother used to say a change is always good even if it's for the worse", Portuguese artist Paula Rego writes. We agree with the mother that change can be liberating. We are less poetic and more critical, and unlike her we clearly distinguish between hegemonization of national populism as a change for the bad and revitalization of citizen's activism as a change for good and assign liberating potential to civic actors and their contestatory and solidary innovations, experiments, and initiatives.

---

[3] It is not a coincidence that the weeks of finalization of the conclusion are marked by environmental and anti-state-capture mobilizations, and an author of the conclusion was moving back and forth between the street and the desk. This back-and-forth has been a constant source of inspiration for all authors' activists.

Reinventing Citizenship for Revitalizing Pluralism and Democracy

"Transgressive citizenship" (Harrington 2014), "urban citizenship" (Nielsen 2008), "e-citizenship" (Krasteva 2013), "graduated citizenship" (Ong 2006), "irregular citizenship" (Nyers 2011), "differentiated citizenship" (Siim and Meret 2016)—the proliferation of forms of citizenship is impressive. The book contributes to conceptualizing and empirically validating four other types of citizenship relevant to the study of countering far-right populism: contestatory, solidary, everyday, and creative.

Contestatory Citizenship as a Democratic Confrontation with Unaccountable Elites

Anti-elitism can be expressed in two opposite forms: populist and democratic. Populist anti-elitism points at different targets: national establishment, Brussels, global "neo-colonial yoke".[4] The populist type of anti-elitism has a triple aim: to impose a simple bipolar structure of society, elite vs. people, to homogenize the "people", and to enthrone itself as the only representative of the "people". Civic anti-elitism does not steer the same target and formulates opposite aims. It targets not a homogenized elite but unaccountable, corrupted, inefficient representatives: a member of Kombinat, a feminist organization in Slovenia, reflected that we are currently experiencing "the abuse of democracy". She refers to corruption, corrupt politicians, and the economic elite who should be stopped and fought against collectively for a kind of catharsis and "a renewal of democracy" (Mojca Pajnik). Citizen's activism aims not to replace one fraction of the elite with another one but to offer alternative policies or ways of doing politics. As Mojca Pajnik emphasizes, social movements are by definition protest movements—they protest against the often illegitimate domination and the (mis)use of resources/power in society (Touraine 1987, p. 221).

The authors of the book develop Aoileann Ni Mhurchu's (2014, p. 119) idea that what is at stake is the ability to recognize citizenship as something that need not be associated with a certain status (a rights-bearing subject) or a particular type of community (along a particular local, national, or global scale) but can be associated with struggles linked to heterogeneous sites and subjectivities. We further advance the under-

---

[4] Term of the Bulgarian extremist party Attack for global capitalism.

standing of the contestatory citizenship as the "must" of the contest in post-democratic politics, indignation as political imagination, and civic disobedience when legality and legitimacy split.

Post-Democracy: When Elites Degrade Democracy into an Empty Shell, Citizens Have No Other Option But to Contest

The "crisis of democracy" is a major concern (Giovanna Campani) of militants across Europe. "Democracy has become a very problematic notion"; "Democracy that used to be a sort of password we used to use when we wanted to say what we want is totally non-functional today. ... It has become clear that what is behind democracy today is a total propaganda machine. ... Democracy, what we expected it to be, does not exist, it only functions as a word for misleading us" (Mojca Pajnik)—two activists from Slovenia clearly summarize the post-democratic turn.

Colin Crouch defines post-democracy as the paradoxical stage when the institutions of democracy still exist, but increasingly become a formal shell. The energy and innovative drive move from the democratic arena into small circles of a politico-economic elite (Crouch 2013). An Italian activist shares the dramatic awareness "that Italian democracy is in a sort of no-way-out situation where 'technocracy' [with reference to Mario Monti's technocratic government] *and* 'populism' face each other – as Scylla and Charybdis, the two horrible monsters – both ready to destroy democracy's frail ship" (Giovanna Campani). This emptiness of the major instruments of democracy is insightfully identified and rejected by activists: "This is the way I see democracy: not as elections, assemblies and not as public opinion pools" (Mojca Pajnik). Activists have such a strong understanding of the void of democracy that some of them feel it as symbolic violence. Slovenian activist has never voted and finds elections "alienating" and "a great violence over my body" (Mojca Pajnik). If during all elections politicians convey the image of the "good citizen" as the one who votes, activists accuse representatives to not represent any more humiliating democracy making it a "swear word": "Democracy has become a swear word because representatives of democracy made this out of it. So I would not speak of a democratic struggle but of struggle to reform this democratic system" (activist in Mojca Pajnik). This radical criticism of the post-democratic emptiness of democracy is logically translated into an activism as a contestation, as a "struggle to reform the democratic system", as experimenting new democratic practices. A feminist activist prefers to focus on "alternative" conceptualizations of democracy, rather than lamenting the disappearance of democracy, and shares her experience from a protest movement "where there were a lot of experiments with decision-making, with the ways of being together, and I thought this was essential for democracy" (Mojca Pajnik).

Occupy: Indignation as Imagination for Experimenting with Democracy

"The problem isn't with people; it's with the system" and "We've had enough of hierarchy. We want direct democracy"—these slogans from the June 2013 protests in Sofia summarize the high ambitions to reject the existing model and invent a new one (Anna Krasteva et al.). The protests have been severely criticized, and two of the criticisms are relevant to our study: the absence of an alternative project and the lack of genuine political change. According to Chantal Mouffe, "the Occupy and similar movements are strategically ineffective since they are not able to develop a counter-hegemonic political project that truly challenges the existing order" (Decreuse et al. 2014, p. 16; Mouffe 2013). The second line of criticism is the failure to yield results: "The same elites took power and reproduced the old model of democracy with a limited civic participation" (Георгиева 2016, p. 259). Analyzing the protests through the lenses of evolving civic agency, Anna Krasteva reached the opposite conclusions: the protests may not have achieved their goals or provided a new democratic model, but they have been a laboratory for citizenship through contestation (Krasteva 2016a, b; Anna Krasteva et al.). During communism citizenship was "occupied" by the state and fixed to status and belonging. Protests "liberated" citizenship and opened it to citizens. This impact is so tangible that Anna Krasteva conceptualizes it as a "second democratic revolution". It did not transform society but it transformed civic agency. "In the first post-communist revolution of the elites, citizens were assigned the role of attending the democratization process; they were second-class actors. In the second, it is the citizens who experiment, innovate, and refound democracy" (Krasteva 2016a, b; Anna Krasteva et al.). Occupy mobilizations are important for our study as laboratory for forming and strengthening the contestatory ethos. Their impact is also symbolically significant in rehabilitating indignation. If populists instrumentalize rage and indignation of mismanaged crises and inefficient governments into politics of fear, civic activists positively transform indignation into struggle and imagination for experimenting and revitalizing democracy.

A second type of "Occupy" is central for our study. It takes place in the same streets/squares, but the actors are different. If in the first case, they are citizens, urban and active protesters, in the second, they are non-citizens, irregular or detained migrants. Birte Siim and Susi Meret analyze the Castaway Souls group of refugees' marches and demonstrations against what they define as "unjust laws and policies that violate our freedom and dignity: 'We have challenged the idea that we cannot be visible, that we do not have the right to have rights, and that we cannot contribute to society'". The Free Movement Network in Finland, with the Occupy movement in its background, fights to empower marginal groups politically and give them a voice with a militant repertoire that includes open confrontations, protests, and demonstrations (Aino Saarinen et al.).

Both kinds of protests catalyze the learning of contestatory repertoires and transform indignation into imagination of alternative democracy and policies.

Civic Disobedience or the Contestatory Repertoires When Legality Does Not Mean Legitimacy

"If you look at it, it was illegal. At the same time what is written as legal is not necessarily legitimate. It is not necessary to comply with the rules and not complying is not something dangerous, it is not necessarily something that some anarchists and extremists do. Rather it is something that we can all do" (Mojca Pajnik). The repertoire of civic disobedience practices is rich, and the book examines interesting and innovative examples like the Global Clinic in Finland which secretly provides health and dental care to undocumented migrants and brings with it even well-institutionalized religious actors, such as the Deaconess Institute: "The Clinic is not only a service but a political project" (Aino Saarinen et al.). A Slovenian activist summarizes and explains the rationale of a widespread practice of radical activism, namely, temporary occupation of a building, in her case, an empty cinema hall: "An assembly was organized to discuss the problematic of empty places, the issue of property and others. The occupation was initiated by activists and was then joined by several other people who got interested and participated in the debates about topics, such as being without a flat, without a place to live, a room to study, work, etc." (Mojca Pajnik).

The contestatory citizenship expresses the transition from the active to the activist citizen, from the citizen who supports the system by his/her vote to the citizen who contests the political establishment by his/her mobilizations. The active citizen is the "good" citizen in time of democratic consolidation. In time of post-democratic decay and mainstreamed populism, the good citizen is the disobedient one who contests the democratic decline.

Solidary Citizenship as Acts of Friendship

The cases when theory and fieldwork fully coincide are relatively rare and privileged moments in research. Such a happy meeting is the conceptualization of solidary citizenship (Krasteva and Vladiislavjevic 2017; Anna Krasteva et al.) and the innovative experiment of the Trampoline House in Copenhagen (Birte Siim and Susi Meret). Anna Krasteva conceptualizes solidary citizenship as symbolic battles against the hegemonization of the discourses of B/Ordering and Othering (van Houtum and Van Naerssen 2002) and the project to transform public space through the alternative discourses of solidarity, human security, inclusion, and acts that are foundational for constituting civic actors through their struggle for human dignity and politics of friendship. Solidary citizenship uplifts citizen's activism to the intersubjective imperative of E. Levinas, where our responsibility towards others makes our own existence meaningful: "Our responsibility for the Other *founds* our subjective being-in-the world by giving it a meaningful direction and orientation" (Levinas 1969, p. 22; Anna Krasteva et al.).

The book develops the conception of solidary citizenship in three perspectives: innovative integration practices, humanitarian actions, and fight for interpretations.

The Trampoline House is both an innovative practice in Copenhagen and a metaphor for solidary citizenship inventing simultaneously sites and subjectivities. It was founded by Danish artists, Morten Goll and Tone Olaf Nielsen, in 2010 with a dual goal: "close the refugee camps" and start integration of refugees and asylum seekers day one. The Trampoline House is conceived as a house where people meet, eat, discuss, enjoy, create art, and feel "at home" (Birte Siim and Susi Meret). This intercultural civic experiment is a solidary citizenship-in-progress. It introduces a radical equality of actors where citizens and non-citizens—Danish volunteers, refugees, non-status migrants, and so on—act together and become activists through shared activities. A stateless women who has been denied asylum visits the Trampoline House every Saturday where she cooks and her son plays (Birte Siim and Susi Meret). The funding from a variety of sources, public and private in changing proportions, happens to be sustainable. The Trampoline House is a "total" space—civic, cultural, intercultural, and social—in the making. The actors experiment, test, and create a new micro-model of society, of being together, based on participation, activity, innovation, responsibility, trust, openness, intercultural sharing, and mutual enrichment.

The Trampoline House is "institutionalized solidarity", but the book also analyzes several ad hoc mobilizations of humanitarian solidarity, for instance, in cases of deportation where communities stand up for families to protect them (Birgit Sauer).

The third perspective for empirically validating the concept of solidary citizenship is the fight for interpretation and the determination to oppose a language of solidarity to the exclusionary discourses. The "Otherers" (concept introduced by Aino Saarinen et al.) label the new Roma "beggars" or "welfare tourists" within a framework of welfare chauvinism. The "pro-actors" or "equalizers" (concepts introduced by Aino Saarinen et al.) propose an alternative discourse naming the new Roma "migrants" in need of help and welfare rights and services (Aino Saarinen et al.).

EVERYDAY CITIZENSHIP OR HOW SMALL INNOVATIVE PRACTICES OF CITIZENSHIP FROM THE PERIPHERY BECOME VIRAL BECAUSE THEY ARE TRANSFORMED INTO A MODEL AND INSPIRATION

The idea of everyday citizenship is based on Ruth Lister's concept of "lived citizenship" as the meaning that citizenship has in people's lives (Lister 2003, p. 3) and on Birte Siim and Susi Meret's concept of "everyday activism". "The notion and practice of everyday activism and learning democracy is influenced by the lived citizenship and particularities of the Danish version of bottom-up democracy, particularly to the tradition for voluntary civil society associations, cooperatives and social movements". "The Friendly People" from the remote town of Hjørring in Denmark illustrate the crucial ideas of everyday citizenship with their innovative and transformative potential. Four of its innovations are worth emphasizing in this concluding section. The first is the impressively easy transition from hospitality towards "Us"—neighbors—to hospitality towards "Them", foreigners, refugees, and asylum seekers. The second is the everyday "translation" of politics of friendship into simple guiding principles: (1) be friendly in the meeting with others; (2) be curious when you meet people who are different from you; (3) meet diversity with respect (Birte Siim and Susi Meret). The symbolic weight of the experiment touches ethical height by defining the symbolic center of the new site of intercultural contact in terms of friendship. The fourth innovation refers to the viral effect and the significant impact as the movement spread across several cities and the Copenhagen area. The diffusion demonstrates that a small everyday practice of citizenship conceived and tested at the periphery, in a small town, can become central because it is transformed into an inspiration and model.

Everyday citizenship is an expression and catalyst of two important transformations: from NGO-ization to citizen's activism and from the professional militant to the "amateur", from active citizen to activist. The first transition mainly characterizes the post-communist societies analyzed in the book; the second has greater validity and encompasses most cases. "Civil society without citizenship" (Krasteva and Vladislavjevic 2017) is the paradoxical formula Anna Krasteva forged to critically assess the NGO-ization of civil society in the post-communist countries. It was the result of the western engineering project of building democracy and civil society through NGOs and professional civic activists. The profile of the NGO expert focused on fundraising and project management is closer to think tanks and business skills than to the spontaneity of civic agency. Our book focuses on another type of civic actor, namely, the "amateur" who is able and willing to experiment, to search, to propose new, "rough" ideas, to make mistakes, to act, to innovate (Krasteva 2009; Anna Krasteva et al.). The book describes a rich spectrum of practices of everyday citizenship: "ordinary" citizens in Finland and elsewhere in Scandinavia offered Roma a place to sleep in their own homes. A one-week "skiing holiday" also provided Roma with short-term private homes (Aino Saarinen et al.).

The idea of the activist as amateur is foundational for everyday citizenship and leads to the second transformation: from the active citizen to the activist (Isin 2008). We demonstrate that every active citizen can become an activist citizen and transform hospitality into politics of friendship and everyday practices of citizenship.

Creative Citizenship: The Aestheticization of Mobilizations as Resistance and Liberation

The women's choir Kombinat[5] fights racism through anti-fascist and anti-racist songs, which they enrich with their own interventions like "We are against suppressors, abusers, homophobes and racists". Kombinat's singer activists express rebellion through music: "Resistance is understood in a wider sense as national liberation resistance, and also as the emancipation of various marginalized groups, particularly women, but also refugees, workers, Roma" (Mojca Pajnik). This mix is a creative expression of the inclusive intersectionality.

Art as a protest and activist repertoire is the first expression of the creative citizenship. Three others are crucial for its understanding—the Aestheticization of mobilizations and civic actions, art as a means for empowerment of vulnerable groups, and the creativity of the very process of reinventing subjectivities and citizenship. Performances accompany several mobilizations like the demonstration in Finland under the slogan "End to racism, roof for Roma", which continued with the "Flowers and beggars", a carnival-like performance where Roma handed out roses to passers-by (Aino Saarinen et al.). The Finnish Free Movement Network employs flamboyant visual symbols and emotive language (Aino Saarinen et al.). Protest came to be seen as an aesthetic of the urban environment. Protest is a celebration of civic ingenuity and sense of humor; it is the urban culture of artistry (Krasteva 2016b).

Art is mobilized as an instrument for empowerment and transformation opening access even to most marginalized, illiterate Europeans. A Finnish musician trained mobile Roma to transform them from "beggars" into "working people", even street artists (Aino Saarinen et al.).

Creativity and politics of transformation are profoundly and genuinely interconnected: social activism is "not just about individual actions of protest, but rather an opportunity to create new ways of thinking and being in the world" (Mojca Pajnik). The aestheticization of protests softens the political clash and the acuteness of the claims. It is not "effective" in the short term with regard to the outcome of the protests, but it is productive in the long term with regard to the development of creative citizenry, capable of thinking differently, of looking for ways out of dead ends, of formulating utopias and political alternatives (Krasteva 2016b; Anna Krasteva et al.).

---

[5] From Slovenia.

The contestatory, solidary, everyday, and creative citizenship differ in objectives, types of actors, and repertoires, but they all confirm Isin and Nyer's idea that "citizenship remains a significant site through which to develop a critique of the pessimism about political possibilities" (Isin and Nyers 2014, p. 9). It is precisely this active and positive potential of citizenship in generating change and change-bearers that the book validates by innovative and creative practices across Europe.

Mapping Citizen's Activism: Contestatory and Solidary Citizenship and the Impact on Politics and Policies

Civic actors in the diversity of their statuses—citizens, minority representatives, (undocumented) migrants—take center stage. What they share despite the large differences in statuses, their position within centrality vs. periphery vs. outside the borders of citizenship, the cause of the struggle—for their rights or for the rights of Others—is citizens' activism and becoming actors through activism. Two guiding ideas inspired our research: Isin and Nielsen's idea of citizenship as producing both acts and subjects (Isin and Nielsen 2008, p. 6) and Hannah's Arendt conception that acting blends together agency, initiative, beginning, and change—of the world and of the active Self: "To act ... means to take an initiative, to begin (as the Greek word *archein*, 'to begin,' 'to lead,' and eventually 'to rule'), to set something into motion. Because they are *initium*, newcomers and beginners ... take initiative, are prompted into action. This beginning is not the same as the beginning of the world; it is not the beginning of something but of somebody, who is a beginner himself" (Arendt 1998, p. 177). The actors we study are "activists" in Isin's sense, those who write scripts and make a difference: "While activist citizens engage in writing scripts and creating the scene, active citizens follow scripts and participate in scenes that are already created. While activist citizens are creative, active citizens are not" (Isin 2008, p. 38). The authors are aware of the potential risk of conveying a rather "heroic" conception of the activist citizens (Neveu 2014, p. 88) and critically overcome it by subscribing to the "acts of citizenship" conception and developing the "everyday citizenship" concept.

The major ambition of the book is to make the civic activists visible, and the chapters offer a diverse and rich panorama of portraits, discourses, mobilizations, activities, and alternatives. In these concluding pages, we will map them in the coordinate system of citizens' activism. The vertical axis spans from contestatory to solidary citizenship. The horizontal axis displays the impact of citizens' activism on the two faces of the political—politics and policies. At the pole of politics, activists aim for a counter-hegemonic strategy; at the other pole, they aspire to impact policies "to *both* contain and combat racism and other forms of discrimination" (Don Flynn and Gabriella Lazaridis) for more inclusiveness and human rights standards. These distinctions are analytical, and the impact is often complex. The impact on legislation and policies also contributes to more moderation in the political and media discourses. Effective counter-hegemonic strategies improve the climate for more progressive legislation and policies.

The map visualizes the cartography of different types of activism. The actors themselves are not placed in a specific part of the diagram as most of them take part in two to three types of activism or at different moments prioritize one or another. During the peak of the refugee/migration crisis, humanitarian activism became the pole of attraction, and some citizens initiated themselves to activism in this acute crisis situation. With the relative stabilization of the migration flows, several humanitarian activists moved to other less urgent forms of pro-diversity activism. Numerous actors take part simultaneously in more than one form of activism. Others are mobile and move across various forms of activism and parts of the map (Fig. 11.1).

The Migration/Refugee Crisis as a Catalyst for the Initiation of Citizens to Activism and Flourishing of Humanitarian Activism

The *upper left* part of the diagram—*impact of solidary citizenship on policies*—is occupied by two types of activism, "urgent" and legal. Humanitarian activism flourished particularly during the migration/refugee crisis when it succeeded in mobilizing both new and experienced activists. Two groups of actors of humanitarian solidarity can be distinguished: citizens and integrated migrants. The migration crisis played a role of catalyst for various forms of urgent solidary actions and initiatives across Europe and for the emergence of new activists. Some had no previous militant experience and were initiated to activism in this intense, dramatic crisis situation. Representatives of Syrian and other already integrated migrant communities

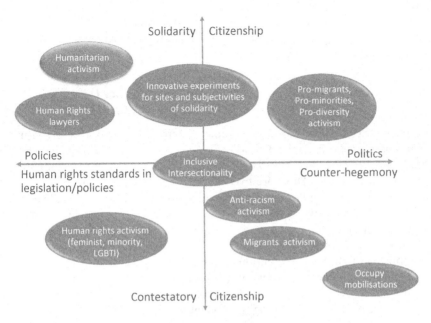

Fig. 11.1 Mapping citizens' activism

(Anna Krasteva et al.) diversified the actors deploying series of humanitarian actions.

The second type of activism in the upper left part of the diagram is human rights lawyers, who have a tangible impact on legislation and the justice system. They defend the rights of the most vulnerable groups, sometimes bringing lawsuits to the European Court of Human Rights as a counter-power to the inability of some anti-discrimination institutions to counteract discrimination (Anna Krasteva et al.).

The *lower left* part of the diagram—the *impact of contestatory citizenship on public policies*—is inhabited by feminist/minority/LGBT activism. Feminist movement in the Slovenian and larger Yugoslav context significantly influenced the institutionalization of gender equality politics. Mojca Pajnik's conclusion on the substantial policy impact of gender activism has great validity not only for Eastern Europe but for most European societies. Policy impact requires broad coalitions, and when civic activists and governmental institutions manage to form them, the results follow. For instance, cooperation between a minority organization and the Ministry of Interior in Bulgaria prevented a new extremist party from entering politics (Anna Krasteva et al.).

Pro-diversity, Pro-migrants, Pro-minority Activism Is the Civic Voice of Those Who Do Not Have a Voice

Pro-diversity, pro-migrants, pro-minorities activism is the central player in the *upper right* part of the diagram of *solidary citizenship with the (im)possible mission to counter far-right populism*. The cause is shared, but the types of actors vary. There are two clusters of actors: the feminist activists and organizations in Slovenia and the minority activist from the Bulgarian chapter, the stateless woman who cooks in the Trampoline House and gives lectures at schools target a specific "adversary"—gender inequality, anti-Semitism, anti-immigration. They are representatives of the target groups and fight for their self-emancipation and anti-discrimination.

The Finns protecting Roma migrants and numerous humanitarian and human rights organizations and initiatives constitute the second group of civic actors fighting for the rights of Others. Those Others are, as a rule, the periphery of the periphery, the poorest of the poor, the most marginalized of the marginalized—Roma, undocumented migrants, and LGBT refugees. The activists' cause and mission is to be the voice of those who have no voice. As a migration lawyer and activist summarizes: "The mission of our organization is to actively protect the rights of disadvantaged groups – mostly refugees, immigrants and asylum seekers – thus becoming the public voice of those who haven't got a voice, promoting justice and truth applied with kindness and compassion" (Anna Krasteva et al.). Working for people is crucial for these vulnerable groups that still need time for self-empowerment and transforming themselves into actors, like the new mobile Roma in Finland or the refugees/asylum seekers in Bulgaria.

Two varieties of overlapping activism are identified: working *with* and/or *for* vulnerable groups. The distinction is relative. Militants "acting for", such as Refugee Welcome and LGBT Asylum (Birte Siim and Susi Meret), also aim at involving vulnerable groups. The Trampoline House is an example of "acting with" people by means of interactive everyday learning, dialogues, and practices (Birte Siim and Susi Meret).

Aino Saarinen conceptualizes these activists as "pro-actors" and "equalizers" for sending a double—analytical and normative—message. Pro-activism produces deeds and doers on both sides of the interaction: the pro-actors as activists and the vulnerable individuals as empowered actors, like a Finn artist teaching Roma new skills and helping to transform them from beggars to working migrants through selling their artifacts. The normative message allows citizens and migrants to "meet in equality" as actors.

Churches and religious associations are powerful solidary actors working for and with vulnerable groups. Religion can be divisive and exclusive, but the book demonstrates the positive potential and activities of numerous religious actors, such as the Lutheran (Aino Saarinen et al.), Catholic, and Valdense churches and Jewish communities (Giovanna Campani) for welcoming refugees and migrants, inter-faith dialogue—especially with Muslims—conflict negotiations, and so on.

Self-Empowered Refugees Transform Themselves from Vulnerable Non-status Individuals into Claimants of Rights

When migrants develop political subjectivities and mobilize for claiming rights, they are analyzed together with anti-racism activism and Occupy in the *right lower* part of the diagram where *contestatory citizenship creates counter-hegemony to populist and extremist discourses*. The transformation of refugees/undocumented migrants from vulnerable people into self-empowered actors is one of the major finding of the book: "The development of refugee-led movements in Germany shows the increasing efforts made by non-status refugees to organize, find autonomous leaders, create alliances, and experiment with democratic and participatory forms of organization" (Susi Meret and Waldemar Diener). "No one is illegal", "Right to stay for everybody", "We are here because you destroyed our countries"—the slogans of refugee mobilizations collected by Susi Meret and Waldemar Diener illustrate two lines of their struggle. The first one is a radical challenge to sovereignty inspired by a utopian idea of global citizenship. The last slogan is an even more radical claim to Western powers to assume responsibility for the conflicts that transform people into forced migrants. The radical messages from the slogans and the varied repertoire of mobilizations reveal the emergence of a strong type of activists not only in Hannah Arendt's terms (the right to have rights) but also in Isin's terms (the right to *claim* rights).

Innovative Experiments for New Sites and Subjectivities of Solidarity Can Be Sustainable and Efficient with a Double Impact on Politics and Policies

As an innovative, sustainable experiment for sites and subjectivities of solidarity, the Trampoline House is central in the solidary citizenship part of the diagram. The impact is double—it contributes to reframing migration and refugee discourses in terms of integration, citizen's activism, and solidarity. The Trampoline House has a tangible impact on policies via its viral effect and the emergence of similar practices in different localities.

Inclusive Intersectionality as "Total Activism" for Countering the Populist Exclusionary Intersectionality

The inclusive intersectionality as "total activism" (Anna Krasteva) takes a central position combining strong elements of both solidary and contestatory citizenship and aiming at impacting both politics and policies. Its high ambition is to counter the exclusionary intersectionality of the new right-wing hegemonic project (Birgit Sauer). The book studies three strategies of inclusive intersectionality: raising awareness of the crucial importance of intersectional mobilizations, the hybrid organizations aimed at transversal politics, and the enlarged transversal understanding of more targeted types of activism.

Intersectionality is the type of alliances to be built—this awareness is in progress in some movements and mobilizations: "Gender, gender minorities' and queer issues are among the problems that need to be equitably implemented in the refugee movements' claims for rights and recognition. Refugee leaders are not only predominately men, but also all straight" (Susi Meret and Waldemar Diener). Raising awareness is the first step on the long way to transform intersectionality into a large spread and efficient strategy.

Hybrid organizations traverse the boundaries between different types of activism like ARCI (Associazione Ricreativa Culturale Italiana), a social and cultural promotion organization that coordinates a network of different associations: "its initiatives aim at promoting active citizenship and democratic participation processes for all people; with special attention to people who have fewer social opportunities in order to promote their autonomy, emancipation, equal dignity and their social inclusion. Migrants are, of course, among them" (Giovanna Campani). Lunaria in Italy is another interesting example of transversal activism aiming at peace, social and economic justice, equality and guarantee of the rights of citizenship, democracy and grassroots participation, and anti-racism and intercultural dialogue (Giovanna Campani).

The second type of strategy is to build inclusive intersectionality upon a previous more targeted activism. This strategy can be particularly effective, as summarized in the UK case: "the most effective voices in generating national legislative changes and influencing political opinion from the early 2000s have been those of 'accidental antibodies'. The term, coined by one of our respondents in a focus group, refers to powerful charities, NGOs, General Medical Council, the Trades Union Congress, individual Unions, and other groups who come to issues of racism, othering and intolerance as part of an extension of their core mission" (Don Flynn and Gabriella Lazaridis). A feminist activist mentions that "Sometimes, misogynist reaction is racist" and "in the Slovenian context racist othering refers to everyone who is not a heterosexual white male, young or middle aged, healthy, of Slovenian nationality and citizenship and a Catholic" (Mojca Pajnik). Activism first deconstructs the patriarchy and racism of exclusionary intersectionality and then constructs "alternative frameworks of meaning and interpretative repertoires" (Karner 2007, p. 85; Birgit Sauer).

The power of national populism is largely due to Othering and Ordering, to the overproduction of Others and the redefinition of social order based on exclusion. Citizen's activism is, by definition, much more fragmented, issue based, ad hoc, and so on. Identifying inclusive intersectionality, the need for civic alliances and coalitions as a crucial way to counter populist exclusionary intersectionality is promising. The strategy is right, but citizens' activism is still at the beginning of the road.

CAN THE COUNTER-HEGEMONIC STRATEGY PRODUCE A CHANGE IN TERMS OF PLURALISM, DEMOCRATIC VITALITY, AND INNOVATIVE CITIZENSHIP?

The conclusions of the book can be summarized in two clusters: the difficulty of countering right-wing populism and the potential of citizens' activism to produce change in terms of pluralism, democratic vitality, and innovative citizenship. The two appear opposite, yet necessary to reconstruct the complex, dynamic, and contradictory scene of solidarity movements in times of post-democracy and populist backlash. Also, it is important to approach the state at various levels as both the target and a partner as the concept of the human rights regime and the case of the City Youth Center in Helsinki shows (Aino Saarinen et al.).

The reasons for the impossibility to definitely combat national populism can be grouped in four clusters: the political and symbolic efficiency of the new wave of populism, the difficulty in working against prejudices, the lack of strategic vision and direction of some movements, and the tensions that divide and weaken civic mobilizations. The political and symbolic efficiency of the new populism, for instance, the "insurgent populism" of Nigel Farage (Don Flynn and Gabriella Lazaridis), has a double negative effect. It undermines the capital of previous civic achievements and deteriorates and poisons the atmosphere for new civic mobilizations: "The later 1990s and 2000s have seen a rich landscape for national, regional and local 'antibody' groups. ...The most vibrant and radical agendas have been driven by bottom-up grass roots groups which have forced local and national political agendas. However, from the early 2000s, the rise of UKIP style identity politics, the reversing of social mobility and the rise of radical Islam poses a toxic systemic threat to the gains already made" (Don Flynn and Gabriella Lazaridis). France is yet another example of the political and symbolic strength of the new populism. Here the government has recently legalized the same-sex marriage, but the French activists point towards the ideological strength and unity of people mobilized in the mass demonstration "Manif pour tout" against the law, contrasted with the weakness, lack of resources, and ideological unity of the LGBT activism (Etienne Pingaud).

"It is getting more and more difficult and complex to argue against right-wing extremist arguments and frames. It is always more difficult to work against prejudices than with them" (Birgit Sauer). Austrian activists summarize the second type of challenges for counter-hegemony against the radical right that are scrutinized in the book. The third cluster of factors is the lack of strategic vision, direction, and sustainability of several mobilizations, as the German chapter demonstrates: "The contemporary refugee movements rarely achieve consolidation, continuity and political and social gains. Some of the reasons are lack of a clear strategic direction, coherence and continuity in the different phases of mobilization" (Susi Meret and Waldemar Diener).

Governmental Elites Use the Old Divide-and-Rule Strategy to Split and Weaken Both Old and New Civic Mobilizations

The fourth group of weaknesses is expressed in the divisions, splits, and frictions among civic actors and organizations. They characterize both old and new types of activism and mobilizations, as illustrated in the UK and German cases: "The tensions between national and regional actors and local campaigning groups have been sustained and considerable, e.g. a periodic sense of betrayal between grassroots organizations and national bodies" (Don Flynn and Gabriella Lazaridis). The recent mobilizations of refugees and pro-refugee actors in Germany experience the same weakness with divisions created on the inside and reinformed from the outside: "We had difficulties … in our movement due to clashes of interests, either strategically or tactically, as well as different demands, from several sides: between refugees and refugees, between refugees and supporters, and between supporters and supporters. These clashes gave the government the chance to try to divide us … The politicians used their divide-and-rule strategy, just like politicians did it in the colonies in Africa" (Susi Meret and Waldemar Diener).

The major theoretical contribution of the book is the study of the opposite transformation: how right-wing populism is met by mobilizations against exclusionary and discriminating policies from civic activists (Birte Siim and Susie Meret). "The only way of genuinely contesting a hegemonic form of politics is to develop a counter-hegemonic strategy" (Stuart Hall 1988, p. 11; Birgit Sauer).

From Politics of Fear to Politics of Friendship and from Hate to Solidarity

So far, citizen's activism has not succeeded in overturning the ascendency of far-right populism, but it does produce a change and its contributions are fivefold. As hegemonic far-right populism aims at delegitimizing different discourses, citizens' activism creates alternative visions, multi-voice agoras, sites and subjectivities of resistance, and solidarity, of ways of being with the Others. Despite an increasingly hostile political and media atmosphere, innovative practices of integration such as the Trampoline House, Refugees Welcome, pro-Roma mobilizations, to name but a few, have been able to expand in terms of participants, activities, visibility, and impact. Activists oppose the politics of friendship to the politics of fear, solidarity to hate, and contribute to transforming the Others from "enemies" to neighbors. Pro-diversity citizens' activism is a laboratory for reimagining and reinventing participatory visions of citizenship, such as contestatory, solidary, everyday, and creative citizenship. Citizenship as acts creates deeds and doers, and the proliferation of new political subjectivities through the transformation of citizens into activists and of vulnerable individuals into civic actors is the double—analytical and normative—message of the book.

References

Arendt, H. (1998). *The human condition*. Chicago/London: University of Chicago Press.

Badie, B. (1995). *La fin des territoires: Essai sur le désordre international et sur l'utilité sociale du respect*. Paris: Fayard.

Balibar, É. (1988). Is there a "neo-racism"? In É. Balibar & I. Wallerstein (Eds.), *Race, nation, class: Ambiguous identities* (pp. 17–28). London: Verso.

Crouch, C. (2013, February 5). Five minutes with Colin Crouch. *British Politics and Policy*. http://blogs.lse.ac.uk/politicsandpolicy/five-minutes-with-colin-crouch/

Decreuse, T., Lievens, M., & Braeckman, A. (2014). Building collective identities: How new social movements try to overcome post-politics. *Parallax, 20*. https://doi.org/10.1080/13534645.2014.896560.

Derrida, J. (1998). *Of grammatology*. Baltimore: The Johns Hopkins University Press.

Hall, S. (1988). *The hard road to renewal: Thatcherism and the crisis of the left*. London/New York: Verso.

Harrington, J. (2014). Navigating global citizenship studies. In E. F. Isin & P. Nyers (Eds.), *Routledge handbook of global citizenship studies* (pp. 12–20). London/New York: Routledge.

Isin, E. F., & Nielsen, G. M. (Eds.). (2008). *Acts of citizenship*. London/New York: Zed Books.

Isin, E. (2009). Citizenship in flux: The figure of the activist citizen. *Subjectivity, 29*, 367–388.

Isin, E. F., & Nyers, P. (2014). Introduction. Globalizing citizenship studies. In E. F. Isin & P. Nyers (Eds.), *Routledge handbook of global citizenship studies* (pp. 1–11). London/New York: Routledge.

Karner, C. (2007). Austrian counter-hegemony. Critiquing ethnic exclusion and globalization. *Ethnicities, 7*, 82–115.

Krasteva, A. (2009). Being a citizen – Not a profession, but a commitment. In K. Hristova-Valtcheva (Ed.), *New actors in a new environment: Accession to the EU, civil society and multi-level governance* (pp. 35–43). Sofia: BECSA.

Krasteva, A. (Ed.). (2013). *E-citoyennetés*. Paris: Harmattan.

Krasteva, A. (2016a). Occupy Bulgaria or the emergence of the post-communist contestatory citizenship. *Southeastern Europe, 40*, 158–187.

Krasteva, A. (2016b). The white piano or the dilemma creative versus contestatory (e-)citizenship. *Digital Icons*, 15. http://www.digitalicons.org/issue15/the-white-piano-or-the-dilemma-of-creative-%E2%80%A8versus-contestatory-%D0%B5-citizenship/

Krasteva, A. (2017a, November). If borders did not exist, Euroscepticism would have invented them, or on post-communist re/de/re/bordering in

Bulgaria. *GeoPolitics*. http://www.tandfonline.com/doi/full/10.1080/1465 0045.2017.1398142

Krasteva, A. (2017b). If crises did not exist, populism would have invented them. In T. Olteanu, T. Spori, F. Jaitner, & H. Asenbaum (Eds.), *Osteuropa transformiert: Sozialismus, Demokratie und Utopie* (pp. 193–210). Wiesbaden: Springer.

Krasteva, A., & Vladisavljević, N. (2017). Securitisation versus citizenship: Populist and authoritarian misuses of security threats and civic responses in the Balkan states. *Global Campus of Human Rights Journal*, 1.2. https://globalcampus.eiuc.org/handle/20.500.11825/423

Laclau, E. (1996). *Emancipation(s)*. London/New York: Verso.

Laclau, E. (2005). *On populist reason*. London: Verso.

Levinas, E. (1969). *Totality and infinity*. Pittsburg: Duquesne University Press.

Lister, R. (2003). *Citizenship: Feminist perspectives* (2nd ed.). Basingstoke: Macmillan.

McNevin, A. (2012). Undocumented citizens? Shifting grounds of citizenship in Los Angeles. In P. Nyers & K. Rygiel (Eds.), *Citizenship, migrant activism and the politics of movement* (pp. 165–183). New York/London: Routledge.

Mezzadra, S. (2011). The gaze of autonomy: Capitalism, migration and social struggles. In V. Squire (Ed.), *The contested politics of mobility: Borderzones of irregularity* (pp. 121–142). London: Routledge.

Mhurchu, A. N. (2014). Citizenship beyond state sovereignty. In E. F. Isin & P. Nyers (Eds.), *Routledge handbook of global citizenship studies* (pp. 119–138). London/New York: Routledge.

Mouffe, C. (2013). *Agonistics: Thinking the world politically*. London/New York: Verso.

Neveu, C. (2014). Practising citizenship from the ordinary to the activist. In E. F. Isin & P. Nyers (Eds.), *Routledge handbook of global citizenship studies* (pp. 86–95). London/New York: Routledge.

Nielsen, G. M. (2008). Answerability with cosmopolitan intent: An ethics-based politics for acts of urban citizenship. In E. F. Isin & G. M. Nielsen (Eds.), *Acts of citizenship* (pp. 266–286). London/New York: Zed Books.

Nyers, P. (2011). Forms of irregular citizenship. In V. Squire (Ed.), *The contested politics of mobility: Borderzones and irregularity* (pp. 184–198). Abingdon: Routledge.

Ong, A. (2006). *Neoliberalism as exception*. Durham: Duke University Press.

Sartre, J.-P. (1946). *Reflexions sur la question juive*. Paris: Gallimard.

Siim, B., & Meret, S. (2016). Right wing populism in Denmark: People, nation and welfare in the construction of the "other". In G. Lazaridis, A. Benveniste, & G. Campani (Eds.), *The rise of the far right in a Europe under crisis*. Houndmills, Basingstoke and Hampshire: Palgrave Macmillan.

Soysal, Y. N. (1994). *Limits of citizenship: Migrants and postnational membership in Europe*. Chicago: The University of Chicago Press.
Sozuk, N. (2014). Global citizenship in an insurrectional era. In E. F. Isin & P. Nyers (Eds.), *Routledge handbook of global citizenship studies* (pp. 49–50). London/New York: Routledge.
Touraine, A. (1987). Social movements: Participation and protest. *Scandinavian Political Studies, 10*, 207–222.
Van Houtum, H., & Van Naerssen, T. (2002). Bordering, ordering and othering. *Tijdschrift voor Economische en Sociale Geografie, 93*, 125–136. https://doi.org/10.1111/tesg.2002.93.issue-2.
Георгиева, В. (2016). *Множества на несъгласните. Антропология на протестните движения в България (2009–2013)*. София: СУ Кл. Охридски.

CHAPTER 12

Activist Citizens: An Afterword

Donatella della Porta

As social movement studies focus mainly on "new, post-materialist" actors, the analysis of social movements for or against forced migrants' rights has rarely been addressed. Social movements on migrants' rights have been instead addressed in citizenship studies, often with a normative concern. In this context, this collection certainly contributes to a dialogue between social movement studies and citizenship studies, pointing at some potential innovations in both. In this afterword, I want to highlight four such contributions that point at contextual opportunities and constraints as well as internal characteristics of the mobilizations.

A Changing Context

Social movement studies have looked at the context of pro-migrant mobilizations by considering, in particular, the specific domestic regime of citizenship (Koopmans et al. 2005) looking at (a) formal access to rights, (b) conditions for access to political representation, and (c) belonging to a political community (Monforte and Dufour 2011). Conditions for access to the nation distinguish civic states (citizenship awarded on the basis of birth) from ethnic states (citizenship awarded on the basis of blood);

D. della Porta (✉)
Scuola Normale Superiore, Florence, Italy

conditions for minorities' access to collective and cultural rights distinguish assimilationist from multicultural states. This research usefully highlights the importance of interactions with the state, as undocumented migrants, even if they are "nonpersons" in legal terms, are nevertheless dependent on state institutions. "Paradoxically, this situation of legal exclusion is also a situation of great dependence on the state: the state alone has the power to legalize their situation and integrate them into the territory's political community or, conversely, to deport them. The question of citizenship is thus at the heart of the undocumented migrant's life" (Monforte and Dufour 2011, p. 206).

While these studies focus on stable opportunities, the contributions to this volume adopt—implicitly or explicitly—a relational perspective by pointing at movement-countermovement dynamics (Lazaridis et al. 2016; Lazaridis and Campani 2016; Pajnik and Sauer 2017). They show indeed that citizens' regimes are transformed in interactions between those who want to make citizenship less inclusive and those who want to make it more inclusive. In general, in recent times, repression broadened from increasing detention and deportation of migrants to legal persecution of activists from grassroots groups and NGOs. Legal provisions for regularization and the granting of asylum have been limited, and terms for expulsions eased even to authoritarian regimes. As, for example, the chapter on Denmark stresses, citizens' regimes undergo big transformations, especially in an exclusive direction as the present political climate makes even advocacy for migrants' rights more difficult. The resonance of right-wing nationalism in countries such as Austria is revived during so-called migration "crises". In particular, the entrepreneurial strategies on the right to single out migration as a main problem revive xenophobic attitudes as basis for national identities. In this sense, acts of citizenship are performed in defense of migrants and (as the chapters on Denmark and Germany show) by the non-status refugees themselves, but citizenship is also redefined on the right.

Moreover, differentiated citizenship (Bauböck 2006) challenges the assessment of similar domestic conditions for mobilization on citizenship rights, breaking, as Siim and Meret observe in their chapter, the triad nation, people, and territory with new forms and practices of inclusion and exclusion of groups of citizens. Thus, movements for migrants' rights have developed from a shifting balance of opportunities and threats. In Europe as well as North America, contentious politics concerning migrant workers' claims for citizenship rights grew after World War II. Later on, protests increased as governments, faced with economic crisis, started to restrict migration and illegalize migrants. Within this exclusionary trend, prospects for regularization also fueled contentious moments (Laubenthal 2007). In the past, protests took specific forms for the migrant workers and naturalized migrants of the Fordist society and then for the illegal (undocumented) migrants of the crisis of that model, and the asylum seekers (but also deported), forced migrants—exiled, *desaparecidos*, corps—produced by the neoliberal need for cheap labor. In particular, the long summer of migration exposed the weakness of the neoliberal migration regime in a moment in which the forced migration of many individuals interacted with the long-lasting consequences of the financial crisis (della Porta 2018). Various chapters in this volume also confirm how the mobilization by and for forced migrants has been influenced by the specific characteristics of migrant groups and their legal status (cf., e.g., Chaps. 2 and 6, which illustrate the differences in the Danish and German asylum systems).

However, all chapters point at a common trend, namely, a crisis in the established definition of citizenship. The relevance of crises has often been mentioned in analyses of poor people's movements. Migrant rights movements have developed in particular around some critical moments as capitalism produces a racially structured society. Neoliberalism has made integration of legal migrants more difficult, as state strategies concerning migrants develop around a mix of ethnic management and territorial encapsulation, but also co-optation and depoliticization (Nicholls and Uitermark 2017). Politics of selective assimilation have been accompanied by growing criminalization, as "Migrants are increasingly cast as the *objects* of securitized fears and anxieties, possessing either an unsavory agency (i.e., they are identity frauds, queue jumpers, people who undermine consent in the polity) or a dangerous agency (i.e., they are criminals, terrorists, agents of insecurity)" (Nyers 2003, p. 1070). In particular, exclusion is visible in the politics of seclusion within closed spaces. Control of migration led to the creation of camps (of first arrival or pre-expulsion detention) as spaces of institutionalized state of exception. In particular, "camps multiply as spatial sites of exclusion: spaces of exception, places apart from the law, whose exclusion from the polis serves to legitimize sovereignty as a power to 'ban' from belonging" (Agamben 2000, p. 39).

The perception of a state of emergency resonates with the perception that citizenship is linked to democracy—and therefore it is of utmost importance to fight the tendency towards illiberal democracy and post-democracy (as observed in Campani's chapter on Italy). As Pajnik stresses for Slovenia (cf. Chap. 10), pro-feminist and anti-racist/anti-discrimination activists are critical of the contemporary state of democracy. They find that democracy has become "a very problematic notion", supported by "a total propaganda machine": "Democracy, what we expected it to be, does not exist, it only functions as a word for misleading us". Acting against the "the abuse of democracy", activists work on "alternative" conceptualizations of democracy: participatory, self-organized, and horizontal.

In this struggle for democracy, mobilizations in solidarity with refugees are influenced by other movements, for instance, anti-austerity movements (della Porta 2015). In Slovenia and Bulgaria, the Occupy protests are perceived in particular as a turning point, which Krasteva et al. refer to as a "second democratic revolution". As they observe, thanks to those empowering experiences, professional top-down activists are now accompanied by amateur civic actors, "able and willing to experiment, to search, to propose new, 'rough' ideas, to make mistakes, to act, to innovate", promoting a second generation of civic mobilizations. The intensity of previous waves of protest is also reflected in the degree of commitment to migrant rights on the left.

Contentious Repertoires

The contributions to this volume point at the plurality and innovation in what social movement studies would define as repertoires of contention during waves of forced migrations. If structure counts, there is agency as well: migrants and citizen activists reacted to restrictions in rights with struggles for more rights. While forced emergencies impose constraints upon acts of solidarity, migrants resist by their moves, crossing borders and breaking fences (Zamponi 2018). Solidarity actions followed these moves, adapting to the needs of the human beings in transit. Visible and invisible acts of resistance challenge the very denial of rights. Acts of citizenship, bringing on new actors as activist citizens, create new sites and scales of struggle (Isin 2008), appropriating citizenship (Moulin and Thomaz 2016) or transgressing citizenship (Rygiel 2016).

Historically, the contentious politics of migrant rights has taken different forms: migrant workers have participated in industrial strikes, house occupations, and rent strikes. Today, "due to their vulnerable status, refugees employ spatial strategies to create visibility against the exclusionary nature of policies, but also as a means to create political conflicts" (Ataç 2016, p. 632). More and more, migrants themselves mobilize inside and against institutional camps, which are transformed into centers for encounters and resistance. Informal camps are also created by migrants along their way, for instance, during the long summer of migration, near the railway stations in Budapest and Vienna, in parks in Serbia, and in Ventimiglia and Calais as they were waiting for crossing options. Invisibility as illegality is challenged by making oneself visible, as protest per se represents a challenge to invisibility (McNevin 2006, p. 144). This point is made in the chapters on the Danish and the German cases as refugees, in the name of the right to have human rights, resist "social, civil, and political death" by becoming visible. As non-status refugees in Denmark mention, they have built, through visible protests, "a community with refugees from other camps, immigrants, Danes and non-Danes who understand that our struggle is legitimate and just. We have brought to public attention the inhumane conditions in Sjælsmark, the deportations, and the unjust laws and policies that violate our freedom and dignity. .... We do not wait for anyone to give us rights. We take the right to participate in the construction of a world where freedom of movement is not a privilege for the few, where the camps are abolished, and where it is unthinkable to create death and destruction".

As this example shows, repertoires of action adapt to the construction of camps and borders, fences, and corridors in countries of arrival, transit, and destination (della Porta 2018). Acts of solidarity and acts of resistance develop inside and around the camps created to imprison the migrants, but also those built by the migrants at the voluntary or forced stops along their routes. While social direct action is an immediate reaction to emergency, political claims are also put forward in disruptive forms of protest by refugees (as in Hamburg or Berlin) as well as by citizens who act to extend rights. An example is the radical refugee-led activism of Castaway Souls, who stated, "We are not criminals. It is not a crime to be a refugee and seek asylum. We are not criminals. Do not treat us like criminals ... Camps are dehumanizing. We demand the closing of camps. We did not flee for our life only to die in your dehumanizing camps", "Stop killing us slowly", "We are here to protest. We have been through a lot without anybody saying anything ... we are punished, forced, treated like criminals ... our life has been taken away from us, we are being killed slowly".

In fact, actions to expand rights take different forms. In the classification suggested by Siim and Meret, there are "a) advocacy citizens 'fighting for' vulnerable groups, for example by providing legal support; b) everyday activism – citizens fighting 'for and with' vulnerable groups sharing everyday activities; c) citizens collectively fighting together for empowerment/self-empowerment; d) civic activism and mobilizations by marginalized people such as refugees, asylum seekers and stateless peoples". In particular, "everyday activism" (as in Friendly Neighbors) is characterized by a "vision of friendship based on curiosity and mutual respect and the practice aimed at changing the everyday lives of refugees and asylum seekers by creating personal friendships by means of local activism". Forms of action include, as in Finland or Denmark, constructing mini-publics to address the definition of migrants as, for example, beggars and welfare tourists. Initiatives offer a political space that, in the Danish case, resonates with tradition of bottom-up democracy based on dialogue.

During the long summer of migration, in countries of first arrival, such as Greece or Italy, the emergencies of the massive arrivals, as well as the dramatic conditions of the people walking long and dangerous routes, "prompted a focus on social direct action oriented to helping the people in need through food and clothing, but also rituals of welcoming. In countries of destination, welcome initiatives aimed at providing housing but also legal information and language skills" (della Porta 2018). Also in cases addressed in this volume, the criminalization of acts of solidarity transformed charity into civil disobedience. Politically oriented claims through marches and protest campaigns tended to become more significant over time.

As in other poor people's movements, resources are developed throughout the mobilization itself, as each event empowers people, strengthens collective identification, and triggers further action (Piven and Cloward 1977). This brings about the empowering feeling by activists, cited for Bulgaria (cf. Chap. 9): "I feel that I can change the world". This happens as action "blends together agency, initiative, beginning, change – of the world and of the active Self", proposing a conception of citizenship as commitment, participation, and transformation.

A Fragmented Organizational Structure

Several contributions in this volume point at the need for but also challenge in building broad coalitions. Social movement studies have often stressed the importance of powerful allies. In particular, the resource mobilization approach has seen social movement organizations as often formed by committed activists who take up the concerns of social constituencies to which they do not belong (McCarthy and Zald 1977), acting out of a sense of solidarity (Giugni and Passy 2001). The mobilization potential for poor people's movements is strengthened by the capacity of building social networks. Given that forced migrants lack material and symbolic resources, supportive organizations—from NGOs to religious groups—provide important help. In various historical periods, immigrant rights organizations have interacted with union activists and community activism (Nicholls and Uitermark 2017).

As critical citizenship studies suggest, however, the challenge to the existing order is often developed by the excluded, who trigger the building of coalitions for an extension of rights (della Porta 2018). Especially since the sans-papiers' struggle in the 1990s in France (Simeant 1998), self-organized migrant groups have gained attention. Speaking-for-oneself spread as a political practice "through which these social actors escape their normalizing representation and paternalistic treatment, as especially NGOs were often criticized for" (Ataç et al. 2015, p. 8). As was noted, "In transit like the migrants themselves, the movement structures seem to be in the making, with resources constructed in action, through the addressing of pressing needs and the building of trust" (della Porta 2018).

Segmented networks of formal and informal, old and new groups, are formed during campaigns in solidarity with refugees. Less politicized (at least initially) collectives of concerned citizens in places of arrival or blockage are described by Siim and Meret in their chapter on Denmark. Like the action repertoires, the organizational structure has been influenced by locations on the migrant route (della Porta 2018). Here, free spaces are created in which different actors interact, cooperate, and compete due to different preferences for action strategies and organizational structures.

Several chapters in this volume highlight the importance—and sometimes difficulty—of building coalitions, pointing at the tensions between advocating for versus acting with, the refusal or acceptance of contacts with institutions, pro-equality versus pro-diversity, contestatory citizenship versus solidarity citizenship (cf. Chap. 9). The lack of mobilization on anti-racism by the unions in Austria (Chap. 5) or by the Roma in Finland is the case in point (Chap. 3). As noted about the Austrian case, "struggles over the meaning of anti-racism – the lack of consensus on an emancipatory anti-racism and an intersectional, transversal anti-racist approach – partly explain the weakness of anti-racist movements in the country". As the case of Slovenia shows, some groups broaden the conception of racism to include "a plethora of discrimination and inequalities", with mobilization against misogyny and ethno-nationalism, suggesting feminist alternatives to patriarchy, neoliberalism, and racism. This helps mobilize support by activists from other social movements, but can also jeopardize alliances with mainstream actors. In the Austrian case, "the focus on racism prevents cooperation with trade unions and the SPÖ as they refuse to talk about it. ... While anti-rightist and anti-racist groups are visible in the Austrian public and have the power to mobilize ad hoc-activities, for instance solidarity with refugees in 2015, their inability to liaise with antineoliberal equality frames obstructs cooperation with trade unions. And vice versa, the trade unions do not actively fight racist common sense". Some chapters highlight the tension between mobilization for migrants and mobilization by migrants (cf. Chap. 2) as well as tensions within migrant organizations (cf. Chap. 6).

While the importance of building cross-national contacts emerges as particularly relevant for a movement that involves people from different nationalities moving to different countries, the construction of transnational ties is certainly a challenge. At the transnational level, co-ordination is also "'on the move' (and in the making). The heterogeneity of organizational structures and visions, as well as the lack of reciprocal acknowledgment between grassroots groups and NGOs, increases the challenges to the construction of a transnational movement. While there is no relevant national co-ordination, transnational ties emerge as networks of national groups and cross-national exchanges between near and distant places" (della Porta 2018).

Despite (or because of) these challenges, there seems to be increasing awareness of the need to develop what Siim and Meret define as an intersectional approach to citizens' activism. Intersectionality should help address the dilemma of integrating equality with diversity; it should function as a methodological approach that stresses "the need to be sensitive to diversity between and within categories". Rainbow alliances do at times develop despite some tensions.

Reframing Citizenship

Social movement studies stress the importance of framing for mobilization by activating cognitive and emotional mechanisms. Several chapters in this volume note how injustice frames are created "in action", as activism itself supports the development of a positive vision of the self (Maurer 2001).

As other "poor people's movements", the refugees' protests challenge a stigmatizing identity and construct an insurgent identity instead. As critical citizenship studies note, acts of citizenship empower the "subalterns" by forming counter-hegemonic visions of the self and the other (Ataç et al. 2016). While the rights of migrant workers were initially claimed in the name of their integration into the national economy, claims for regularization, for naturalization, and against deportation were also based on long-lasting relations between migrants and host country and their assimilation into it (Laubenthal 2007). Neoliberal displacement led to the development of frames of resistance pointing at common humanity (Meret and Della Corte 2016).

Research on the long summer of migration has shown that the framing of the issue cleaves the pro-refugee field between hospitality and solidarity, between humanitarian and political visions, between claims for integration and for the right to move (della Porta 2018). Tensions within the networks of support have been noted, with humanitarian narratives promoting a compassionate welcome opposed to claims of solidarity across borders. As for the diagnostic frames, the degree of politicization varies among groups and countries and is influenced by the presence of anti-austerity and other social movements. As for prognostic frames, especially within a more politicized vision, a tension emerges between claims for integration and for freedom of movement with a dilemma between assimilation and autonomy:

> The immigrant protests that have erupted across the globe in the last decade are a response to the "exclusions, inequalities, hierarchies, securitizations" which have been affected by this refashioning of citizenship. Yet, inevitably, one of the main strategies of migrants and pro-migrant activists is to demand the rights of citizenship, however problematic or precarious this citizenship may have become. Driven by immediate humanitarian considerations, many migrant advocacy movements focus on challenging existing legal and political frameworks in order to gain migrants' rights and access to legal aid, welfare, and education ... immigrant protests are "acts" against the exclusionary technologies of citizenship, which aim to make visible the violence of citizenship as regimes of control. However, in order to effect material changes, protestors are compelled to make their demands in the idiom of the regime of citizenship they are contesting. (Tyler and Marciniak 2013, p. 146)

However, an emerging vision, detaching rights from citizenship, developed within the approach of the autonomy of migration which "understands migration as a social and political movement forming against attempts to control and govern it" (Ataç et al. 2015, p. 10). So, the very definition of migrants, especially the distinction between "forced" and "economic" migrants, is challenged by the claim that all humans move in order to survive (Arendt 1951).

These tensions are manifest in the radical Danish refugee-led Castaway Souls, whose refugee manifesto demanded, "1) the right of all migrants to be free and decide over their future; 2) the right to have rights (to work, to move freely, to stay, to education, to healthcare, voice, etc.; 3) the right to move free or stay and not to be forcefully confined to Sjælsmark, nor deported by force; 4) the right to resist deportation; 5) the demand to close camps like Sjælsmark where people are criminalized and forced to live without dignity, in a state of intolerable uncertainty, poverty and isolation; 6) the right to resist the criminalization of refugees and their being represented as the source of all evils and problems in society" (see Chap. 2).

In fact, the right to stay is bridged to the right to move. The Lampedusa in Hamburg and their supporters expressed, as Meret and Diener noted, "1) A call against structural problems such as racism, discrimination, and against the Western European colonial mentality (We are Here Because You are There; United Against Colonial Injustice, In the name of democracy and human rights: Stop this hypocrisy!, Self-determination and freedom for the people of the world), 2) a call for the promotion of new fundamental rights (Open Borders, Right to Stay for Everybody, Freedom of Movement, Solidarity without Borders, Kein Mensch Ist Illegal, No Borders, No Nations, No Deportations, etc.); 3) a call of awareness for the role played by European countries in the Libyan war and more generally in the African conflicts".

Conclusion

The research presented in this volume contributes to both social movement studies and citizenship studies. The contribution to social movement studies is in the empirical investigations of a social movement that has rarely been studied through the toolkit of concepts and theories of social movement studies. For critical citizenship studies, the research goes beyond what is usually seen as acts of solidarity and looks more broadly to what Monforte and Dufour (2013) call "acts of emancipation" and Walters

(2008) labels "acts of demonstrations". It is all the more important, then, to look at how acts of resistance interact with acts of solidarity within mobilized networks in which new actors emerge as central for the struggle over citizenship bringing in their specific practices and ideas.

REFERENCES

Agamben, G. (2000). *Means without end: Notes of politics*. Minneapolis: The University of Minnesota Press.
Arendt, H. (1951). *The origin of totalitarianism*. New York: Harvard Law School.
Ataç, I. (2016). "Refugee protest camp Vienna": Making citizens through locations of the protest movement. *Citizenship Studies, 20*, 629–646.
Ataç, I., Kron, S., Schilliger, S., Schwiertz, H., & Stierl, M. (2015). Struggles of migration as in-/visible politics: Introduction. *Movements. Journal für kritische Migrations- und Grenzregimeforschung, 1*(2). http://movements-journal.org/issues/02.kaempfe/01.ataç,kron,schilliger,schwiertz,stierl--einleitung~en.html
Ataç, I., Rygiel, K., & Stierl, M. (2016). Introduction: The contentious politics of refugee and migrant protest and solidarity movements: Remaking citizenship from the margins. *Citizenship Studies, 20*, 527–544.
Bauböck, R. (2006). Citizenship and migration – Concepts and controversies. In R. Bauboeck (Ed.), *Migration and citizenship. Legal status, rights and political participation, IMISCOE reports* (pp. 15–32). Amsterdam: Amsterdam University Press.
della Porta, D. (2015). *Social movements in times of austerity*. Cambridge: Polity.
della Porta, D. (2018). Contentious moves: Some conclusions. In D. della Porta (Ed.), *Solidarity mobilizations in the "refugee crisis": Contentious moves*. London: Palgrave. forthcoming.
Giugni, M., & Passy, F. (Eds.). (2001). *Political altruism? Solidarity movements in international perspective*. Lanham: Rowman and Littlefield.
Isin, E. F. (2008). Theorizing acts of citizenship. In E. F. Isin & G. M. Nielsen (Eds.), *Acts of citizenship* (pp. 15–43). London: Zed Books.
Koopmans, R., Statham, P., & Giugni, M. (2005). *Contested citizenship: Immigration and cultural diversity in Europe*. Minneapolis: University of Minnesota Press.
Laubenthal, B. (2007). The emergence of pro-regularisation movements in Western Europe. *International Migration, 45*, 101–133.
Lazaridis, G., & Campani, G. (2016). *Understanding the populist shift: Othering in a Europe in crisis*. Milton Keynes: Routledge.
Lazaridis, G., Benveniste, A., & Campani, G. (Eds.). (2016). *The rise of the far right in a Europe under crisis*. London: Palgrave Macmillan.

Maurer, S. (2001). *Les chômeurs en action (décembre 1997–mars 1998): Mobilisation collective et ressources compensatoires.* Paris: L'Harmattan.

McCarthy, J., & Zald, M. (1977). Resource mobilization and social movements: A partial theory. *American Journal of Sociology, 82,* 1212–1241.

McNevin, A. (2006). Political belonging in a neoliberal era: The struggle of the sans-papiers. *Citizenship Studies, 10,* 135–151.

Meret, S., & Della Corte, E. (2016). Spaces of resistance and re-actuality of Gramsci in refugees' struggles for rights? The "Lampedusa in Hamburg" between exit and voice. In Ó. G. Augustín & M. B. Jørgensen (Eds.), *Solidarity without borders: Gramscian perspectives on migration and civil society alliances.* London: Pluto Press.

Monforte, P., & Dufour, P. (2011). Mobilizing in borderline citizenship regimes: A comparative analysis of undocumented migrants' collective actions. *Politics & Society, 39,* 203–232.

Monforte, P., & Dufour, P. (2013). Comparing the protests of undocumented migrants beyond contexts: Collective actions as acts of emancipation. *European Political Science Review, 5,* 83–104.

Moulin, C., & Thomaz, D. (2016). The tactical politics of "humanitarian" immigration: Negotiating stasis, enacting mobility. *Citizenship Studies, 20,* 595–609.

Nicholls, W. J., & Uitermark, J. (2017). *Cities and social movements: Immigrant rights activism in the US, France, and the Netherlands, 1970–2015.* Oxford: Wiley.

Nyers, P. (2003). Abject cosmopolitanism: The politics of protection in the anti-deportation movement. *Third World Quarterly, 24,* 1069–1093.

Pajnik, M., & Sauer, B. (2017). *Populism and the web: Communicative practices of parties and movements in Europe.* Milton Keynes: Routledge.

Piven, F. F., & Cloward, R. (1977). *Poor people's movements.* New York: Pantheon.

Rygiel, K. (2016). Dying to live: Migrant deaths and citizenship politics along European borders: Transgressions, disruptions, and mobilizations. *Citizenship Studies, 20,* 545–560.

Simeant, J. (1998). *La cause des sans-papiers.* Paris: Presses de Sciences Po.

Tyler, I., & Marciniak, K. (2013). Immigrant protest: An introduction. *Citizenship Studies, 17,* 143–156.

Walters, W. (2008). Acts of demonstration: Mapping the territory of (non-)citizenship. In E. F. Isin & G. M. Nielsen (Eds.), *Acts of citizenship* (pp. 182–205). London: Zed Books.

Zamponi, L. (2018, forthcoming). From border to border: Refugee solidarity activism in Italy across space, time and practices. In D. della Porta (Ed.), *Solidarity mobilizations in the "refugee crisis": Contentious moves.* London: Palgrave.

Index

A
Activism modes, 55–56, 71
Activist citizenship, 14, 30, 32, 43–44, 46–47, 56
Actor-centered methodology, 271
Acts of citizenship, 214, 217, 244–245, 248–249, 270, 281, 294, 296, 301
Acts of friendship, 23–24, 43–44, 71, 297
Advocacy activism, 55, 60, 69
Agency, 29, 31, 36, 44, 214–216, 218–220, 275, 279, 281, 295–296, 298
Antibodies, 79–80, 94–95, 97–99, 101, 104, 108, 113, 172, 192–193
Anti-discrimination, 28, 32, 113–114, 121–122, 125, 131, 167–212
Anti-racism, 28, 114, 115, 117, 121–125, 127–129, 132–133, 235–237, 239, 252, 255, 258, 261, 283, 285, 287, 299

Arendt, Hannah, 5–6, 29, 47, 214, 219, 221, 224, 285
Asylum seekers, 28–37, 41, 43, 45–47, 52, 63, 91, 116–118, 120–122, 125, 131–132, 140, 145–146, 258, 277, 279, 284–285
Austria, 111–136
Authoritarian populism, 81–82, 108

B
"Beggars," 54, 57, 66, 68–69
Berlin Refugee Strike Movement, 139, 154, 159
Bulgaria, 213–239

C
Civic self-organization, 55, 65, 69, 70
Civil disobedience, 19, 55, 59–60, 64, 66, 70
Civil society, 42, 69, 81, 94–95, 113–115, 117, 127, 130, 138, 207, 209–216, 243–245, 247–248

Civil society organizations (CSO), 28, 31–32, 95, 113, 117, 119–121, 123, 127–128, 131–133, 188, 193, 196, 198
Class, 31, 81–84, 93–94, 99–100, 103, 107, 112, 117, 123, 130, 133, 141–142, 155, 162, 194, 196, 200, 208, 219, 228, 244, 247, 255, 269–270, 275
Comparative RAGE-project, the, 12
Conservative counter movements, 167–168
Contestatory citizenship, 214, 218–219, 221, 225, 236–238, 266, 271, 273–274, 277, 281–286, 289
Counter-forces, 19–20, 113
Counter-hegemonic strategy, 271, 282, 287, 289
Creative citizenship, 214, 271, 280–281, 289
Critical citizenship studies, 266–268, 271–299, 301–302

D
Danish People's Party, the, 26–27
Deliberative mini-publics, 11
della Porta, Donatella, 6, 20, 47, 54, 68, 214
Denmark, 25–50
Differentiated citizenship, 26, 30–31, 45, 47, 156, 273, 294
Discrimination shift, the, 167, 170

E
Eastern European Roma, 51, 54, 61, 63
Econocracy, 189, 193, 195–196, 205
Equality, social justice, 29–31, 38–39
Equal Opportunities and Antidiscrimination Commission, the (HALDE), 171–172

European Union, 87, 92
Event observation, 69
Everyday
    activism, 32, 35–37, 43–46
    citizenship, 8, 278–279, 281
Exclusionary
    intersectionality, 112–113, 119, 123, 126, 130, 268–271, 286–287
    welfare nationalism, 45
Exclusive intersectionality, 112, 129
Experimenting with democracy, 275

F
Feminist movements, 243–261
    the Feminist Manifesto, 260
Fighting racism, 257
Finland, 51–78
Finnish Roma, 52, 54, 57, 62, 64, 66, 71
Finns, the, 52, 61, 67, 69, 284
The Five Star Movement/Beppo Grillo's Five Star Movement, 188–189, 194–196, 202–205, 208
Focus group discussion, 55, 66, 69, 71
France, 167–184
Fraser, Nancy, 5, 6, 8, 55, 57, 62, 65, 67, 72, 247
Freiheitliche Partei Österreich (FPÖ), 112–118, 126, 129, 132
French backlash, 168, 183
Friendly Neighbors, the, 29, 33, 36, 298

G
Gender
    equality, 243, 245, 248–251, 259
    inequality, 257
Germany, 137–166

Globalization, 107, 138, 205, 217, 266, 269
Green citizenship, 216

H
Hegemony, 111–113, 126–127, 130–131
  right-wing, 126
Homophobia, 174–183
Human rights, 56–63, 66–70, 216, 220, 222, 224, 230, 232, 235
Hybrid organizations, 120, 123, 125, 132

I
Insurgent populism, 89, 95
Intersectionality, 6–7, 112–114, 119, 123, 126, 130, 132
  inclusive, 280, 283, 286–287
  political, 119
Isin, Engin, 6, 9, 11, 30, 47, 53, 127, 137, 140, 214, 217, 232, 244, 248, 249, 271, 281, 285
Italy, 185–212

L
La Manif pour tous, 173, 176–179, 181
Lampedusa in Hamburg, 139, 141, 144, 146, 162
Learning democracy, 31, 44–45
"Left behind" citizens, 93
Legal approach to discrimination, the, 173
Le Pen, Marine, 168
LGBT, 28–29, 32–33, 45, 47
  focus groups, 173–174
  movement, 173–174, 176–177, 179, 181–182
  rights, 167–169, 174, 177, 179–181, 183, 186

Liquid and dynamic citizenship, 19–20
Local activism, 298

M
Methodological nationalism, 5
Movement's networking, 256
Mudde, Cas, 1, 3, 7, 10, 59, 70

N
Nationalism/nativism, 27
Neo-liberal economy, 205
Neoliberalism, 117
Non-governmental organizations (NGOs), 28, 214–216, 224, 231, 237, 249, 250, 253, 256, 258, 261
Nielsen, G. M., 9, 11, 53, 127, 137, 140, 214, 217, 232, 244, 248, 249, 281
Northern League, the, 189

O
Occupy movement, 5, 215–216, 218–219, 235–238, 275–276, 283, 285, 296

P
Periodic mass mobilization, 55, 67, 69, 70
Political subjectivation, 138, 140, 149
Politics
  of courage, 232–233
  of fear, 45, 232–234, 276, 289
  of friendship, 277, 279, 289
  of transformation, 215, 221, 225, 232, 234
Populism
  authoritarian, 81–82, 108
  far-right, 196, 214, 265, 272–273, 284, 289

Populism (*cont.*)
  insurgent, 89, 95, 288
  national, 215, 219, 227, 233, 238, 266, 270–272, 287–288
  progressive, 85–86, 189
  right-wing, 27–28, 31–32, 44–47
Post-communism, 214
Post-democracy, 188–189, 195, 205
Pro-diversity activism, 282
Progressive populism, 85–86
Pro-refugee, 28, 35, 40, 42, 45
Protest, 215, 217–218, 226, 235, 243, 245–247, 253, 256
  camps, 137, 141
Public, the, 246–247

R
Race equality directive, 170
Racism, 113–133, 184, 244, 251, 254–258, 261
Radical (underground) activism, 55, 59, 63, 66, 69, 71
Refugee
  crisis, 282
  movements, 139–141, 145, 160–161
  pro-refugee, 28, 35, 40, 42, 45
Romanophobia, 51, 53, 66, 69

S
Same-sex marriage, 168, 173, 175–179, 182–183
Securitization, 139, 235, 301
Service activism, 55–56, 69
Slovenia, 243–264
Social justice, 6
Social movement, 5, 17–20, 145–146, 243, 245–251, 256, 261

Solidarity, 269, 272, 277, 283, 286, 289, 296, 299
Solidary citizenship, 214, 219–221, 225, 227–228, 233, 236–237, 277–278, 281–282, 284, 286
State capture, 226, 235–238

T
Transnational civil society, 5
Transversal
  dialogue, 56, 67, 70
  framing, 114, 123, 127, 129–130, 132–133
  politics, 114, 119, 120, 123–124, 126

U
UK Independence Party (UKIP), 89–93
United Kingdom (UK), 79–110

W
Welfare
  chauvinism, 169
  exclusionism, 2
  national chauvinism, 2
  nationalism, 26–69

X
Xenophobia, 188, 196

Y
Yuval-Davis, Nira, 6, 12, 56, 67, 114, 119

CPSIA information can be obtained
at www.ICGtesting.com
Printed in the USA
LVOW13*1939120718
583543LV00018B/438/P